scrum bums

Other Books by Darby Conley

The Dog Is Not a Toy (House Rule #4)

Fuzzy Logic: Get Fuzzy 2

Groovitude: A Get Fuzzy Treasury

The Get Fuzzy Experience: Are You Bucksperienced

I Would Have Bought You a Cat, But . . .

Blueprint for Disaster

Bucky Katt's Big Book of Fun

Say Cheesy

scrum bums

A GET FUZZY Collection

by darby conley

Andrews McMeel
Publishing

Kansas City

Get Fuzzy is distributed internationally by United Feature Syndicate.

Scrum Bums copyright © 2005 by Darby Conley. All rights reserved. Printed in the United States of America. No part of this book may be used or reproduced in any manner whatsoever without written permission except in the case of reprints in the context of reviews. For information, write Andrews McMeel Publishing, an Andrews McMeel Universal company, 4520 Main Street, Kansas City, Missouri 64111.

05 06 07 08 09 BBG 10 9 8 7 6 5 4 3 2 1

ISBN-13: 978-0-7407-5001-4
ISBN-10: 0-7407-5001-1

Library of Congress Control Number: 2005925658

Get Fuzzy can be viewed on the Internet at

www.comics.com/comics/getfuzzy.

━━━ **ATTENTION: SCHOOLS AND BUSINESSES** ━━━

Andrews McMeel books are available at quantity discounts with bulk purchase for educational, business, or sales promotional use. For information, please write to: Special Sales Department, Andrews McMeel Publishing, 4520 Main Street, Kansas City, Missouri 64111.

For Stephan

what else?
this is what else, man.

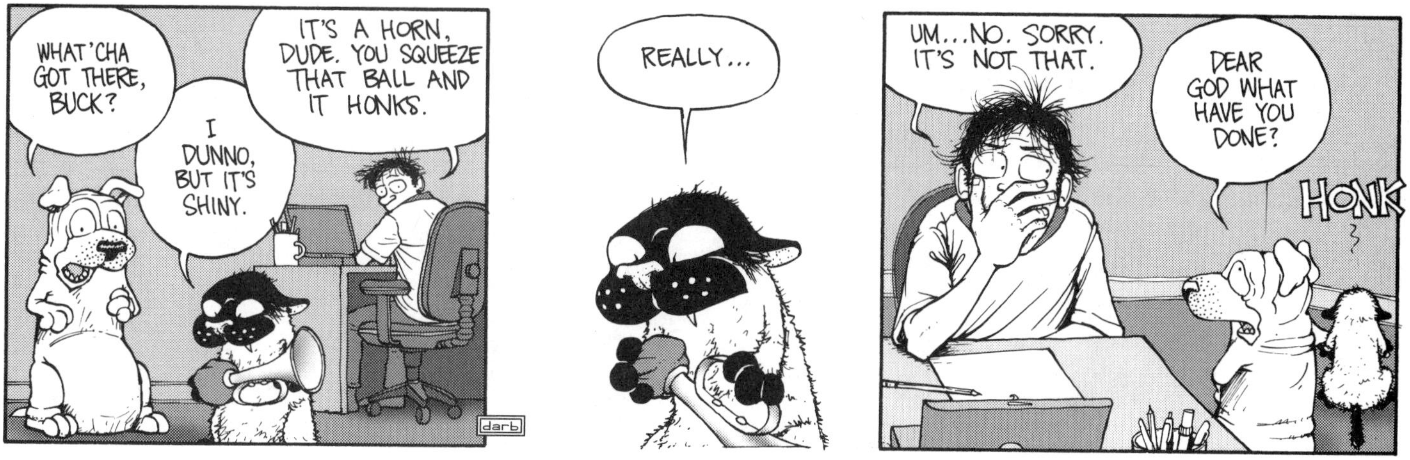
WHAT'CHA GOT THERE, BUCK?
I DUNNO, BUT IT'S SHINY.
IT'S A HORN, DUDE. YOU SQUEEZE THAT BALL AND IT HONKS.
REALLY...
UM...NO. SORRY. IT'S NOT THAT.
DEAR GOD WHAT HAVE YOU DONE?
HONK
darb

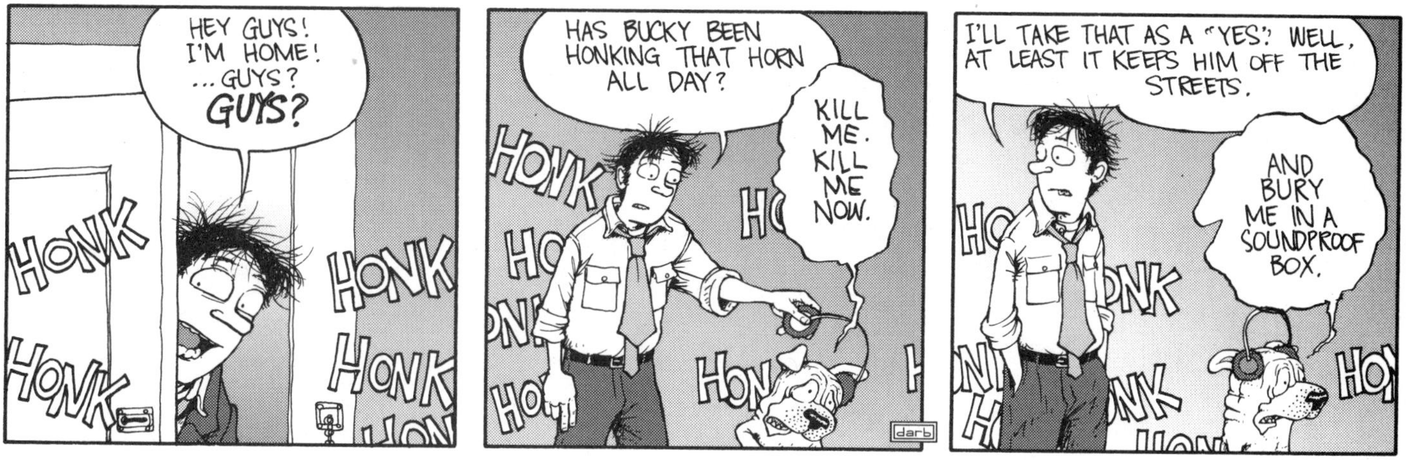
HEY GUYS! I'M HOME! ...GUYS? GUYS?
HONK
HONK
HONK
HONK
HAS BUCKY BEEN HONKING THAT HORN ALL DAY?
KILL ME. KILL ME NOW.
HONK
HON
I'LL TAKE THAT AS A "YES." WELL, AT LEAST IT KEEPS HIM OFF THE STREETS.
AND BURY ME IN A SOUNDPROOF BOX.
darb

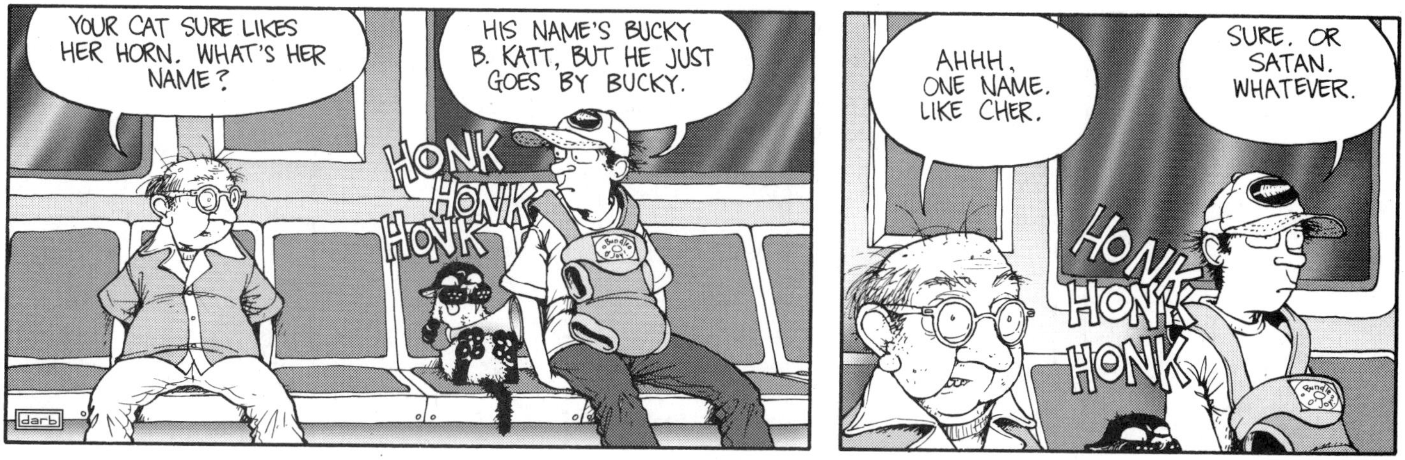
YOUR CAT SURE LIKES HER HORN. WHAT'S HER NAME?
HIS NAME'S BUCKY B. KATT, BUT HE JUST GOES BY BUCKY.
HONK
HONK
HONK
AHHH, ONE NAME. LIKE CHER.
SURE. OR SATAN. WHATEVER.
HONK
HONK
HONK
darb

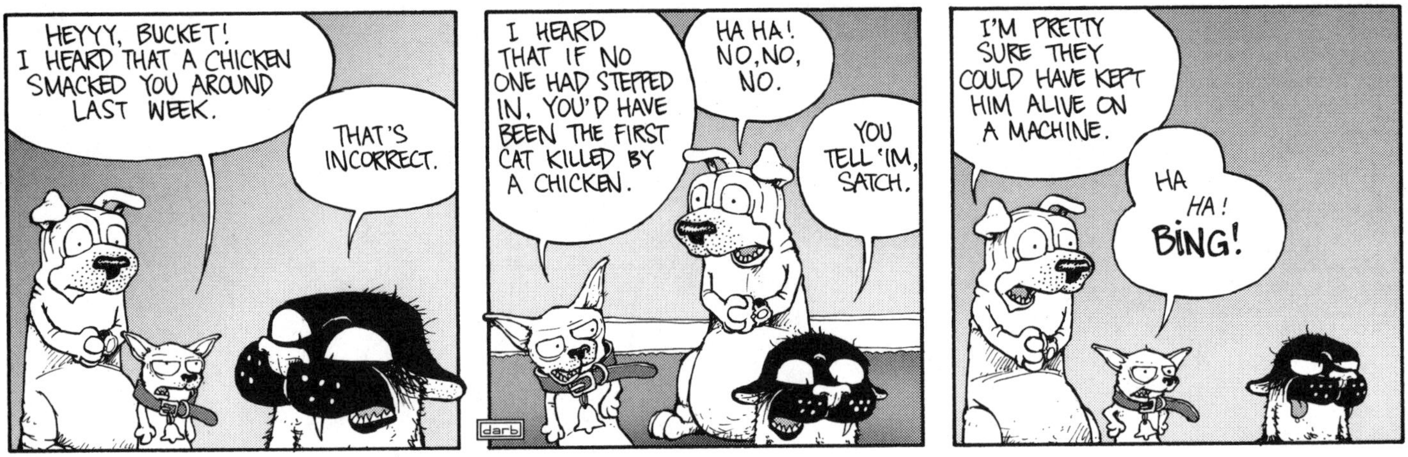
HEYYY, BUCKET! I HEARD THAT A CHICKEN SMACKED YOU AROUND LAST WEEK.
THAT'S INCORRECT.
I HEARD THAT IF NO ONE HAD STEPPED IN, YOU'D HAVE BEEN THE FIRST CAT KILLED BY A CHICKEN.
HA HA! NO, NO, NO.
YOU TELL 'IM, SATCH.
darb
I'M PRETTY SURE THEY COULD HAVE KEPT HIM ALIVE ON A MACHINE.
HA HA! BING!

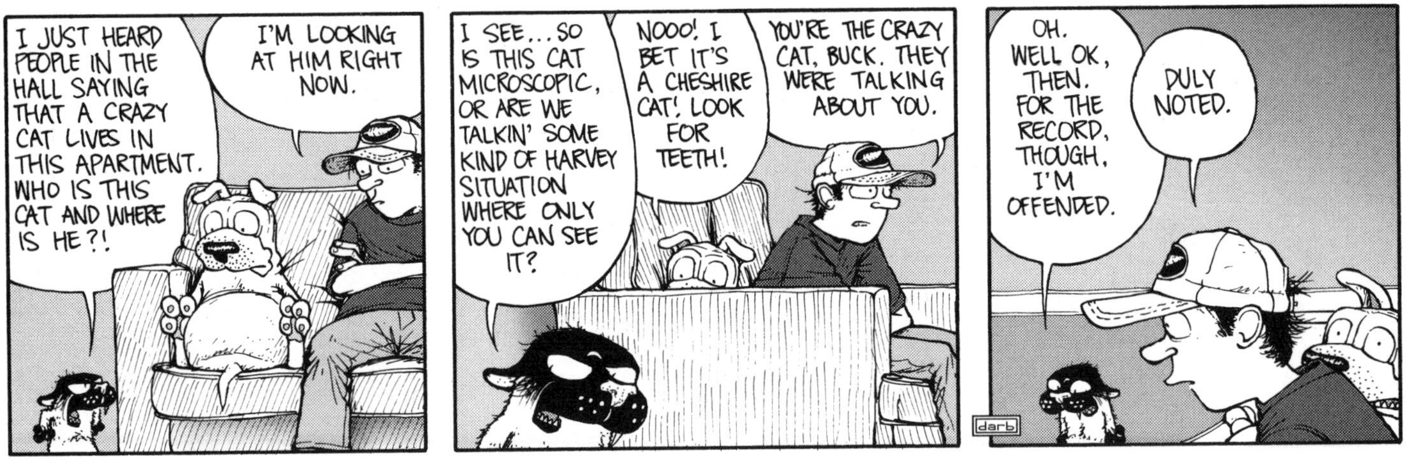
I JUST HEARD PEOPLE IN THE HALL SAYING THAT A CRAZY CAT LIVES IN THIS APARTMENT. WHO IS THIS CAT AND WHERE IS HE?!
I'M LOOKING AT HIM RIGHT NOW.
I SEE... SO IS THIS CAT MICROSCOPIC, OR ARE WE TALKIN' SOME KIND OF HARVEY SITUATION WHERE ONLY YOU CAN SEE IT?
NOOO! I BET IT'S A CHESHIRE CAT! LOOK FOR TEETH!
YOU'RE THE CRAZY CAT, BUCK. THEY WERE TALKING ABOUT YOU.
darb
OH. WELL OK, THEN. FOR THE RECORD, THOUGH, I'M OFFENDED.
DULY NOTED.

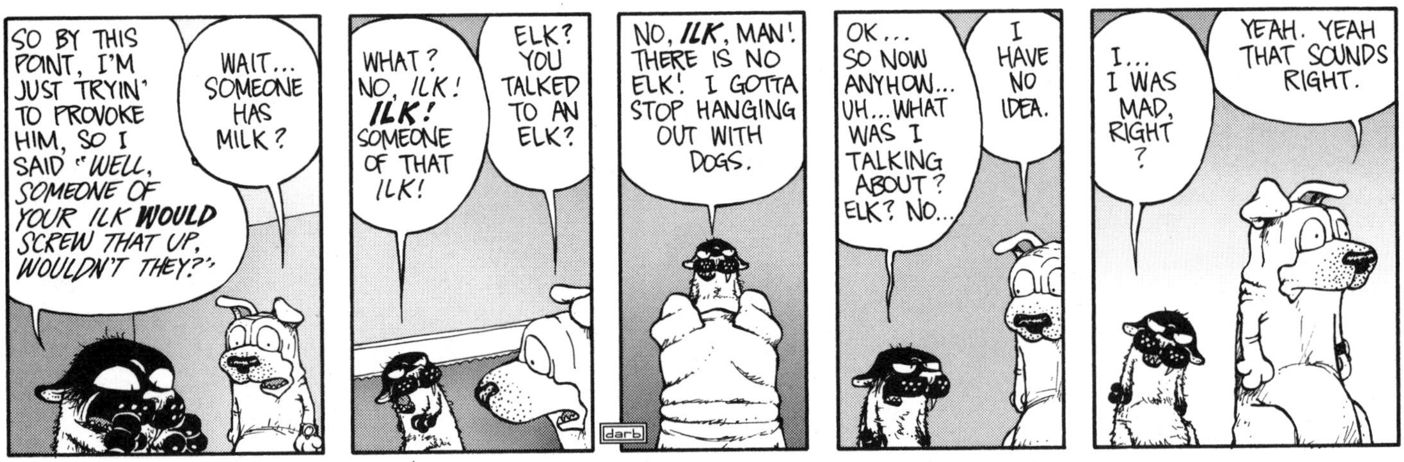
SO BY THIS POINT, I'M JUST TRYIN' TO PROVOKE HIM, SO I SAID "WELL, SOMEONE OF YOUR ILK WOULD SCREW THAT UP, WOULDN'T THEY?"
WAIT... SOMEONE HAS MILK?
WHAT? NO, ILK! ILK! SOMEONE OF THAT ILK!
ELK? YOU TALKED TO AN ELK?
darb
NO, ILK, MAN! THERE IS NO ELK! I GOTTA STOP HANGING OUT WITH DOGS.
OK... SO NOW ANYHOW... UH... WHAT WAS I TALKING ABOUT? ELK? NO...
I HAVE NO IDEA.
I... I WAS MAD, RIGHT?
YEAH. YEAH THAT SOUNDS RIGHT.

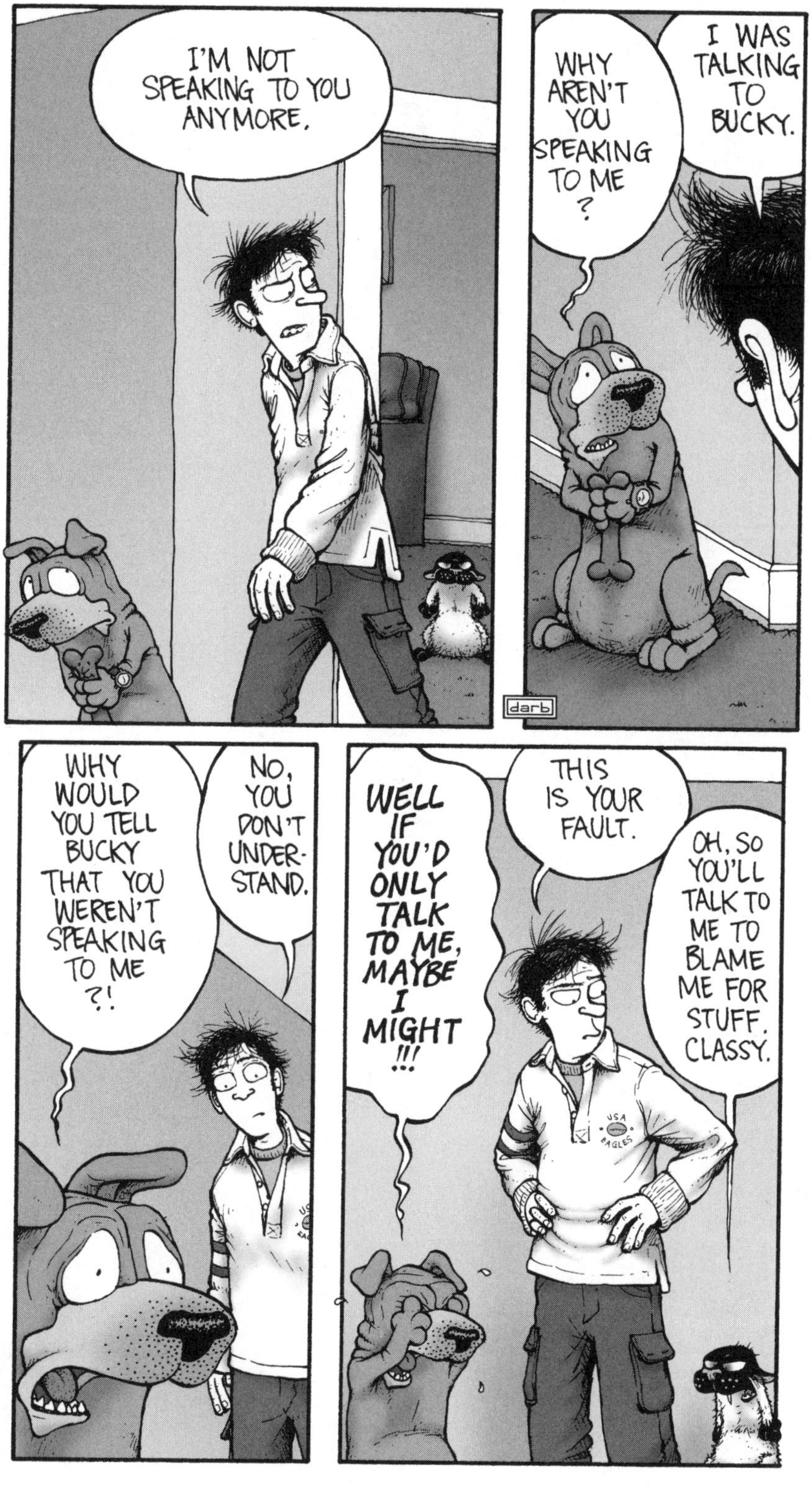
I'M NOT SPEAKING TO YOU ANYMORE.
WHY AREN'T YOU SPEAKING TO ME ?
I WAS TALKING TO BUCKY.
darb
WHY WOULD YOU TELL BUCKY THAT YOU WEREN'T SPEAKING TO ME ?!
NO, YOU DON'T UNDER-STAND.
WELL IF YOU'D ONLY TALK TO ME, MAYBE I MIGHT !!!
THIS IS YOUR FAULT.
OH, SO YOU'LL TALK TO ME TO BLAME ME FOR STUFF. CLASSY.
USA EAGLES

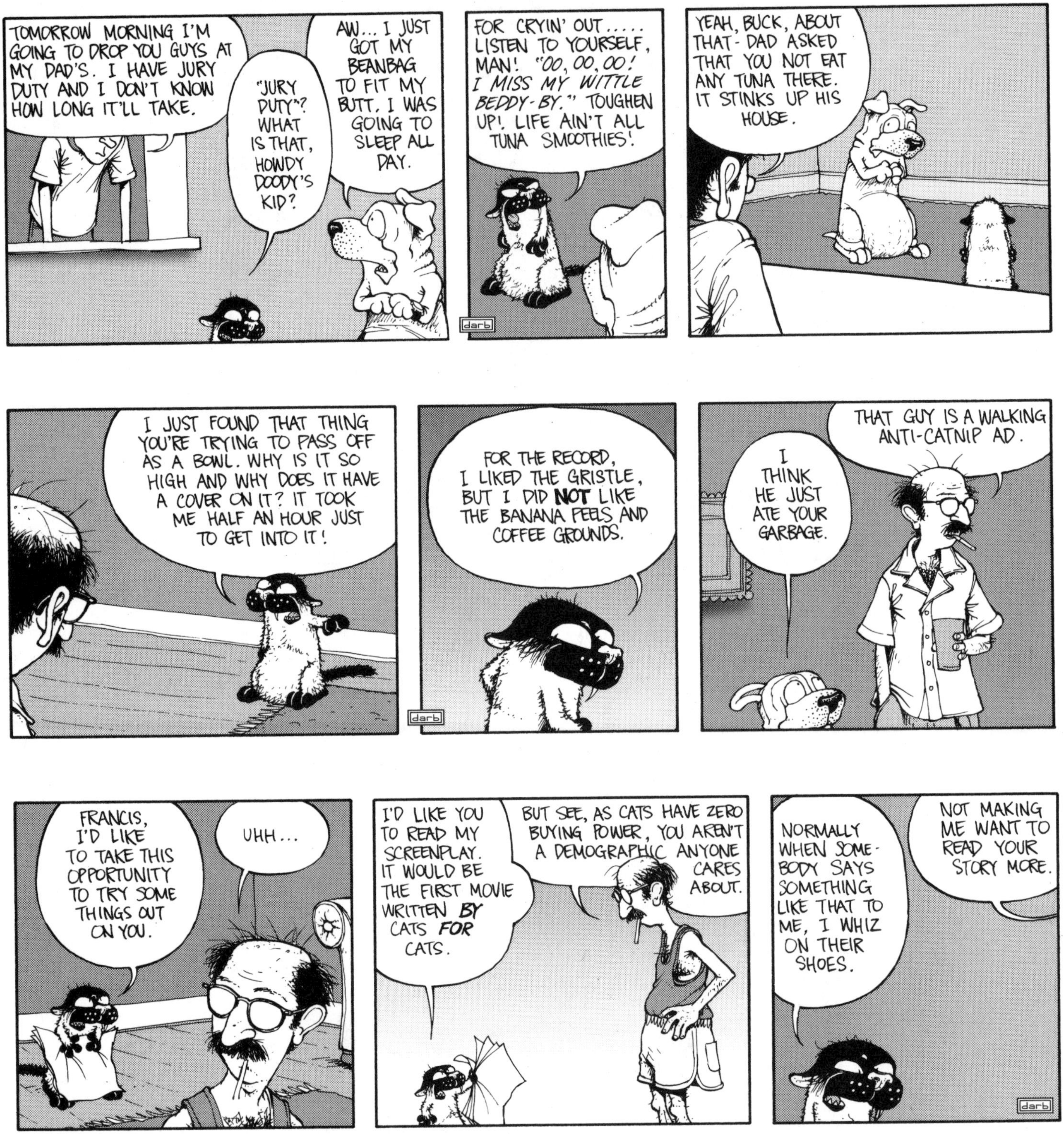
TOMORROW MORNING I'M GOING TO DROP YOU GUYS AT MY DAD'S. I HAVE JURY DUTY AND I DON'T KNOW HOW LONG IT'LL TAKE.
"JURY DUTY"? WHAT IS THAT, HOWDY DOODY'S KID?
AW... I JUST GOT MY BEANBAG TO FIT MY BUTT. I WAS GOING TO SLEEP ALL DAY.
darb
FOR CRYIN' OUT..... LISTEN TO YOURSELF, MAN! "OO, OO, OO! I MISS MY WITTLE BEDDY-BY." TOUGHEN UP! LIFE AIN'T ALL TUNA SMOOTHIES!
YEAH, BUCK, ABOUT THAT- DAD ASKED THAT YOU NOT EAT ANY TUNA THERE. IT STINKS UP HIS HOUSE.
I JUST FOUND THAT THING YOU'RE TRYING TO PASS OFF AS A BOWL. WHY IS IT SO HIGH AND WHY DOES IT HAVE A COVER ON IT? IT TOOK ME HALF AN HOUR JUST TO GET INTO IT!
darb
FOR THE RECORD, I LIKED THE GRISTLE, BUT I DID NOT LIKE THE BANANA PEELS AND COFFEE GROUNDS.
I THINK HE JUST ATE YOUR GARBAGE.
THAT GUY IS A WALKING ANTI-CATNIP AD.
FRANCIS, I'D LIKE TO TAKE THIS OPPORTUNITY TO TRY SOME THINGS OUT ON YOU.
UHH...
I'D LIKE YOU TO READ MY SCREENPLAY. IT WOULD BE THE FIRST MOVIE WRITTEN BY CATS FOR CATS.
BUT SEE, AS CATS HAVE ZERO BUYING POWER, YOU AREN'T A DEMOGRAPHIC ANYONE CARES ABOUT.
NORMALLY WHEN SOMEBODY SAYS SOMETHING LIKE THAT TO ME, I WHIZ ON THEIR SHOES.
NOT MAKING ME WANT TO READ YOUR STORY MORE.
darb

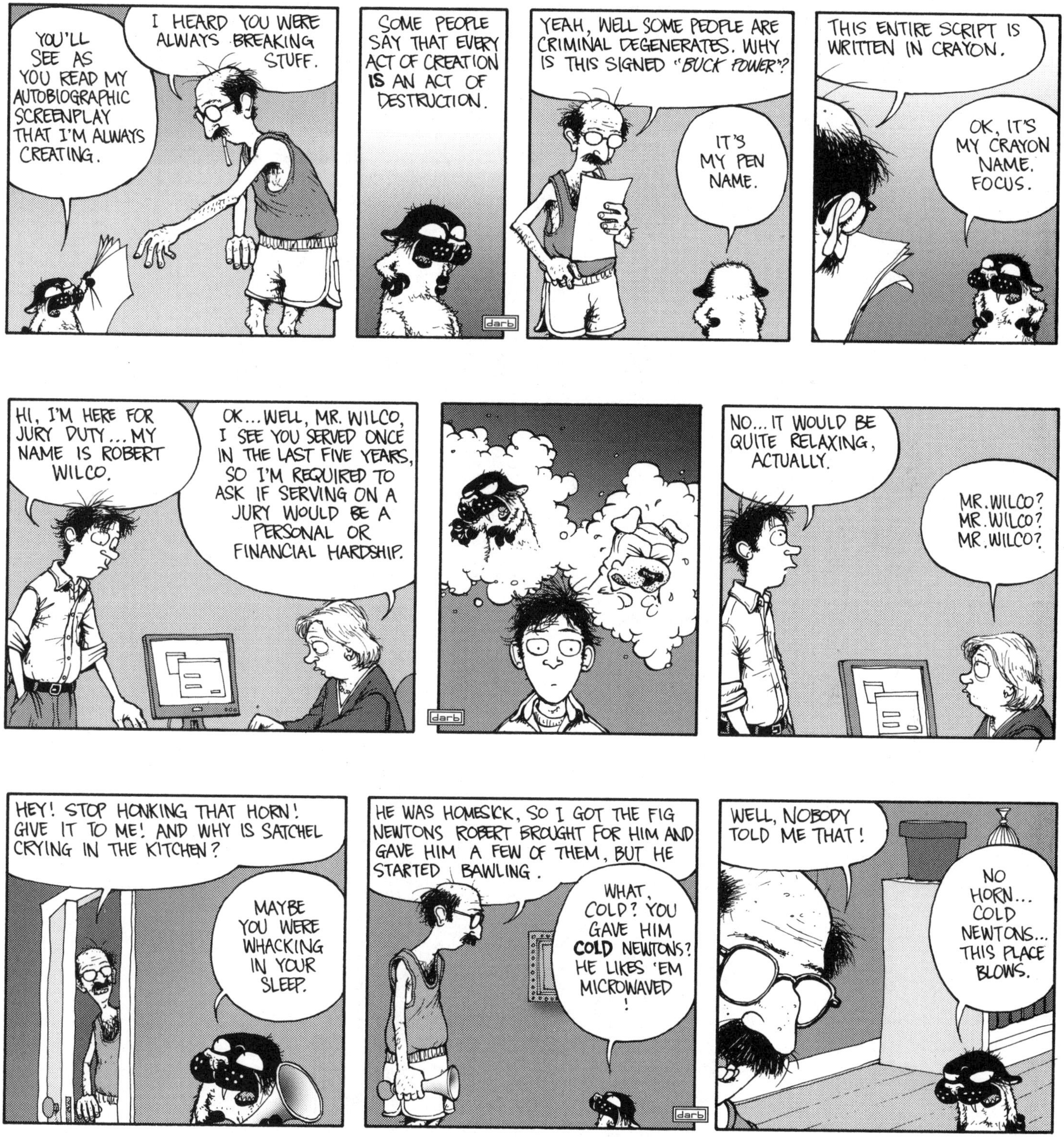
YOU'LL SEE AS YOU READ MY AUTOBIOGRAPHIC SCREENPLAY THAT I'M ALWAYS CREATING.
I HEARD YOU WERE ALWAYS BREAKING STUFF.
SOME PEOPLE SAY THAT EVERY ACT OF CREATION IS AN ACT OF DESTRUCTION.
darb
YEAH, WELL SOME PEOPLE ARE CRIMINAL DEGENERATES. WHY IS THIS SIGNED "BUCK POWER"?
IT'S MY PEN NAME.
THIS ENTIRE SCRIPT IS WRITTEN IN CRAYON.
OK, IT'S MY CRAYON NAME. FOCUS.
HI, I'M HERE FOR JURY DUTY... MY NAME IS ROBERT WILCO.
OK... WELL, MR. WILCO, I SEE YOU SERVED ONCE IN THE LAST FIVE YEARS, SO I'M REQUIRED TO ASK IF SERVING ON A JURY WOULD BE A PERSONAL OR FINANCIAL HARDSHIP.
darb
NO... IT WOULD BE QUITE RELAXING, ACTUALLY.
MR. WILCO? MR. WILCO? MR. WILCO?
HEY! STOP HONKING THAT HORN! GIVE IT TO ME! AND WHY IS SATCHEL CRYING IN THE KITCHEN?
MAYBE YOU WERE WHACKING IN YOUR SLEEP.
HE WAS HOMESICK, SO I GOT THE FIG NEWTONS ROBERT BROUGHT FOR HIM AND GAVE HIM A FEW OF THEM, BUT HE STARTED BAWLING.
WHAT, COLD? YOU GAVE HIM COLD NEWTONS? HE LIKES 'EM MICROWAVED!
darb
WELL, NOBODY TOLD ME THAT!
NO HORN... COLD NEWTONS... THIS PLACE BLOWS.

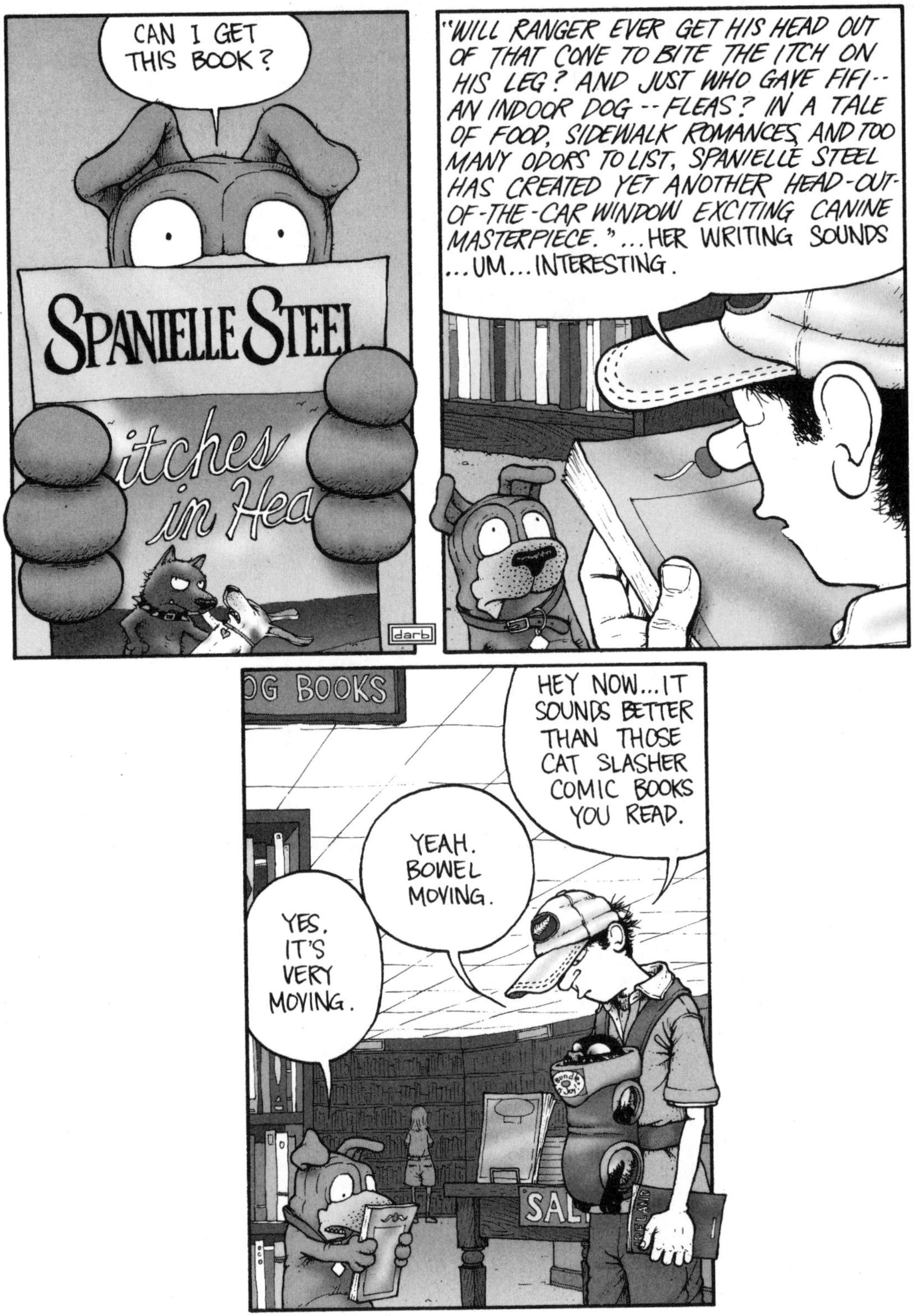
CAN I GET THIS BOOK?
SPANIELLE STEEL
itches
in Hea
darb
"WILL RANGER EVER GET HIS HEAD OUT OF THAT CONE TO BITE THE ITCH ON HIS LEG? AND JUST WHO GAVE FIFI -- AN INDOOR DOG -- FLEAS? IN A TALE OF FOOD, SIDEWALK ROMANCES, AND TOO MANY ODORS TO LIST, SPANIELLE STEEL HAS CREATED YET ANOTHER HEAD-OUT-OF-THE-CAR WINDOW EXCITING CANINE MASTERPIECE."... HER WRITING SOUNDS ...UM... INTERESTING.
OG BOOKS
HEY NOW... IT SOUNDS BETTER THAN THOSE CAT SLASHER COMIC BOOKS YOU READ.
YEAH. BOWEL MOVING.
YES. IT'S VERY MOVING.
SAL

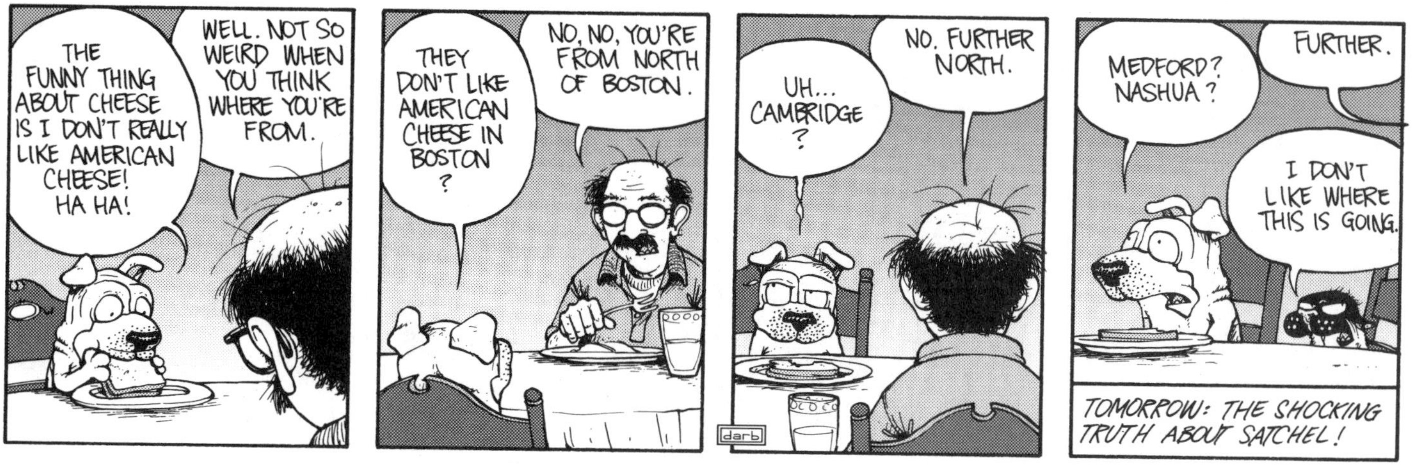
THE FUNNY THING ABOUT CHEESE IS I DON'T REALLY LIKE AMERICAN CHEESE! HA HA!
WELL. NOT SO WEIRD WHEN YOU THINK WHERE YOU'RE FROM.
THEY DON'T LIKE AMERICAN CHEESE IN BOSTON ?
NO, NO, YOU'RE FROM NORTH OF BOSTON.
UH... CAMBRIDGE ?
NO. FURTHER NORTH.
MEDFORD? NASHUA?
FURTHER.
I DON'T LIKE WHERE THIS IS GOING.
TOMORROW: THE SHOCKING TRUTH ABOUT SATCHEL!

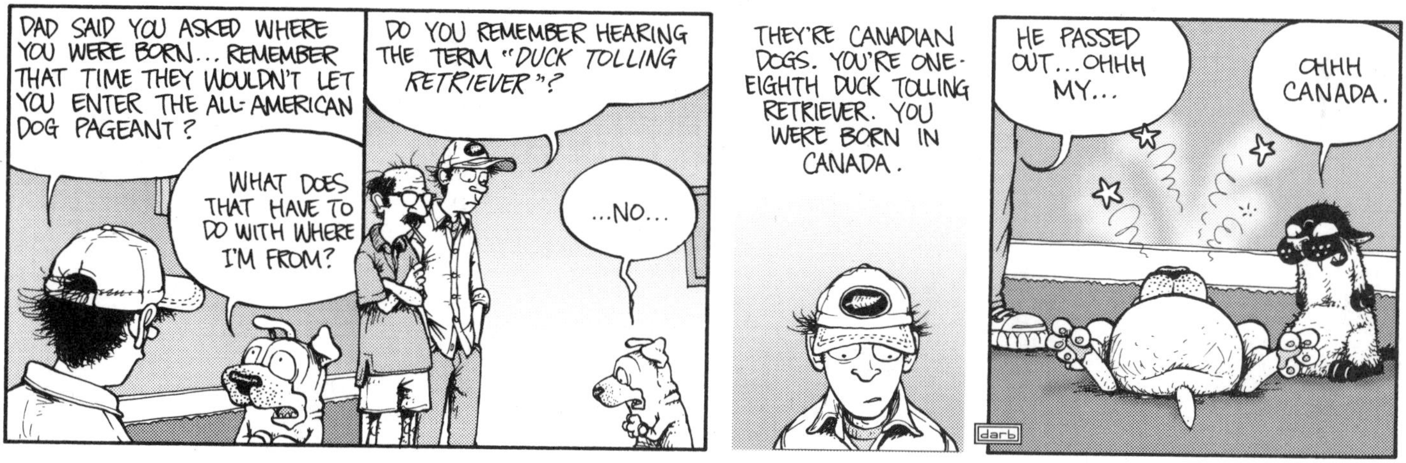
DAD SAID YOU ASKED WHERE YOU WERE BORN... REMEMBER THAT TIME THEY WOULDN'T LET YOU ENTER THE ALL-AMERICAN DOG PAGEANT?
WHAT DOES THAT HAVE TO DO WITH WHERE I'M FROM?
DO YOU REMEMBER HEARING THE TERM "*DUCK TOLLING RETRIEVER*"?
...NO...
THEY'RE CANADIAN DOGS. YOU'RE ONE-EIGHTH DUCK TOLLING RETRIEVER. YOU WERE BORN IN CANADA.
HE PASSED OUT...OHHH MY...
OHHH CANADA.

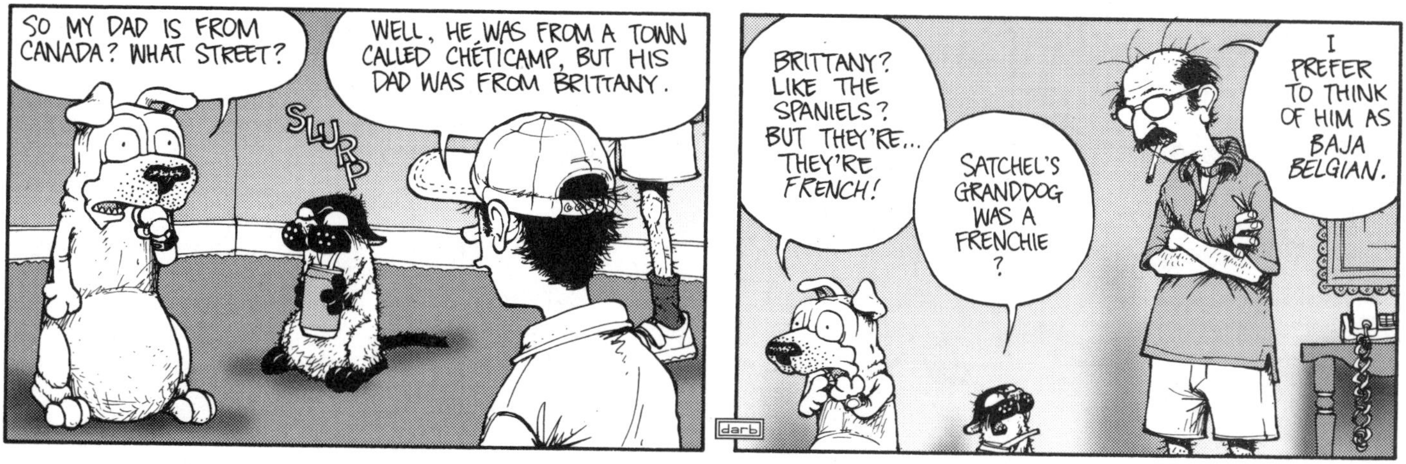
SO MY DAD IS FROM CANADA? WHAT STREET?
SLURP
WELL, HE WAS FROM A TOWN CALLED CHÉTICAMP, BUT HIS DAD WAS FROM BRITTANY.
BRITTANY? LIKE THE SPANIELS? BUT THEY'RE... THEY'RE *FRENCH!*
SATCHEL'S GRANDDOG WAS A FRENCHIE ?
I PREFER TO THINK OF HIM AS *BAJA BELGIAN.*

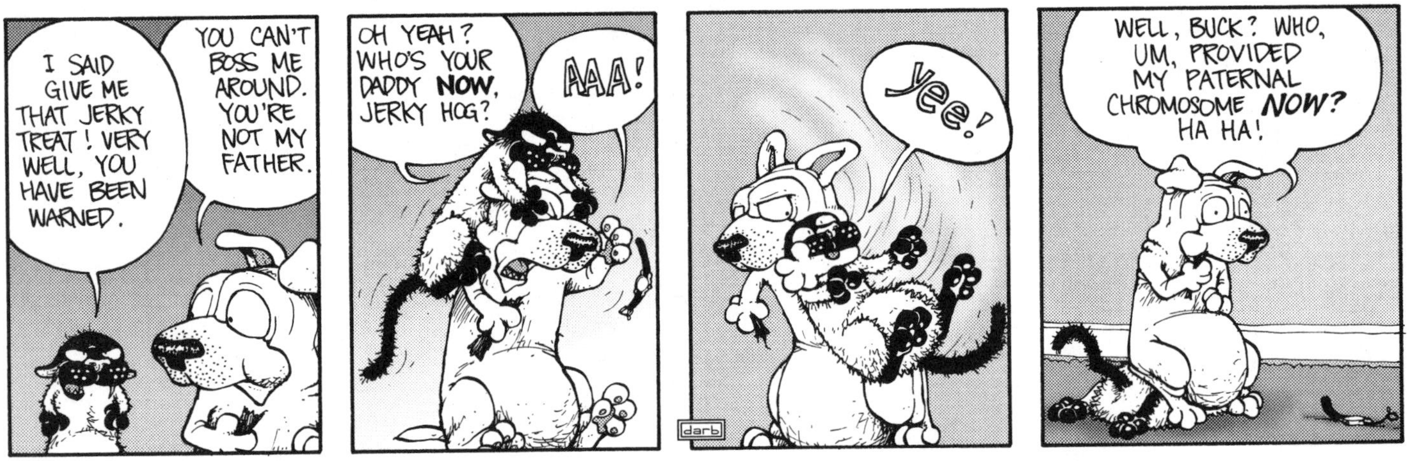
I SAID GIVE ME THAT JERKY TREAT! VERY WELL, YOU HAVE BEEN WARNED.
YOU CAN'T BOSS ME AROUND. YOU'RE NOT MY FATHER.
OH YEAH? WHO'S YOUR DADDY **NOW**, JERKY HOG?
AAA!
YEE!
WELL, BUCK? WHO, UM, PROVIDED MY PATERNAL CHROMOSOME ***NOW?*** HA HA!
darb

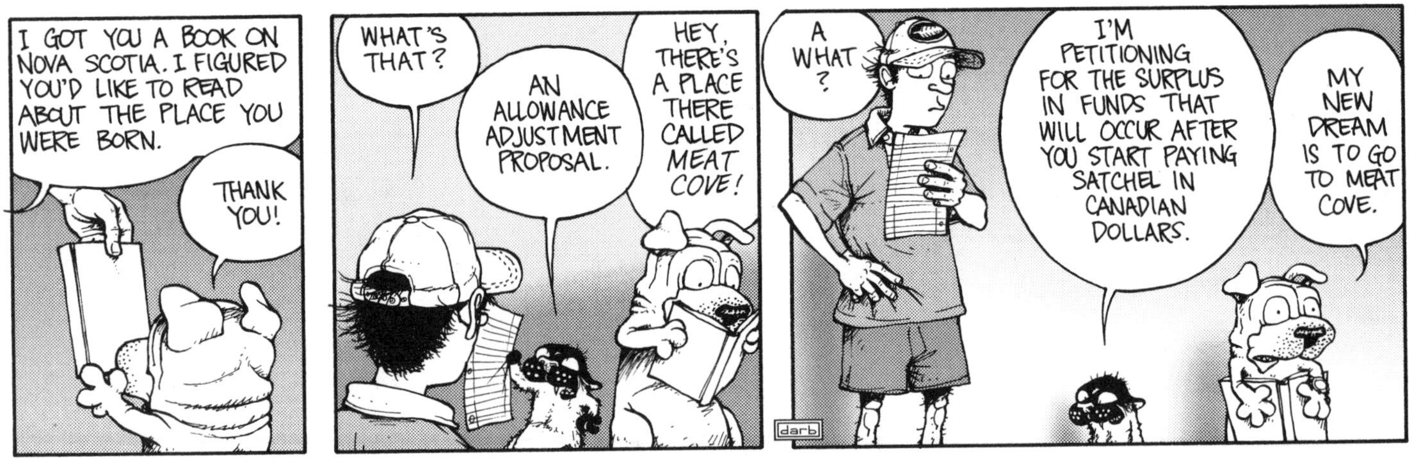
I GOT YOU A BOOK ON NOVA SCOTIA. I FIGURED YOU'D LIKE TO READ ABOUT THE PLACE YOU WERE BORN.
THANK YOU!
WHAT'S THAT?
AN ALLOWANCE ADJUSTMENT PROPOSAL.
HEY, THERE'S A PLACE THERE CALLED *MEAT COVE!*
A WHAT?
I'M PETITIONING FOR THE SURPLUS IN FUNDS THAT WILL OCCUR AFTER YOU START PAYING SATCHEL IN CANADIAN DOLLARS.
MY NEW DREAM IS TO GO TO MEAT COVE.
darb

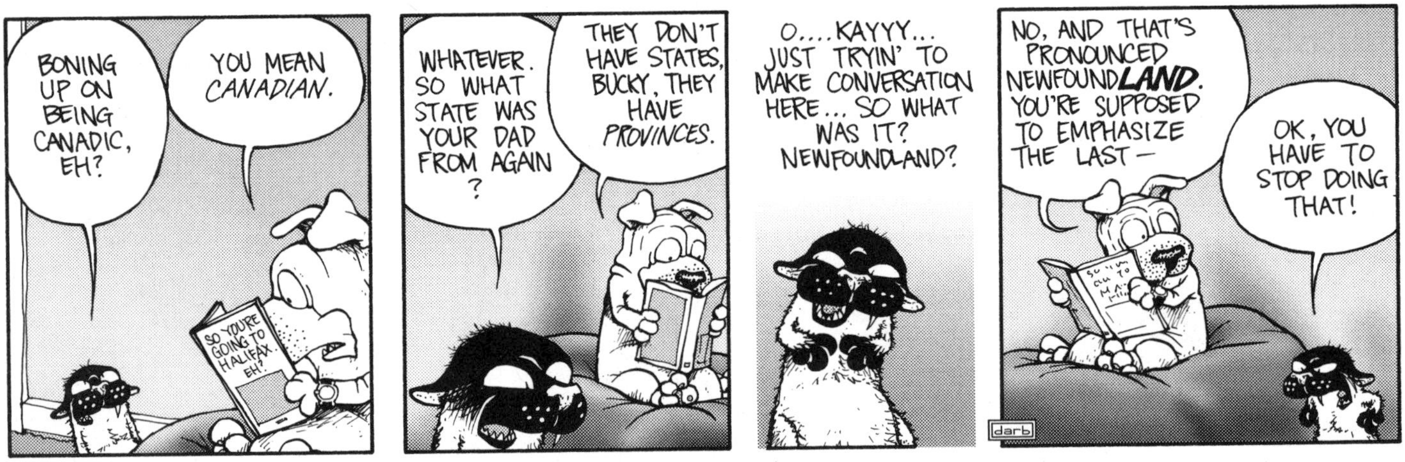
BONING UP ON BEING CANADIC, EH?
YOU MEAN *CANADIAN.*
SO YOU'RE GOING TO HALIFAX, EH?
WHATEVER. SO WHAT STATE WAS YOUR DAD FROM AGAIN?
THEY DON'T HAVE STATES, BUCKY. THEY HAVE *PROVINCES.*
O.... KAYYY... JUST TRYIN' TO MAKE CONVERSATION HERE... SO WHAT WAS IT? NEWFOUNDLAND?
NO, AND THAT'S PRONOUNCED NEWFOUND***LAND***. YOU'RE SUPPOSED TO EMPHASIZE THE LAST—
OK, YOU HAVE TO STOP DOING THAT!
darb

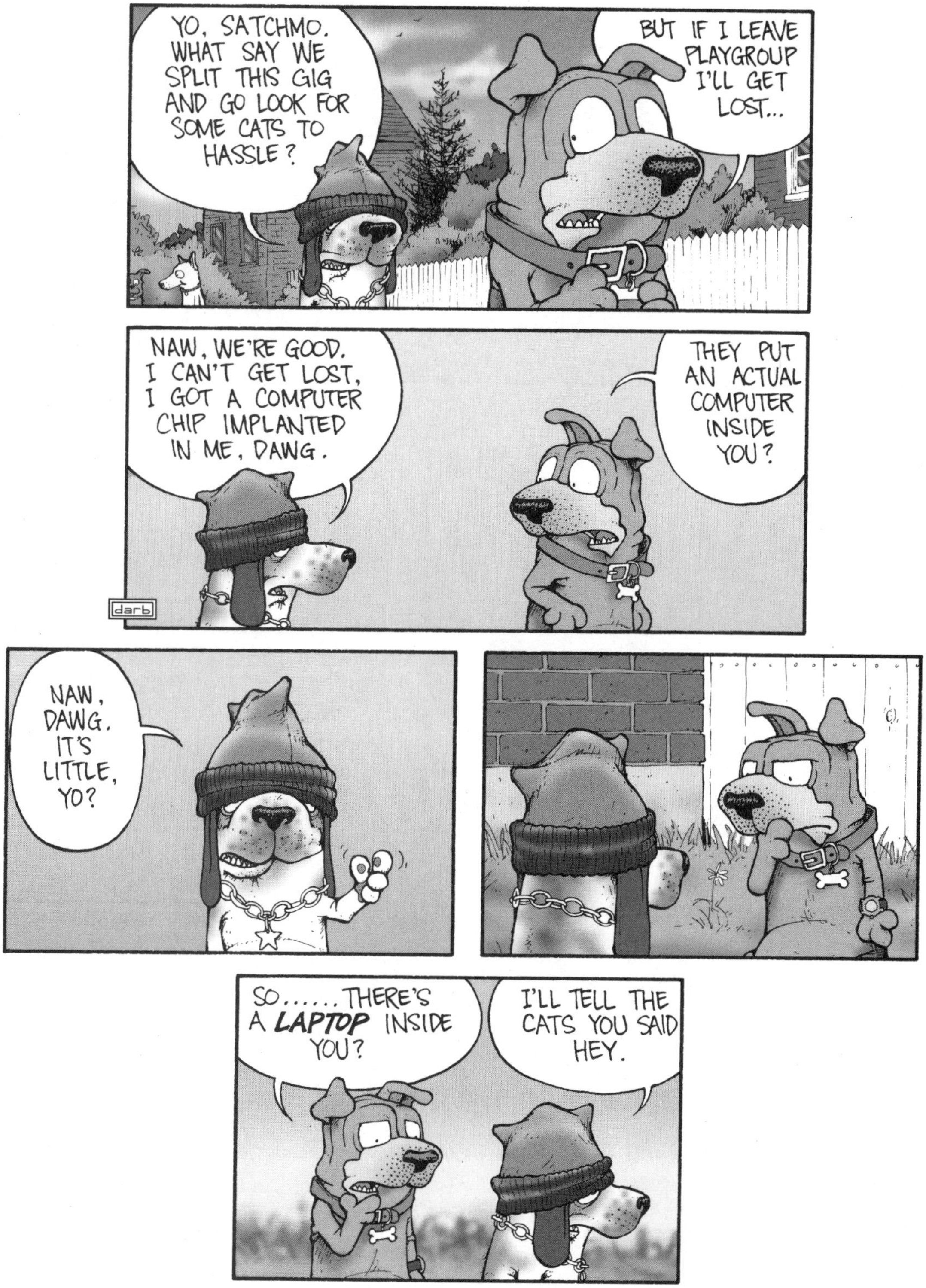
YO, SATCHMO. WHAT SAY WE SPLIT THIS GIG AND GO LOOK FOR SOME CATS TO HASSLE?
BUT IF I LEAVE PLAYGROUP I'LL GET LOST...
NAW, WE'RE GOOD. I CAN'T GET LOST, I GOT A COMPUTER CHIP IMPLANTED IN ME, DAWG.
THEY PUT AN ACTUAL COMPUTER INSIDE YOU?
darb
NAW, DAWG. IT'S LITTLE, YO?
SO......THERE'S A *LAPTOP* INSIDE YOU?
I'LL TELL THE CATS YOU SAID HEY.

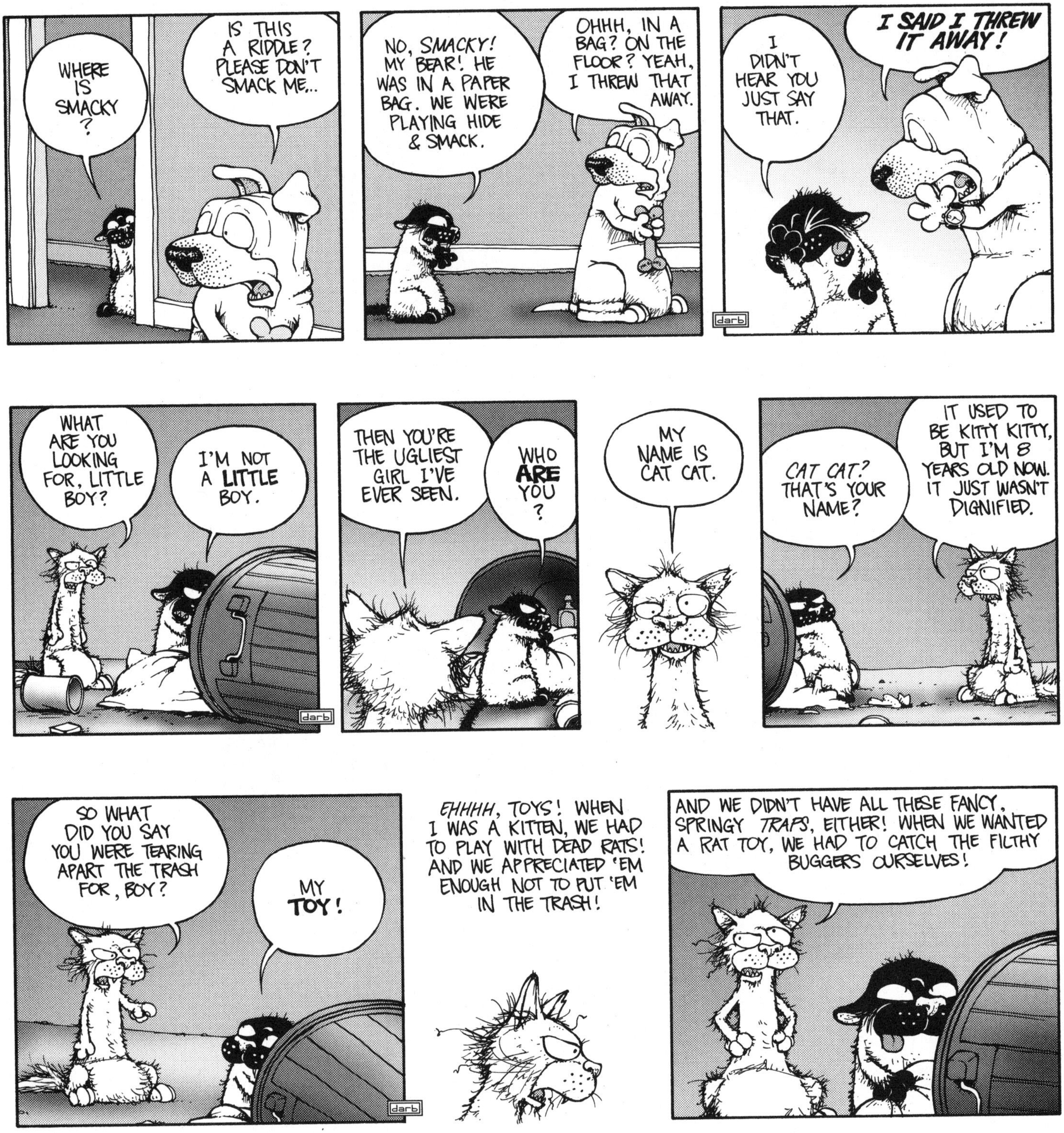
WHERE IS SMACKY?
IS THIS A RIDDLE? PLEASE DON'T SMACK ME...
NO, SMACKY! MY BEAR! HE WAS IN A PAPER BAG. WE WERE PLAYING HIDE & SMACK.
OHHH, IN A BAG? ON THE FLOOR? YEAH, I THREW THAT AWAY.
I DIDN'T HEAR YOU JUST SAY THAT.
I SAID I THREW IT AWAY!
darb
WHAT ARE YOU LOOKING FOR, LITTLE BOY?
I'M NOT A LITTLE BOY.
darb
THEN YOU'RE THE UGLIEST GIRL I'VE EVER SEEN.
WHO ARE YOU?
MY NAME IS CAT CAT.
CAT CAT? THAT'S YOUR NAME?
IT USED TO BE KITTY KITTY, BUT I'M 8 YEARS OLD NOW. IT JUST WASN'T DIGNIFIED.
SO WHAT DID YOU SAY YOU WERE TEARING APART THE TRASH FOR, BOY?
MY TOY!
darb
EHHHH, TOYS! WHEN I WAS A KITTEN, WE HAD TO PLAY WITH DEAD RATS! AND WE APPRECIATED 'EM ENOUGH NOT TO PUT 'EM IN THE TRASH!
AND WE DIDN'T HAVE ALL THESE FANCY, SPRINGY TRAPS, EITHER! WHEN WE WANTED A RAT TOY, WE HAD TO CATCH THE FILTHY BUGGERS OURSELVES!

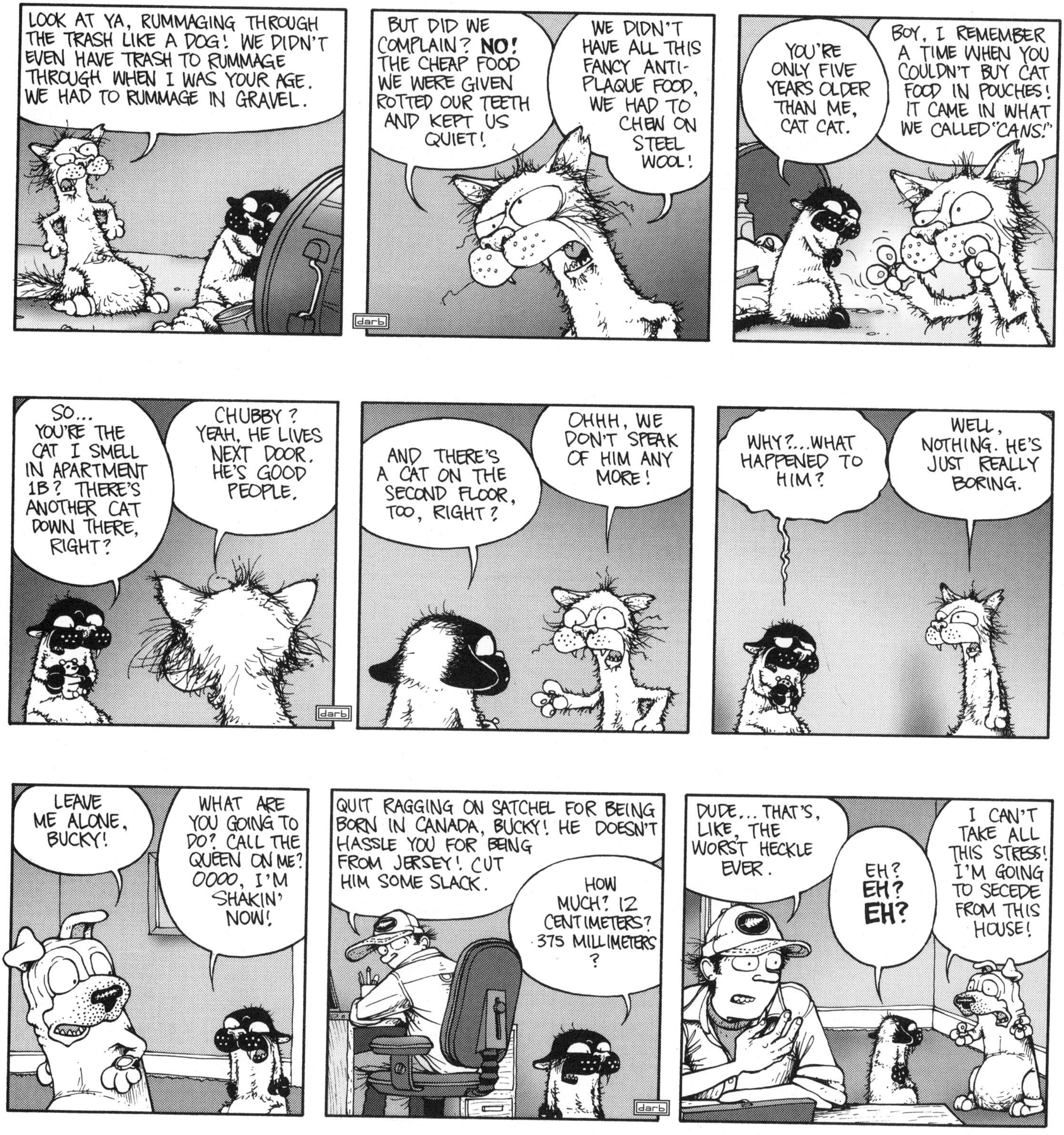
LOOK AT YA, RUMMAGING THROUGH THE TRASH LIKE A DOG! WE DIDN'T EVEN HAVE TRASH TO RUMMAGE THROUGH WHEN I WAS YOUR AGE. WE HAD TO RUMMAGE IN GRAVEL.
BUT DID WE COMPLAIN? **NO!** THE CHEAP FOOD WE WERE GIVEN ROTTED OUR TEETH AND KEPT US QUIET!
WE DIDN'T HAVE ALL THIS FANCY ANTI-PLAQUE FOOD, WE HAD TO CHEW ON STEEL WOOL!
darb
BOY, I REMEMBER A TIME WHEN YOU COULDN'T BUY CAT FOOD IN POUCHES! IT CAME IN WHAT WE CALLED "CANS!"
YOU'RE ONLY FIVE YEARS OLDER THAN ME, CAT CAT.
SO... YOU'RE THE CAT I SMELL IN APARTMENT 1B? THERE'S ANOTHER CAT DOWN THERE, RIGHT?
CHUBBY? YEAH, HE LIVES NEXT DOOR. HE'S GOOD PEOPLE.
darb
AND THERE'S A CAT ON THE SECOND FLOOR, TOO, RIGHT?
OHHH, WE DON'T SPEAK OF HIM ANY MORE!
WHY?...WHAT HAPPENED TO HIM?
WELL, NOTHING. HE'S JUST REALLY BORING.
LEAVE ME ALONE, BUCKY!
WHAT ARE YOU GOING TO DO? CALL THE QUEEN ON ME? OOOO, I'M SHAKIN' NOW!
QUIT RAGGING ON SATCHEL FOR BEING BORN IN CANADA, BUCKY! HE DOESN'T HASSLE YOU FOR BEING FROM JERSEY! CUT HIM SOME SLACK.
HOW MUCH? 12 CENTIMETERS? 375 MILLIMETERS?
darb
DUDE... THAT'S, LIKE, THE WORST HECKLE EVER.
EH? **EH? EH?**
I CAN'T TAKE ALL THIS STRESS! I'M GOING TO SECEDE FROM THIS HOUSE!

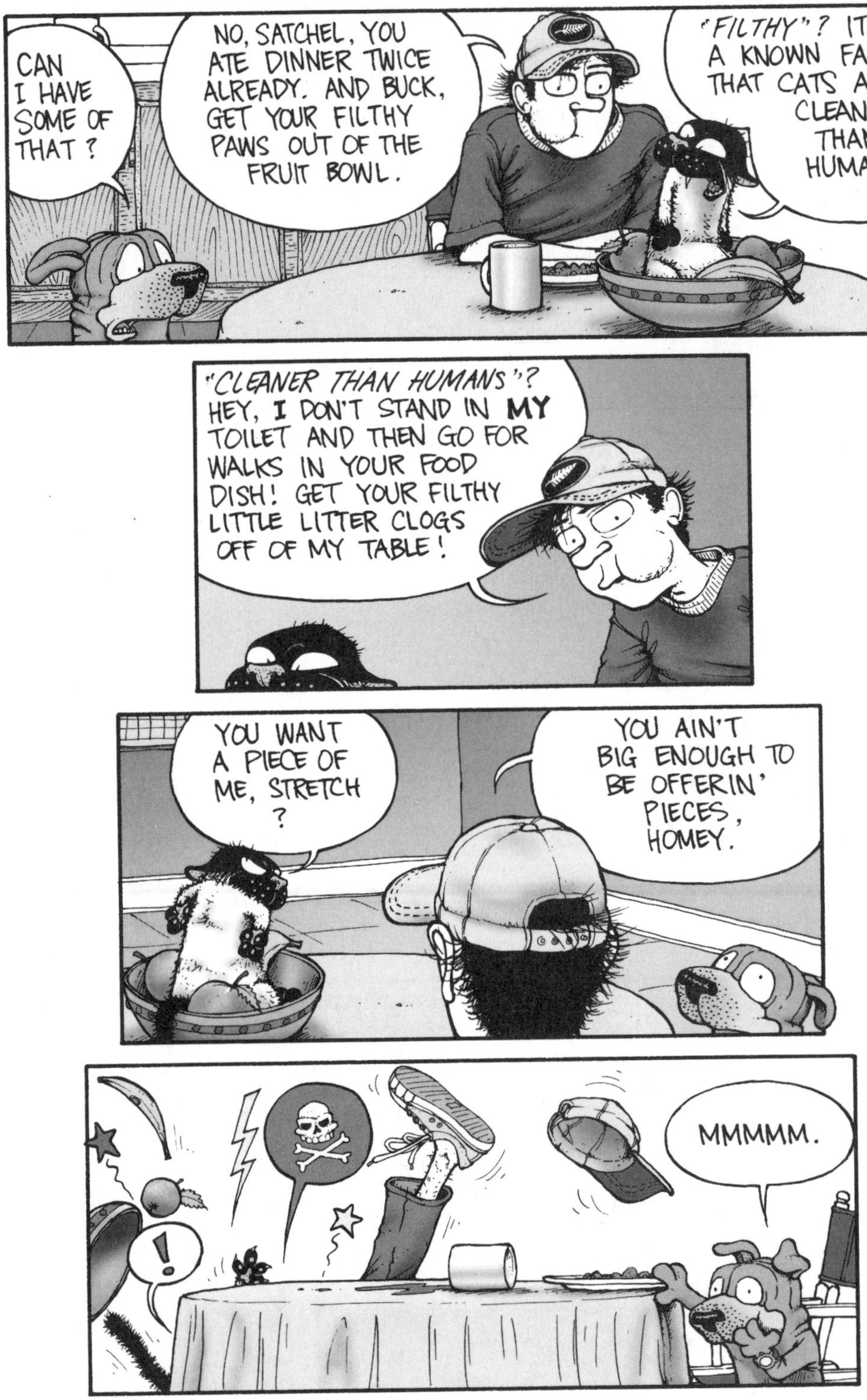
CAN I HAVE SOME OF THAT?
NO, SATCHEL, YOU ATE DINNER TWICE ALREADY. AND BUCK, GET YOUR FILTHY PAWS OUT OF THE FRUIT BOWL.
"FILTHY"? IT IS A KNOWN FACT THAT CATS ARE CLEANER THAN HUMANS.
darb
"CLEANER THAN HUMANS"? HEY, I DON'T STAND IN MY TOILET AND THEN GO FOR WALKS IN YOUR FOOD DISH! GET YOUR FILTHY LITTLE LITTER CLOGS OFF OF MY TABLE!
YOU WANT A PIECE OF ME, STRETCH?
YOU AIN'T BIG ENOUGH TO BE OFFERIN' PIECES, HOMEY.
!
MMMMM.

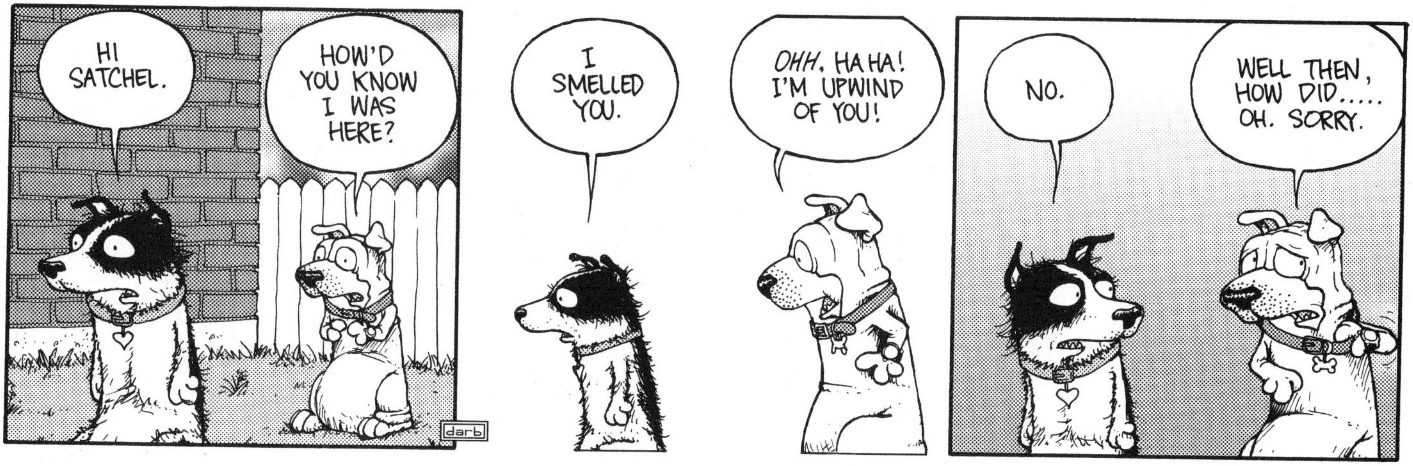
HI SATCHEL.
HOW'D YOU KNOW I WAS HERE?
darb
I SMELLED YOU.
OHH, HA HA! I'M UPWIND OF YOU!
NO.
WELL THEN, HOW DID..... OH. SORRY.

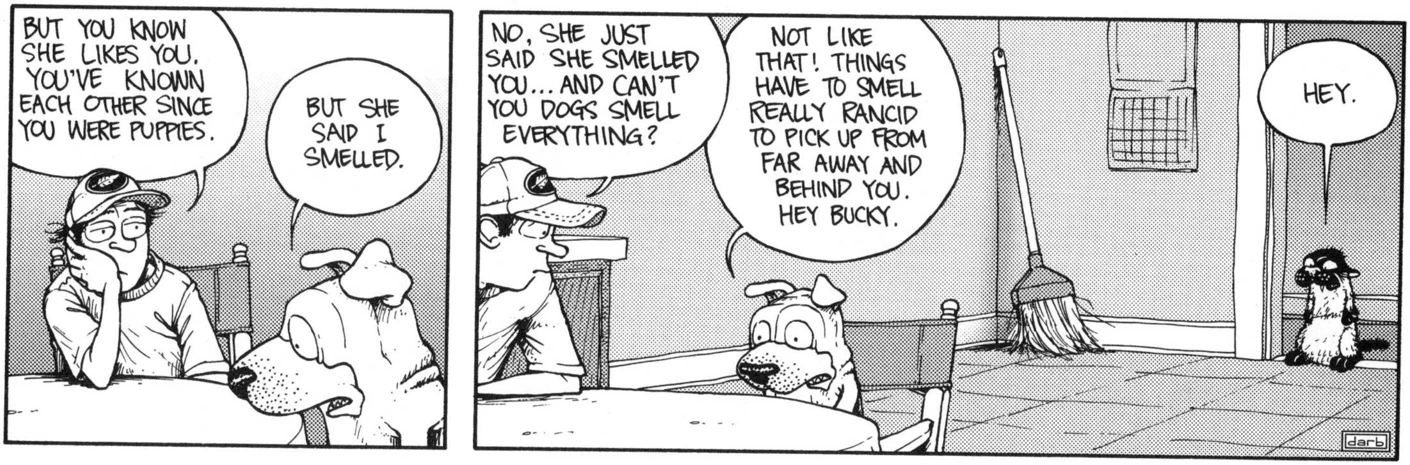
BUT YOU KNOW SHE LIKES YOU. YOU'VE KNOWN EACH OTHER SINCE YOU WERE PUPPIES.
BUT SHE SAID I SMELLED.
NO, SHE JUST SAID SHE SMELLED YOU... AND CAN'T YOU DOGS SMELL EVERYTHING?
NOT LIKE THAT! THINGS HAVE TO SMELL REALLY RANCID TO PICK UP FROM FAR AWAY AND BEHIND YOU. HEY BUCKY.
HEY.
darb

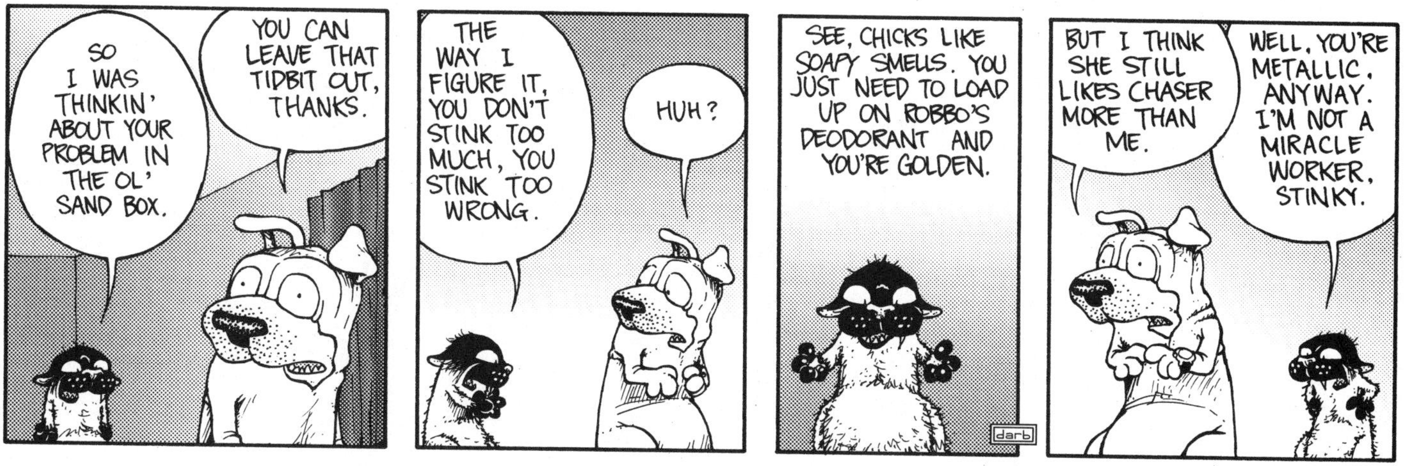
SO I WAS THINKIN' ABOUT YOUR PROBLEM IN THE OL' SAND BOX.
YOU CAN LEAVE THAT TIDBIT OUT, THANKS.
THE WAY I FIGURE IT, YOU DON'T STINK TOO MUCH, YOU STINK TOO WRONG.
HUH?
SEE, CHICKS LIKE SOAPY SMELLS. YOU JUST NEED TO LOAD UP ON ROBBO'S DEODORANT AND YOU'RE GOLDEN.
darb
BUT I THINK SHE STILL LIKES CHASER MORE THAN ME.
WELL, YOU'RE METALLIC, ANYWAY. I'M NOT A MIRACLE WORKER, STINKY.

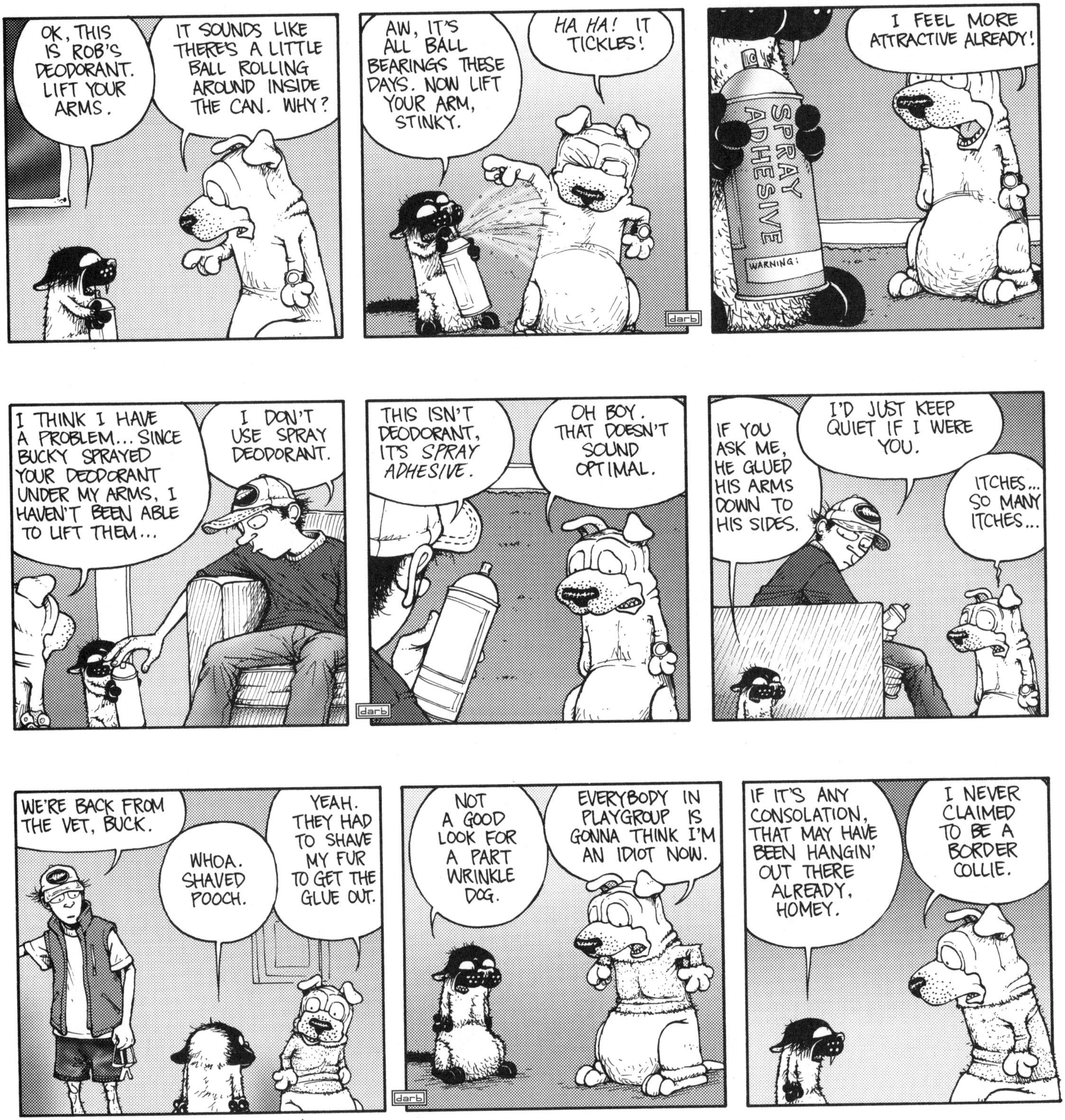
OK, THIS IS ROB'S DEODORANT. LIFT YOUR ARMS.
IT SOUNDS LIKE THERE'S A LITTLE BALL ROLLING AROUND INSIDE THE CAN. WHY?
AW, IT'S ALL BALL BEARINGS THESE DAYS. NOW LIFT YOUR ARM, STINKY.
HA HA! IT TICKLES!
SPRAY ADHESIVE
WARNING:
I FEEL MORE ATTRACTIVE ALREADY!
darb
I THINK I HAVE A PROBLEM... SINCE BUCKY SPRAYED YOUR DEODORANT UNDER MY ARMS, I HAVEN'T BEEN ABLE TO LIFT THEM...
I DON'T USE SPRAY DEODORANT.
THIS ISN'T DEODORANT, IT'S SPRAY ADHESIVE.
OH BOY. THAT DOESN'T SOUND OPTIMAL.
IF YOU ASK ME, HE GLUED HIS ARMS DOWN TO HIS SIDES.
I'D JUST KEEP QUIET IF I WERE YOU.
ITCHES... SO MANY ITCHES...
darb
WE'RE BACK FROM THE VET, BUCK.
WHOA. SHAVED POOCH.
YEAH. THEY HAD TO SHAVE MY FUR TO GET THE GLUE OUT.
NOT A GOOD LOOK FOR A PART WRINKLE DOG.
EVERYBODY IN PLAYGROUP IS GONNA THINK I'M AN IDIOT NOW.
IF IT'S ANY CONSOLATION, THAT MAY HAVE BEEN HANGIN' OUT THERE ALREADY, HOMEY.
I NEVER CLAIMED TO BE A BORDER COLLIE.
darb

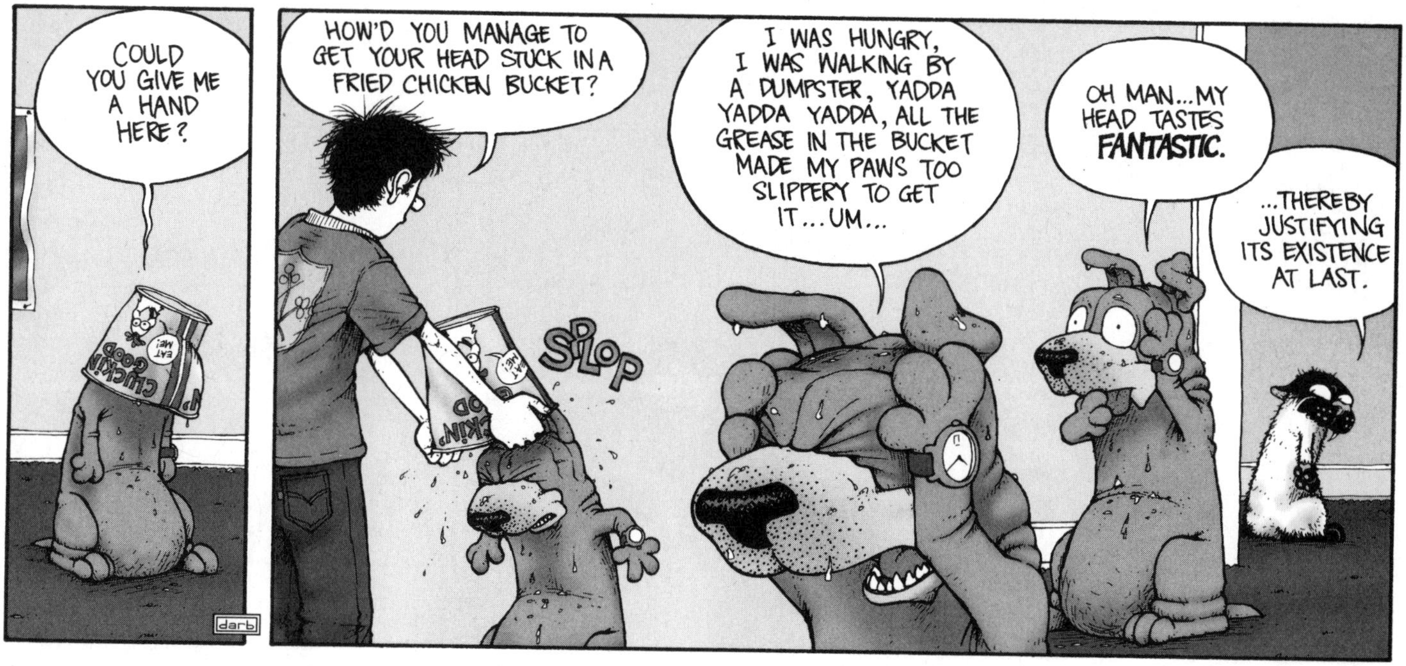
COULD YOU GIVE ME A HAND HERE?
CLUCKIN' GOOD
EAT ME!
darb
HOW'D YOU MANAGE TO GET YOUR HEAD STUCK IN A FRIED CHICKEN BUCKET?
SPLOP
I WAS HUNGRY, I WAS WALKING BY A DUMPSTER, YADDA YADDA YADDA, ALL THE GREASE IN THE BUCKET MADE MY PAWS TOO SLIPPERY TO GET IT... UM...
OH MAN... MY HEAD TASTES **FANTASTIC.**
...THEREBY JUSTIFYING ITS EXISTENCE AT LAST.

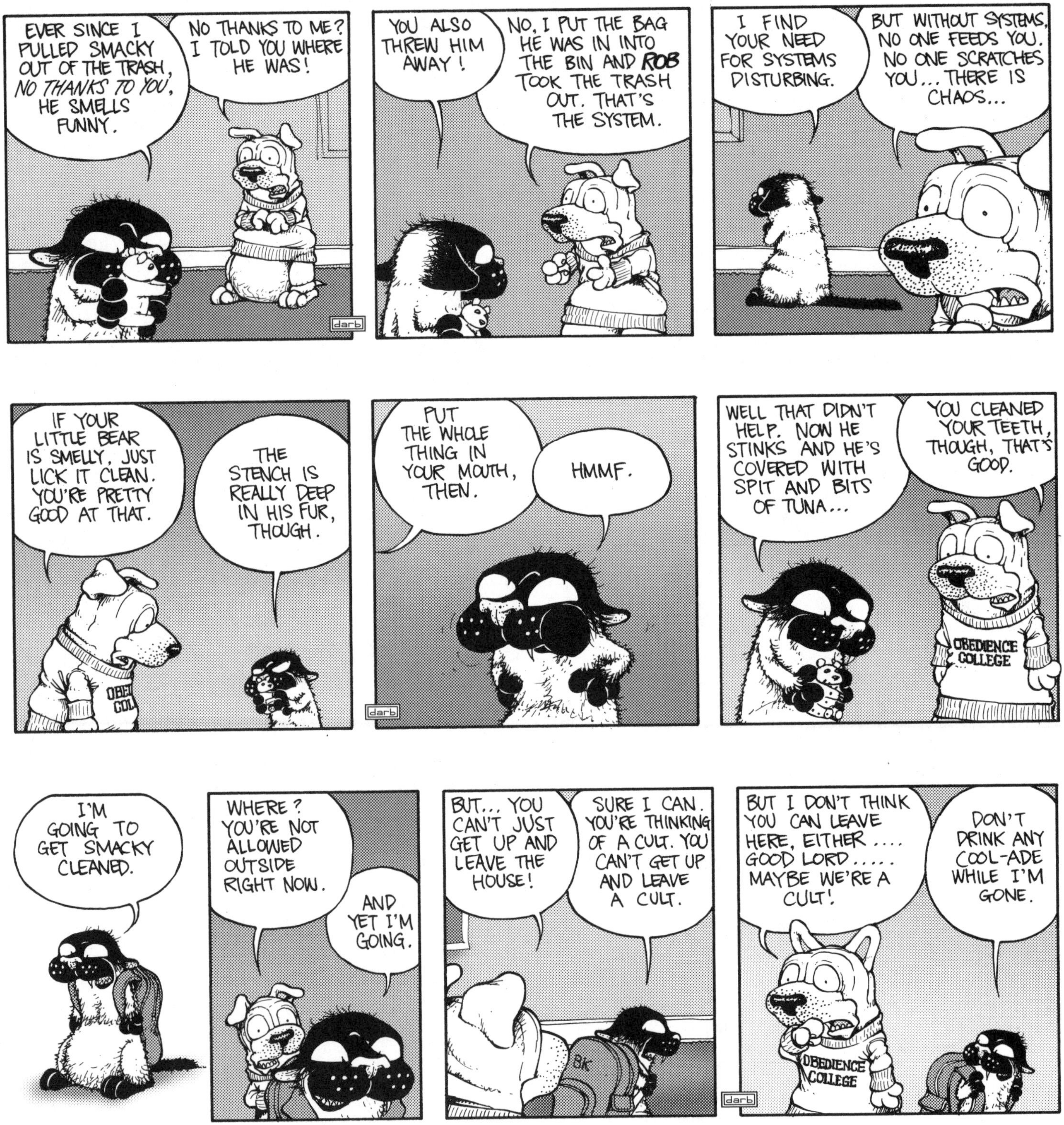
EVER SINCE I PULLED SMACKY OUT OF THE TRASH, *NO THANKS TO YOU*, HE SMELLS FUNNY.
NO THANKS TO ME? I TOLD YOU WHERE HE WAS!
darb
YOU ALSO THREW HIM AWAY!
NO, I PUT THE BAG HE WAS IN INTO THE BIN AND **ROB** TOOK THE TRASH OUT. THAT'S THE SYSTEM.
I FIND YOUR NEED FOR SYSTEMS DISTURBING.
BUT WITHOUT SYSTEMS, NO ONE FEEDS YOU. NO ONE SCRATCHES YOU... THERE IS CHAOS...
IF YOUR LITTLE BEAR IS SMELLY, JUST LICK IT CLEAN. YOU'RE PRETTY GOOD AT THAT.
THE STENCH IS REALLY DEEP IN HIS FUR, THOUGH.
darb
PUT THE WHOLE THING IN YOUR MOUTH, THEN.
HMMF.
WELL THAT DIDN'T HELP. NOW HE STINKS AND HE'S COVERED WITH SPIT AND BITS OF TUNA...
YOU CLEANED YOUR TEETH, THOUGH, THAT'S GOOD.
OBEDIENCE COLLEGE
I'M GOING TO GET SMACKY CLEANED.
WHERE? YOU'RE NOT ALLOWED OUTSIDE RIGHT NOW.
AND YET I'M GOING.
BUT... YOU CAN'T JUST GET UP AND LEAVE THE HOUSE!
SURE I CAN. YOU'RE THINKING OF A CULT. YOU CAN'T GET UP AND LEAVE A CULT.
BK
BUT I DON'T THINK YOU CAN LEAVE HERE, EITHER.... GOOD LORD..... MAYBE WE'RE A CULT!
DON'T DRINK ANY COOL-ADE WHILE I'M GONE.
OBEDIENCE COLLEGE
darb

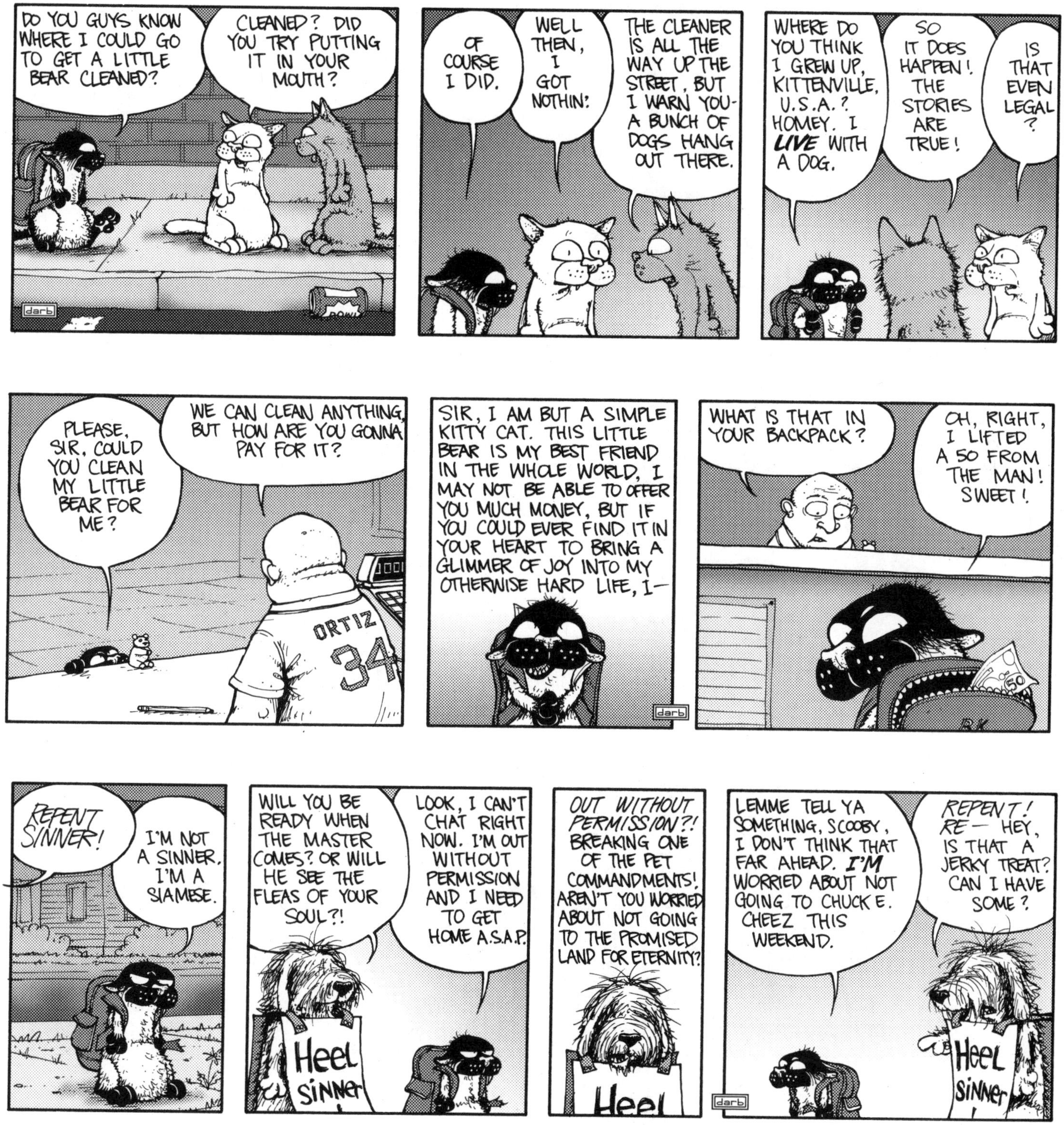
DO YOU GUYS KNOW WHERE I COULD GO TO GET A LITTLE BEAR CLEANED?
CLEANED? DID YOU TRY PUTTING IT IN YOUR MOUTH?
darb
OF COURSE I DID.
WELL THEN, I GOT NOTHIN'.
THE CLEANER IS ALL THE WAY UP THE STREET, BUT I WARN YOU- A BUNCH OF DOGS HANG OUT THERE.
WHERE DO YOU THINK I GREW UP, KITTENVILLE, U.S.A.? HOMEY, I **LIVE** WITH A DOG.
SO IT DOES HAPPEN! THE STORIES ARE TRUE!
IS THAT EVEN LEGAL?
PLEASE, SIR, COULD YOU CLEAN MY LITTLE BEAR FOR ME?
WE CAN CLEAN ANYTHING, BUT HOW ARE YOU GONNA PAY FOR IT?
ORTIZ 34
SIR, I AM BUT A SIMPLE KITTY CAT. THIS LITTLE BEAR IS MY BEST FRIEND IN THE WHOLE WORLD, I MAY NOT BE ABLE TO OFFER YOU MUCH MONEY, BUT IF YOU COULD EVER FIND IT IN YOUR HEART TO BRING A GLIMMER OF JOY INTO MY OTHERWISE HARD LIFE, I—
darb
WHAT IS THAT IN YOUR BACKPACK?
OH, RIGHT, I LIFTED A 50 FROM THE MAN! SWEET!
50
REPENT SINNER!
I'M NOT A SINNER, I'M A SIAMESE.
WILL YOU BE READY WHEN THE MASTER COMES? OR WILL HE SEE THE FLEAS OF YOUR SOUL?!
LOOK, I CAN'T CHAT RIGHT NOW. I'M OUT WITHOUT PERMISSION AND I NEED TO GET HOME A.S.A.P.
Heel sinner
OUT WITHOUT PERMISSION?! BREAKING ONE OF THE PET COMMANDMENTS! AREN'T YOU WORRIED ABOUT NOT GOING TO THE PROMISED LAND FOR ETERNITY?
darb
LEMME TELL YA SOMETHING, SCOOBY, I DON'T THINK THAT FAR AHEAD. **I'M** WORRIED ABOUT NOT GOING TO CHUCK E. CHEEZ THIS WEEKEND.
REPENT! RE— HEY, IS THAT A JERKY TREAT? CAN I HAVE SOME?
Heel sinner

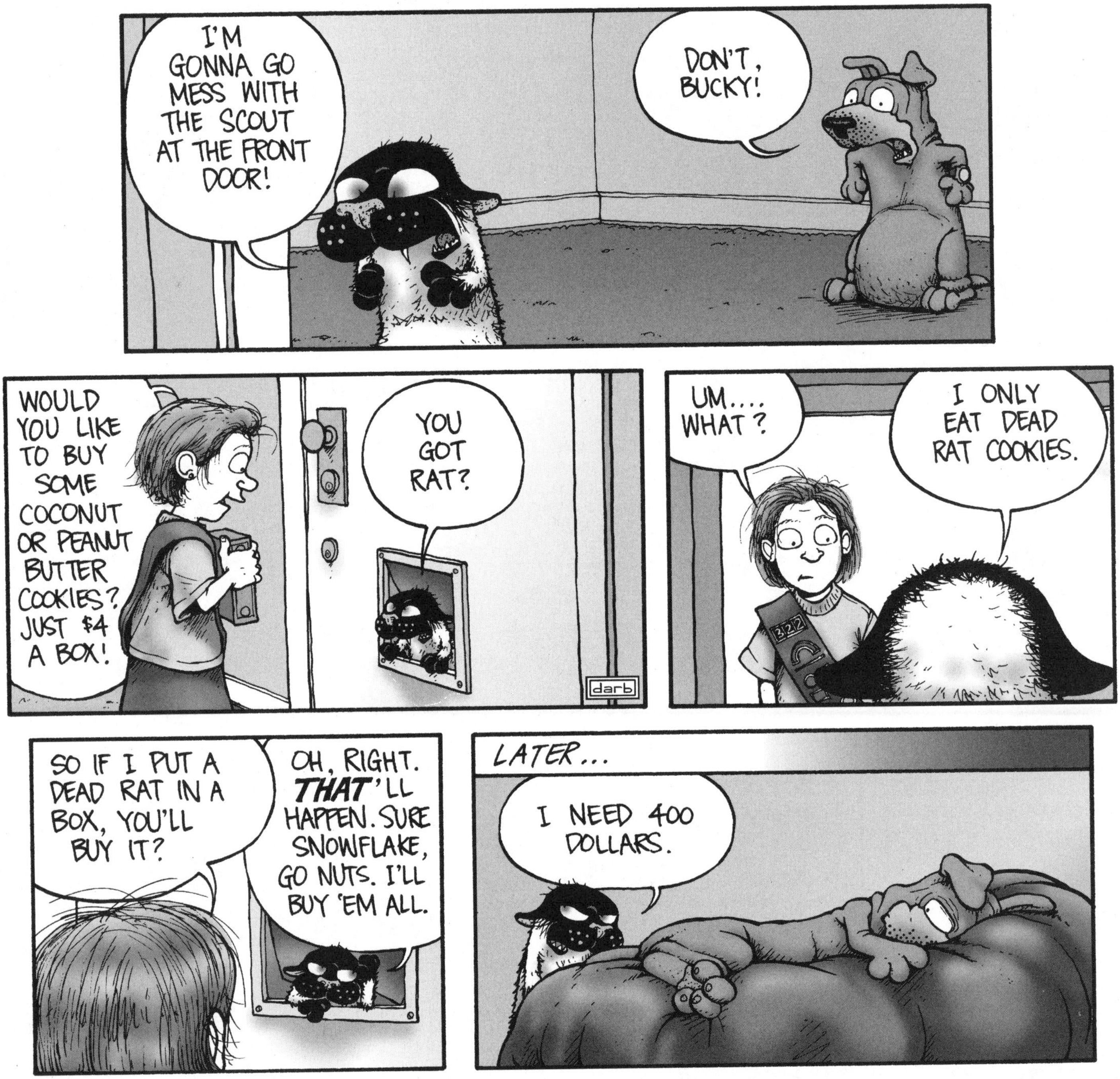
I'M GONNA GO MESS WITH THE SCOUT AT THE FRONT DOOR!
DON'T, BUCKY!
WOULD YOU LIKE TO BUY SOME COCONUT OR PEANUT BUTTER COOKIES? JUST $4 A BOX!
YOU GOT RAT?
darb
UM.... WHAT?
I ONLY EAT DEAD RAT COOKIES.
SO IF I PUT A DEAD RAT IN A BOX, YOU'LL BUY IT?
OH, RIGHT. **THAT**'LL HAPPEN. SURE SNOWFLAKE, GO NUTS. I'LL BUY 'EM ALL.
LATER...
I NEED 400 DOLLARS.

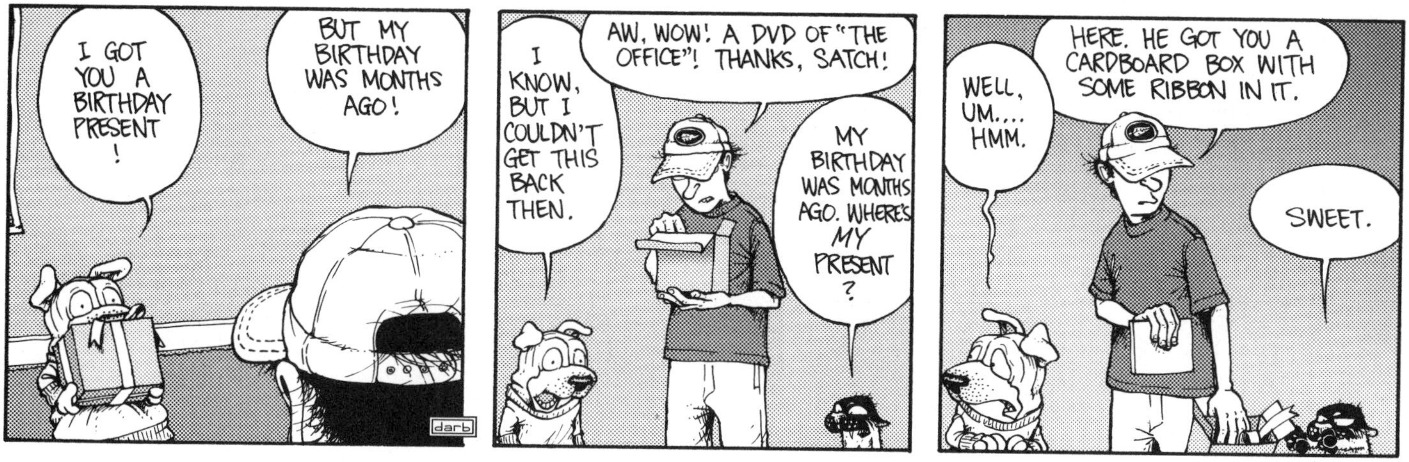
I GOT YOU A BIRTHDAY PRESENT!
BUT MY BIRTHDAY WAS MONTHS AGO!
I KNOW, BUT I COULDN'T GET THIS BACK THEN.
AW, WOW! A DVD OF "THE OFFICE"! THANKS, SATCH!
MY BIRTHDAY WAS MONTHS AGO. WHERE'S *MY* PRESENT?
WELL, UM.... HMM.
HERE. HE GOT YOU A CARDBOARD BOX WITH SOME RIBBON IN IT.
SWEET.
darb

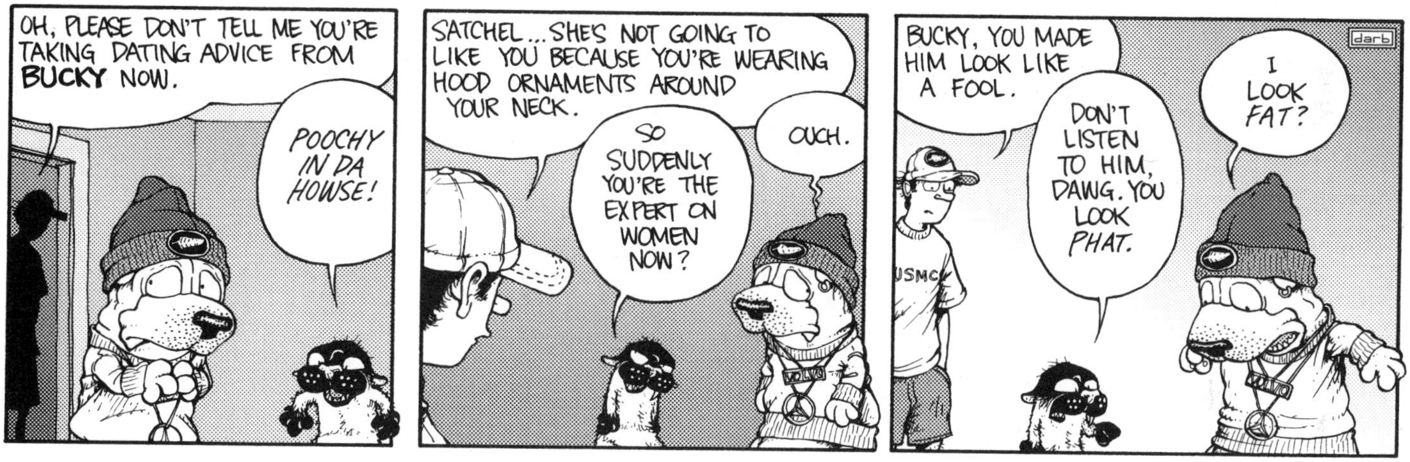
OH, PLEASE DON'T TELL ME YOU'RE TAKING DATING ADVICE FROM **BUCKY** NOW.
POOCHY IN DA HOWSE!
SATCHEL... SHE'S NOT GOING TO LIKE YOU BECAUSE YOU'RE WEARING HOOD ORNAMENTS AROUND YOUR NECK.
SO SUDDENLY YOU'RE THE EXPERT ON WOMEN NOW?
OUCH.
darb
BUCKY, YOU MADE HIM LOOK LIKE A FOOL.
I LOOK *FAT?*
DON'T LISTEN TO HIM, DAWG. YOU LOOK *PHAT.*
USMC

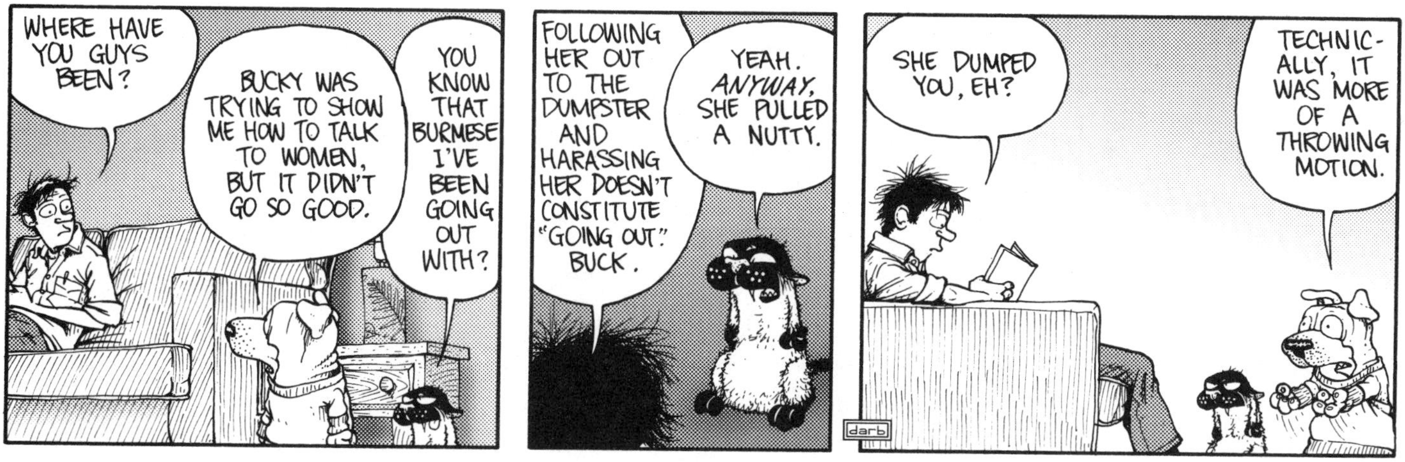
WHERE HAVE YOU GUYS BEEN?
BUCKY WAS TRYING TO SHOW ME HOW TO TALK TO WOMEN, BUT IT DIDN'T GO SO GOOD.
YOU KNOW THAT BURMESE I'VE BEEN GOING OUT WITH?
FOLLOWING HER OUT TO THE DUMPSTER AND HARASSING HER DOESN'T CONSTITUTE "GOING OUT," BUCK.
YEAH. *ANYWAY,* SHE PULLED A NUTTY.
darb
SHE DUMPED YOU, EH?
TECHNICALLY, IT WAS MORE OF A THROWING MOTION.

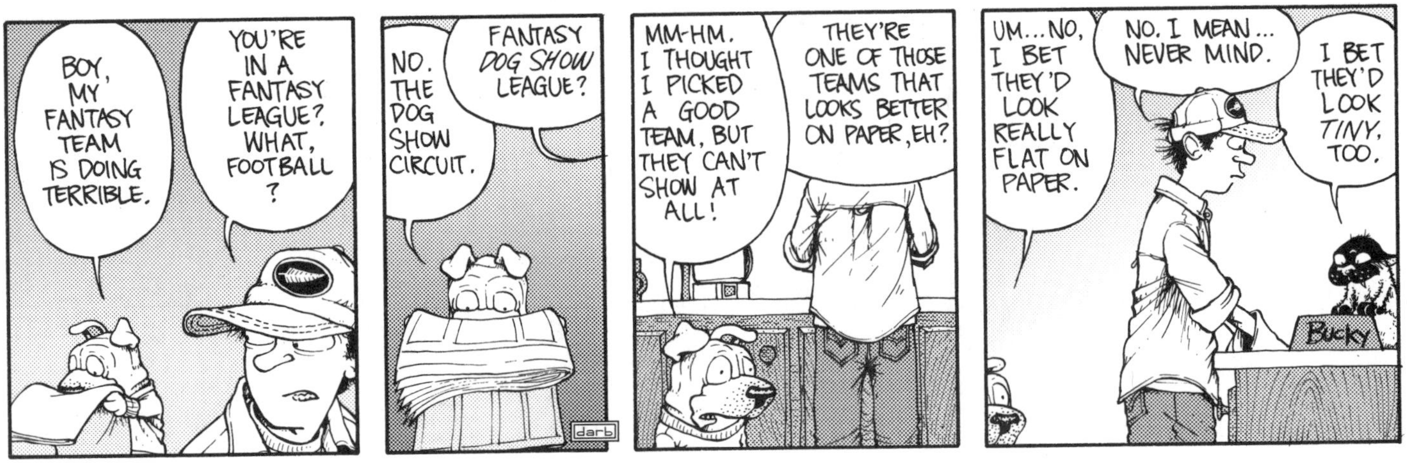
BOY, MY FANTASY TEAM IS DOING TERRIBLE.
YOU'RE IN A FANTASY LEAGUE? WHAT, FOOTBALL?
NO. THE DOG SHOW CIRCUIT.
FANTASY *DOG SHOW* LEAGUE?
darb
MM-HM. I THOUGHT I PICKED A GOOD TEAM, BUT THEY CAN'T SHOW AT ALL!
THEY'RE ONE OF THOSE TEAMS THAT LOOKS BETTER ON PAPER, EH?
UM...NO, I BET THEY'D LOOK REALLY FLAT ON PAPER.
NO. I MEAN... NEVER MIND.
I BET THEY'D LOOK *TINY*, TOO.
Bucky

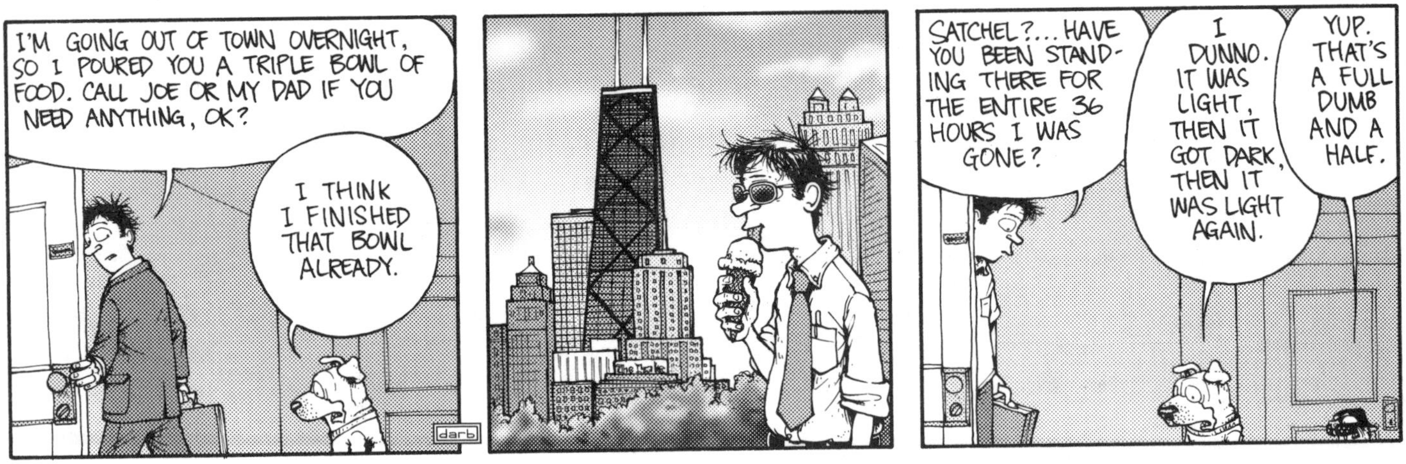
I'M GOING OUT OF TOWN OVERNIGHT, SO I POURED YOU A TRIPLE BOWL OF FOOD. CALL JOE OR MY DAD IF YOU NEED ANYTHING, OK?
I THINK I FINISHED THAT BOWL ALREADY.
darb
SATCHEL?... HAVE YOU BEEN STANDING THERE FOR THE ENTIRE 36 HOURS I WAS GONE?
I DUNNO. IT WAS LIGHT, THEN IT GOT DARK, THEN IT WAS LIGHT AGAIN.
YUP. THAT'S A FULL DUMB AND A HALF.

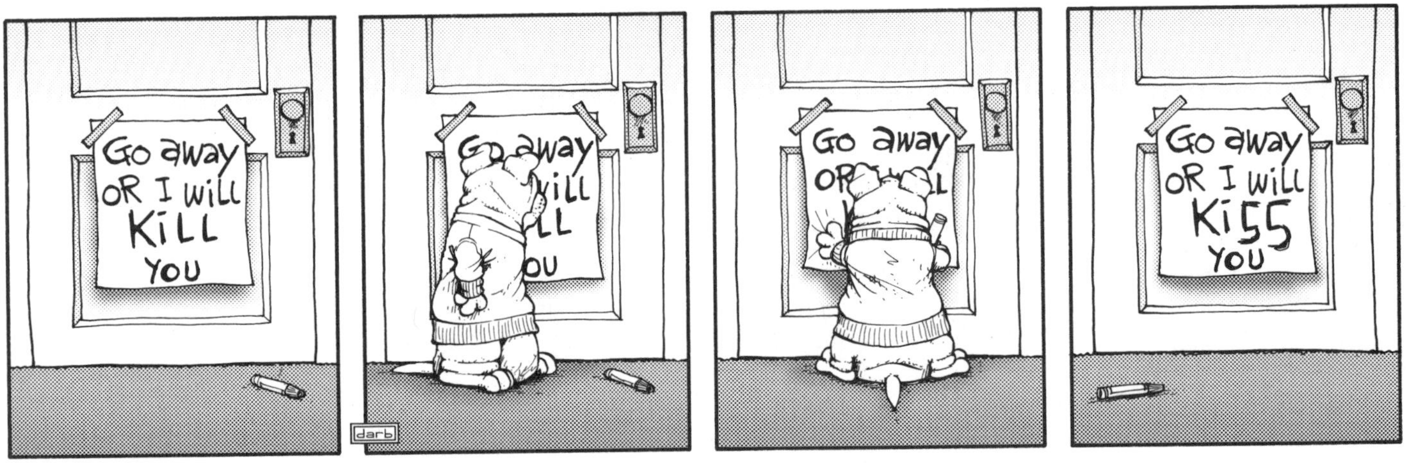
Go away OR I will KiLL YOU
darb
Go away OR I will KiSS YOU

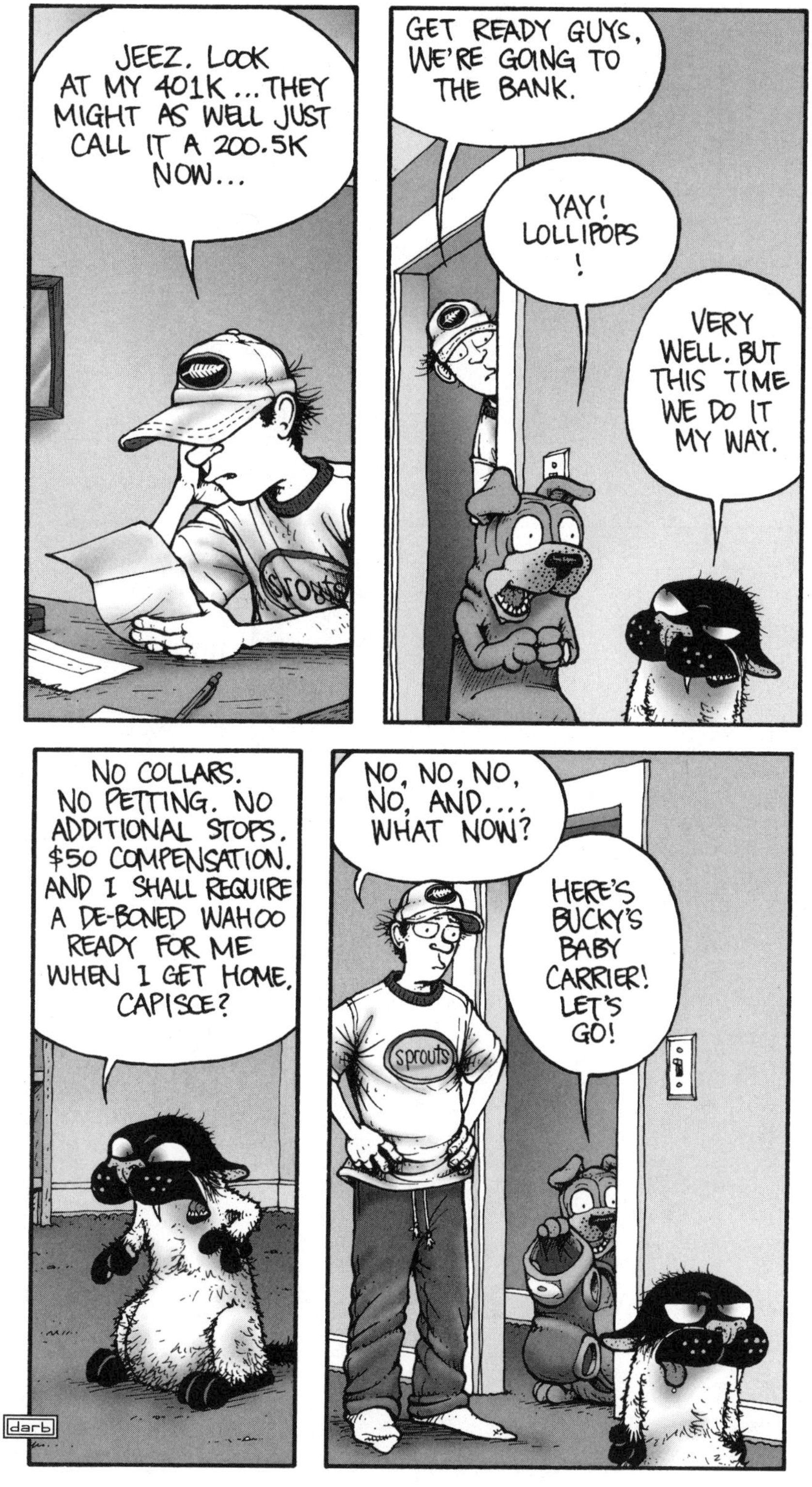
JEEZ. LOOK AT MY 401K ... THEY MIGHT AS WELL JUST CALL IT A 200.5K NOW...
GET READY GUYS, WE'RE GOING TO THE BANK.
YAY! LOLLIPOPS !
VERY WELL. BUT THIS TIME WE DO IT MY WAY.
NO COLLARS. NO PETTING. NO ADDITIONAL STOPS. $50 COMPENSATION. AND I SHALL REQUIRE A DE-BONED WAHOO READY FOR ME WHEN I GET HOME, CAPISCE?
NO, NO, NO, NO, AND.... WHAT NOW?
HERE'S BUCKY'S BABY CARRIER! LET'S GO!
sprouts
darb

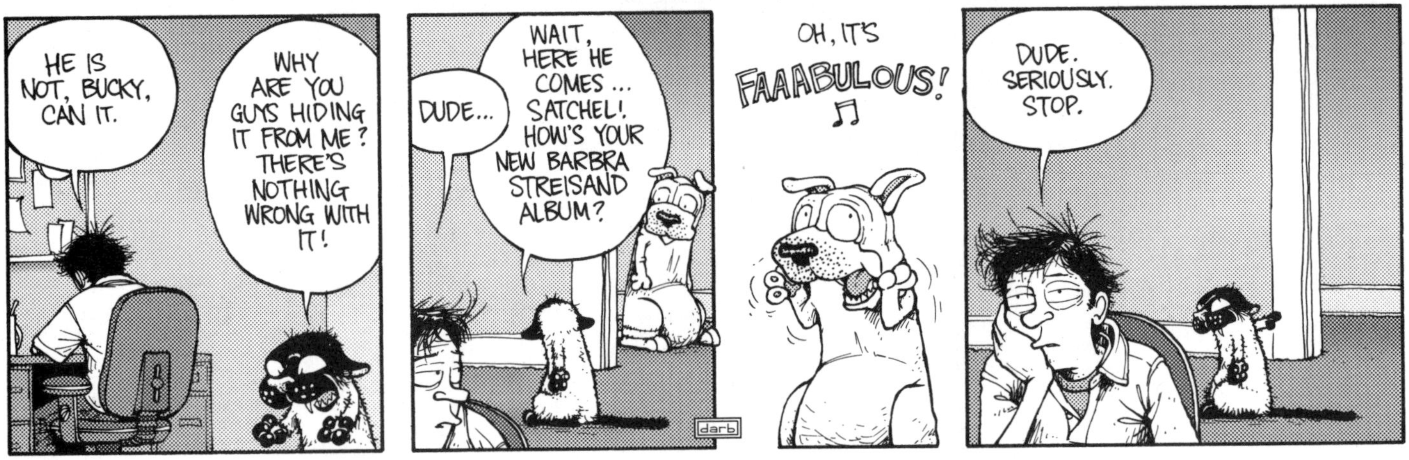
HE IS NOT, BUCKY, CAN IT.
WHY ARE YOU GUYS HIDING IT FROM ME? THERE'S NOTHING WRONG WITH IT!
DUDE...
WAIT, HERE HE COMES... SATCHEL! HOW'S YOUR NEW BARBRA STREISAND ALBUM?
darb
OH, IT'S FAAABULOUS!
DUDE. SERIOUSLY. STOP.

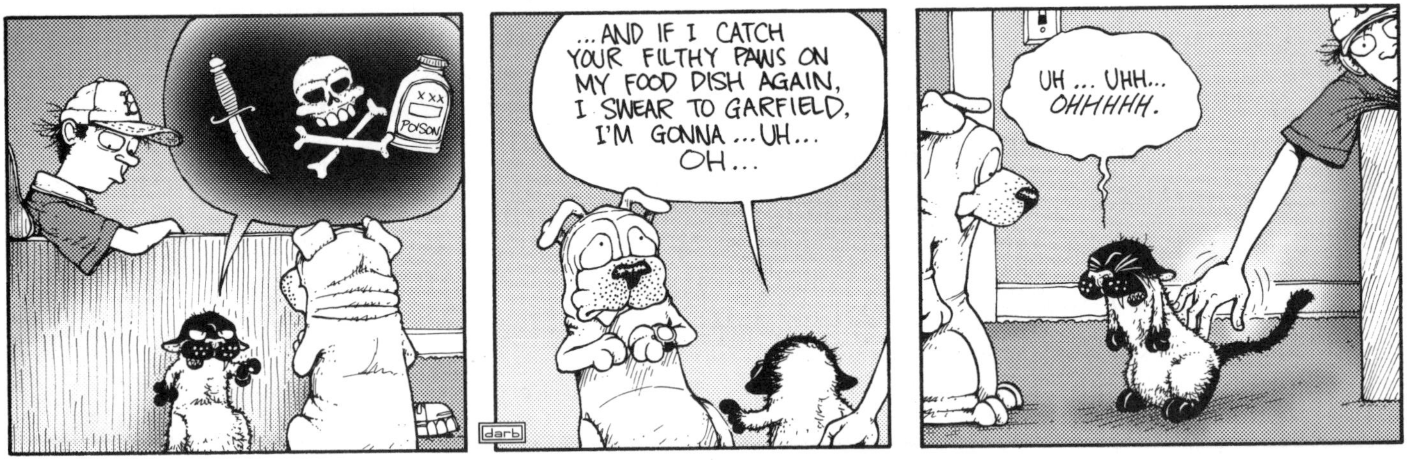
POISON
darb
...AND IF I CATCH YOUR FILTHY PAWS ON MY FOOD DISH AGAIN, I SWEAR TO GARFIELD, I'M GONNA...UH... OH...
UH... UHH... OHHHHH.

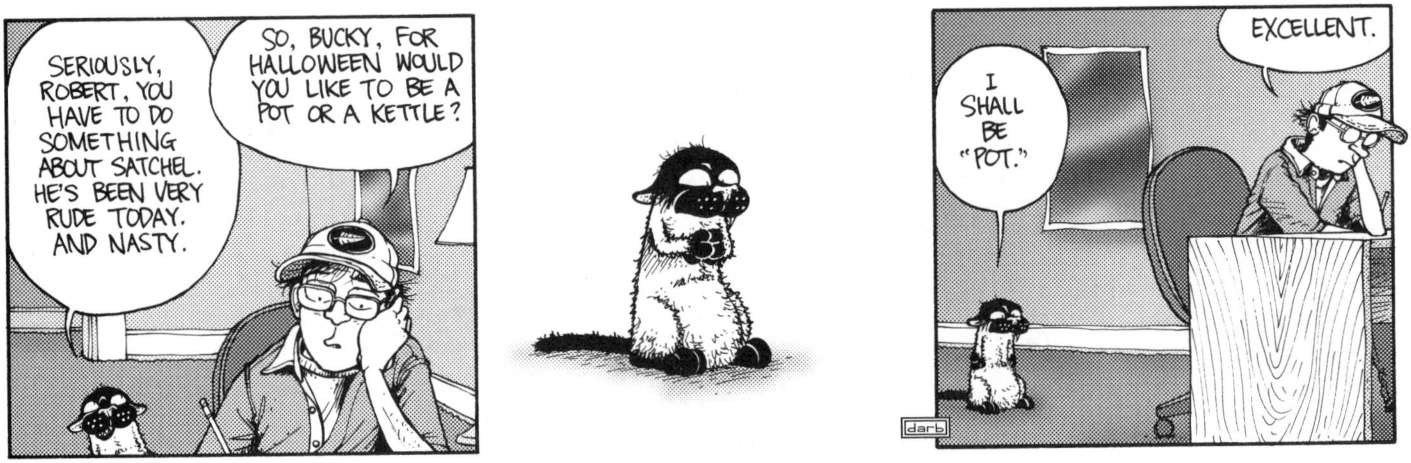
SERIOUSLY, ROBERT, YOU HAVE TO DO SOMETHING ABOUT SATCHEL. HE'S BEEN VERY RUDE TODAY. AND NASTY.
SO, BUCKY, FOR HALLOWEEN WOULD YOU LIKE TO BE A POT OR A KETTLE?
I SHALL BE "POT."
EXCELLENT.
darb

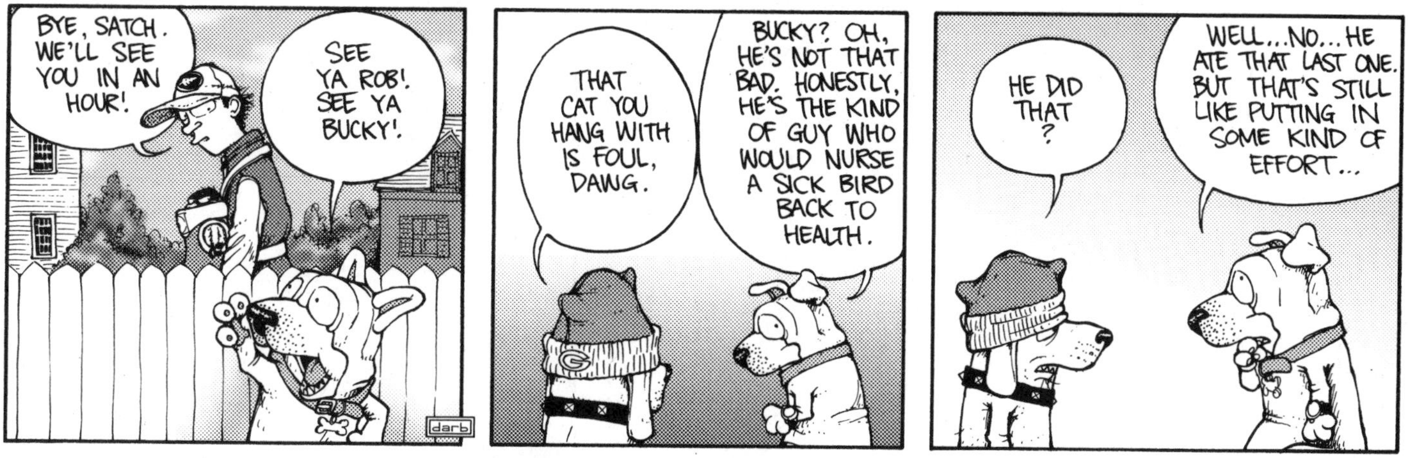
BYE, SATCH. WE'LL SEE YOU IN AN HOUR!
SEE YA ROB! SEE YA BUCKY!
darb
THAT CAT YOU HANG WITH IS FOUL, DAWG.
BUCKY? OH, HE'S NOT THAT BAD. HONESTLY, HE'S THE KIND OF GUY WHO WOULD NURSE A SICK BIRD BACK TO HEALTH.
HE DID THAT?
WELL... NO... HE ATE THAT LAST ONE. BUT THAT'S STILL LIKE PUTTING IN SOME KIND OF EFFORT...

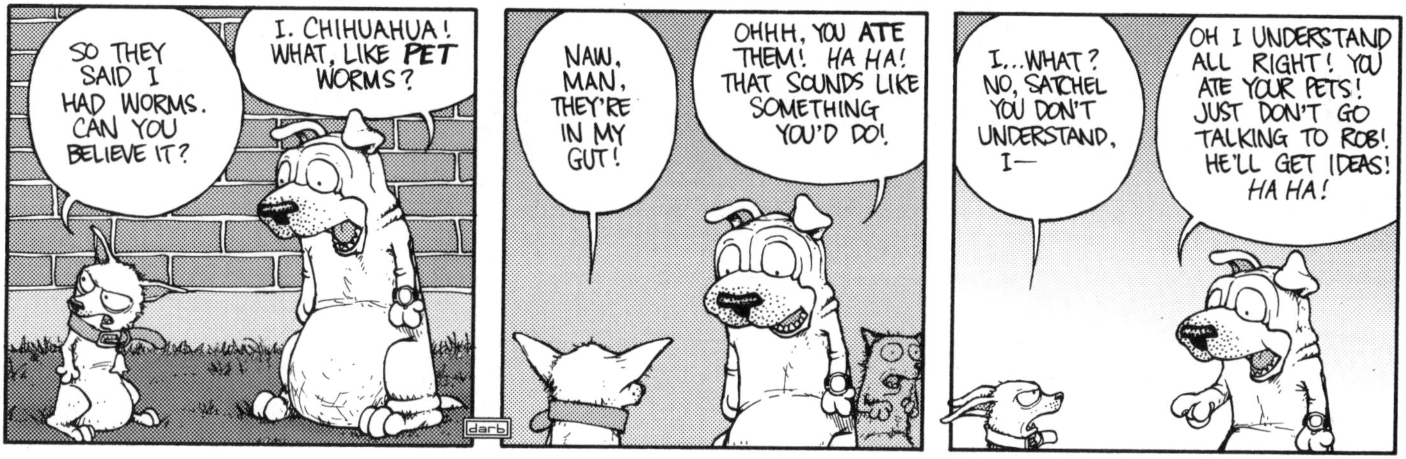
SO THEY SAID I HAD WORMS. CAN YOU BELIEVE IT?
I. CHIHUAHUA! WHAT, LIKE **PET** WORMS?
darb
NAW, MAN, THEY'RE IN MY GUT!
OHHH, YOU **ATE** THEM! *HA HA!* THAT SOUNDS LIKE SOMETHING YOU'D DO!
I... WHAT? NO, SATCHEL YOU DON'T UNDERSTAND, I—
OH I UNDERSTAND ALL RIGHT! YOU ATE YOUR PETS! JUST DON'T GO TALKING TO ROB! HE'LL GET IDEAS! *HA HA!*

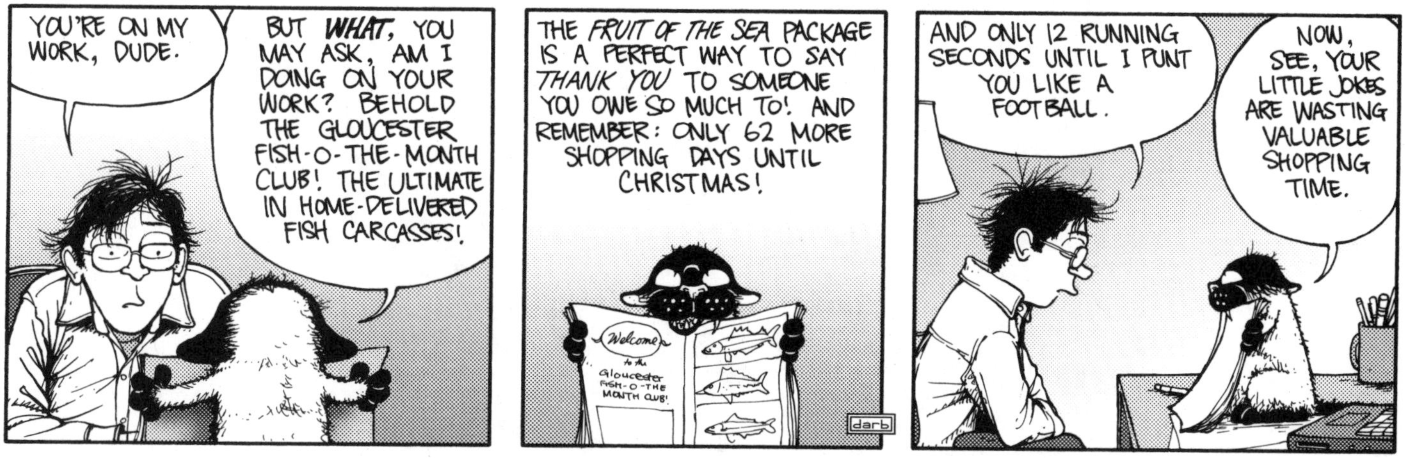
YOU'RE ON MY WORK, DUDE.
BUT ***WHAT,*** YOU MAY ASK, AM I DOING ON YOUR WORK? BEHOLD THE GLOUCESTER FISH-O-THE-MONTH CLUB! THE ULTIMATE IN HOME-DELIVERED FISH CARCASSES!
THE *FRUIT OF THE SEA* PACKAGE IS A PERFECT WAY TO SAY *THANK YOU* TO SOMEONE YOU OWE SO MUCH TO! AND REMEMBER: ONLY 62 MORE SHOPPING DAYS UNTIL CHRISTMAS!
Welcome to the Gloucester FISH-O-THE MONTH CLUB!
darb
AND ONLY 12 RUNNING SECONDS UNTIL I PUNT YOU LIKE A FOOTBALL.
NOW, SEE, YOUR LITTLE JOKES ARE WASTING VALUABLE SHOPPING TIME.

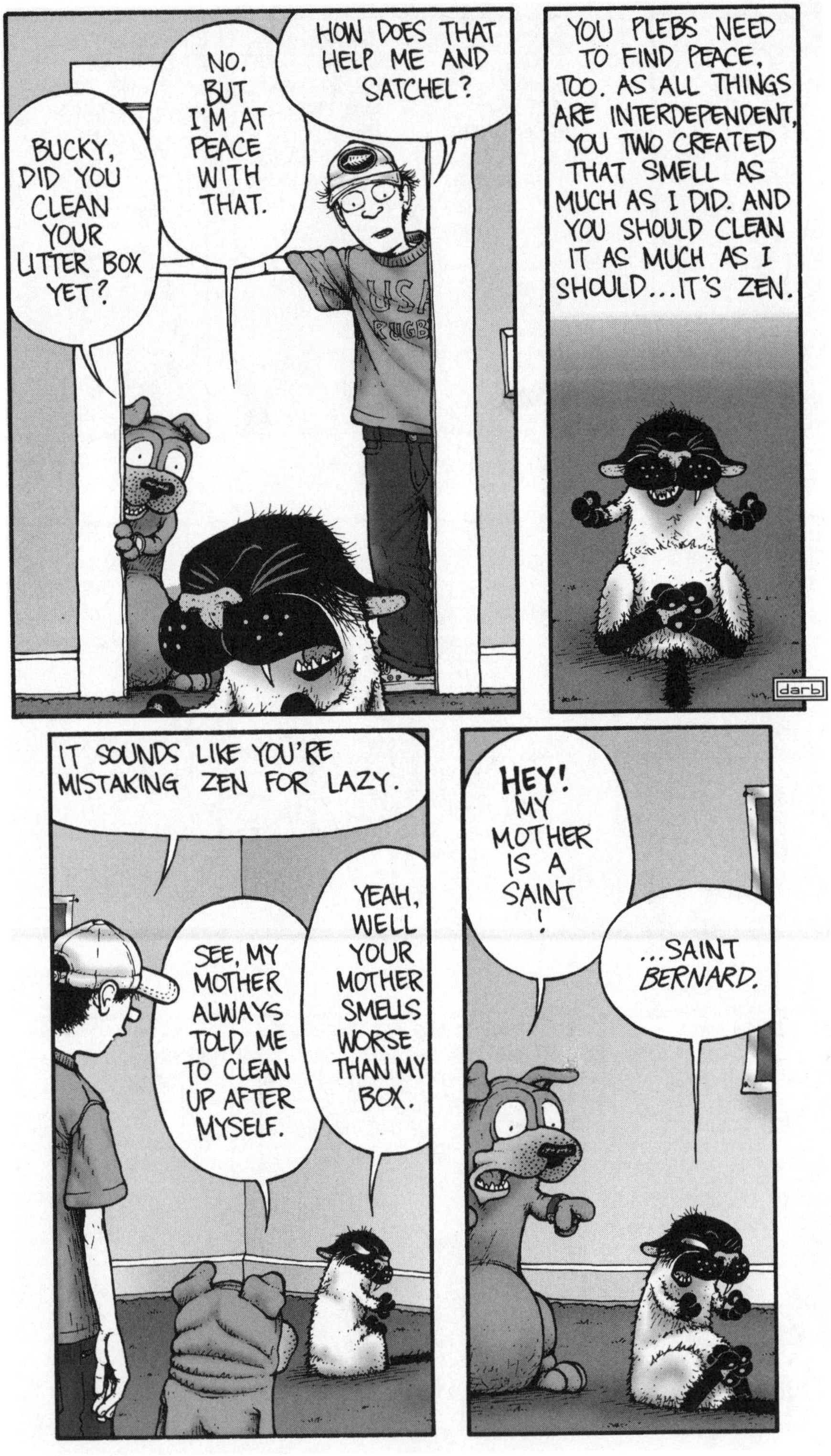
BUCKY, DID YOU CLEAN YOUR LITTER BOX YET?
NO. BUT I'M AT PEACE WITH THAT.
HOW DOES THAT HELP ME AND SATCHEL?
YOU PLEBS NEED TO FIND PEACE, TOO. AS ALL THINGS ARE INTERDEPENDENT, YOU TWO CREATED THAT SMELL AS MUCH AS I DID. AND YOU SHOULD CLEAN IT AS MUCH AS I SHOULD...IT'S ZEN.
darb
IT SOUNDS LIKE YOU'RE MISTAKING ZEN FOR LAZY.
SEE, MY MOTHER ALWAYS TOLD ME TO CLEAN UP AFTER MYSELF.
YEAH, WELL YOUR MOTHER SMELLS WORSE THAN MY BOX.
HEY! MY MOTHER IS A SAINT!
...SAINT *BERNARD.*

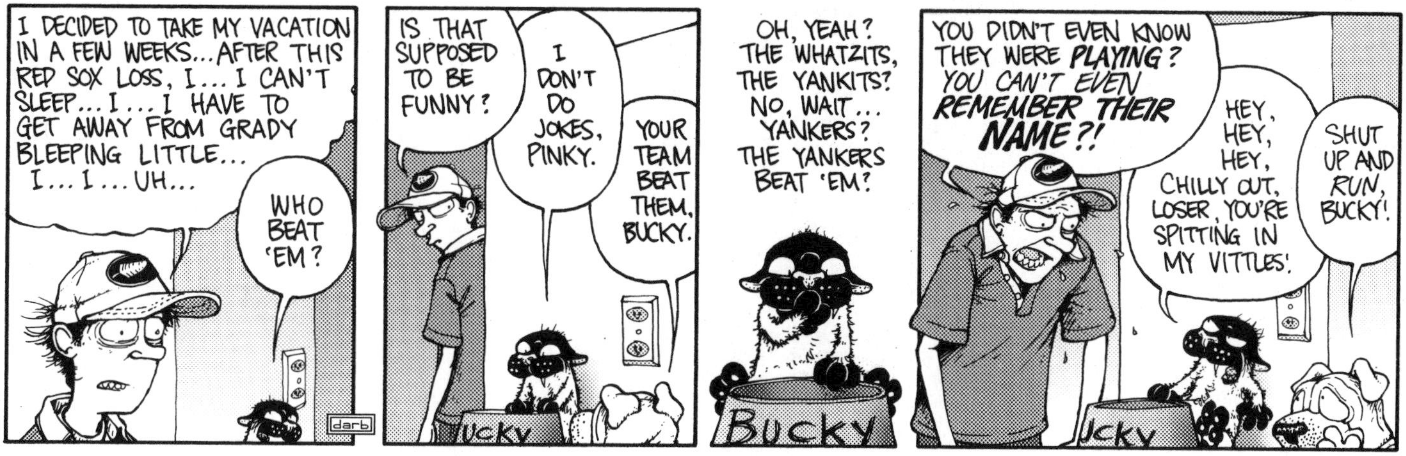
I DECIDED TO TAKE MY VACATION IN A FEW WEEKS... AFTER THIS RED SOX LOSS, I... I CAN'T SLEEP... I... I HAVE TO GET AWAY FROM GRADY BLEEPING LITTLE... I... I... UH...
WHO BEAT 'EM?
IS THAT SUPPOSED TO BE FUNNY?
I DON'T DO JOKES, PINKY.
YOUR TEAM BEAT THEM, BUCKY.
OH, YEAH? THE WHATZITS, THE YANKITS? NO, WAIT... YANKERS? THE YANKERS BEAT 'EM?
BUCKY
YOU DIDN'T EVEN KNOW THEY WERE PLAYING? YOU CAN'T EVEN REMEMBER THEIR NAME?!
HEY, HEY, HEY, CHILLY OUT, LOSER, YOU'RE SPITTING IN MY VITTLES!
SHUT UP AND RUN, BUCKY!

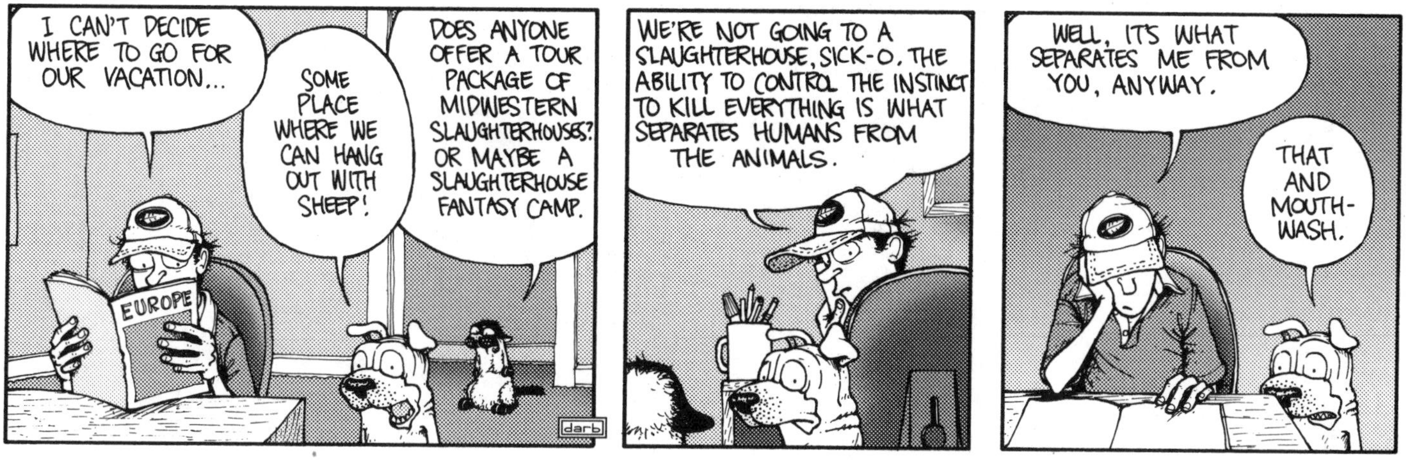
I CAN'T DECIDE WHERE TO GO FOR OUR VACATION...
SOME PLACE WHERE WE CAN HANG OUT WITH SHEEP!
DOES ANYONE OFFER A TOUR PACKAGE OF MIDWESTERN SLAUGHTERHOUSES? OR MAYBE A SLAUGHTERHOUSE FANTASY CAMP.
EUROPE
WE'RE NOT GOING TO A SLAUGHTERHOUSE, SICK-O. THE ABILITY TO CONTROL THE INSTINCT TO KILL EVERYTHING IS WHAT SEPARATES HUMANS FROM THE ANIMALS.
WELL, IT'S WHAT SEPARATES ME FROM YOU, ANYWAY.
THAT AND MOUTH-WASH.

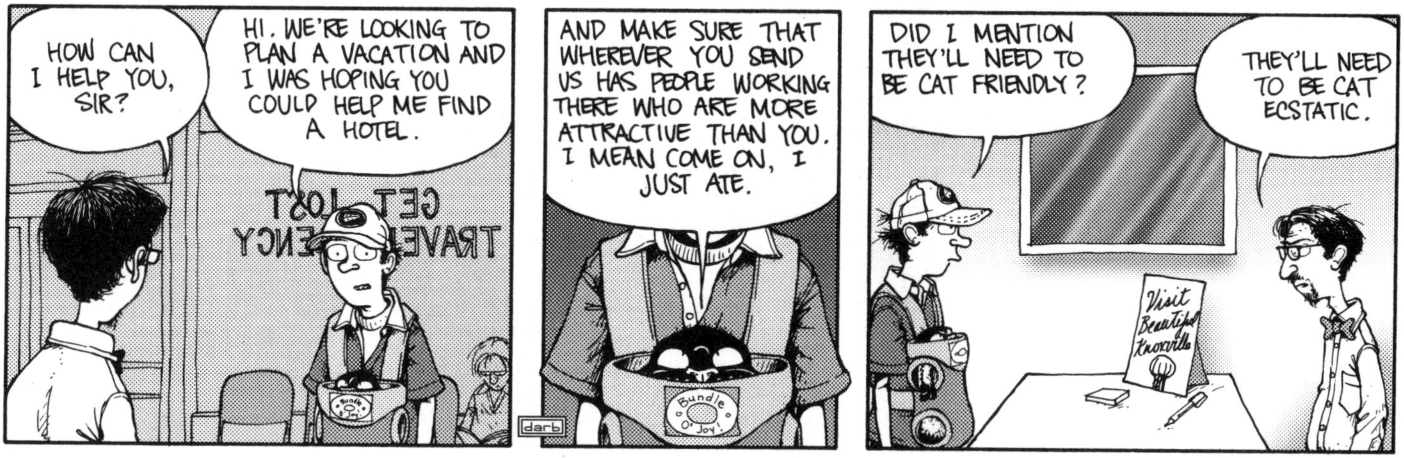
HOW CAN I HELP YOU, SIR?
HI. WE'RE LOOKING TO PLAN A VACATION AND I WAS HOPING YOU COULD HELP ME FIND A HOTEL.
AND MAKE SURE THAT WHEREVER YOU SEND US HAS PEOPLE WORKING THERE WHO ARE MORE ATTRACTIVE THAN YOU. I MEAN COME ON, I JUST ATE.
Bundle O' Joy!
DID I MENTION THEY'LL NEED TO BE CAT FRIENDLY?
THEY'LL NEED TO BE CAT ECSTATIC.
Visit Beautiful Knoxville

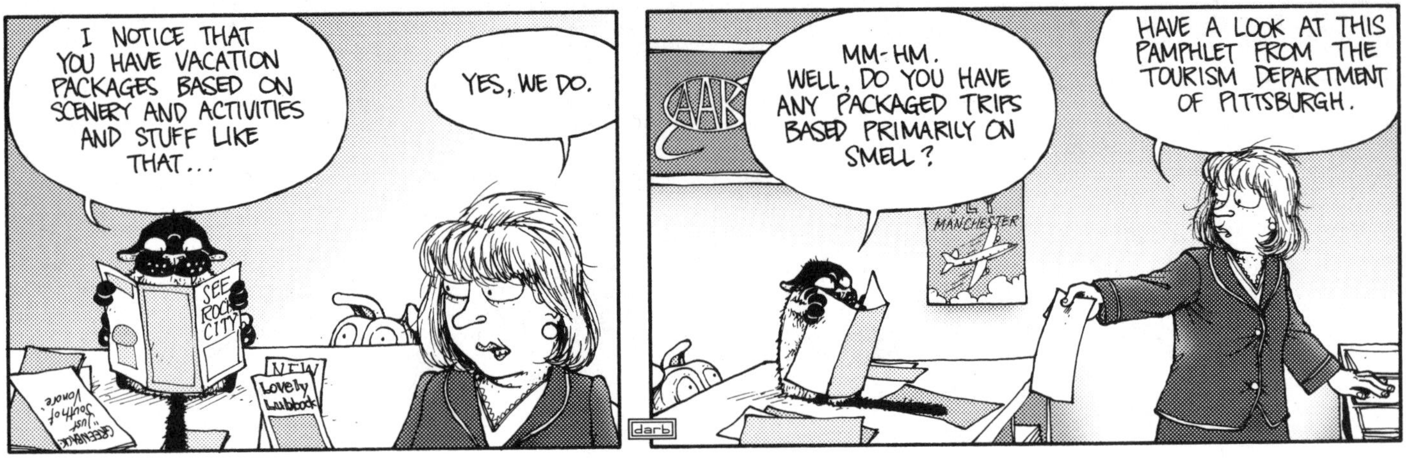
I NOTICE THAT YOU HAVE VACATION PACKAGES BASED ON SCENERY AND ACTIVITIES AND STUFF LIKE THAT...
YES, WE DO.
SEE ROCK CITY
NEW
Lovely Lubbock
darb
MM-HM. WELL, DO YOU HAVE ANY PACKAGED TRIPS BASED PRIMARILY ON SMELL?
HAVE A LOOK AT THIS PAMPHLET FROM THE TOURISM DEPARTMENT OF PITTSBURGH.
MANCHESTER

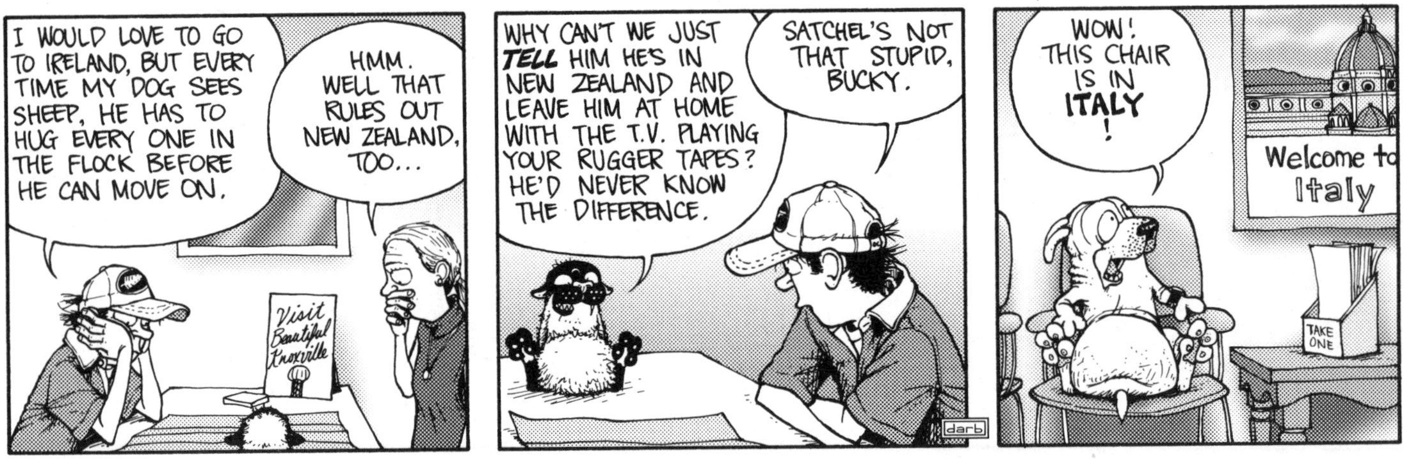
I WOULD LOVE TO GO TO IRELAND, BUT EVERY TIME MY DOG SEES SHEEP, HE HAS TO HUG EVERY ONE IN THE FLOCK BEFORE HE CAN MOVE ON.
HMM. WELL THAT RULES OUT NEW ZEALAND, TOO...
Visit Beautiful Knoxville
WHY CAN'T WE JUST TELL HIM HE'S IN NEW ZEALAND AND LEAVE HIM AT HOME WITH THE T.V. PLAYING YOUR RUGGER TAPES? HE'D NEVER KNOW THE DIFFERENCE.
SATCHEL'S NOT THAT STUPID, BUCKY.
darb
WOW! THIS CHAIR IS IN ITALY!
Welcome to Italy
TAKE ONE

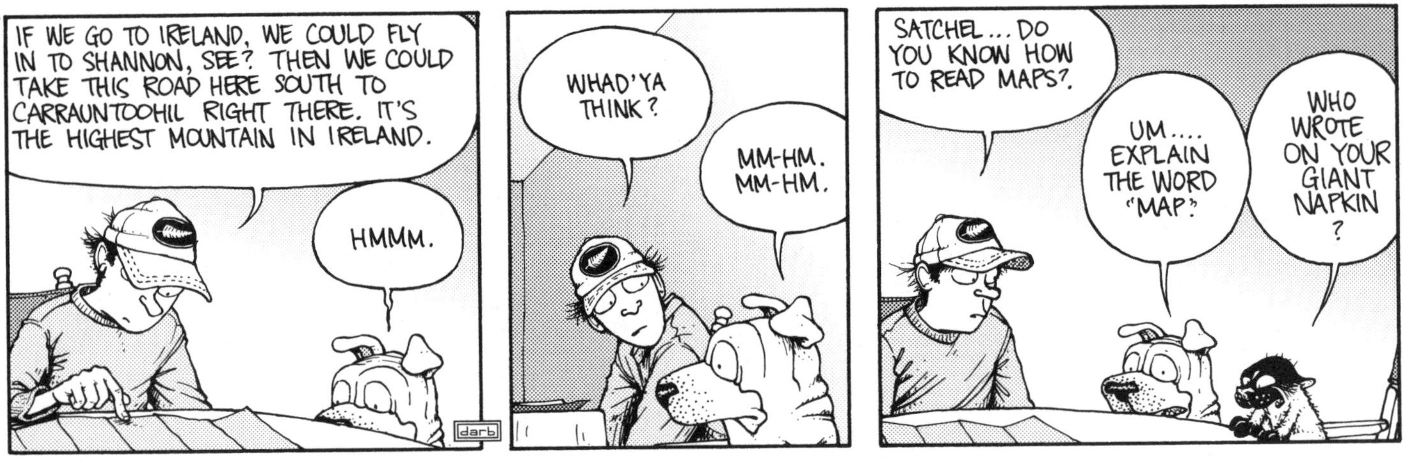
IF WE GO TO IRELAND, WE COULD FLY IN TO SHANNON, SEE? THEN WE COULD TAKE THIS ROAD HERE SOUTH TO CARRAUNTOOHIL RIGHT THERE. IT'S THE HIGHEST MOUNTAIN IN IRELAND.
HMMM.
darb
WHAD'YA THINK?
MM-HM. MM-HM.
SATCHEL... DO YOU KNOW HOW TO READ MAPS?
UM.... EXPLAIN THE WORD "MAP."
WHO WROTE ON YOUR GIANT NAPKIN?

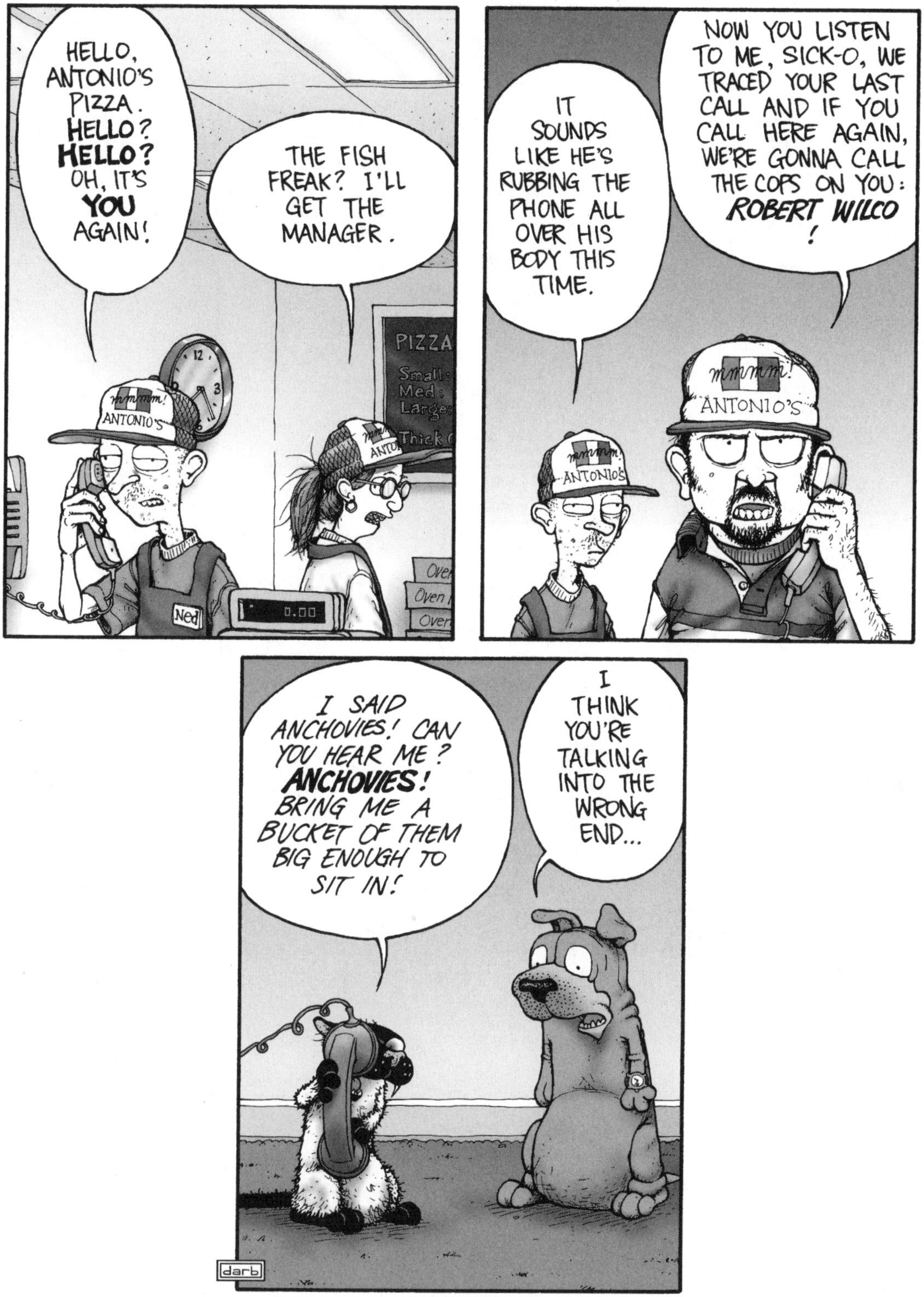
HELLO, ANTONIO'S PIZZA. HELLO? HELLO? OH, IT'S YOU AGAIN!
THE FISH FREAK? I'LL GET THE MANAGER.
PIZZA
Small:
Med:
Large:
Thick
Ned
0.00
Oven
Oven
Over
IT SOUNDS LIKE HE'S RUBBING THE PHONE ALL OVER HIS BODY THIS TIME.
NOW YOU LISTEN TO ME, SICK-O, WE TRACED YOUR LAST CALL AND IF YOU CALL HERE AGAIN, WE'RE GONNA CALL THE COPS ON YOU: ROBERT WILCO!
I SAID ANCHOVIES! CAN YOU HEAR ME? ANCHOVIES! BRING ME A BUCKET OF THEM BIG ENOUGH TO SIT IN!
I THINK YOU'RE TALKING INTO THE WRONG END...
darb

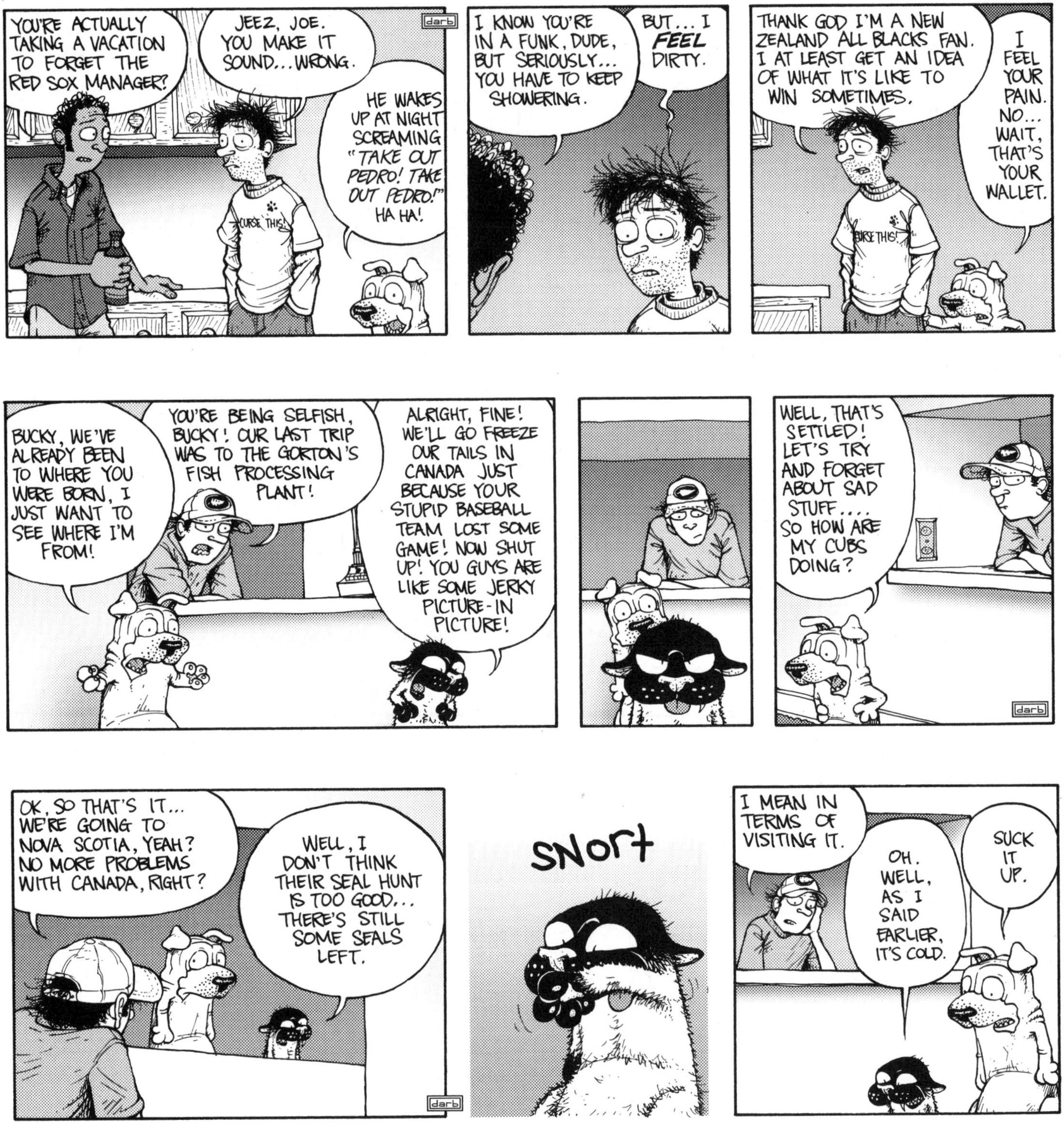
YOU'RE ACTUALLY TAKING A VACATION TO FORGET THE RED SOX MANAGER?
JEEZ, JOE. YOU MAKE IT SOUND... WRONG.
HE WAKES UP AT NIGHT SCREAMING "TAKE OUT PEDRO! TAKE OUT PEDRO!" HA HA!
CURSE THIS!
I KNOW YOU'RE IN A FUNK, DUDE, BUT SERIOUSLY... YOU HAVE TO KEEP SHOWERING.
BUT... I FEEL DIRTY.
THANK GOD I'M A NEW ZEALAND ALL BLACKS FAN. I AT LEAST GET AN IDEA OF WHAT IT'S LIKE TO WIN SOMETIMES.
I FEEL YOUR PAIN. NO... WAIT, THAT'S YOUR WALLET.
CURSE THIS!
BUCKY, WE'VE ALREADY BEEN TO WHERE YOU WERE BORN, I JUST WANT TO SEE WHERE I'M FROM!
YOU'RE BEING SELFISH, BUCKY! OUR LAST TRIP WAS TO THE GORTON'S FISH PROCESSING PLANT!
ALRIGHT, FINE! WE'LL GO FREEZE OUR TAILS IN CANADA JUST BECAUSE YOUR STUPID BASEBALL TEAM LOST SOME GAME! NOW SHUT UP! YOU GUYS ARE LIKE SOME JERKY PICTURE-IN PICTURE!
WELL, THAT'S SETTLED! LET'S TRY AND FORGET ABOUT SAD STUFF.... SO HOW ARE MY CUBS DOING?
OK, SO THAT'S IT... WE'RE GOING TO NOVA SCOTIA, YEAH? NO MORE PROBLEMS WITH CANADA, RIGHT?
WELL, I DON'T THINK THEIR SEAL HUNT IS TOO GOOD... THERE'S STILL SOME SEALS LEFT.
SNort
I MEAN IN TERMS OF VISITING IT.
OH. WELL, AS I SAID EARLIER, IT'S COLD.
SUCK IT UP.

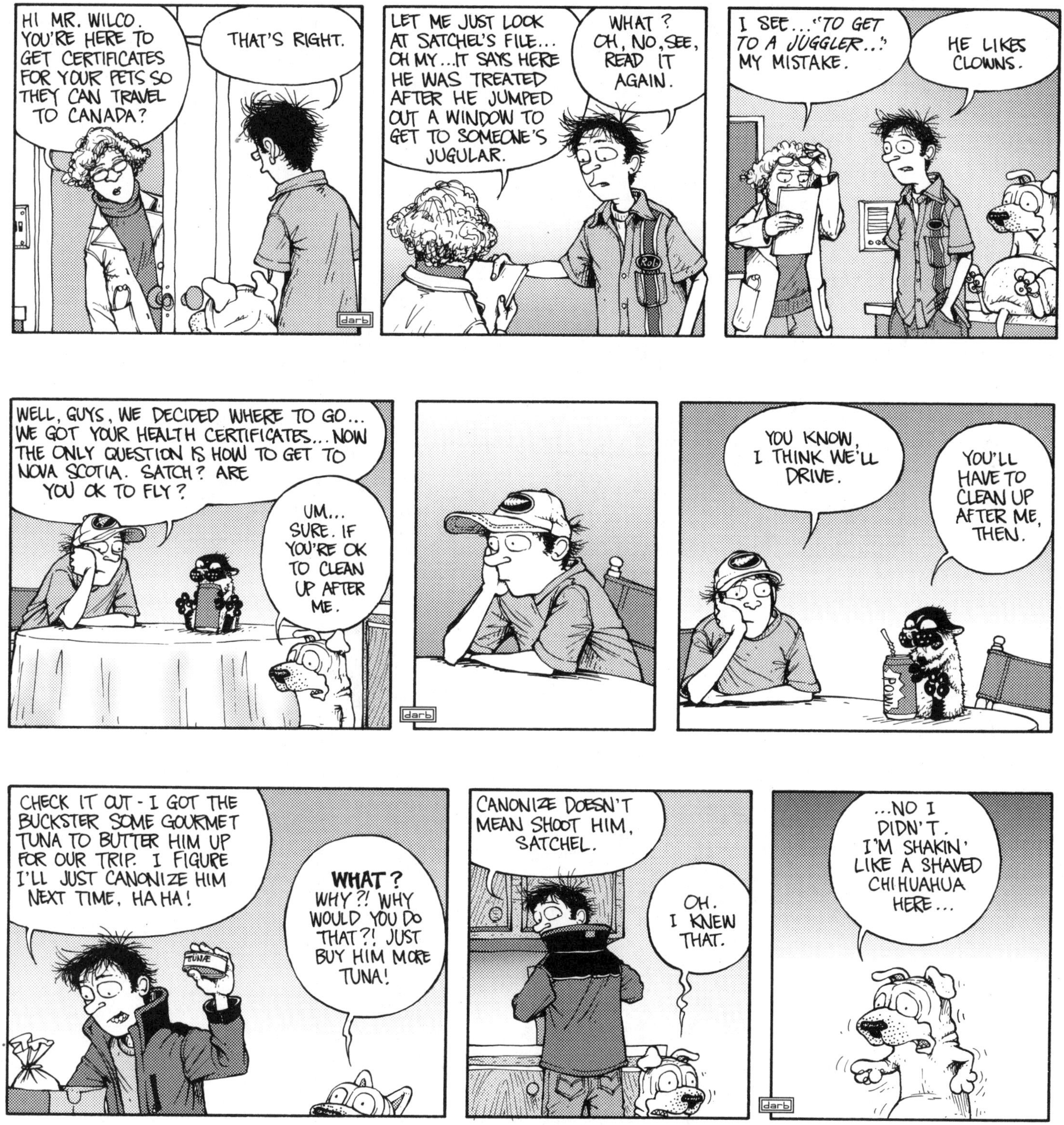
HI MR. WILCO. YOU'RE HERE TO GET CERTIFICATES FOR YOUR PETS SO THEY CAN TRAVEL TO CANADA?
THAT'S RIGHT.
darb
LET ME JUST LOOK AT SATCHEL'S FILE... OH MY...IT SAYS HERE HE WAS TREATED AFTER HE JUMPED OUT A WINDOW TO GET TO SOMEONE'S JUGULAR.
WHAT? OH, NO, SEE, READ IT AGAIN.
Rob
I SEE... "TO GET TO A JUGGLER..." MY MISTAKE.
HE LIKES CLOWNS.
WELL, GUYS, WE DECIDED WHERE TO GO... WE GOT YOUR HEALTH CERTIFICATES... NOW THE ONLY QUESTION IS HOW TO GET TO NOVA SCOTIA. SATCH? ARE YOU OK TO FLY?
UM... SURE. IF YOU'RE OK TO CLEAN UP AFTER ME.
darb
YOU KNOW, I THINK WE'LL DRIVE.
YOU'LL HAVE TO CLEAN UP AFTER ME, THEN.
POW
CHECK IT OUT - I GOT THE BUCKSTER SOME GOURMET TUNA TO BUTTER HIM UP FOR OUR TRIP. I FIGURE I'LL JUST CANONIZE HIM NEXT TIME, HA HA!
TUNA
WHAT? WHY?! WHY WOULD YOU DO THAT?! JUST BUY HIM MORE TUNA!
CANONIZE DOESN'T MEAN SHOOT HIM, SATCHEL.
OH. I KNEW THAT.
...NO I DIDN'T. I'M SHAKIN' LIKE A SHAVED CHIHUAHUA HERE...
darb

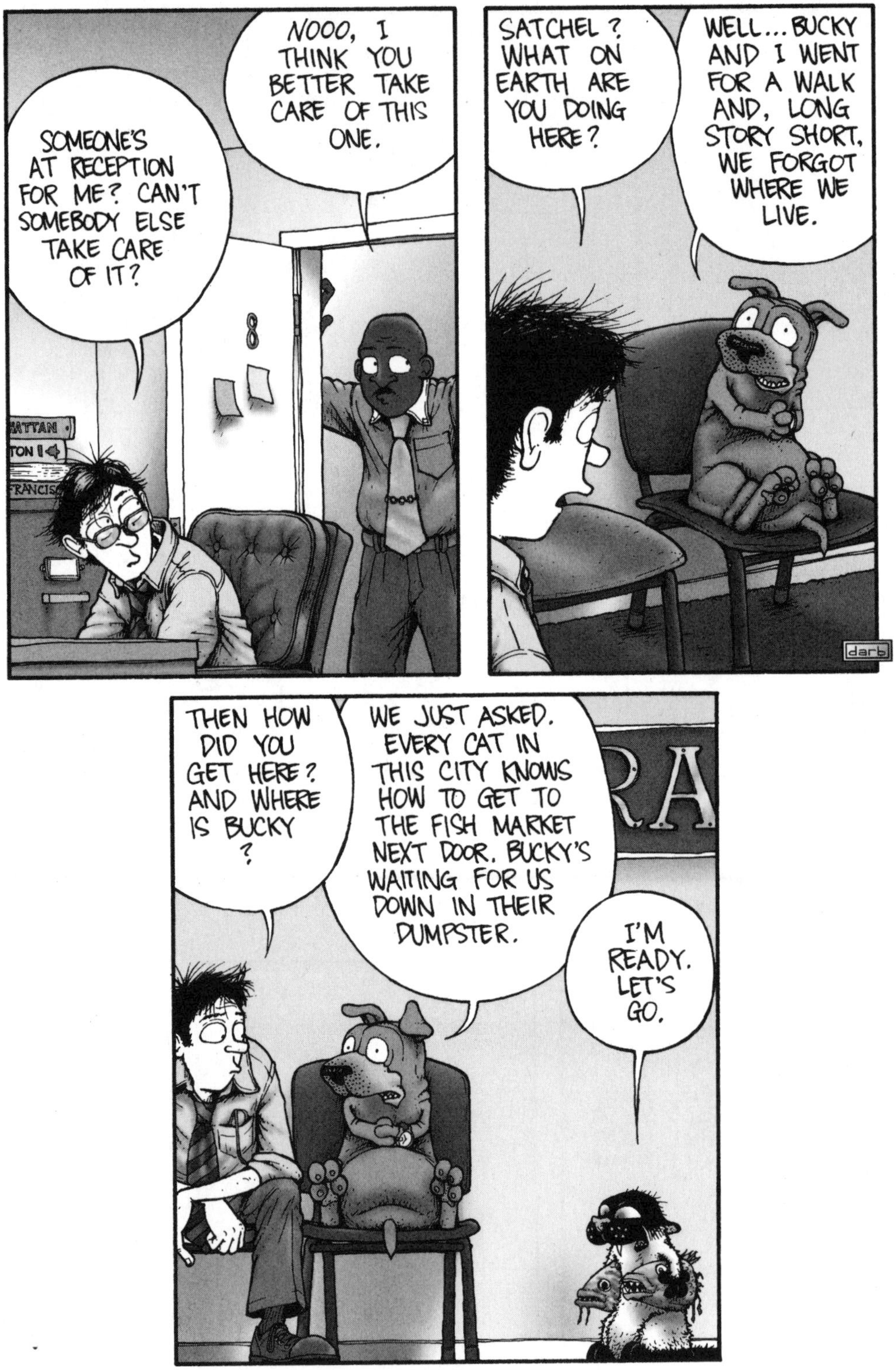
SOMEONE'S AT RECEPTION FOR ME? CAN'T SOMEBODY ELSE TAKE CARE OF IT?
NOOO, I THINK YOU BETTER TAKE CARE OF THIS ONE.
SATCHEL? WHAT ON EARTH ARE YOU DOING HERE?
WELL... BUCKY AND I WENT FOR A WALK AND, LONG STORY SHORT, WE FORGOT WHERE WE LIVE.
THEN HOW DID YOU GET HERE? AND WHERE IS BUCKY?
WE JUST ASKED. EVERY CAT IN THIS CITY KNOWS HOW TO GET TO THE FISH MARKET NEXT DOOR. BUCKY'S WAITING FOR US DOWN IN THEIR DUMPSTER.
I'M READY. LET'S GO.

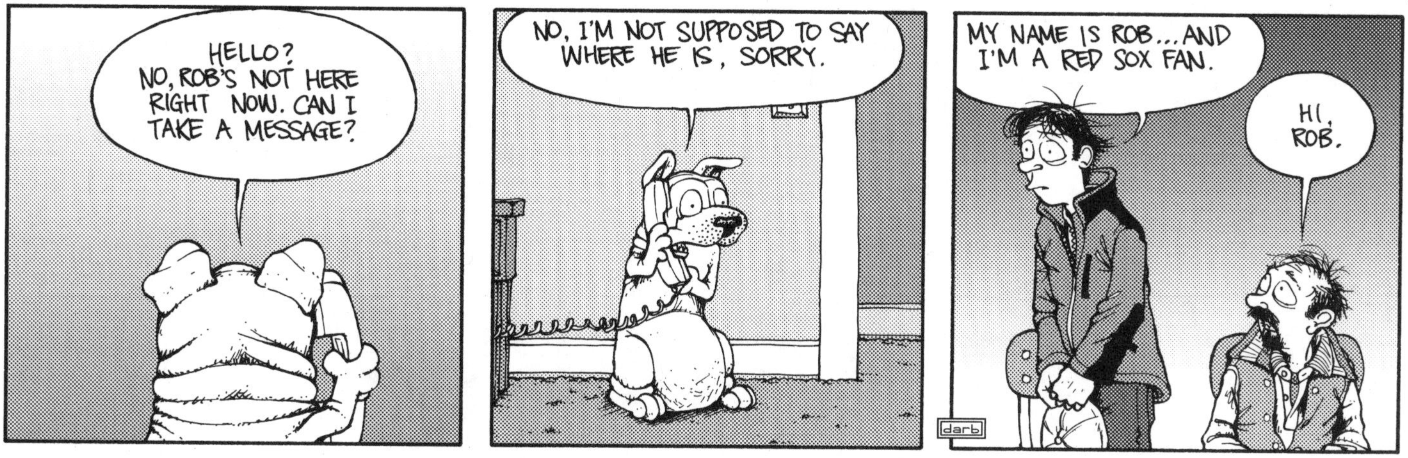
HELLO? NO, ROB'S NOT HERE RIGHT NOW. CAN I TAKE A MESSAGE?
NO, I'M NOT SUPPOSED TO SAY WHERE HE IS, SORRY.
MY NAME IS ROB... AND I'M A RED SOX FAN.
HI, ROB.
darb

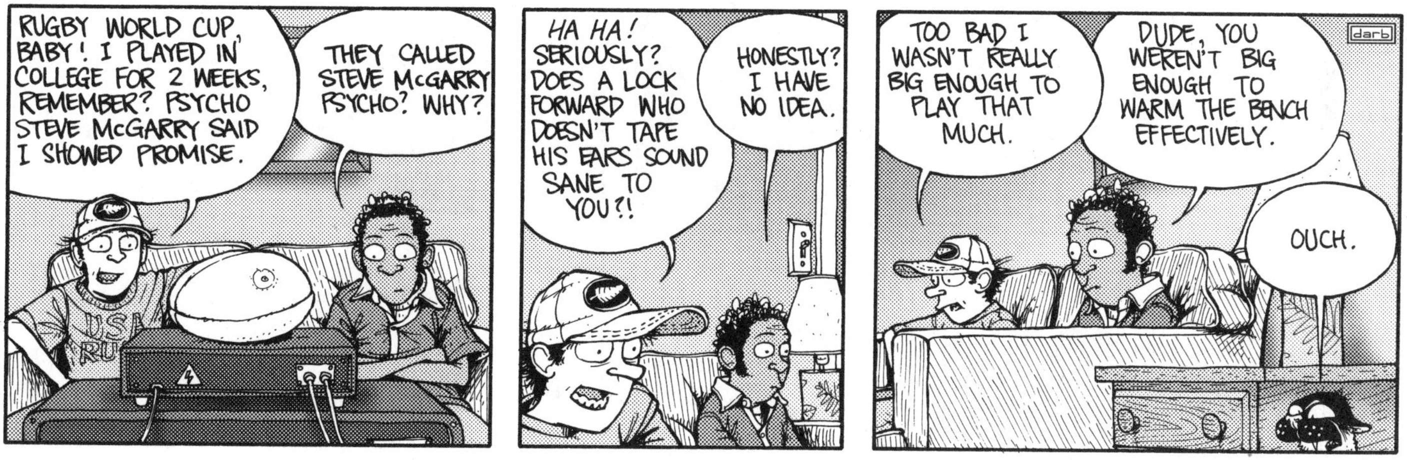
RUGBY WORLD CUP, BABY! I PLAYED IN COLLEGE FOR 2 WEEKS, REMEMBER? PSYCHO STEVE McGARRY SAID I SHOWED PROMISE.
THEY CALLED STEVE McGARRY PSYCHO? WHY?
HA HA! SERIOUSLY? DOES A LOCK FORWARD WHO DOESN'T TAPE HIS EARS SOUND SANE TO YOU?!
HONESTLY? I HAVE NO IDEA.
TOO BAD I WASN'T REALLY BIG ENOUGH TO PLAY THAT MUCH.
DUDE, YOU WEREN'T BIG ENOUGH TO WARM THE BENCH EFFECTIVELY.
OUCH.
darb

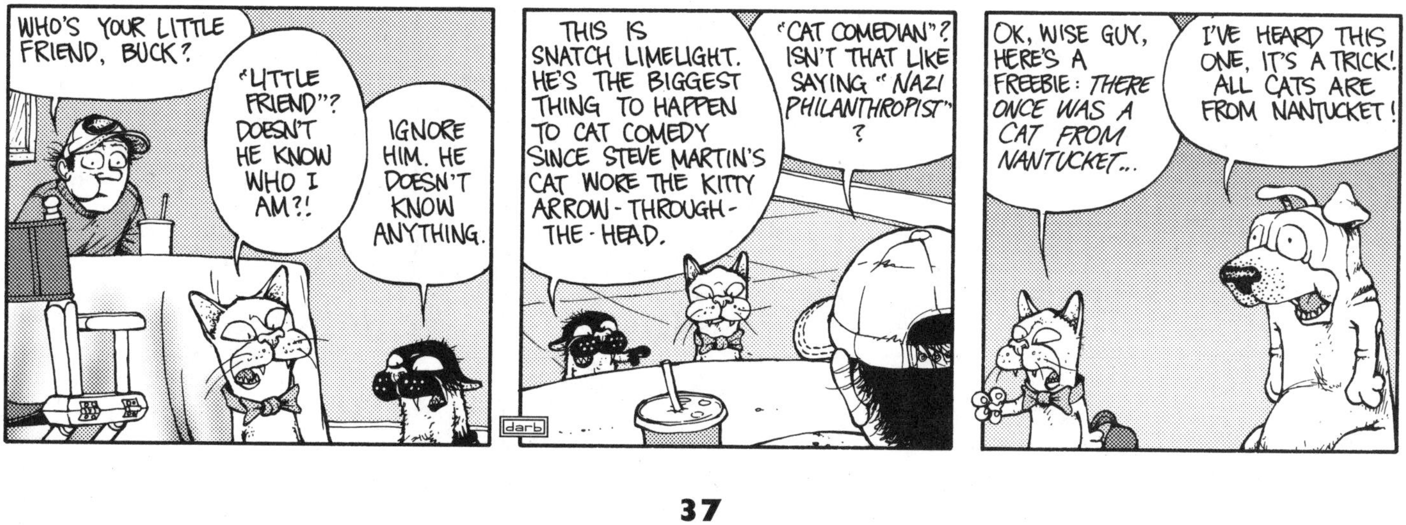
WHO'S YOUR LITTLE FRIEND, BUCK?
"LITTLE FRIEND"? DOESN'T HE KNOW WHO I AM?!
IGNORE HIM. HE DOESN'T KNOW ANYTHING.
THIS IS SNATCH LIMELIGHT. HE'S THE BIGGEST THING TO HAPPEN TO CAT COMEDY SINCE STEVE MARTIN'S CAT WORE THE KITTY ARROW-THROUGH-THE-HEAD.
"CAT COMEDIAN"? ISN'T THAT LIKE SAYING "NAZI PHILANTHROPIST"?
OK, WISE GUY, HERE'S A FREEBIE: THERE ONCE WAS A CAT FROM NANTUCKET...
I'VE HEARD THIS ONE, IT'S A TRICK! ALL CATS ARE FROM NANTUCKET!
darb

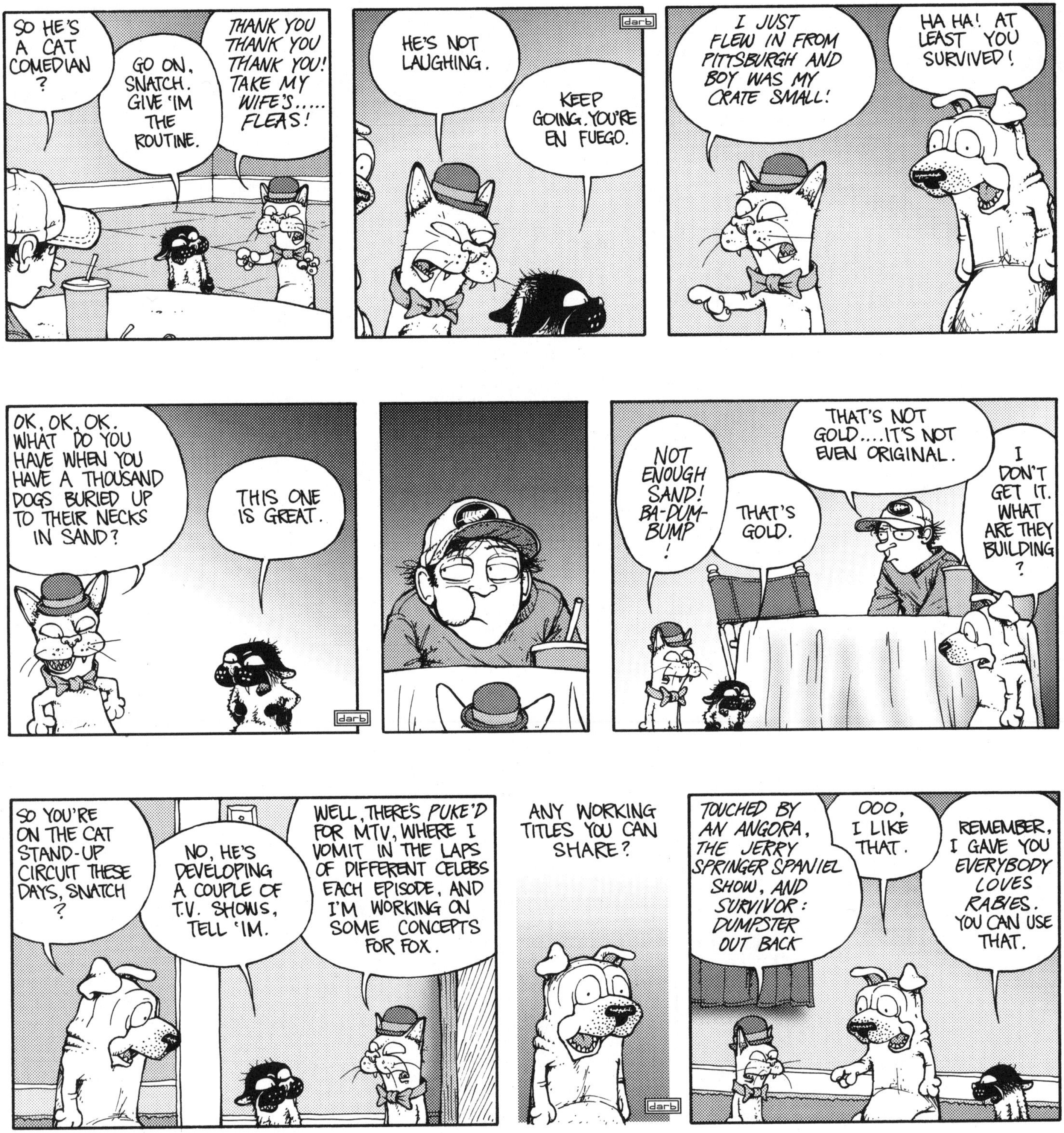
SO HE'S A CAT COMEDIAN ?
GO ON, SNATCH. GIVE 'IM THE ROUTINE.
THANK YOU THANK YOU THANK YOU! TAKE MY WIFE'S..... FLEAS!
HE'S NOT LAUGHING.
KEEP GOING. YOU'RE EN FUEGO.
I JUST FLEW IN FROM PITTSBURGH AND BOY WAS MY CRATE SMALL!
HA HA! AT LEAST YOU SURVIVED!
OK, OK, OK. WHAT DO YOU HAVE WHEN YOU HAVE A THOUSAND DOGS BURIED UP TO THEIR NECKS IN SAND?
THIS ONE IS GREAT.
NOT ENOUGH SAND! BA-DUM-BUMP!
THAT'S GOLD.
THAT'S NOT GOLD....IT'S NOT EVEN ORIGINAL.
I DON'T GET IT. WHAT ARE THEY BUILDING?
SO YOU'RE ON THE CAT STAND-UP CIRCUIT THESE DAYS, SNATCH?
NO, HE'S DEVELOPING A COUPLE OF T.V. SHOWS, TELL 'IM.
WELL, THERE'S PUKE'D FOR MTV, WHERE I VOMIT IN THE LAPS OF DIFFERENT CELEBS EACH EPISODE, AND I'M WORKING ON SOME CONCEPTS FOR FOX.
ANY WORKING TITLES YOU CAN SHARE?
TOUCHED BY AN ANGORA, THE JERRY SPRINGER SPANIEL SHOW, AND SURVIVOR: DUMPSTER OUT BACK
OOO, I LIKE THAT.
REMEMBER, I GAVE YOU EVERYBODY LOVES RABIES. YOU CAN USE THAT.

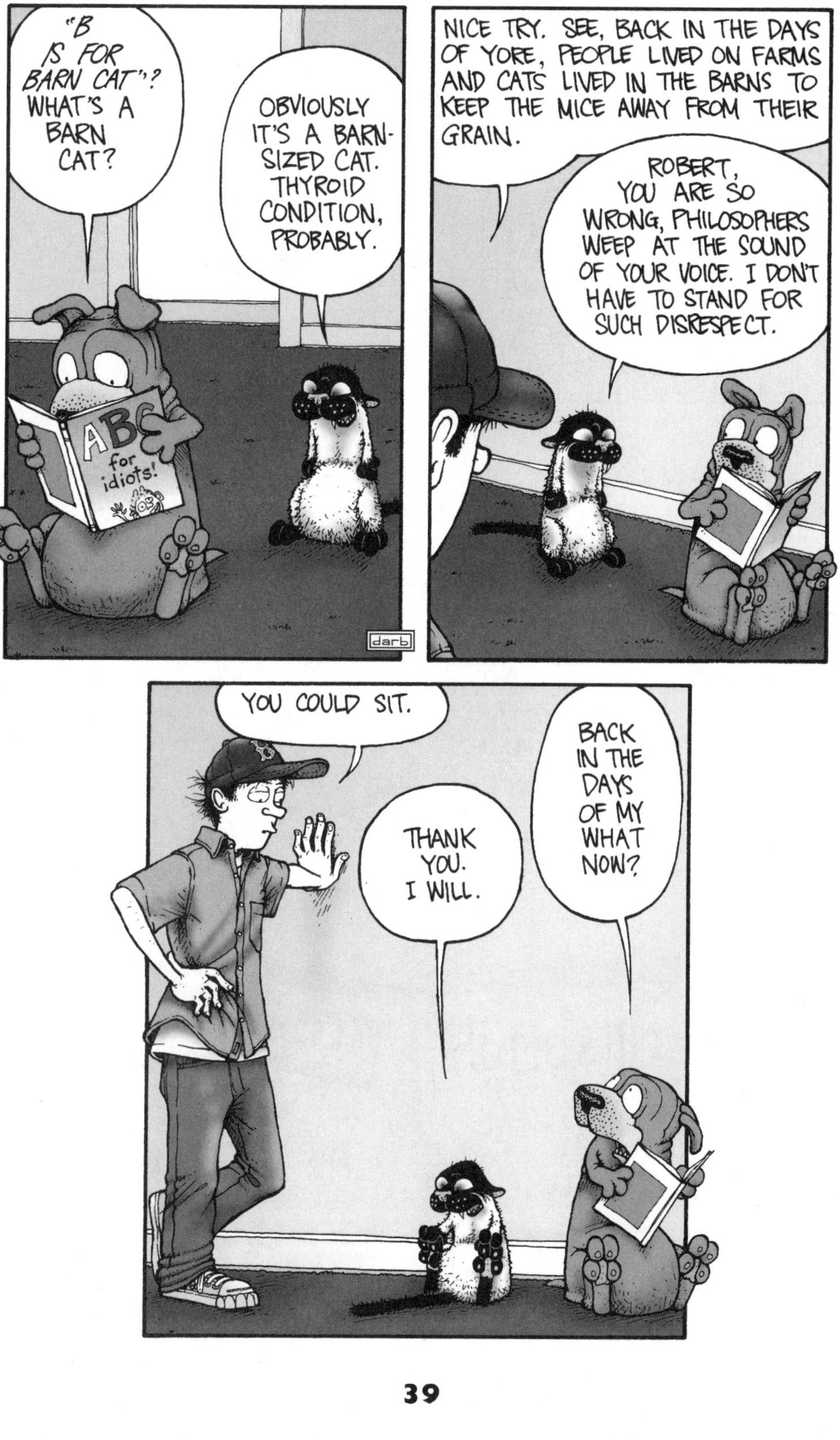
"B IS FOR BARN CAT"? WHAT'S A BARN CAT?
OBVIOUSLY IT'S A BARN-SIZED CAT. THYROID CONDITION, PROBABLY.
ABC for idiots!
darb
NICE TRY. SEE, BACK IN THE DAYS OF YORE, PEOPLE LIVED ON FARMS AND CATS LIVED IN THE BARNS TO KEEP THE MICE AWAY FROM THEIR GRAIN.
ROBERT, YOU ARE SO WRONG, PHILOSOPHERS WEEP AT THE SOUND OF YOUR VOICE. I DON'T HAVE TO STAND FOR SUCH DISRESPECT.
YOU COULD SIT.
THANK YOU. I WILL.
BACK IN THE DAYS OF MY WHAT NOW?

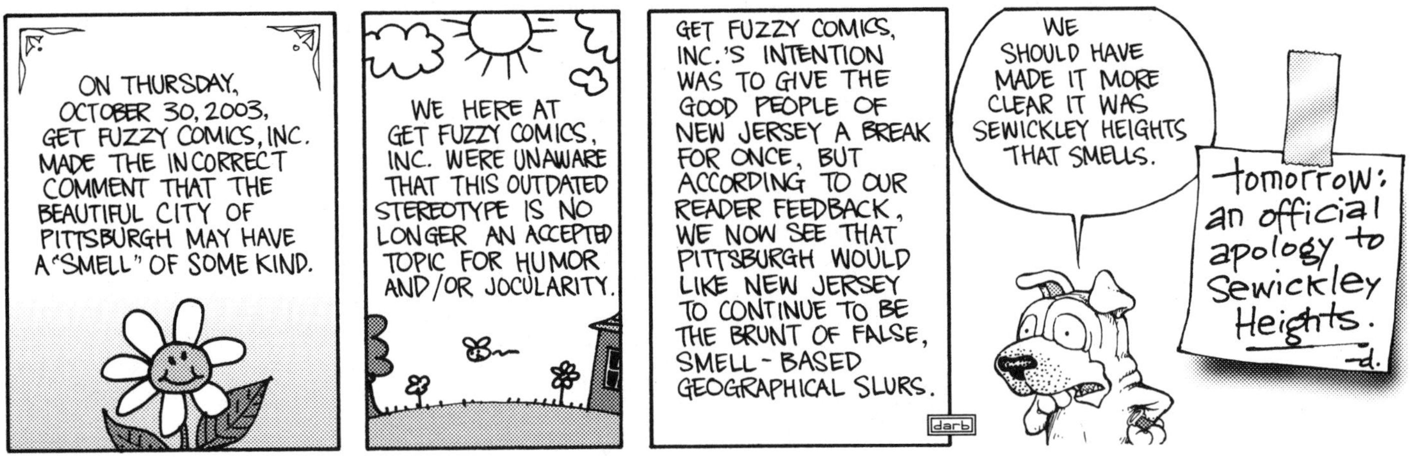
ON THURSDAY, OCTOBER 30, 2003, GET FUZZY COMICS, INC. MADE THE INCORRECT COMMENT THAT THE BEAUTIFUL CITY OF PITTSBURGH MAY HAVE A "SMELL" OF SOME KIND.
WE HERE AT GET FUZZY COMICS, INC. WERE UNAWARE THAT THIS OUTDATED STEREOTYPE IS NO LONGER AN ACCEPTED TOPIC FOR HUMOR AND/OR JOCULARITY.
GET FUZZY COMICS, INC.'S INTENTION WAS TO GIVE THE GOOD PEOPLE OF NEW JERSEY A BREAK FOR ONCE, BUT ACCORDING TO OUR READER FEEDBACK, WE NOW SEE THAT PITTSBURGH WOULD LIKE NEW JERSEY TO CONTINUE TO BE THE BRUNT OF FALSE, SMELL-BASED GEOGRAPHICAL SLURS.
darb
WE SHOULD HAVE MADE IT MORE CLEAR IT WAS SEWICKLEY HEIGHTS THAT SMELLS.
tomorrow: an official apology to Sewickley Heights. -d.

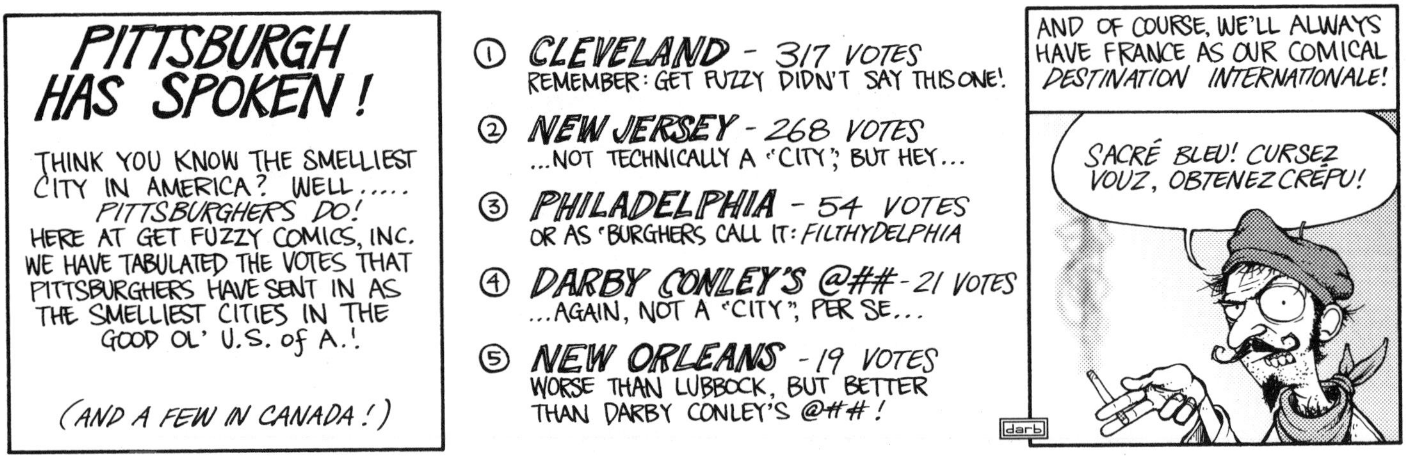
PITTSBURGH HAS SPOKEN!
THINK YOU KNOW THE SMELLIEST CITY IN AMERICA? WELL..... PITTSBURGHERS DO! HERE AT GET FUZZY COMICS, INC. WE HAVE TABULATED THE VOTES THAT PITTSBURGHERS HAVE SENT IN AS THE SMELLIEST CITIES IN THE GOOD OL' U.S. of A.!
(AND A FEW IN CANADA!)
① CLEVELAND - 317 VOTES REMEMBER: GET FUZZY DIDN'T SAY THIS ONE!
② NEW JERSEY - 268 VOTES ...NOT TECHNICALLY A "CITY", BUT HEY...
③ PHILADELPHIA - 54 VOTES OR AS 'BURGHERS CALL IT: FILTHYDELPHIA
④ DARBY CONLEY'S @## - 21 VOTES ...AGAIN, NOT A "CITY", PER SE...
⑤ NEW ORLEANS - 19 VOTES WORSE THAN LUBBOCK, BUT BETTER THAN DARBY CONLEY'S @##!
darb
AND OF COURSE, WE'LL ALWAYS HAVE FRANCE AS OUR COMICAL DESTINATION INTERNATIONALE!
SACRÉ BLEU! CURSEZ VOUZ, OBTENEZ CRÉPU!

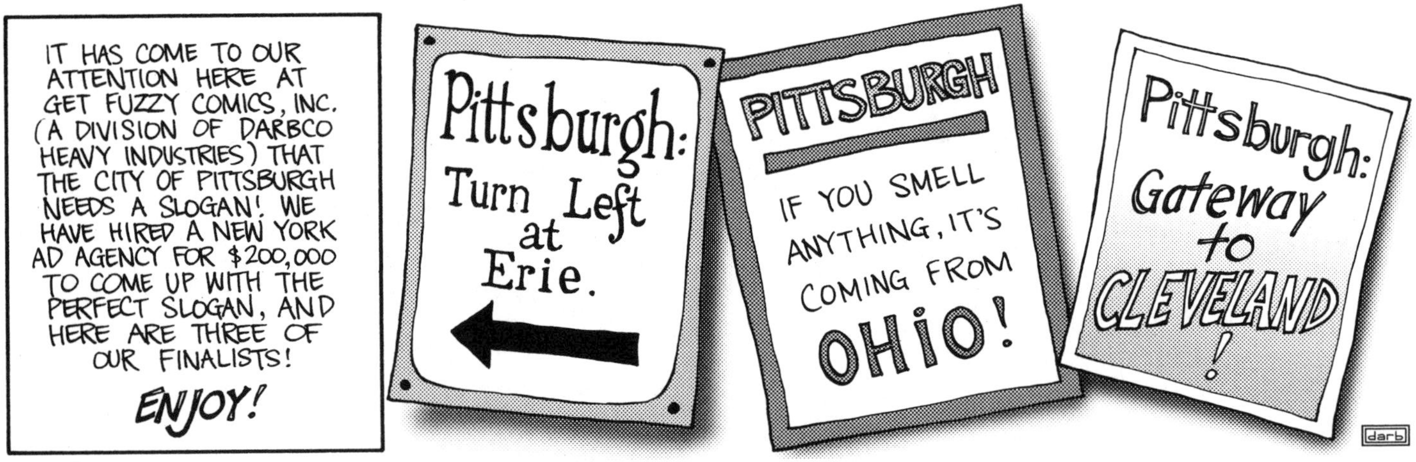
IT HAS COME TO OUR ATTENTION HERE AT GET FUZZY COMICS, INC. (A DIVISION OF DARBCO HEAVY INDUSTRIES) THAT THE CITY OF PITTSBURGH NEEDS A SLOGAN! WE HAVE HIRED A NEW YORK AD AGENCY FOR $200,000 TO COME UP WITH THE PERFECT SLOGAN, AND HERE ARE THREE OF OUR FINALISTS!
ENJOY!
Pittsburgh: Turn Left at Erie.
PITTSBURGH
IF YOU SMELL ANYTHING, IT'S COMING FROM OHIO!
Pittsburgh: Gateway to CLEVELAND!
darb

YOU ASKED FOR 'EM, NOW HERE THEY ARE! SATCHEL AND BUCKY TRADING CARDS!

CUT 'EM OUT AND TRADE 'EM WITH YOUR FRIENDS!

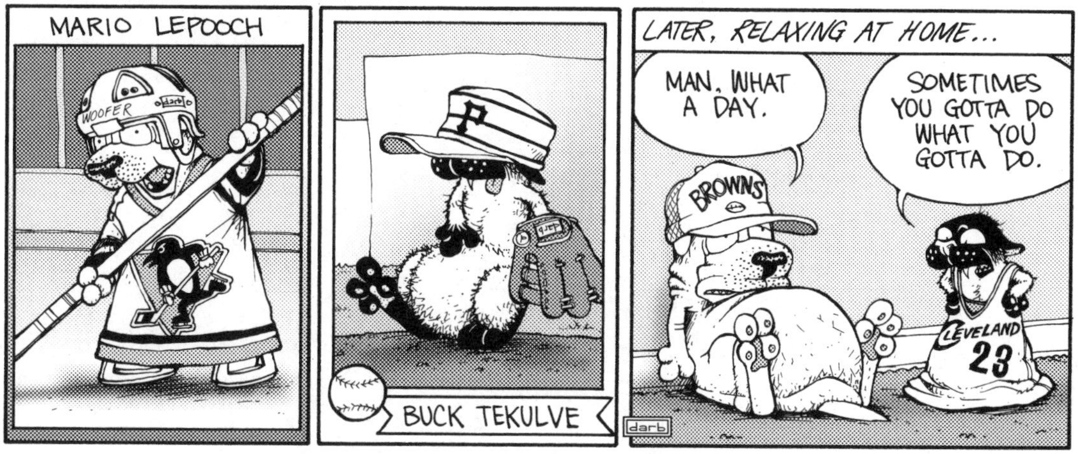
MARIO LEPOOCH
WOOFER
BUCK TEKULVE
LATER, RELAXING AT HOME...
MAN, WHAT A DAY.
SOMETIMES YOU GOTTA DO WHAT YOU GOTTA DO.
BROWNS
CLEVELAND 23

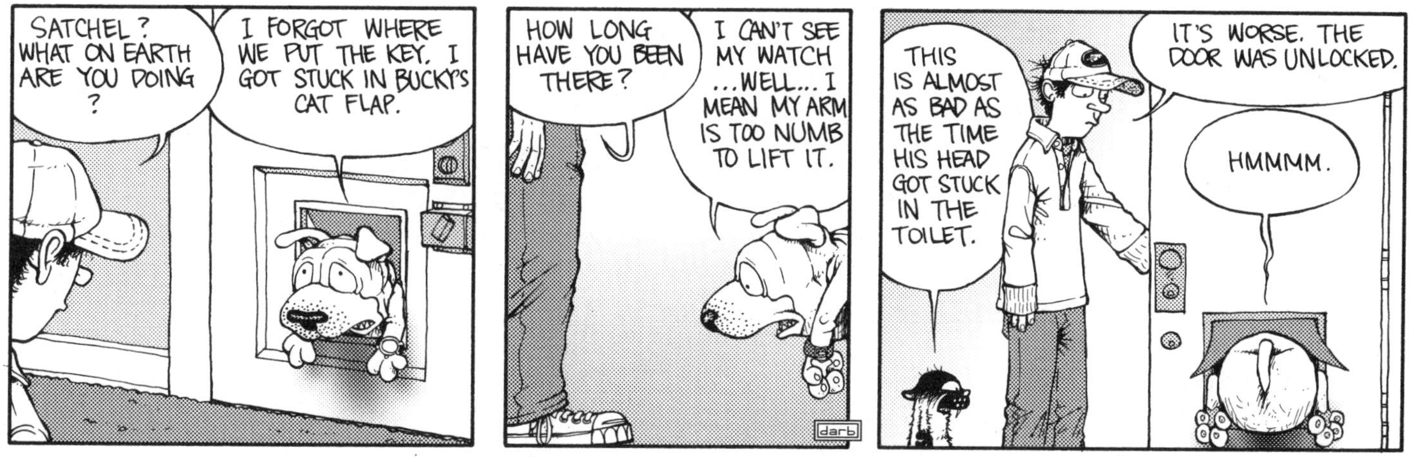
SATCHEL? WHAT ON EARTH ARE YOU DOING?
I FORGOT WHERE WE PUT THE KEY. I GOT STUCK IN BUCKY'S CAT FLAP.
HOW LONG HAVE YOU BEEN THERE?
I CAN'T SEE MY WATCH ...WELL... I MEAN MY ARM IS TOO NUMB TO LIFT IT.
THIS IS ALMOST AS BAD AS THE TIME HIS HEAD GOT STUCK IN THE TOILET.
IT'S WORSE. THE DOOR WAS UNLOCKED.
HMMMM.

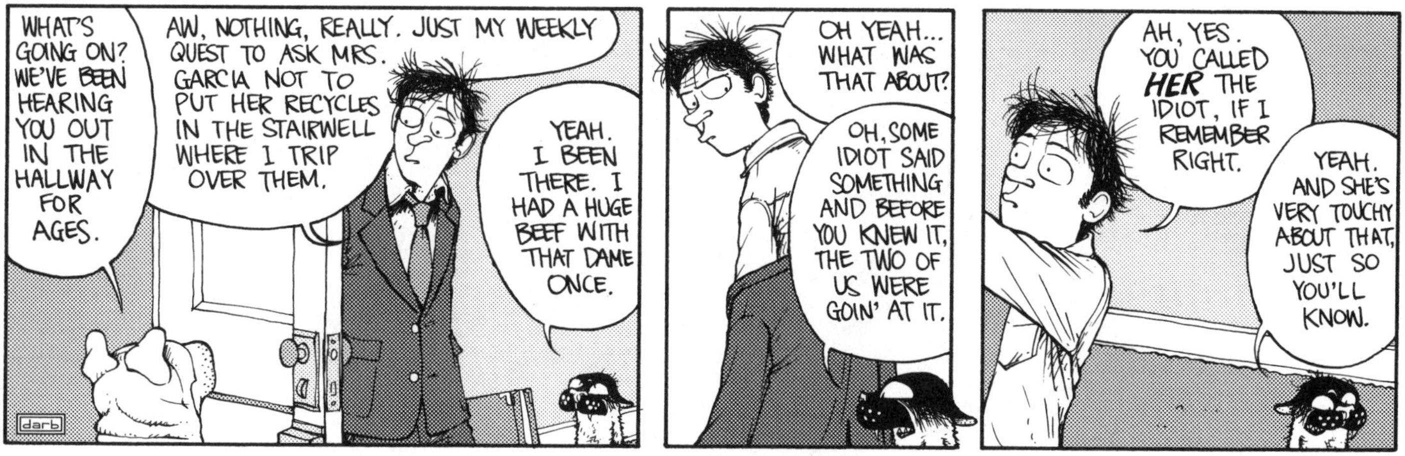
WHAT'S GOING ON? WE'VE BEEN HEARING YOU OUT IN THE HALLWAY FOR AGES.
AW, NOTHING, REALLY. JUST MY WEEKLY QUEST TO ASK MRS. GARCIA NOT TO PUT HER RECYCLES IN THE STAIRWELL WHERE I TRIP OVER THEM.
YEAH. I BEEN THERE. I HAD A HUGE BEEF WITH THAT DAME ONCE.
OH YEAH... WHAT WAS THAT ABOUT?
OH, SOME IDIOT SAID SOMETHING AND BEFORE YOU KNEW IT, THE TWO OF US WERE GOIN' AT IT.
AH, YES. YOU CALLED HER THE IDIOT, IF I REMEMBER RIGHT.
YEAH. AND SHE'S VERY TOUCHY ABOUT THAT, JUST SO YOU'LL KNOW.

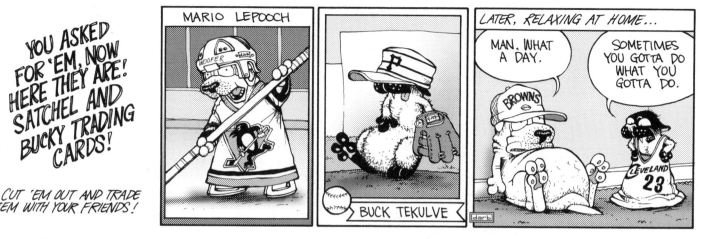

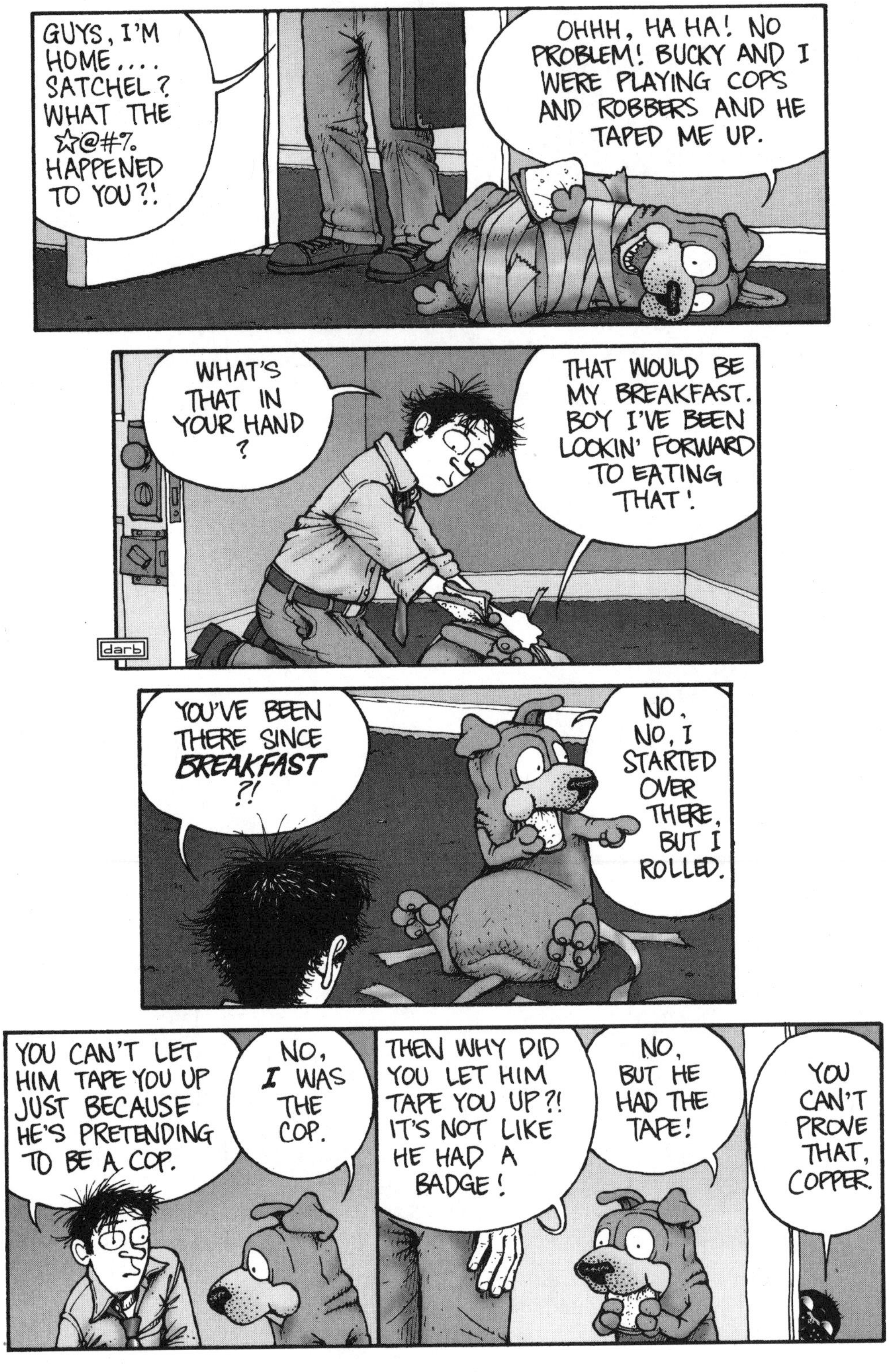
GUYS, I'M HOME.... SATCHEL? WHAT THE ☆@#%. HAPPENED TO YOU?!
OHHH, HA HA! NO PROBLEM! BUCKY AND I WERE PLAYING COPS AND ROBBERS AND HE TAPED ME UP.
WHAT'S THAT IN YOUR HAND?
THAT WOULD BE MY BREAKFAST. BOY I'VE BEEN LOOKIN' FORWARD TO EATING THAT!
darb
YOU'VE BEEN THERE SINCE BREAKFAST?!
NO, NO, I STARTED OVER THERE, BUT I ROLLED.
YOU CAN'T LET HIM TAPE YOU UP JUST BECAUSE HE'S PRETENDING TO BE A COP.
NO, I WAS THE COP.
THEN WHY DID YOU LET HIM TAPE YOU UP?! IT'S NOT LIKE HE HAD A BADGE!
NO, BUT HE HAD THE TAPE!
YOU CAN'T PROVE THAT, COPPER.

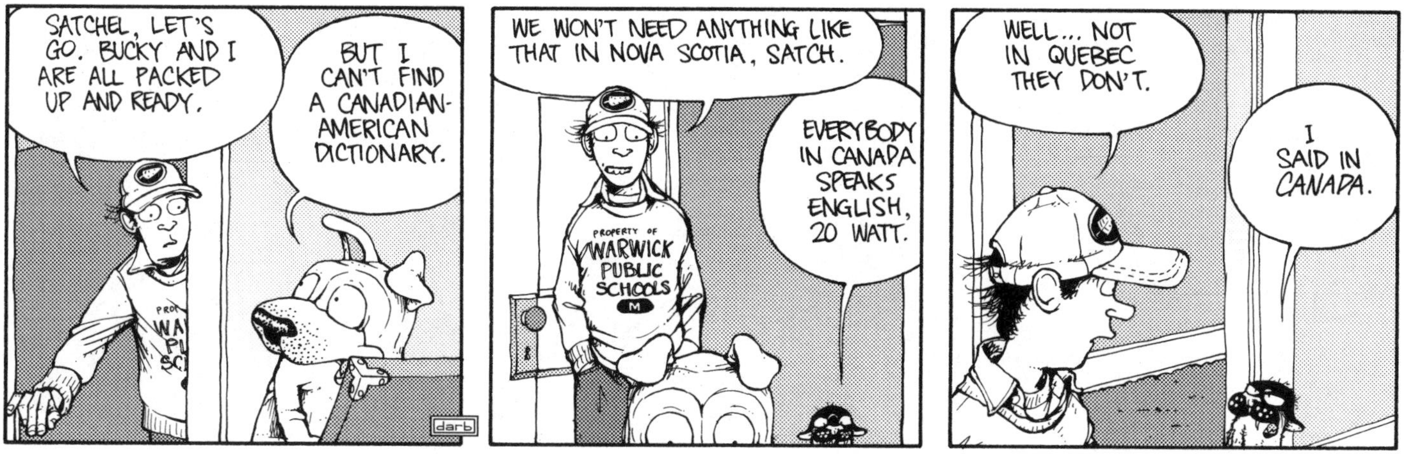
SATCHEL, LET'S GO. BUCKY AND I ARE ALL PACKED UP AND READY.
BUT I CAN'T FIND A CANADIAN-AMERICAN DICTIONARY.
WE WON'T NEED ANYTHING LIKE THAT IN NOVA SCOTIA, SATCH.
PROPERTY OF WARWICK PUBLIC SCHOOLS
EVERYBODY IN CANADA SPEAKS ENGLISH, 20 WATT.
WELL... NOT IN QUEBEC THEY DON'T.
I SAID IN *CANADA*.

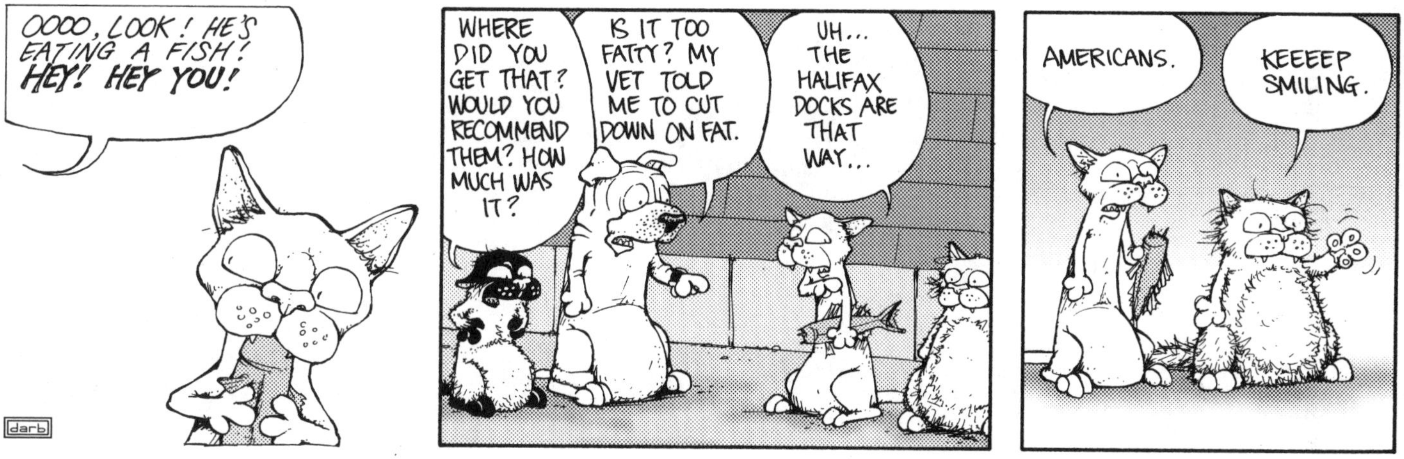
OOOO, LOOK! HE'S EATING A FISH! ***HEY! HEY YOU!***
WHERE DID YOU GET THAT? WOULD YOU RECOMMEND THEM? HOW MUCH WAS IT?
IS IT TOO FATTY? MY VET TOLD ME TO CUT DOWN ON FAT.
UH... THE HALIFAX DOCKS ARE THAT WAY...
AMERICANS.
KEEEEP SMILING.

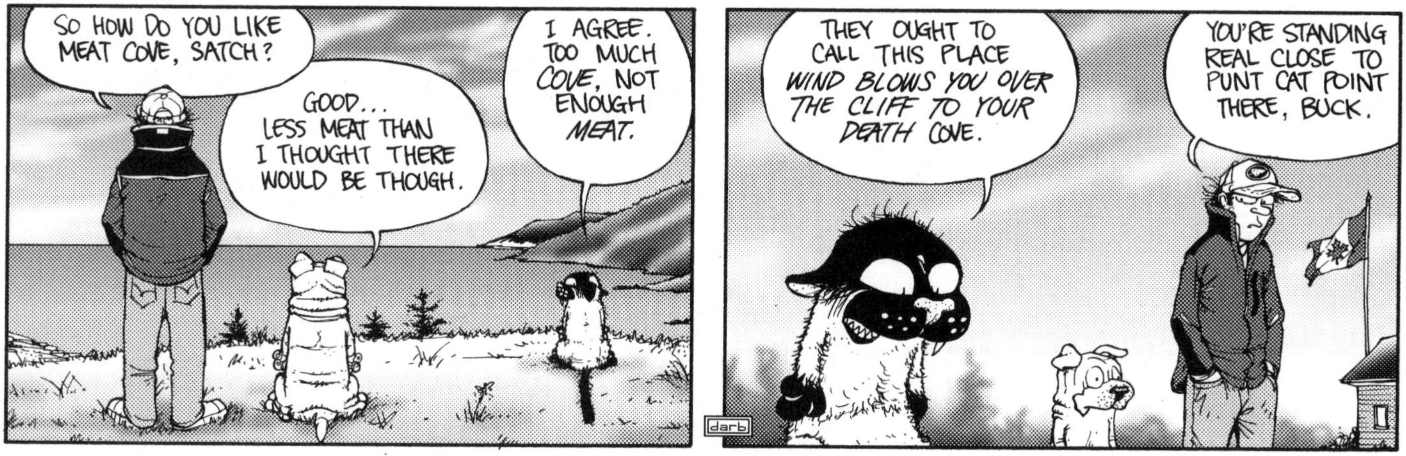
SO HOW DO YOU LIKE MEAT COVE, SATCH?
GOOD... LESS MEAT THAN I THOUGHT THERE WOULD BE THOUGH.
I AGREE. TOO MUCH *COVE*, NOT ENOUGH *MEAT*.
THEY OUGHT TO CALL THIS PLACE *WIND BLOWS YOU OVER THE CLIFF TO YOUR DEATH* COVE.
YOU'RE STANDING REAL CLOSE TO PUNT CAT POINT THERE, BUCK.

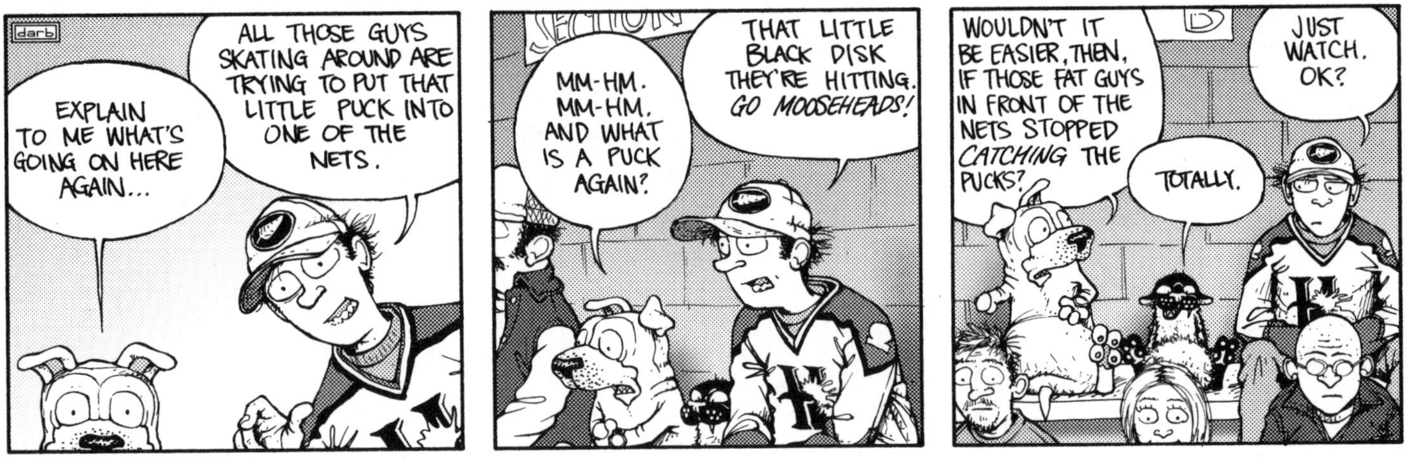
EXPLAIN TO ME WHAT'S GOING ON HERE AGAIN...
ALL THOSE GUYS SKATING AROUND ARE TRYING TO PUT THAT LITTLE PUCK INTO ONE OF THE NETS.
MM-HM. MM-HM. AND WHAT IS A PUCK AGAIN?
THAT LITTLE BLACK DISK THEY'RE HITTING. *GO MOOSEHEADS!*
WOULDN'T IT BE EASIER, THEN, IF THOSE FAT GUYS IN FRONT OF THE NETS STOPPED *CATCHING* THE PUCKS?
TOTALLY.
JUST WATCH. OK?

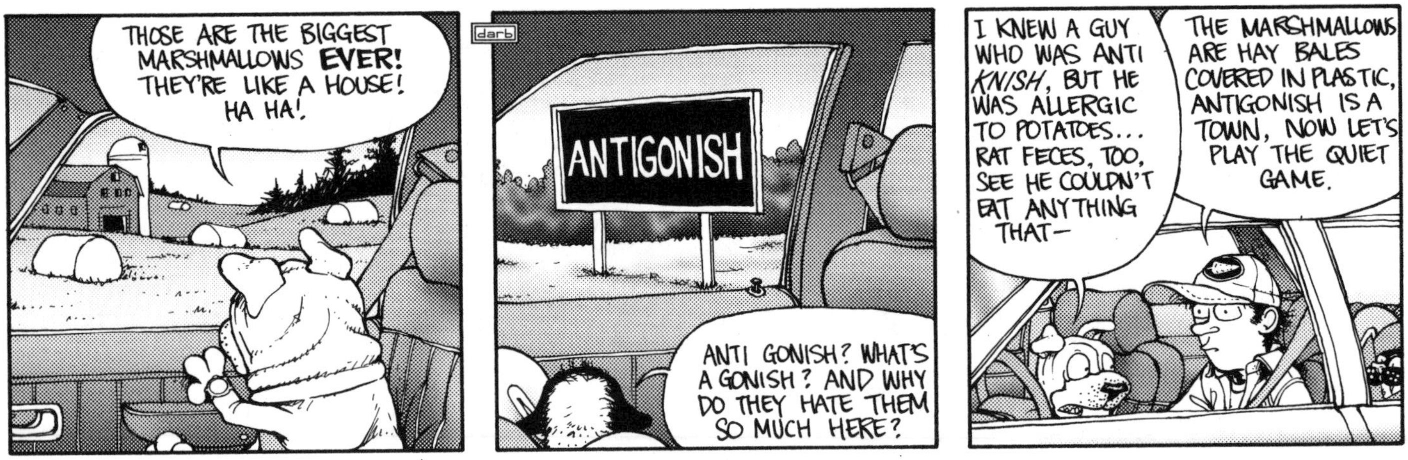
THOSE ARE THE BIGGEST MARSHMALLOWS **EVER!** THEY'RE LIKE A HOUSE! HA HA!
ANTIGONISH
ANTI GONISH? WHAT'S A GONISH? AND WHY DO THEY HATE THEM SO MUCH HERE?
I KNEW A GUY WHO WAS ANTI *KNISH*, BUT HE WAS ALLERGIC TO POTATOES... RAT FECES, TOO, SEE HE COULDN'T EAT ANYTHING THAT—
THE MARSHMALLOWS ARE HAY BALES COVERED IN PLASTIC, ANTIGONISH IS A TOWN, NOW LET'S PLAY THE QUIET GAME.

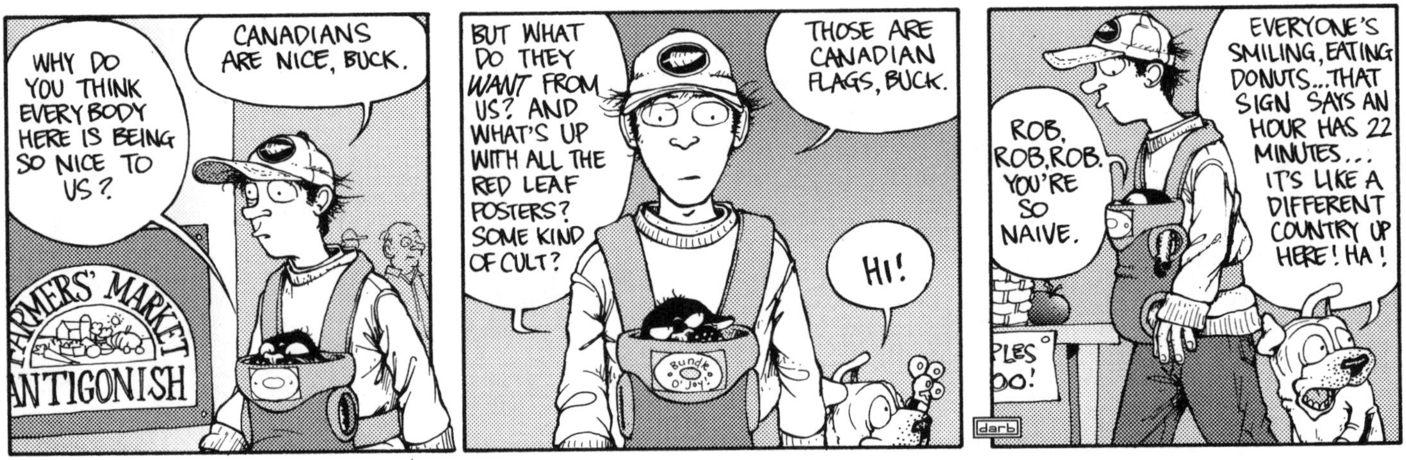
WHY DO YOU THINK EVERYBODY HERE IS BEING SO NICE TO US?
CANADIANS ARE NICE, BUCK.
FARMERS' MARKET
ANTIGONISH
BUT WHAT DO THEY *WANT* FROM US? AND WHAT'S UP WITH ALL THE RED LEAF POSTERS? SOME KIND OF CULT?
THOSE ARE CANADIAN FLAGS, BUCK.
HI!
Bundle O' Joy
ROB, ROB, ROB. YOU'RE SO NAIVE.
EVERYONE'S SMILING, EATING DONUTS... THAT SIGN SAYS AN HOUR HAS 22 MINUTES... IT'S LIKE A DIFFERENT COUNTRY UP HERE! HA!

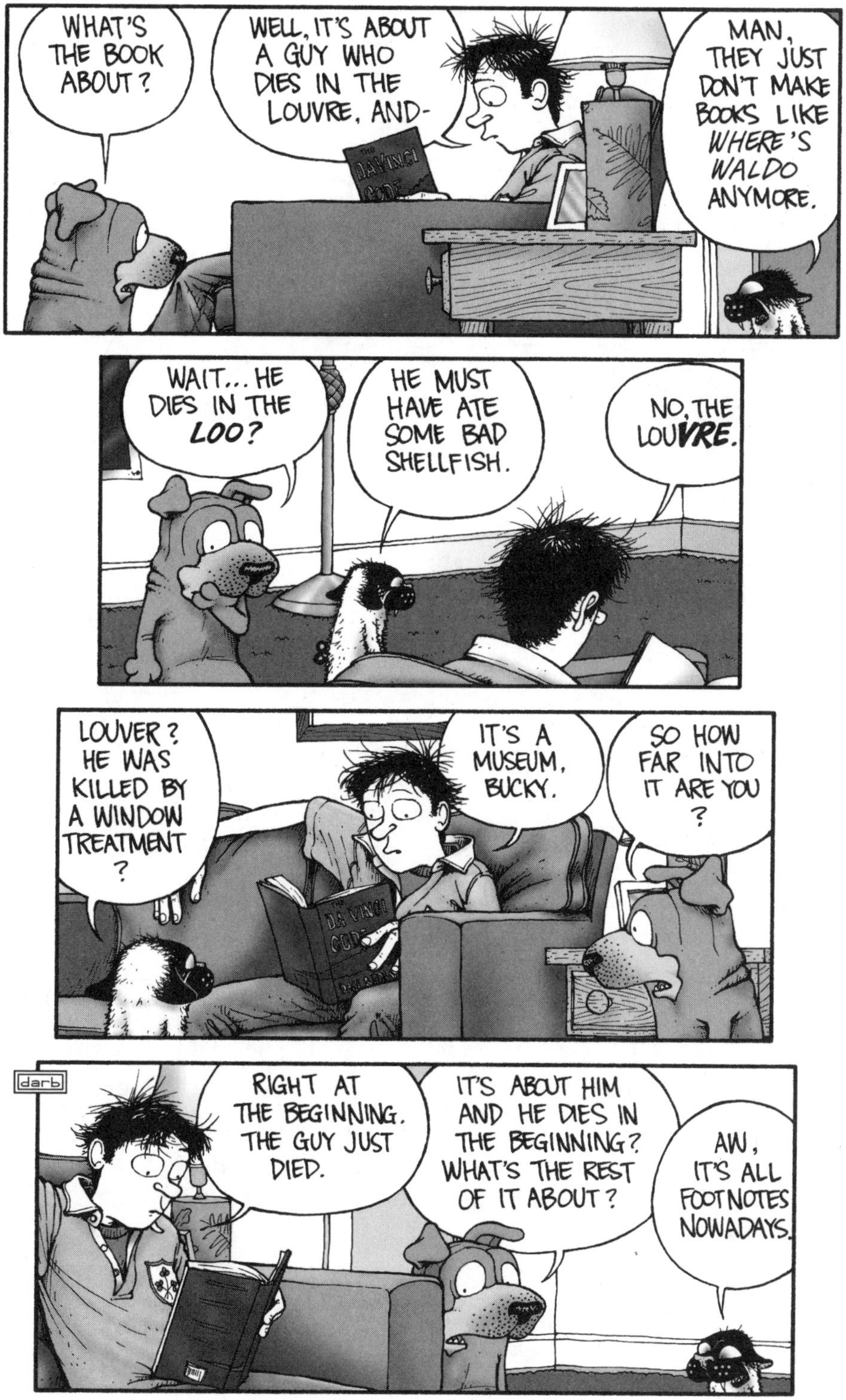
WHAT'S THE BOOK ABOUT?
WELL, IT'S ABOUT A GUY WHO DIES IN THE LOUVRE, AND-
MAN, THEY JUST DON'T MAKE BOOKS LIKE *WHERE'S WALDO* ANYMORE.
WAIT... HE DIES IN THE ***LOO?***
HE MUST HAVE ATE SOME BAD SHELLFISH.
NO, THE LOU***VRE.***
LOUVER? HE WAS KILLED BY A WINDOW TREATMENT?
IT'S A MUSEUM, BUCKY.
SO HOW FAR INTO IT ARE YOU?
darb
RIGHT AT THE BEGINNING. THE GUY JUST DIED.
IT'S ABOUT HIM AND HE DIES IN THE BEGINNING? WHAT'S THE REST OF IT ABOUT?
AW, IT'S ALL FOOTNOTES NOWADAYS.

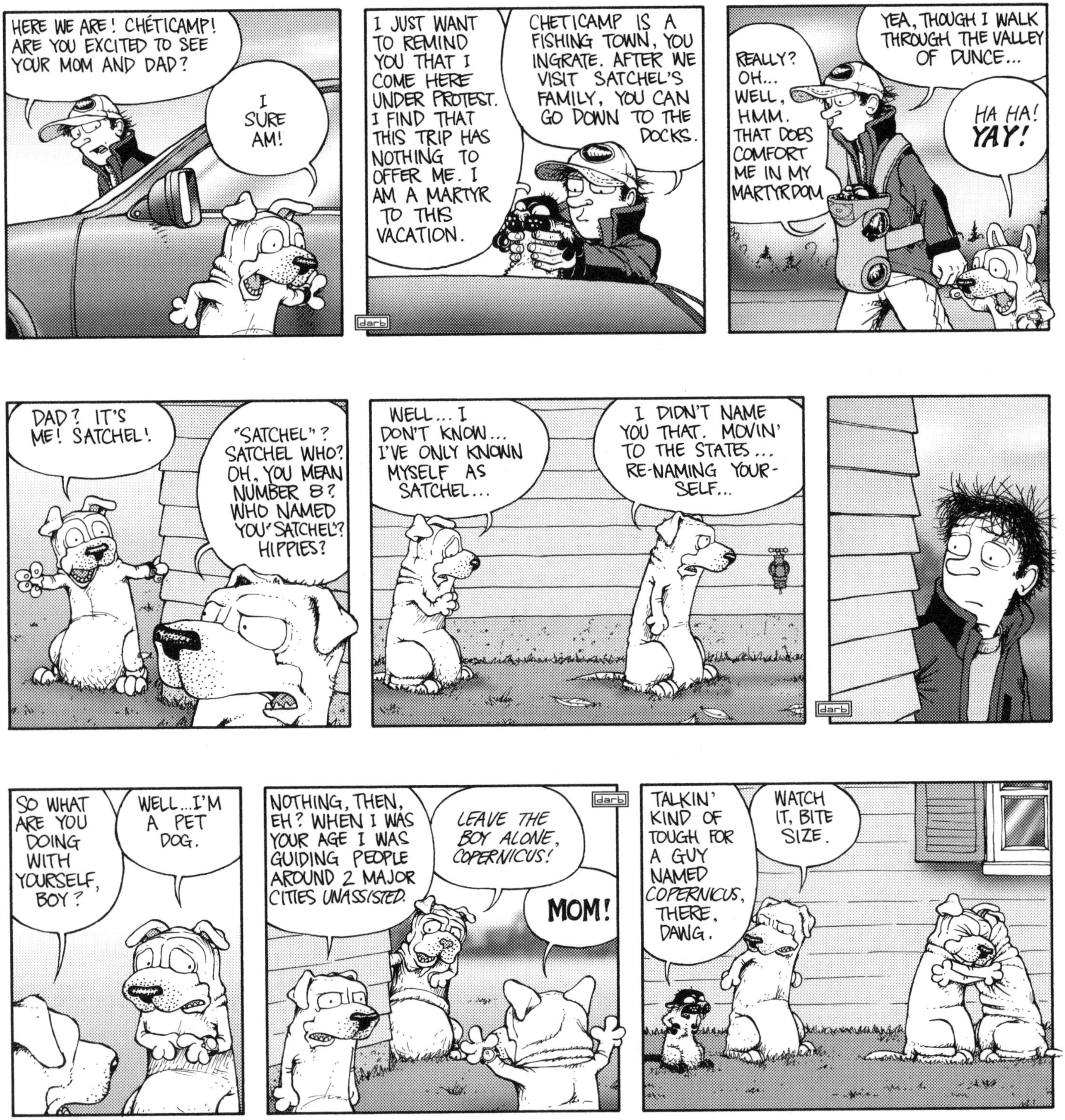

HERE WE ARE! CHÉTICAMP! ARE YOU EXCITED TO SEE YOUR MOM AND DAD?
I SURE AM!
I JUST WANT TO REMIND YOU THAT I COME HERE UNDER PROTEST. I FIND THAT THIS TRIP HAS NOTHING TO OFFER ME. I AM A MARTYR TO THIS VACATION.
CHETICAMP IS A FISHING TOWN, YOU INGRATE. AFTER WE VISIT SATCHEL'S FAMILY, YOU CAN GO DOWN TO THE DOCKS.
darb
REALLY? OH... WELL, HMM. THAT DOES COMFORT ME IN MY MARTYRDOM.
YEA, THOUGH I WALK THROUGH THE VALLEY OF DUNCE...
HA HA! YAY!
DAD? IT'S ME! SATCHEL!
"SATCHEL"? SATCHEL WHO? OH, YOU MEAN NUMBER 8? WHO NAMED YOU "SATCHEL"? HIPPIES?
WELL... I DON'T KNOW... I'VE ONLY KNOWN MYSELF AS SATCHEL...
I DIDN'T NAME YOU THAT. MOVIN' TO THE STATES... RE-NAMING YOURSELF...
darb
SO WHAT ARE YOU DOING WITH YOURSELF, BOY?
WELL...I'M A PET DOG.
NOTHING, THEN, EH? WHEN I WAS YOUR AGE I WAS GUIDING PEOPLE AROUND 2 MAJOR CITIES UNASSISTED.
LEAVE THE BOY ALONE, COPERNICUS!
MOM!
darb
TALKIN' KIND OF TOUGH FOR A GUY NAMED COPERNICUS, THERE, DAWG.
WATCH IT, BITE SIZE.

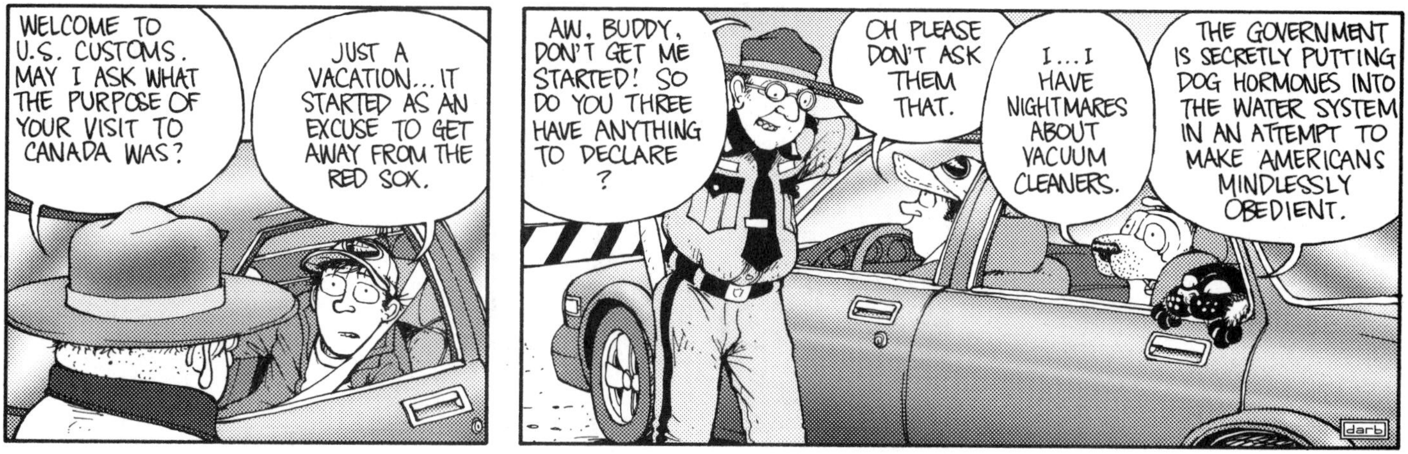
WELCOME TO U.S. CUSTOMS. MAY I ASK WHAT THE PURPOSE OF YOUR VISIT TO CANADA WAS?
JUST A VACATION... IT STARTED AS AN EXCUSE TO GET AWAY FROM THE RED SOX.
AW, BUDDY, DON'T GET ME STARTED! SO DO YOU THREE HAVE ANYTHING TO DECLARE?
OH PLEASE DON'T ASK THEM THAT.
I... I HAVE NIGHTMARES ABOUT VACUUM CLEANERS.
THE GOVERNMENT IS SECRETLY PUTTING DOG HORMONES INTO THE WATER SYSTEM IN AN ATTEMPT TO MAKE AMERICANS MINDLESSLY OBEDIENT.
darb

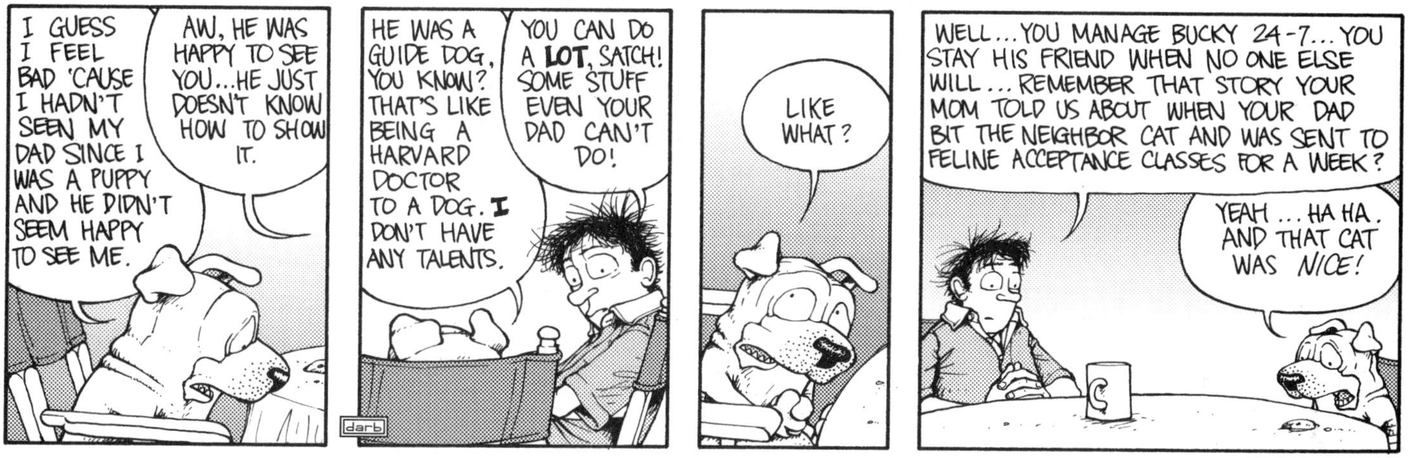
I GUESS I FEEL BAD 'CAUSE I HADN'T SEEN MY DAD SINCE I WAS A PUPPY AND HE DIDN'T SEEM HAPPY TO SEE ME.
AW, HE WAS HAPPY TO SEE YOU... HE JUST DOESN'T KNOW HOW TO SHOW IT.
darb
HE WAS A GUIDE DOG, YOU KNOW? THAT'S LIKE BEING A HARVARD DOCTOR TO A DOG. **I** DON'T HAVE ANY TALENTS.
YOU CAN DO A **LOT**, SATCH! SOME STUFF EVEN YOUR DAD CAN'T DO!
LIKE WHAT?
WELL... YOU MANAGE BUCKY 24-7... YOU STAY HIS FRIEND WHEN NO ONE ELSE WILL... REMEMBER THAT STORY YOUR MOM TOLD US ABOUT WHEN YOUR DAD BIT THE NEIGHBOR CAT AND WAS SENT TO FELINE ACCEPTANCE CLASSES FOR A WEEK?
YEAH... HA HA. AND THAT CAT WAS *NICE*!

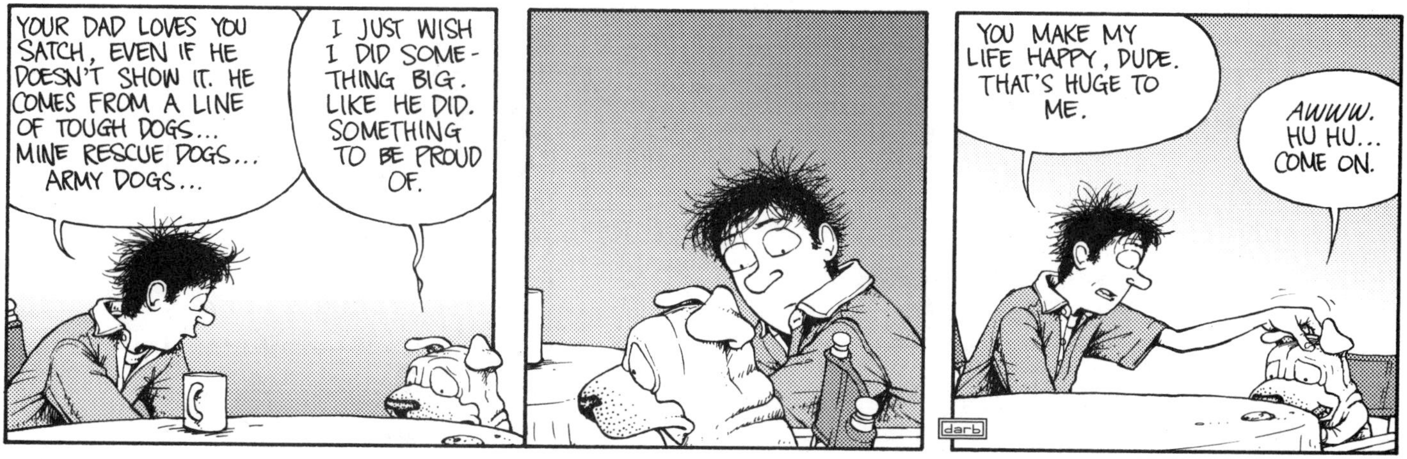
YOUR DAD LOVES YOU SATCH, EVEN IF HE DOESN'T SHOW IT. HE COMES FROM A LINE OF TOUGH DOGS... MINE RESCUE DOGS... ARMY DOGS...
I JUST WISH I DID SOMETHING BIG. LIKE HE DID. SOMETHING TO BE PROUD OF.
YOU MAKE MY LIFE HAPPY, DUDE. THAT'S HUGE TO ME.
AWWW. HU HU... COME ON.
darb

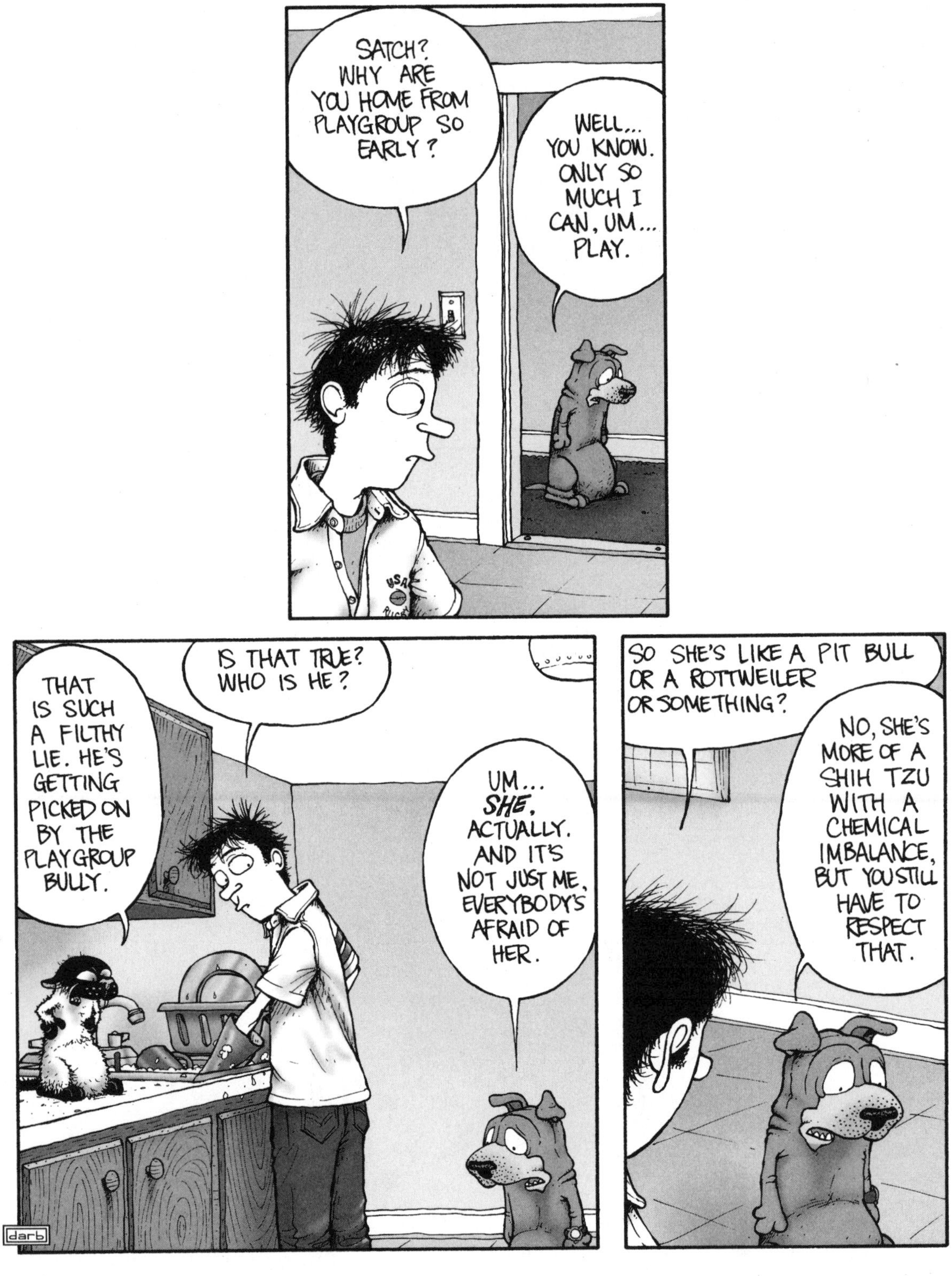
SATCH? WHY ARE YOU HOME FROM PLAYGROUP SO EARLY?
WELL... YOU KNOW. ONLY SO MUCH I CAN, UM... PLAY.
THAT IS SUCH A FILTHY LIE. HE'S GETTING PICKED ON BY THE PLAYGROUP BULLY.
IS THAT TRUE? WHO IS HE?
UM... *SHE*, ACTUALLY. AND IT'S NOT JUST ME, EVERYBODY'S AFRAID OF HER.
darb
SO SHE'S LIKE A PIT BULL OR A ROTTWEILER OR SOMETHING?
NO, SHE'S MORE OF A SHIH TZU WITH A CHEMICAL IMBALANCE, BUT YOU STILL HAVE TO RESPECT THAT.

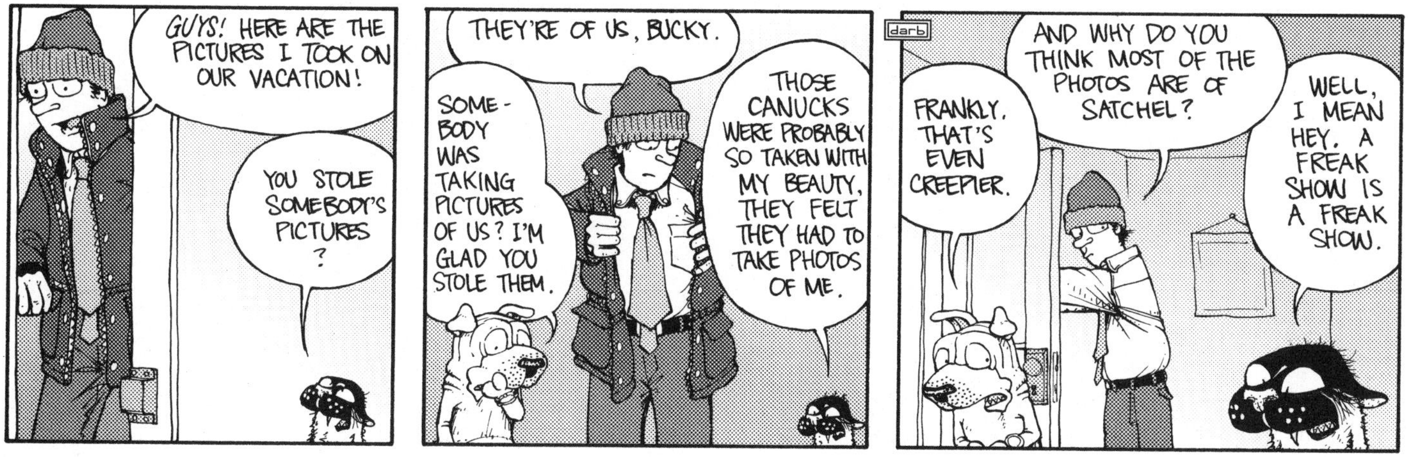
GUYS! HERE ARE THE PICTURES I TOOK ON OUR VACATION!
YOU STOLE SOMEBODY'S PICTURES ?
THEY'RE OF US, BUCKY.
SOMEBODY WAS TAKING PICTURES OF US? I'M GLAD YOU STOLE THEM.
THOSE CANUCKS WERE PROBABLY SO TAKEN WITH MY BEAUTY, THEY FELT THEY HAD TO TAKE PHOTOS OF ME.
darb
FRANKLY, THAT'S EVEN CREEPIER.
AND WHY DO YOU THINK MOST OF THE PHOTOS ARE OF SATCHEL?
WELL, I MEAN HEY, A FREAK SHOW IS A FREAK SHOW.

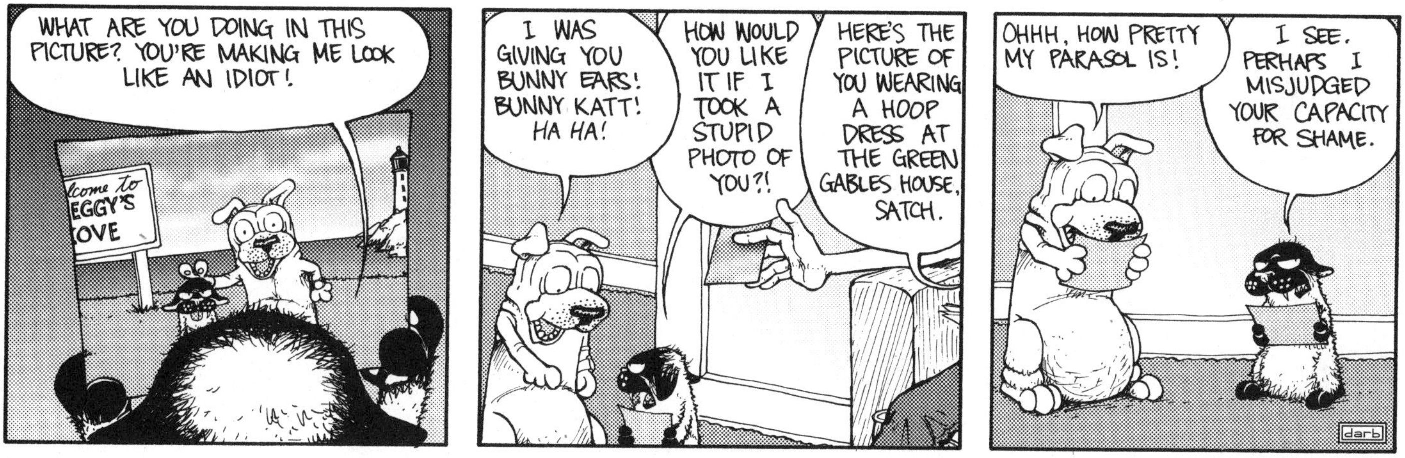
WHAT ARE YOU DOING IN THIS PICTURE? YOU'RE MAKING ME LOOK LIKE AN IDIOT!
I WAS GIVING YOU BUNNY EARS! BUNNY KATT! HA HA!
HOW WOULD YOU LIKE IT IF I TOOK A STUPID PHOTO OF YOU?!
HERE'S THE PICTURE OF YOU WEARING A HOOP DRESS AT THE GREEN GABLES HOUSE, SATCH.
OHHH, HOW PRETTY MY PARASOL IS!
I SEE. PERHAPS I MISJUDGED YOUR CAPACITY FOR SHAME.
darb

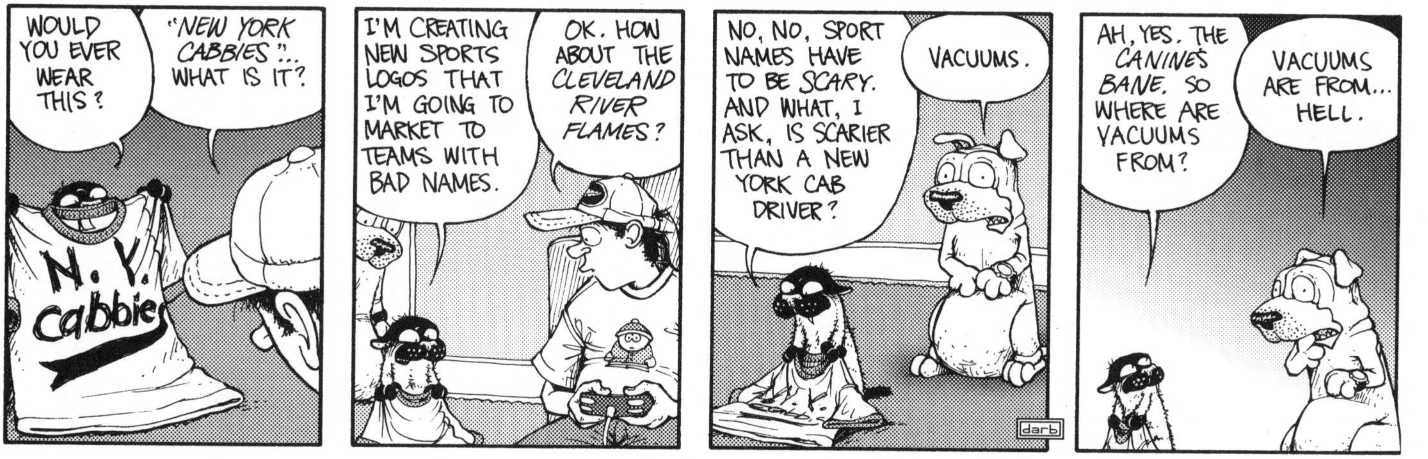
WOULD YOU EVER WEAR THIS?
"NEW YORK CABBIES"... WHAT IS IT?
N.Y. cabbie
I'M CREATING NEW SPORTS LOGOS THAT I'M GOING TO MARKET TO TEAMS WITH BAD NAMES.
OK. HOW ABOUT THE CLEVELAND RIVER FLAMES?
NO, NO, SPORT NAMES HAVE TO BE SCARY. AND WHAT, I ASK, IS SCARIER THAN A NEW YORK CAB DRIVER?
VACUUMS.
darb
AH, YES. THE CANINE'S BANE. SO WHERE ARE VACUUMS FROM?
VACUUMS ARE FROM... HELL.

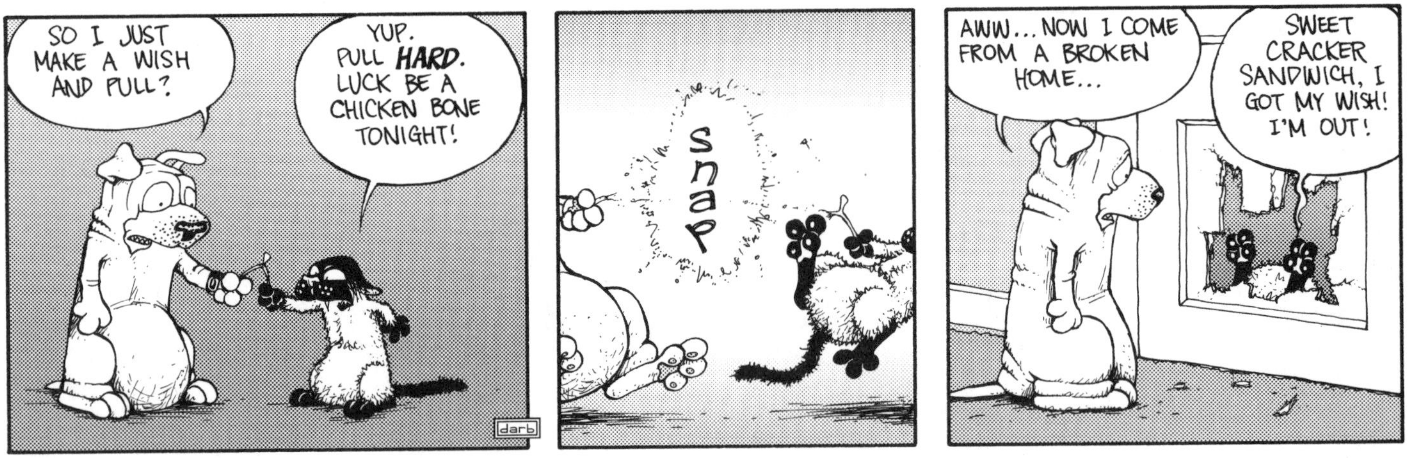
SO I JUST MAKE A WISH AND PULL?
YUP. PULL HARD. LUCK BE A CHICKEN BONE TONIGHT!
SNAP
AWW... NOW I COME FROM A BROKEN HOME...
SWEET CRACKER SANDWICH, I GOT MY WISH! I'M OUT!
darb

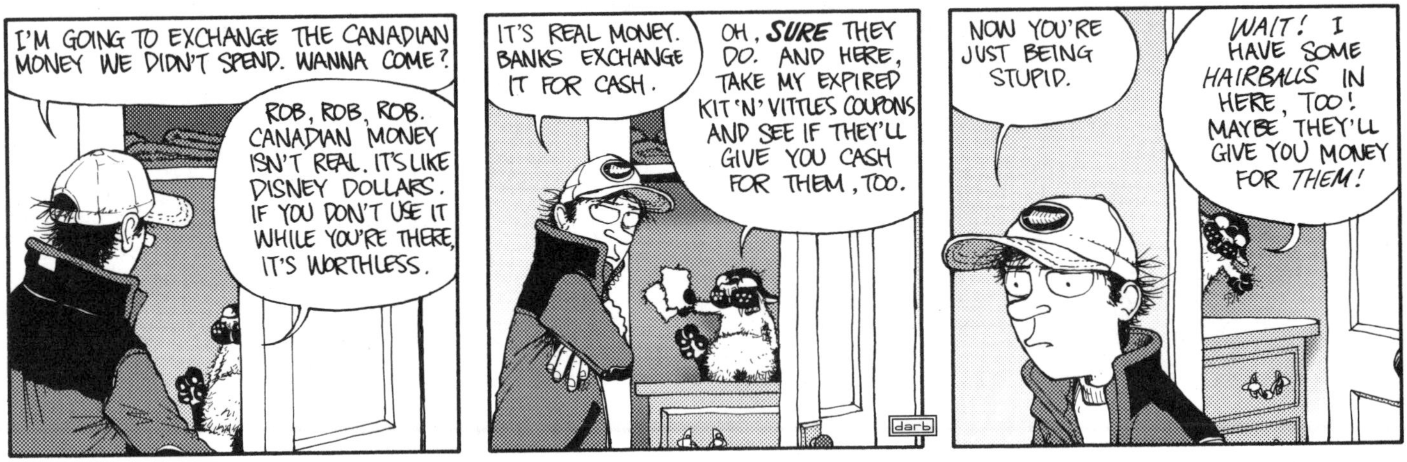
I'M GOING TO EXCHANGE THE CANADIAN MONEY WE DIDN'T SPEND. WANNA COME?
ROB, ROB, ROB. CANADIAN MONEY ISN'T REAL. IT'S LIKE DISNEY DOLLARS. IF YOU DON'T USE IT WHILE YOU'RE THERE, IT'S WORTHLESS.
IT'S REAL MONEY. BANKS EXCHANGE IT FOR CASH.
OH, SURE THEY DO. AND HERE, TAKE MY EXPIRED KIT 'N' VITTLES COUPONS AND SEE IF THEY'LL GIVE YOU CASH FOR THEM, TOO.
darb
NOW YOU'RE JUST BEING STUPID.
WAIT! I HAVE SOME HAIRBALLS IN HERE, TOO! MAYBE THEY'LL GIVE YOU MONEY FOR THEM!

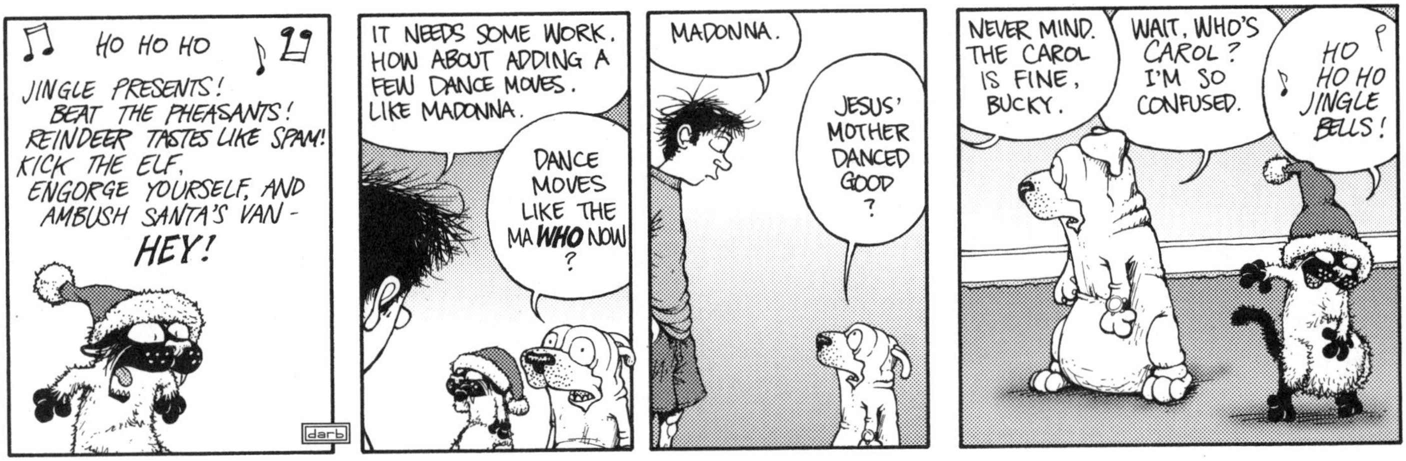
HO HO HO
JINGLE PRESENTS! BEAT THE PHEASANTS! REINDEER TASTES LIKE SPAM! KICK THE ELF, ENGORGE YOURSELF, AND AMBUSH SANTA'S VAN -
HEY!
darb
IT NEEDS SOME WORK. HOW ABOUT ADDING A FEW DANCE MOVES. LIKE MADONNA.
DANCE MOVES LIKE THE MA WHO NOW?
MADONNA.
JESUS' MOTHER DANCED GOOD?
NEVER MIND. THE CAROL IS FINE, BUCKY.
WAIT, WHO'S CAROL? I'M SO CONFUSED.
HO HO HO JINGLE BELLS!

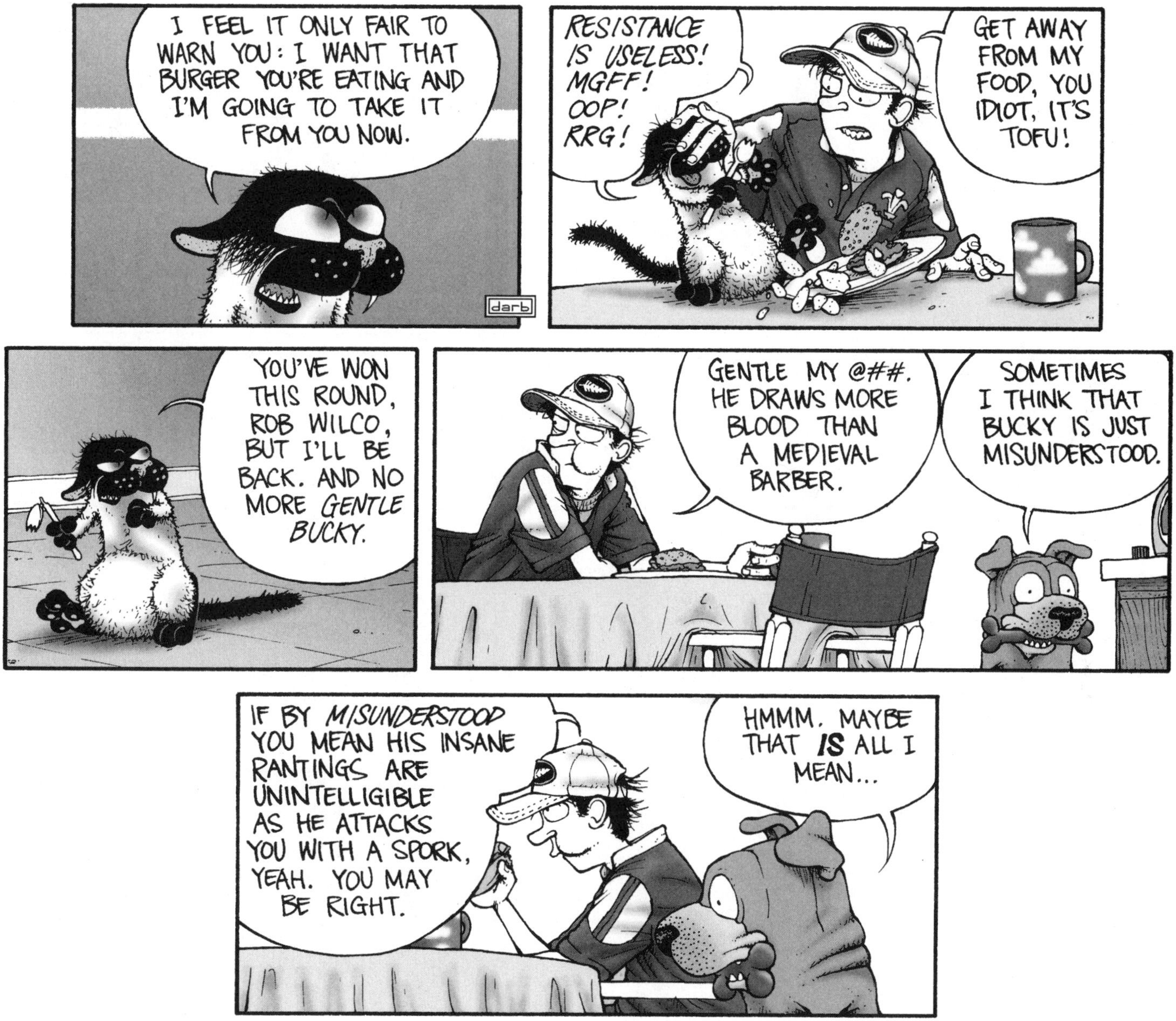
I FEEL IT ONLY FAIR TO WARN YOU: I WANT THAT BURGER YOU'RE EATING AND I'M GOING TO TAKE IT FROM YOU NOW.
darb
RESISTANCE IS USELESS! MGFF! OOP! RRG!
GET AWAY FROM MY FOOD, YOU IDIOT, IT'S TOFU!
YOU'VE WON THIS ROUND, ROB WILCO, BUT I'LL BE BACK. AND NO MORE *GENTLE BUCKY*.
SOMETIMES I THINK THAT BUCKY IS JUST MISUNDERSTOOD.
GENTLE MY @##. HE DRAWS MORE BLOOD THAN A MEDIEVAL BARBER.
IF BY *MISUNDERSTOOD* YOU MEAN HIS INSANE RANTINGS ARE UNINTELLIGIBLE AS HE ATTACKS YOU WITH A SPORK, YEAH. YOU MAY BE RIGHT.
HMMM. MAYBE THAT **IS** ALL I MEAN...

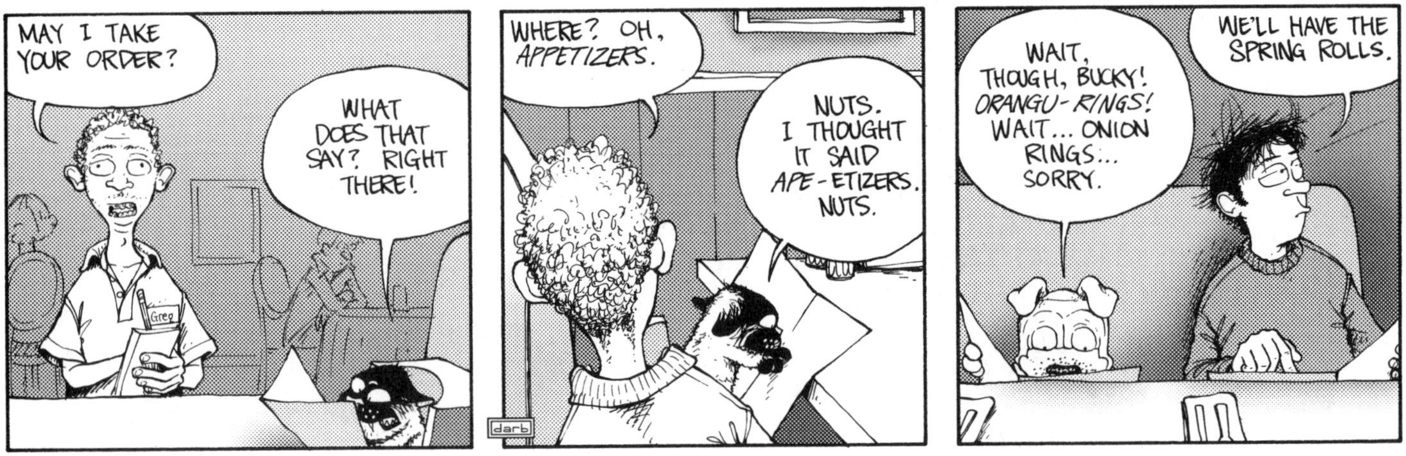
MAY I TAKE YOUR ORDER?
WHAT DOES THAT SAY? RIGHT THERE!
WHERE? OH, *APPETIZERS*.
NUTS. I THOUGHT IT SAID *APE*-ETIZERS. NUTS.
WAIT, THOUGH, BUCKY! *ORANGU-RINGS!* WAIT... ONION RINGS... SORRY.
WE'LL HAVE THE SPRING ROLLS.

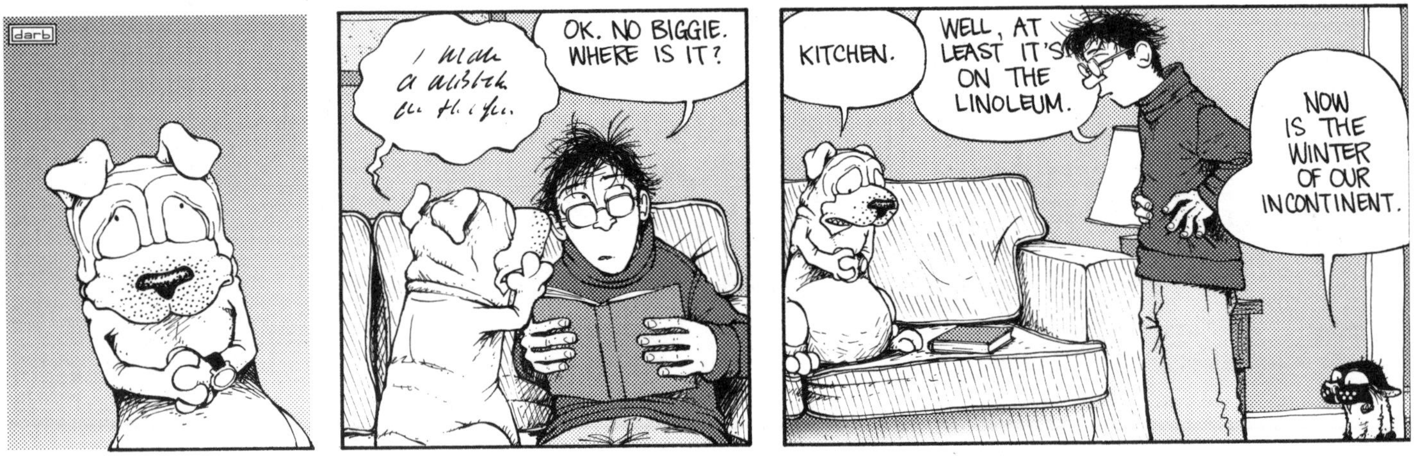
OK. NO BIGGIE. WHERE IS IT?
KITCHEN.
WELL, AT LEAST IT'S ON THE LINOLEUM.
NOW IS THE WINTER OF OUR INCONTINENT.

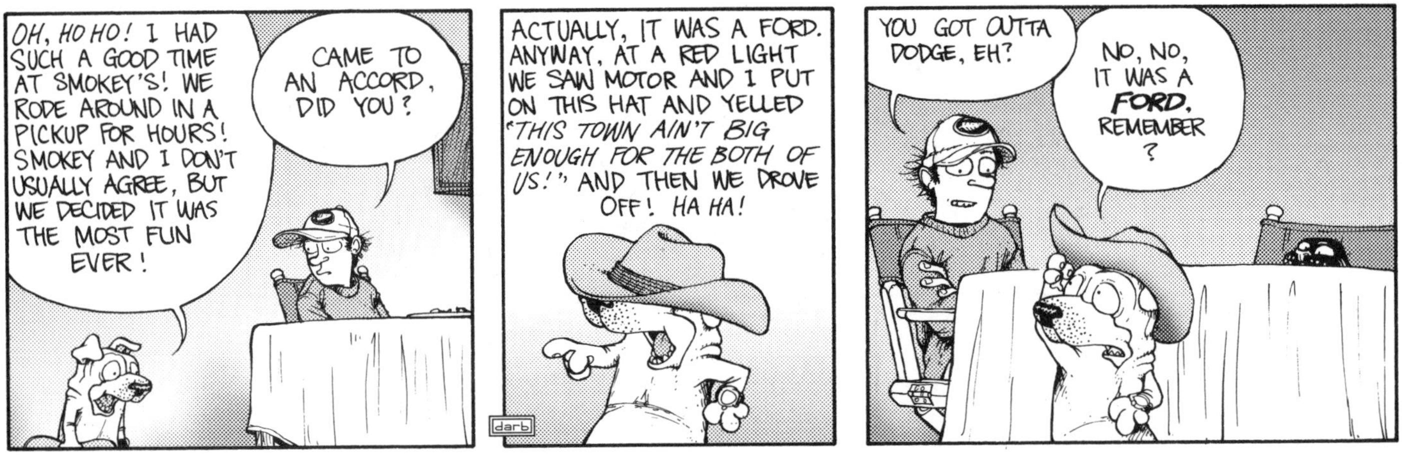
OH, HO HO! I HAD SUCH A GOOD TIME AT SMOKEY'S! WE RODE AROUND IN A PICKUP FOR HOURS! SMOKEY AND I DON'T USUALLY AGREE, BUT WE DECIDED IT WAS THE MOST FUN EVER!
CAME TO AN ACCORD, DID YOU?
ACTUALLY, IT WAS A FORD. ANYWAY, AT A RED LIGHT WE SAW MOTOR AND I PUT ON THIS HAT AND YELLED *"THIS TOWN AIN'T BIG ENOUGH FOR THE BOTH OF US!"* AND THEN WE DROVE OFF! *HA HA!*
YOU GOT OUTTA DODGE, EH?
NO, NO, IT WAS A **FORD**, REMEMBER?

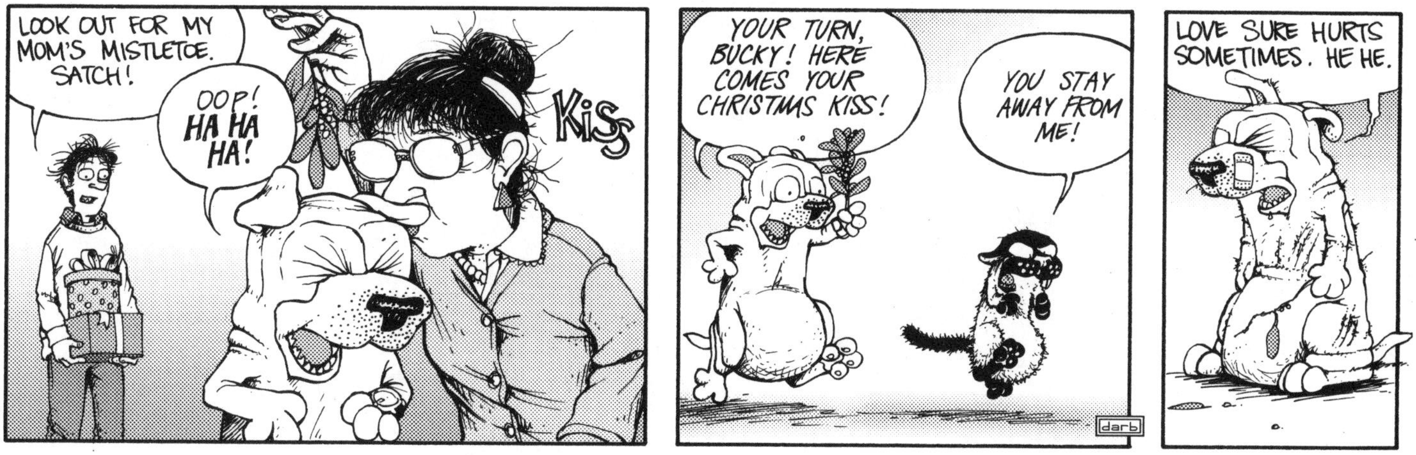
LOOK OUT FOR MY MOM'S MISTLETOE. SATCH!
OOP! HA HA HA!
KISS
YOUR TURN, BUCKY! HERE COMES YOUR CHRISTMAS KISS!
YOU STAY AWAY FROM ME!
darb
LOVE SURE HURTS SOMETIMES. HE HE.

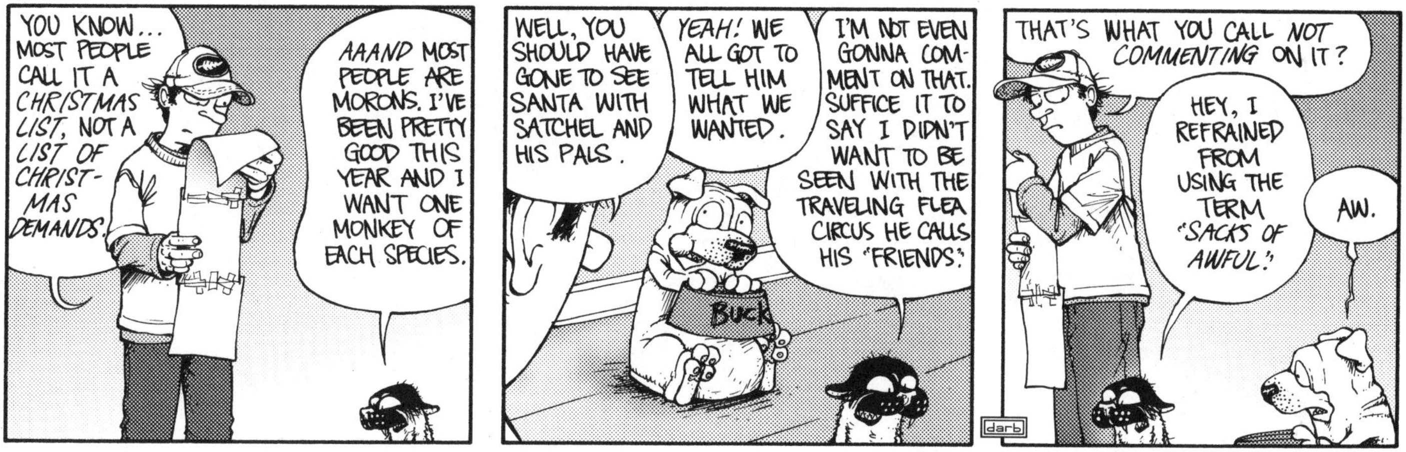
YOU KNOW... MOST PEOPLE CALL IT A CHRISTMAS LIST, NOT A LIST OF CHRISTMAS DEMANDS.
AAAND MOST PEOPLE ARE MORONS. I'VE BEEN PRETTY GOOD THIS YEAR AND I WANT ONE MONKEY OF EACH SPECIES.
WELL, YOU SHOULD HAVE GONE TO SEE SANTA WITH SATCHEL AND HIS PALS.
YEAH! WE ALL GOT TO TELL HIM WHAT WE WANTED.
I'M NOT EVEN GONNA COMMENT ON THAT. SUFFICE IT TO SAY I DIDN'T WANT TO BE SEEN WITH THE TRAVELING FLEA CIRCUS HE CALLS HIS "FRIENDS."
BUCK
darb
THAT'S WHAT YOU CALL NOT COMMENTING ON IT?
HEY, I REFRAINED FROM USING THE TERM "SACKS OF AWFUL."
AW.

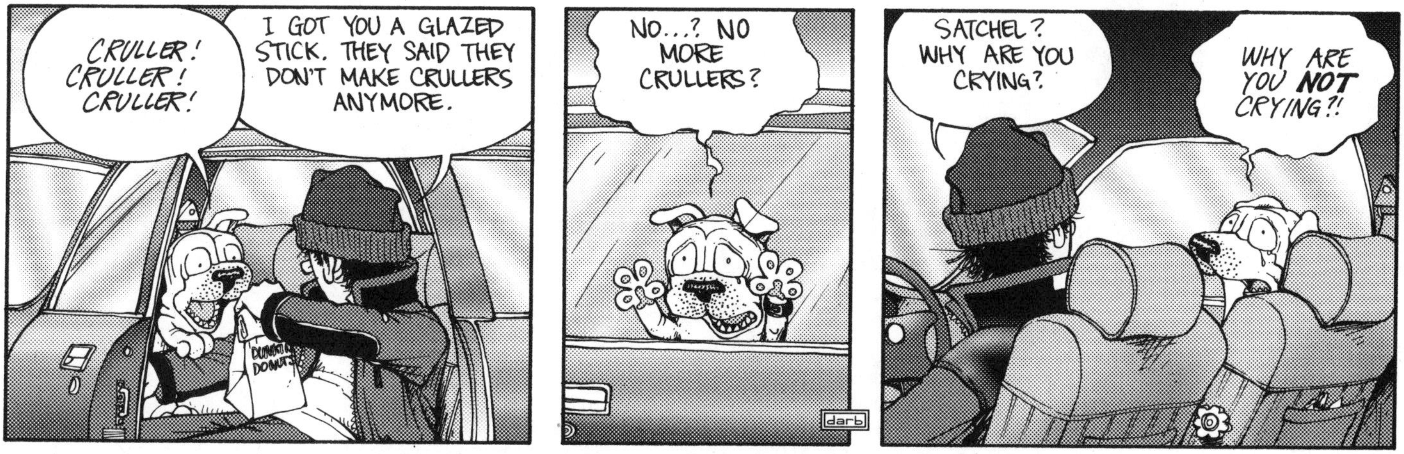
CRULLER! CRULLER! CRULLER!
I GOT YOU A GLAZED STICK. THEY SAID THEY DON'T MAKE CRULLERS ANYMORE.
DUNKIN DONUTS
NO...? NO MORE CRULLERS?
darb
SATCHEL? WHY ARE YOU CRYING?
WHY ARE YOU NOT CRYING?!

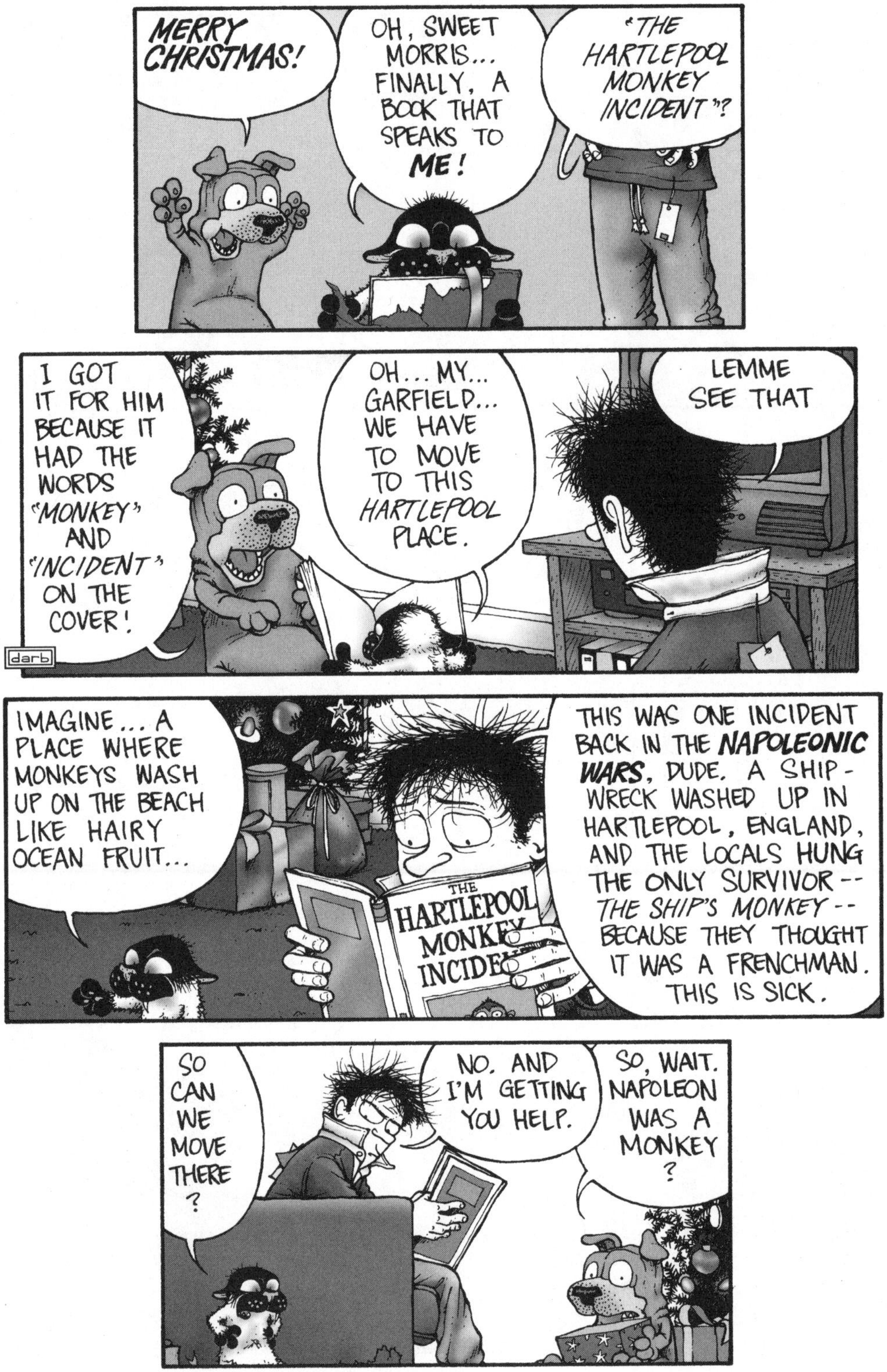
MERRY CHRISTMAS!
OH, SWEET MORRIS... FINALLY, A BOOK THAT SPEAKS TO ME!
"THE HARTLEPOOL MONKEY INCIDENT"?
I GOT IT FOR HIM BECAUSE IT HAD THE WORDS "MONKEY" AND "INCIDENT" ON THE COVER!
OH... MY... GARFIELD... WE HAVE TO MOVE TO THIS HARTLEPOOL PLACE.
LEMME SEE THAT
darb
IMAGINE... A PLACE WHERE MONKEYS WASH UP ON THE BEACH LIKE HAIRY OCEAN FRUIT...
THE HARTLEPOOL MONKEY INCIDE
THIS WAS ONE INCIDENT BACK IN THE NAPOLEONIC WARS, DUDE. A SHIP-WRECK WASHED UP IN HARTLEPOOL, ENGLAND, AND THE LOCALS HUNG THE ONLY SURVIVOR -- THE SHIP'S MONKEY -- BECAUSE THEY THOUGHT IT WAS A FRENCHMAN. THIS IS SICK.
SO CAN WE MOVE THERE?
NO. AND I'M GETTING YOU HELP.
SO, WAIT. NAPOLEON WAS A MONKEY?

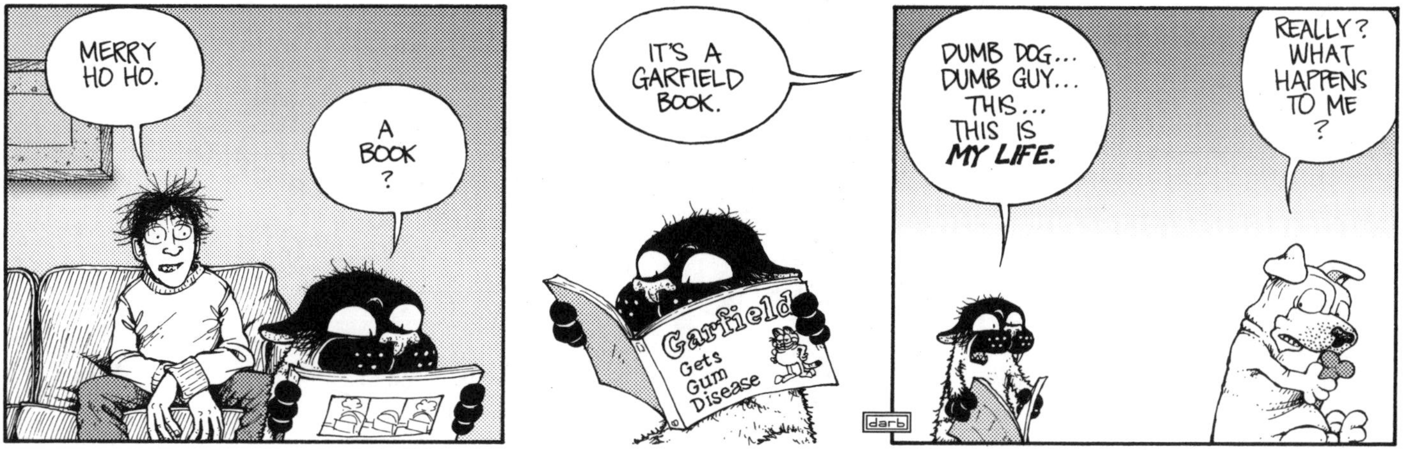
MERRY HO HO.
A BOOK ?
IT'S A GARFIELD BOOK.
Garfield Gets Gum Disease
DUMB DOG... DUMB GUY... THIS... THIS IS *MY LIFE.*
REALLY? WHAT HAPPENS TO ME ?

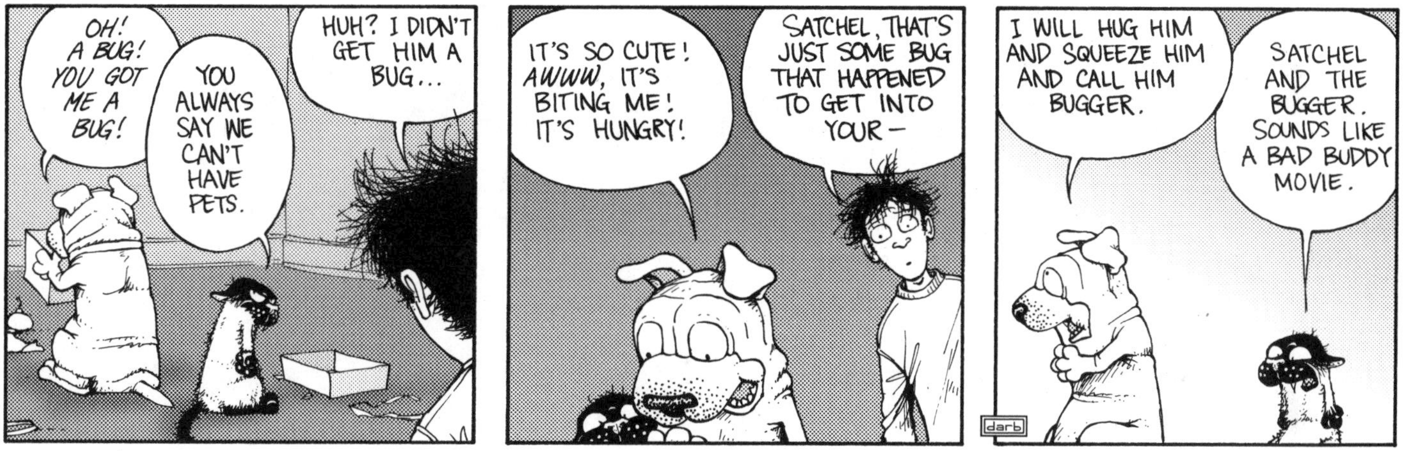
OH! A BUG! YOU GOT ME A BUG!
YOU ALWAYS SAY WE CAN'T HAVE PETS.
HUH? I DIDN'T GET HIM A BUG...
IT'S SO CUTE! *AWWW*, IT'S BITING ME! IT'S HUNGRY!
SATCHEL, THAT'S JUST SOME BUG THAT HAPPENED TO GET INTO YOUR—
I WILL HUG HIM AND SQUEEZE HIM AND CALL HIM BUGGER.
SATCHEL AND THE BUGGER. SOUNDS LIKE A BAD BUDDY MOVIE.

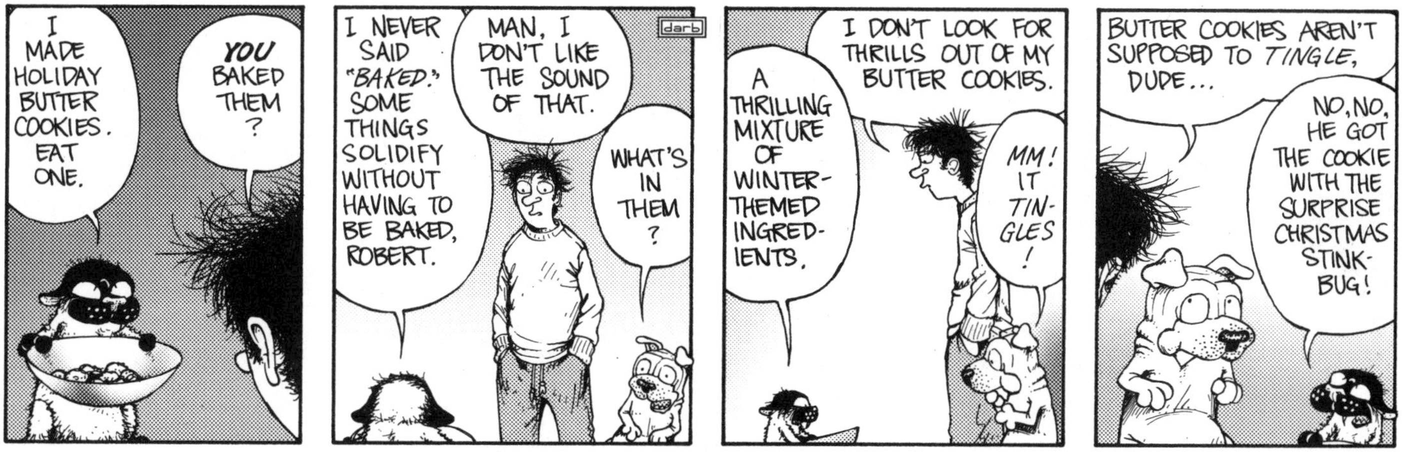
I MADE HOLIDAY BUTTER COOKIES. EAT ONE.
YOU BAKED THEM ?
I NEVER SAID "*BAKED*." SOME THINGS SOLIDIFY WITHOUT HAVING TO BE BAKED, ROBERT.
MAN, I DON'T LIKE THE SOUND OF THAT.
WHAT'S IN THEM ?
A THRILLING MIXTURE OF WINTER-THEMED INGREDIENTS.
I DON'T LOOK FOR THRILLS OUT OF MY BUTTER COOKIES.
MM! IT TINGLES!
BUTTER COOKIES AREN'T SUPPOSED TO *TINGLE*, DUDE...
NO, NO, HE GOT THE COOKIE WITH THE SURPRISE CHRISTMAS STINK-BUG!

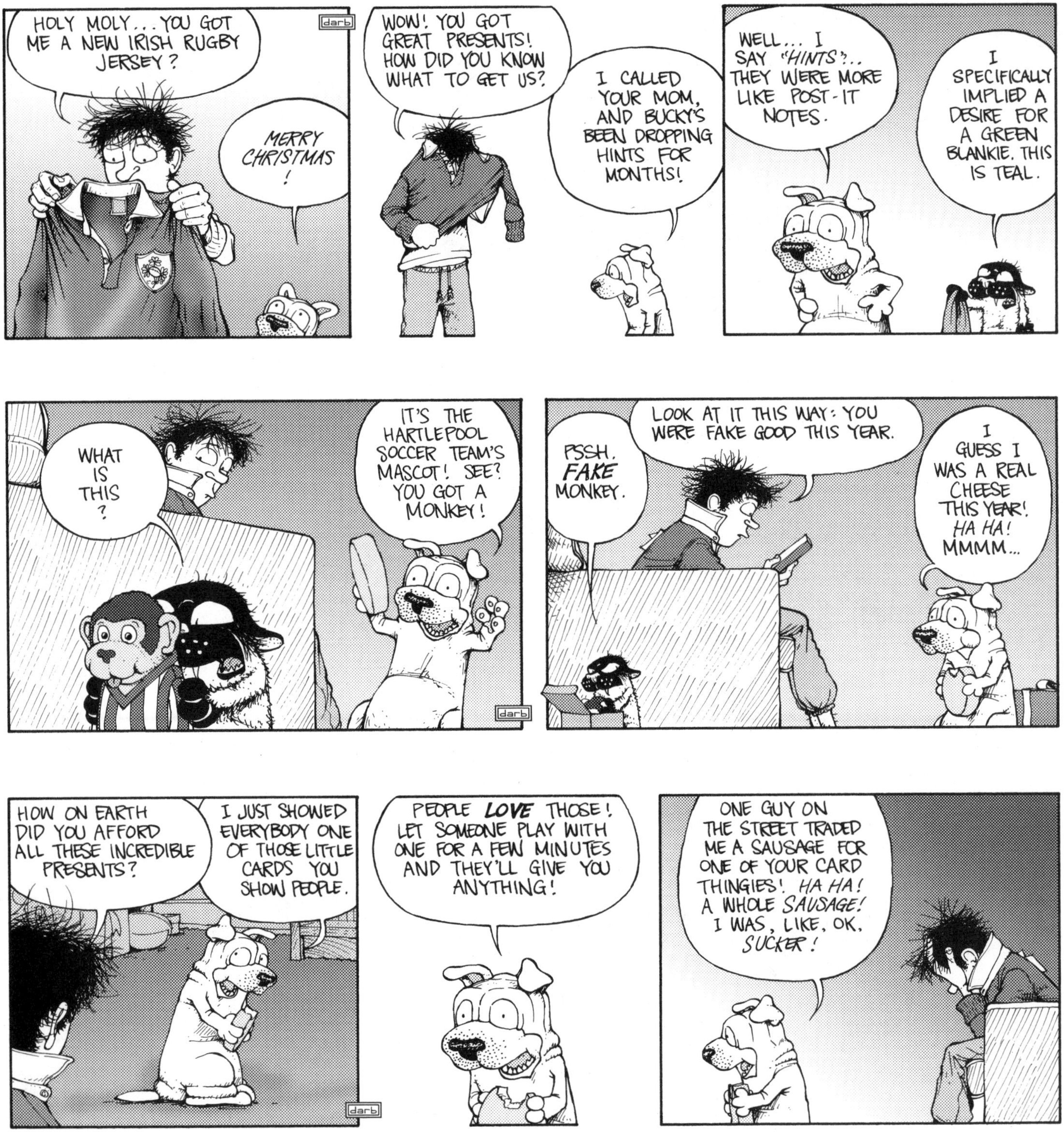
darb
HOLY MOLY... YOU GOT ME A NEW IRISH RUGBY JERSEY?
MERRY CHRISTMAS!
WOW! YOU GOT GREAT PRESENTS! HOW DID YOU KNOW WHAT TO GET US?
I CALLED YOUR MOM, AND BUCKY'S BEEN DROPPING HINTS FOR MONTHS!
WELL... I SAY "HINTS"... THEY WERE MORE LIKE POST-IT NOTES.
I SPECIFICALLY IMPLIED A DESIRE FOR A GREEN BLANKIE. THIS IS TEAL.
WHAT IS THIS?
IT'S THE HARTLEPOOL SOCCER TEAM'S MASCOT! SEE? YOU GOT A MONKEY!
darb
PSSH. FAKE MONKEY.
LOOK AT IT THIS WAY: YOU WERE FAKE GOOD THIS YEAR.
I GUESS I WAS A REAL CHEESE THIS YEAR! HA HA! MMMM...
HOW ON EARTH DID YOU AFFORD ALL THESE INCREDIBLE PRESENTS?
I JUST SHOWED EVERYBODY ONE OF THOSE LITTLE CARDS YOU SHOW PEOPLE.
darb
PEOPLE LOVE THOSE! LET SOMEONE PLAY WITH ONE FOR A FEW MINUTES AND THEY'LL GIVE YOU ANYTHING!
ONE GUY ON THE STREET TRADED ME A SAUSAGE FOR ONE OF YOUR CARD THINGIES! HA HA! A WHOLE SAUSAGE! I WAS, LIKE, OK. SUCKER!

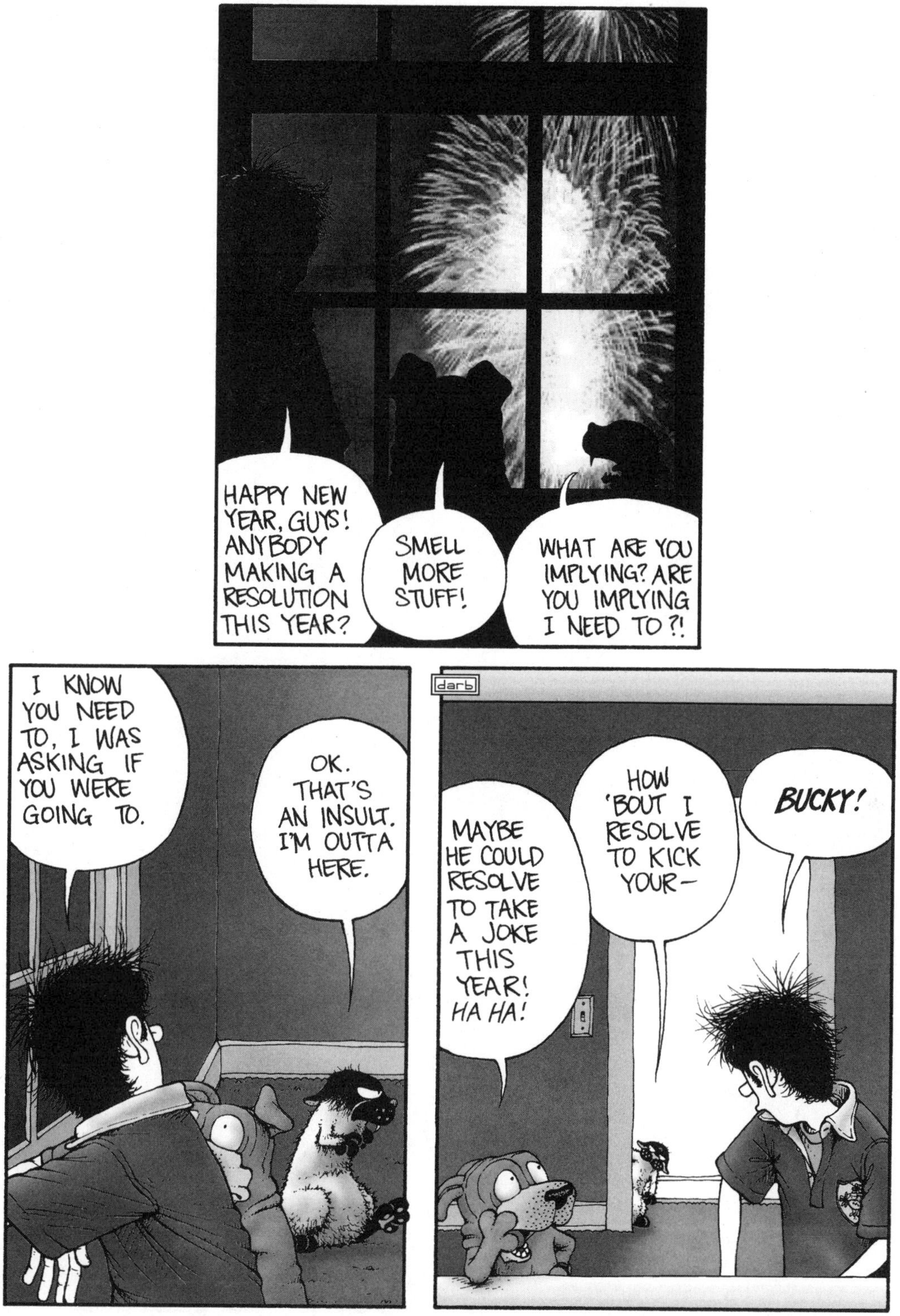
HAPPY NEW YEAR, GUYS! ANYBODY MAKING A RESOLUTION THIS YEAR?
SMELL MORE STUFF!
WHAT ARE YOU IMPLYING? ARE YOU IMPLYING I NEED TO?!
I KNOW YOU NEED TO, I WAS ASKING IF YOU WERE GOING TO.
OK. THAT'S AN INSULT. I'M OUTTA HERE.
MAYBE HE COULD RESOLVE TO TAKE A JOKE THIS YEAR! HA HA!
HOW 'BOUT I RESOLVE TO KICK YOUR—
BUCKY!

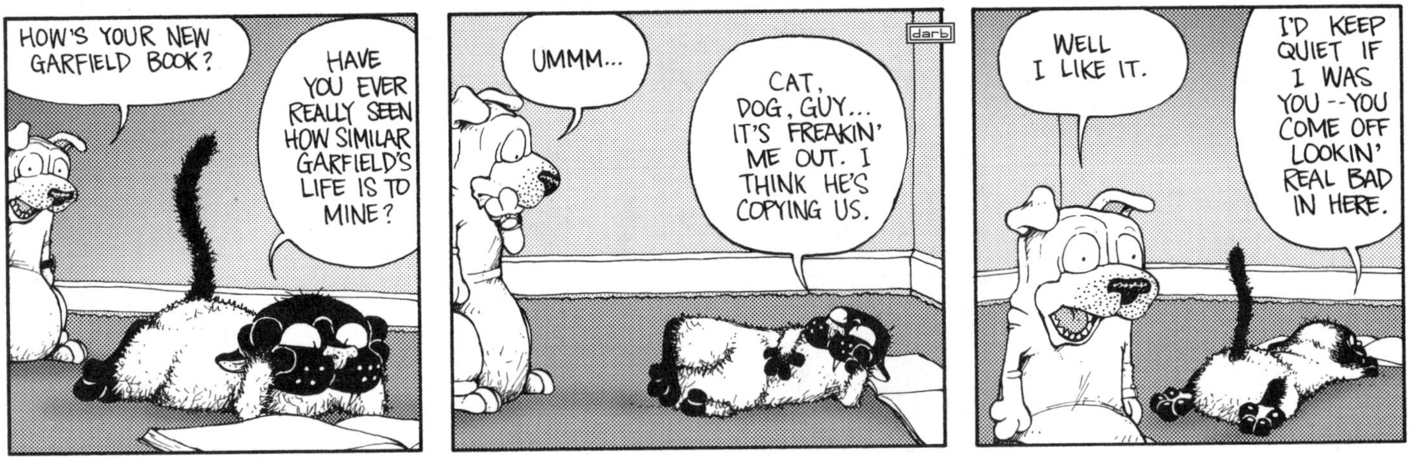
HOW'S YOUR NEW GARFIELD BOOK?
HAVE YOU EVER REALLY SEEN HOW SIMILAR GARFIELD'S LIFE IS TO MINE?
darb
UMMM...
CAT, DOG, GUY... IT'S FREAKIN' ME OUT. I THINK HE'S COPYING US.
WELL I LIKE IT.
I'D KEEP QUIET IF I WAS YOU --YOU COME OFF LOOKIN' REAL BAD IN HERE.

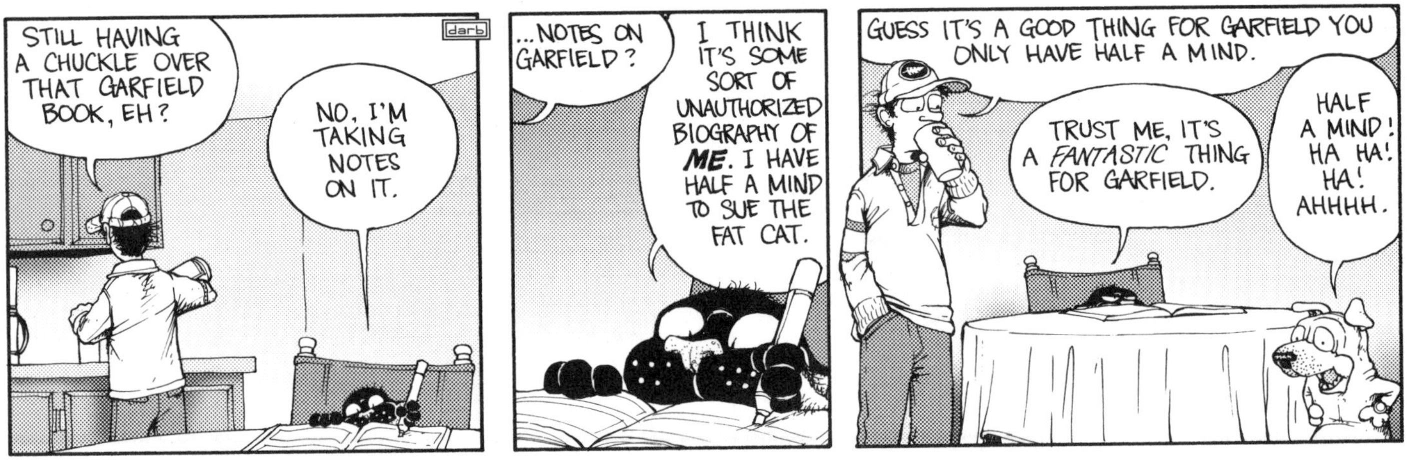
darb
STILL HAVING A CHUCKLE OVER THAT GARFIELD BOOK, EH?
NO, I'M TAKING NOTES ON IT.
...NOTES ON GARFIELD?
I THINK IT'S SOME SORT OF UNAUTHORIZED BIOGRAPHY OF ME. I HAVE HALF A MIND TO SUE THE FAT CAT.
GUESS IT'S A GOOD THING FOR GARFIELD YOU ONLY HAVE HALF A MIND.
TRUST ME, IT'S A FANTASTIC THING FOR GARFIELD.
HALF A MIND! HA HA! HA! AHHHH.

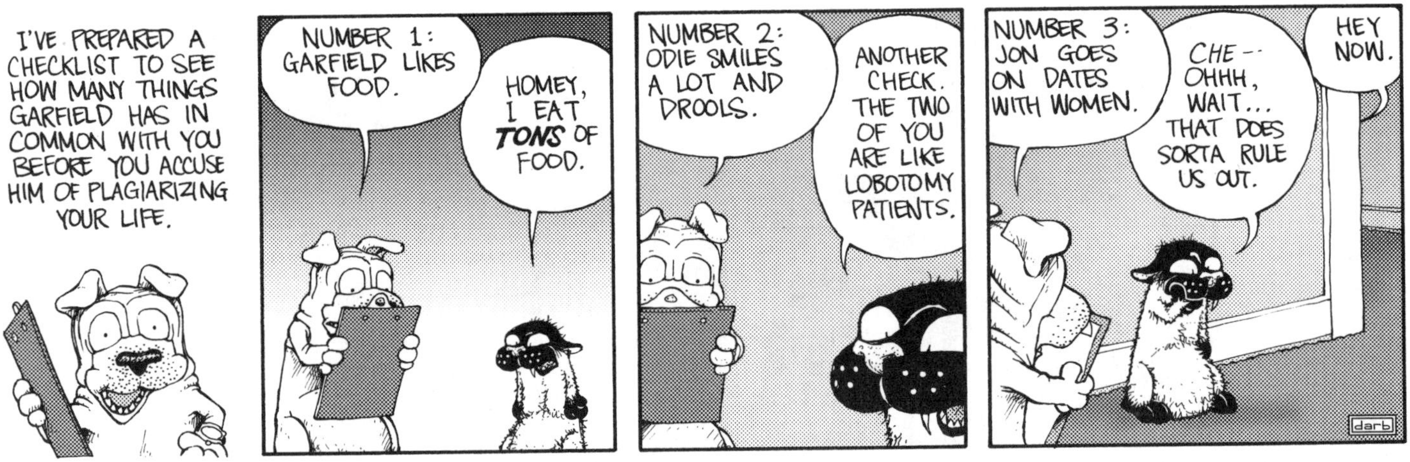
I'VE PREPARED A CHECKLIST TO SEE HOW MANY THINGS GARFIELD HAS IN COMMON WITH YOU BEFORE YOU ACCUSE HIM OF PLAGIARIZING YOUR LIFE.
NUMBER 1: GARFIELD LIKES FOOD.
HOMEY, I EAT TONS OF FOOD.
NUMBER 2: ODIE SMILES A LOT AND DROOLS.
ANOTHER CHECK. THE TWO OF YOU ARE LIKE LOBOTOMY PATIENTS.
NUMBER 3: JON GOES ON DATES WITH WOMEN.
CHE-- OHHH, WAIT... THAT DOES SORTA RULE US OUT.
HEY NOW.
darb

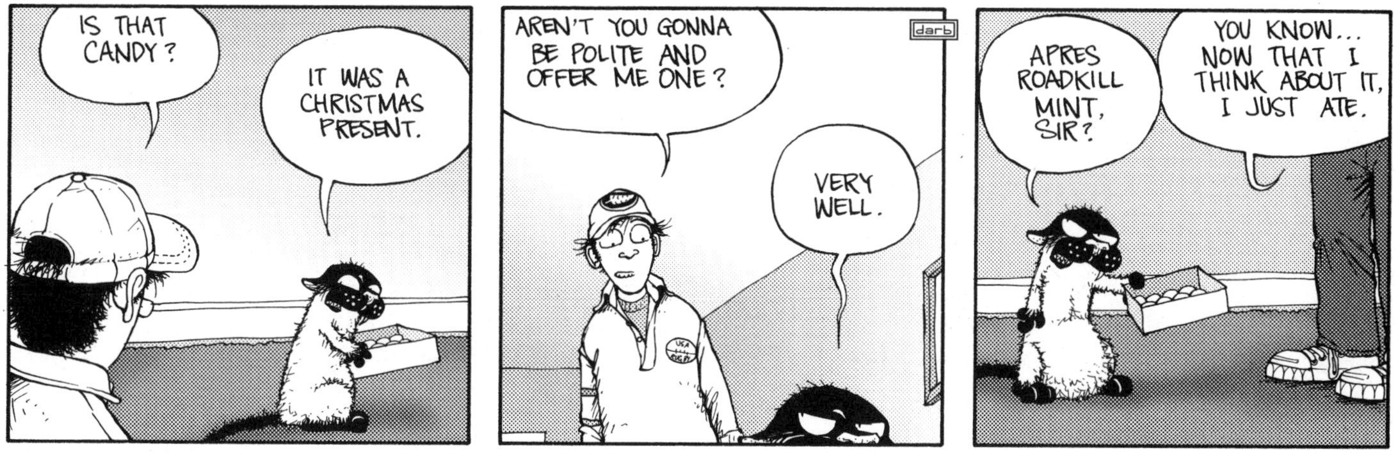
IS THAT CANDY?
IT WAS A CHRISTMAS PRESENT.
AREN'T YOU GONNA BE POLITE AND OFFER ME ONE?
VERY WELL.
APRES ROADKILL MINT, SIR?
YOU KNOW... NOW THAT I THINK ABOUT IT, I JUST ATE.
darb

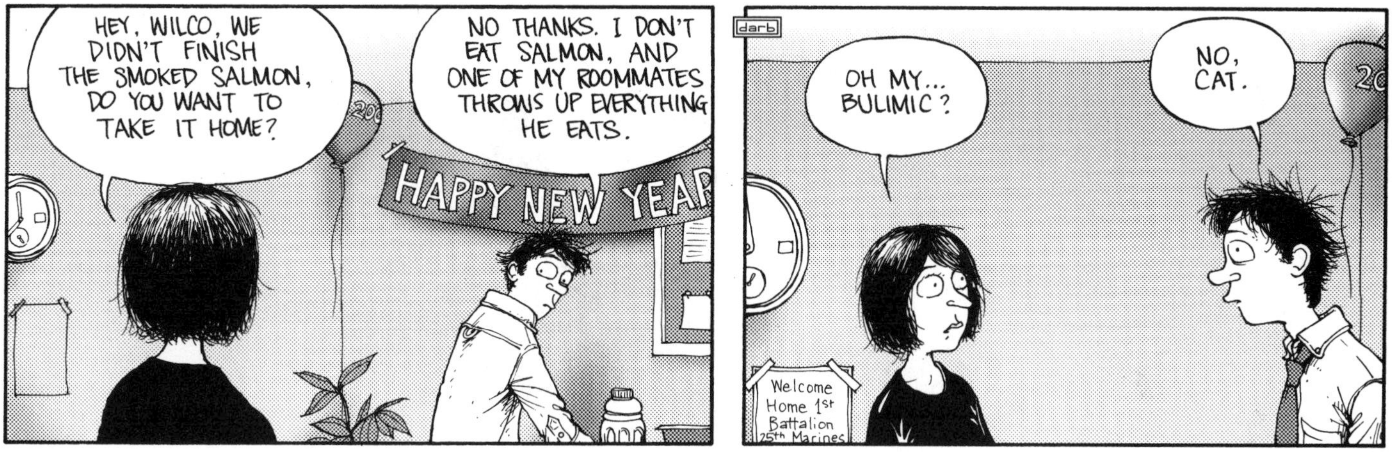
HEY, WILCO, WE DIDN'T FINISH THE SMOKED SALMON, DO YOU WANT TO TAKE IT HOME?
NO THANKS. I DON'T EAT SALMON, AND ONE OF MY ROOMMATES THROWS UP EVERYTHING HE EATS.
HAPPY NEW YEAR
OH MY... BULIMIC?
NO, CAT.
Welcome Home 1st Battalion 25th Marines
darb

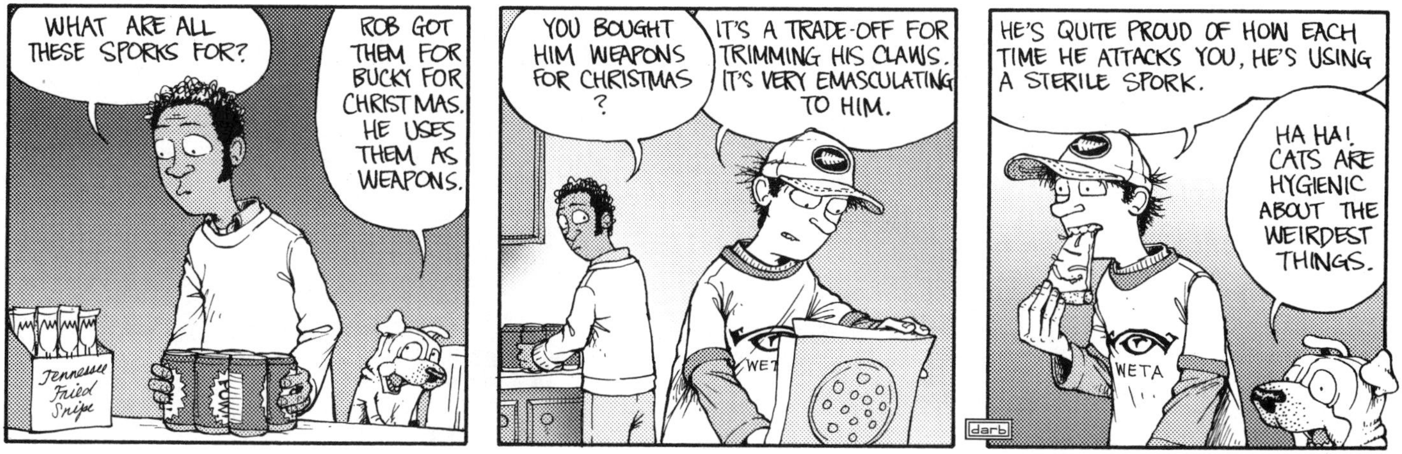
WHAT ARE ALL THESE SPORKS FOR?
ROB GOT THEM FOR BUCKY FOR CHRISTMAS. HE USES THEM AS WEAPONS.
Tennessee Fried Snipe
YOU BOUGHT HIM WEAPONS FOR CHRISTMAS?
IT'S A TRADE-OFF FOR TRIMMING HIS CLAWS. IT'S VERY EMASCULATING TO HIM.
HE'S QUITE PROUD OF HOW EACH TIME HE ATTACKS YOU, HE'S USING A STERILE SPORK.
HA HA! CATS ARE HYGIENIC ABOUT THE WEIRDEST THINGS.
WETA
darb

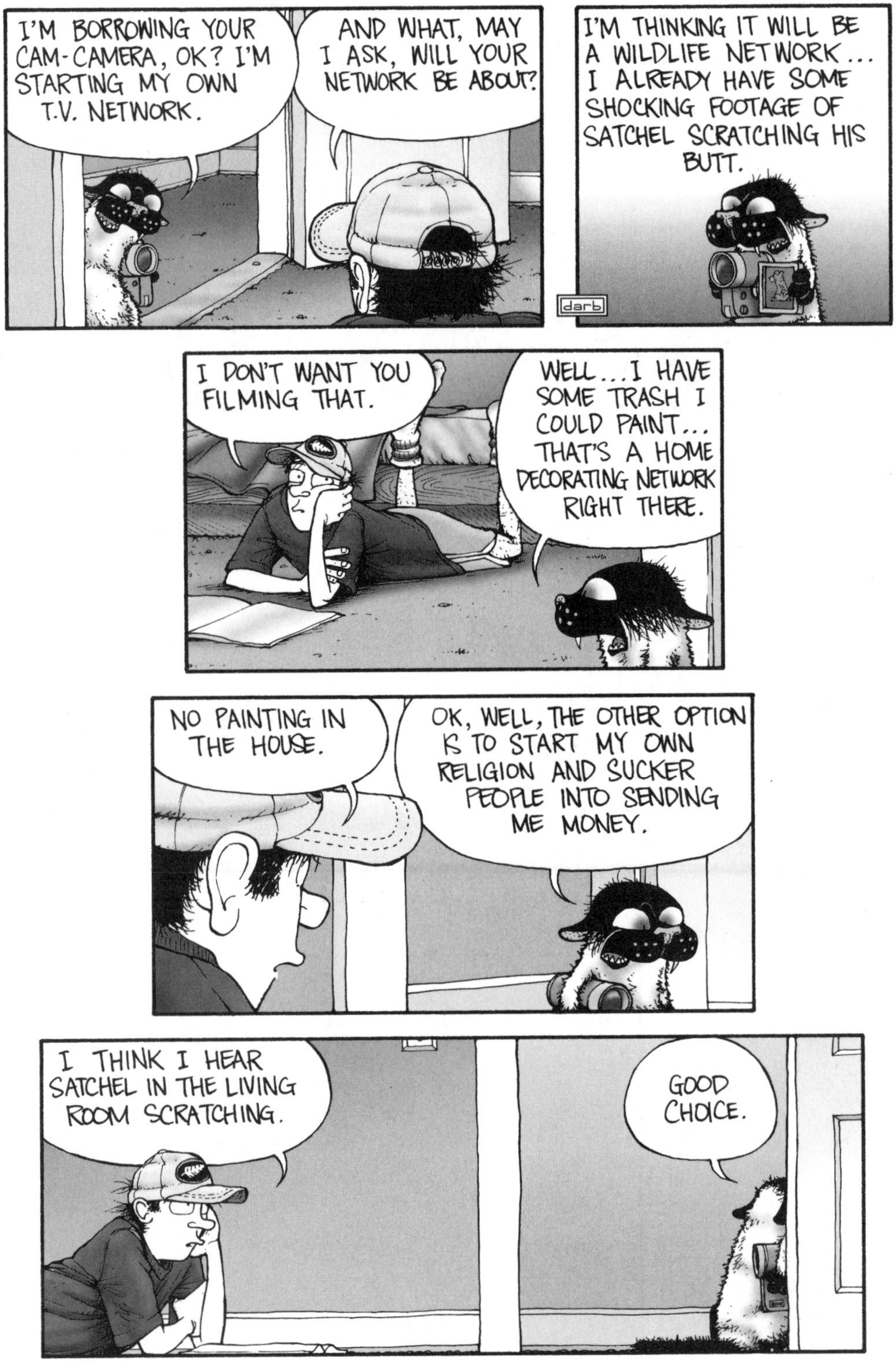
I'M BORROWING YOUR CAM-CAMERA, OK? I'M STARTING MY OWN T.V. NETWORK.
AND WHAT, MAY I ASK, WILL YOUR NETWORK BE ABOUT?
I'M THINKING IT WILL BE A WILDLIFE NETWORK... I ALREADY HAVE SOME SHOCKING FOOTAGE OF SATCHEL SCRATCHING HIS BUTT.
darb
I DON'T WANT YOU FILMING THAT.
WELL... I HAVE SOME TRASH I COULD PAINT... THAT'S A HOME DECORATING NETWORK RIGHT THERE.
NO PAINTING IN THE HOUSE.
OK, WELL, THE OTHER OPTION IS TO START MY OWN RELIGION AND SUCKER PEOPLE INTO SENDING ME MONEY.
I THINK I HEAR SATCHEL IN THE LIVING ROOM SCRATCHING.
GOOD CHOICE.

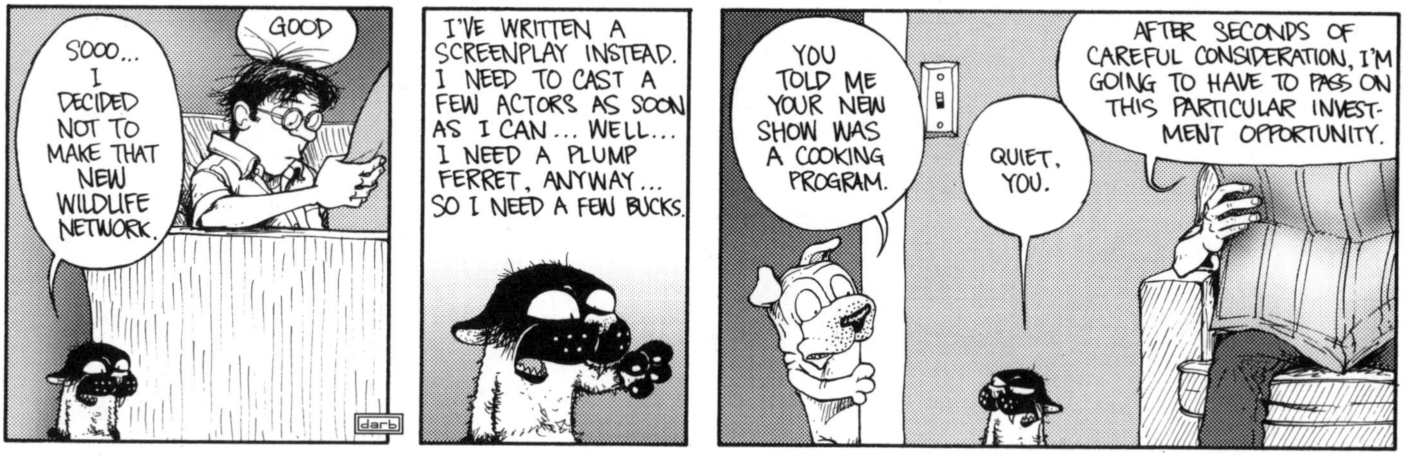
SOOO... I DECIDED NOT TO MAKE THAT NEW WILDLIFE NETWORK.
GOOD
I'VE WRITTEN A SCREENPLAY INSTEAD. I NEED TO CAST A FEW ACTORS AS SOON AS I CAN... WELL... I NEED A PLUMP FERRET, ANYWAY... SO I NEED A FEW BUCKS.
YOU TOLD ME YOUR NEW SHOW WAS A COOKING PROGRAM.
QUIET, YOU.
AFTER SECONDS OF CAREFUL CONSIDERATION, I'M GOING TO HAVE TO PASS ON THIS PARTICULAR INVEST-MENT OPPORTUNITY.
darb

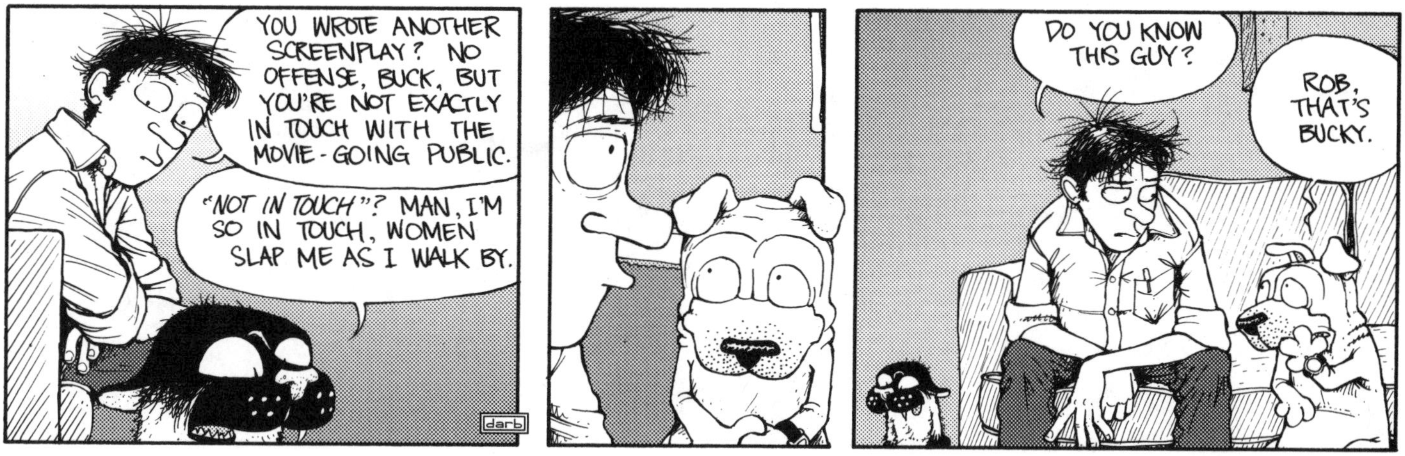
YOU WROTE ANOTHER SCREENPLAY? NO OFFENSE, BUCK, BUT YOU'RE NOT EXACTLY IN TOUCH WITH THE MOVIE-GOING PUBLIC.
"NOT IN TOUCH"? MAN, I'M SO IN TOUCH, WOMEN SLAP ME AS I WALK BY.
darb
DO YOU KNOW THIS GUY?
ROB, THAT'S BUCKY.

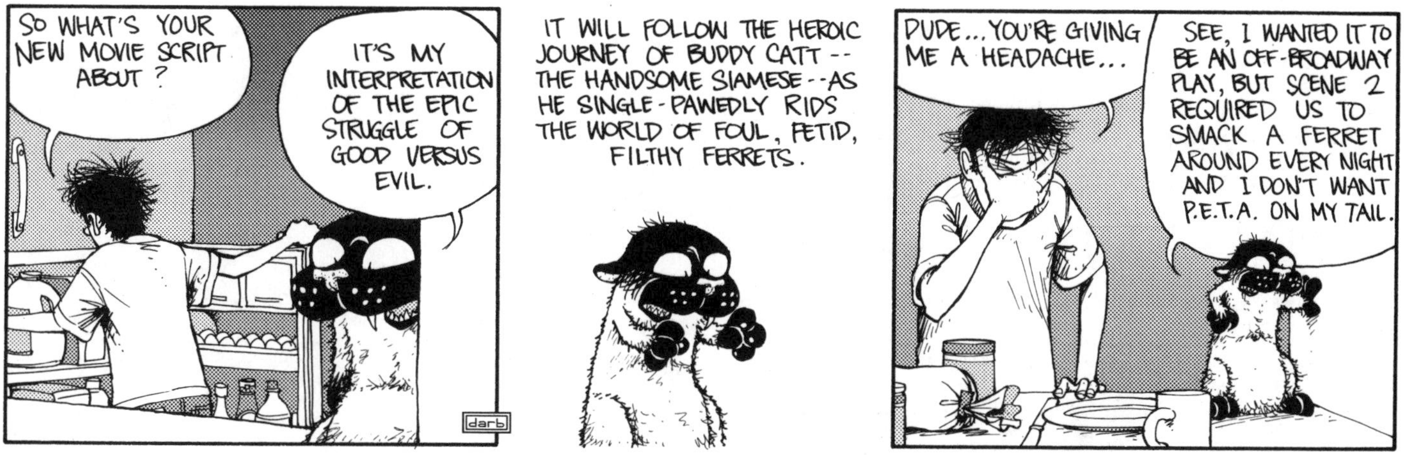
SO WHAT'S YOUR NEW MOVIE SCRIPT ABOUT?
IT'S MY INTERPRETATION OF THE EPIC STRUGGLE OF GOOD VERSUS EVIL.
darb
IT WILL FOLLOW THE HEROIC JOURNEY OF BUDDY CATT -- THE HANDSOME SIAMESE -- AS HE SINGLE-PAWEDLY RIDS THE WORLD OF FOUL, FETID, FILTHY FERRETS.
DUDE... YOU'RE GIVING ME A HEADACHE...
SEE, I WANTED IT TO BE AN OFF-BROADWAY PLAY, BUT SCENE 2 REQUIRED US TO SMACK A FERRET AROUND EVERY NIGHT AND I DON'T WANT P.E.T.A. ON MY TAIL.

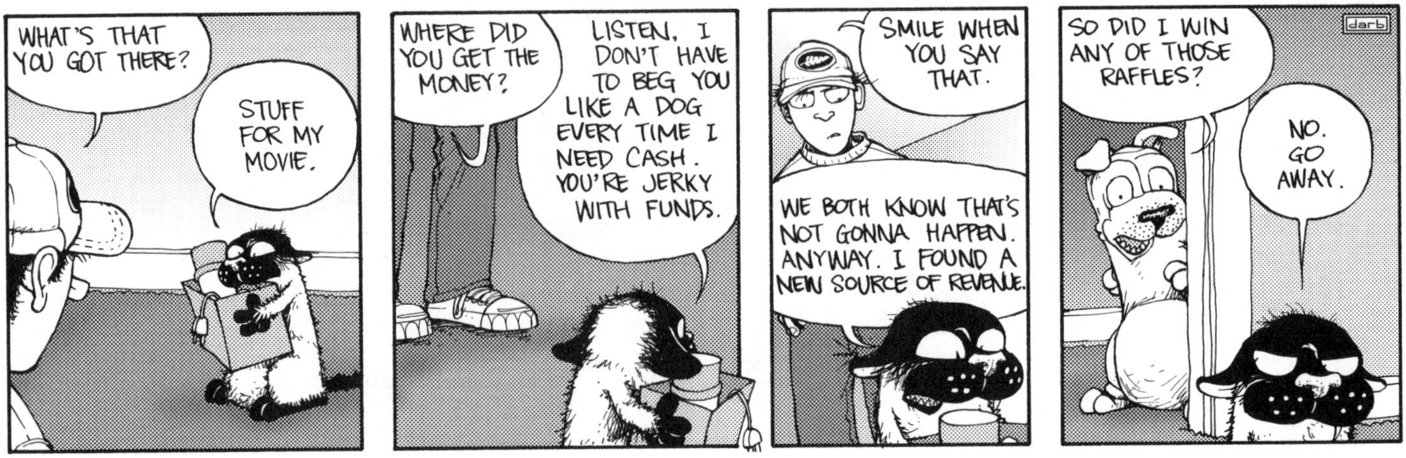
WHAT'S THAT YOU GOT THERE?
STUFF FOR MY MOVIE.
WHERE DID YOU GET THE MONEY?
LISTEN, I DON'T HAVE TO BEG YOU LIKE A DOG EVERY TIME I NEED CASH. YOU'RE JERKY WITH FUNDS.
SMILE WHEN YOU SAY THAT.
WE BOTH KNOW THAT'S NOT GONNA HAPPEN. ANYWAY, I FOUND A NEW SOURCE OF REVENUE.
SO DID I WIN ANY OF THOSE RAFFLES?
NO. GO AWAY.
darb

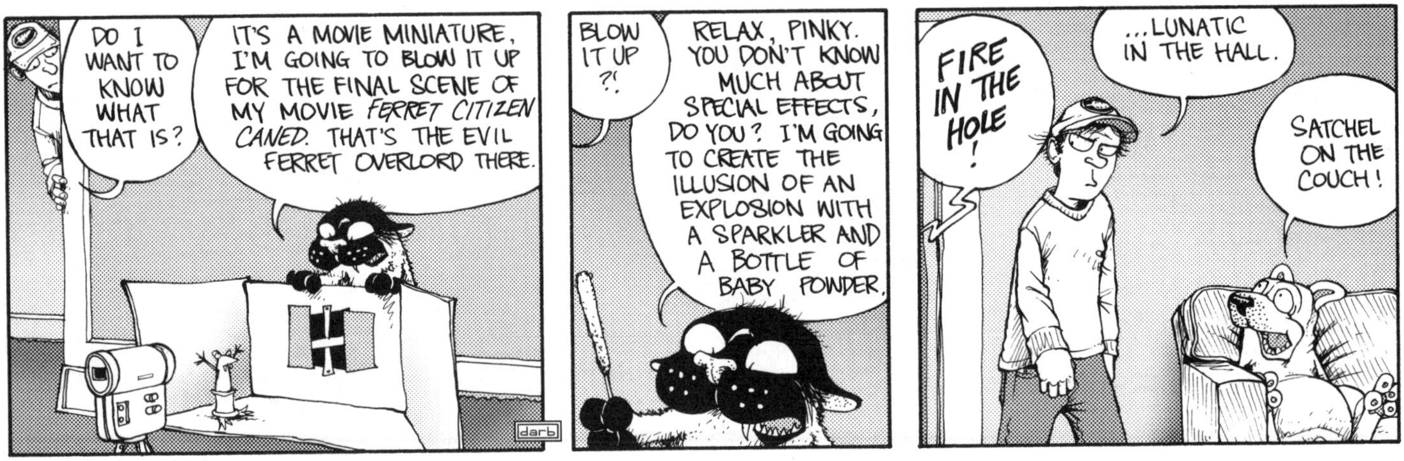
DO I WANT TO KNOW WHAT THAT IS?
IT'S A MOVIE MINIATURE, I'M GOING TO BLOW IT UP FOR THE FINAL SCENE OF MY MOVIE FERRET CITIZEN CANED. THAT'S THE EVIL FERRET OVERLORD THERE.
darb
BLOW IT UP ?!
RELAX, PINKY. YOU DON'T KNOW MUCH ABOUT SPECIAL EFFECTS, DO YOU? I'M GOING TO CREATE THE ILLUSION OF AN EXPLOSION WITH A SPARKLER AND A BOTTLE OF BABY POWDER.
FIRE IN THE HOLE!
...LUNATIC IN THE HALL.
SATCHEL ON THE COUCH!

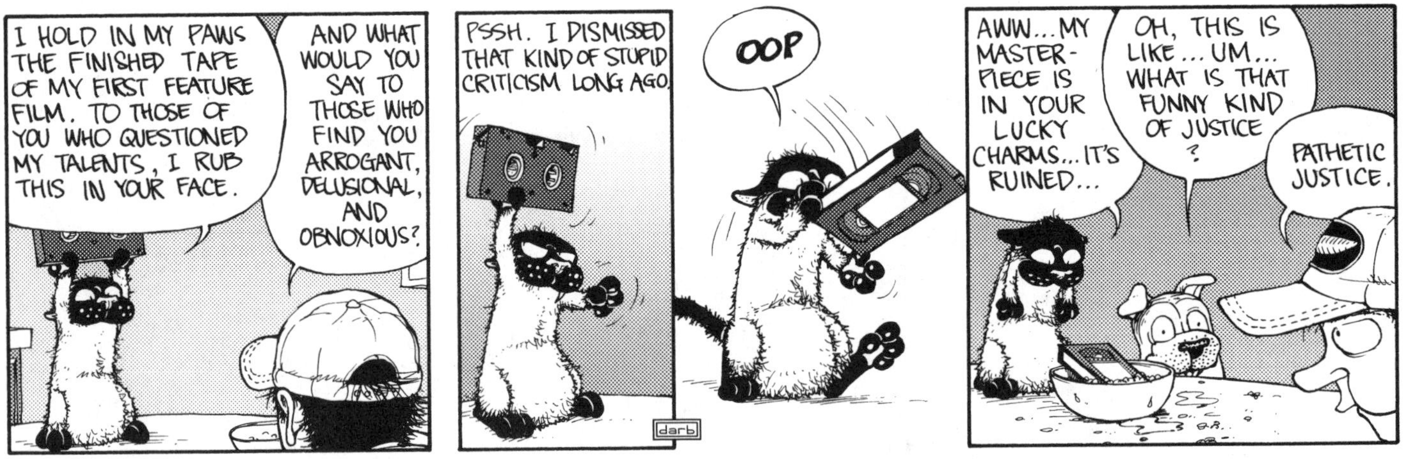
I HOLD IN MY PAWS THE FINISHED TAPE OF MY FIRST FEATURE FILM. TO THOSE OF YOU WHO QUESTIONED MY TALENTS, I RUB THIS IN YOUR FACE.
AND WHAT WOULD YOU SAY TO THOSE WHO FIND YOU ARROGANT, DELUSIONAL, AND OBNOXIOUS?
PSSH. I DISMISSED THAT KIND OF STUPID CRITICISM LONG AGO.
darb
OOP
AWW...MY MASTER-PIECE IS IN YOUR LUCKY CHARMS... IT'S RUINED...
OH, THIS IS LIKE... UM... WHAT IS THAT FUNNY KIND OF JUSTICE ?
PATHETIC JUSTICE.

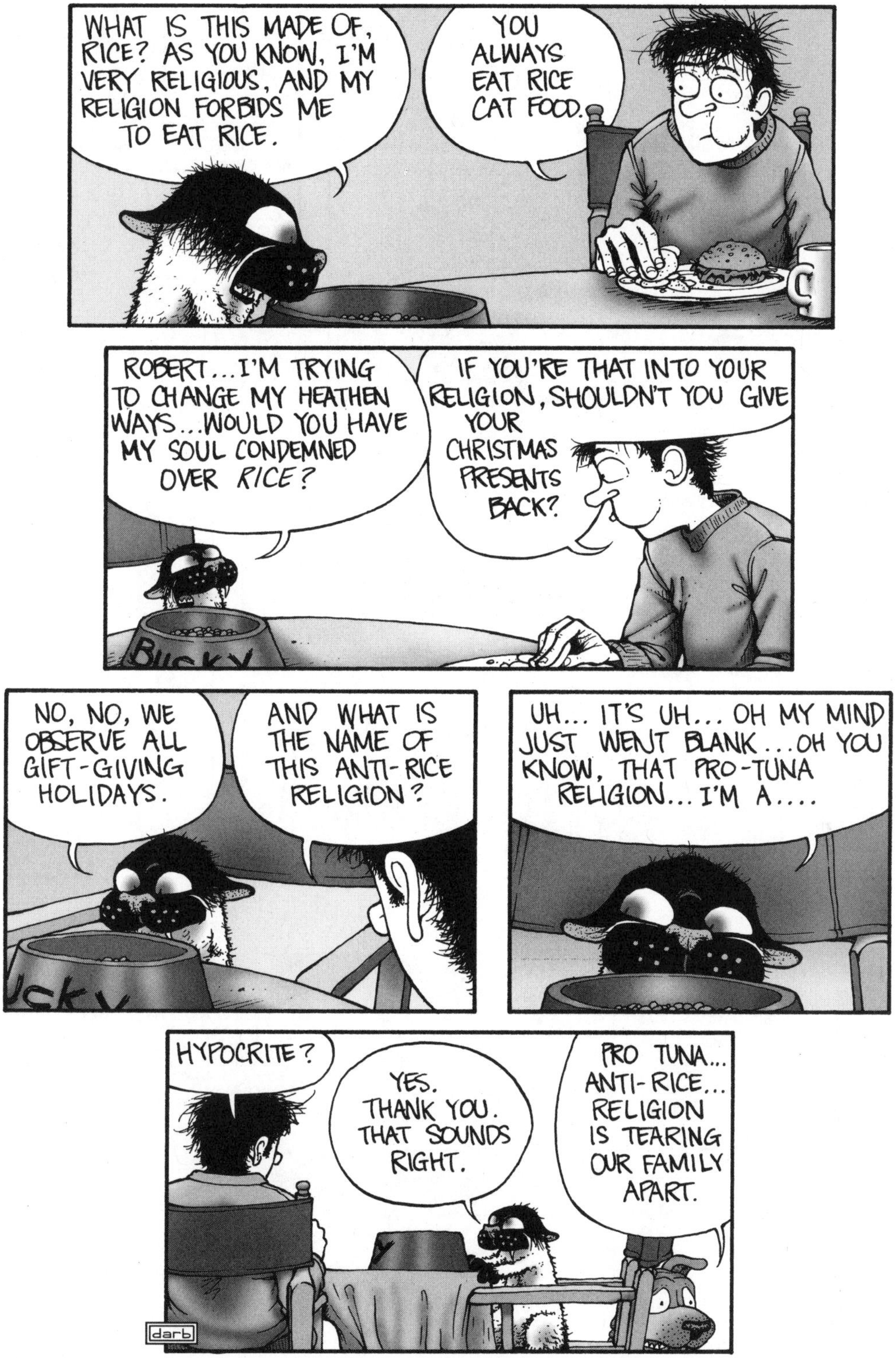
WHAT IS THIS MADE OF, RICE? AS YOU KNOW, I'M VERY RELIGIOUS, AND MY RELIGION FORBIDS ME TO EAT RICE.
YOU ALWAYS EAT RICE CAT FOOD.
ROBERT... I'M TRYING TO CHANGE MY HEATHEN WAYS... WOULD YOU HAVE MY SOUL CONDEMNED OVER *RICE*?
IF YOU'RE THAT INTO YOUR RELIGION, SHOULDN'T YOU GIVE YOUR CHRISTMAS PRESENTS BACK?
NO, NO, WE OBSERVE ALL GIFT-GIVING HOLIDAYS.
AND WHAT IS THE NAME OF THIS ANTI-RICE RELIGION?
UH... IT'S UH... OH MY MIND JUST WENT BLANK... OH YOU KNOW, THAT PRO-TUNA RELIGION... I'M A....
HYPOCRITE?
YES. THANK YOU. THAT SOUNDS RIGHT.
PRO TUNA... ANTI-RICE... RELIGION IS TEARING OUR FAMILY APART.
darb

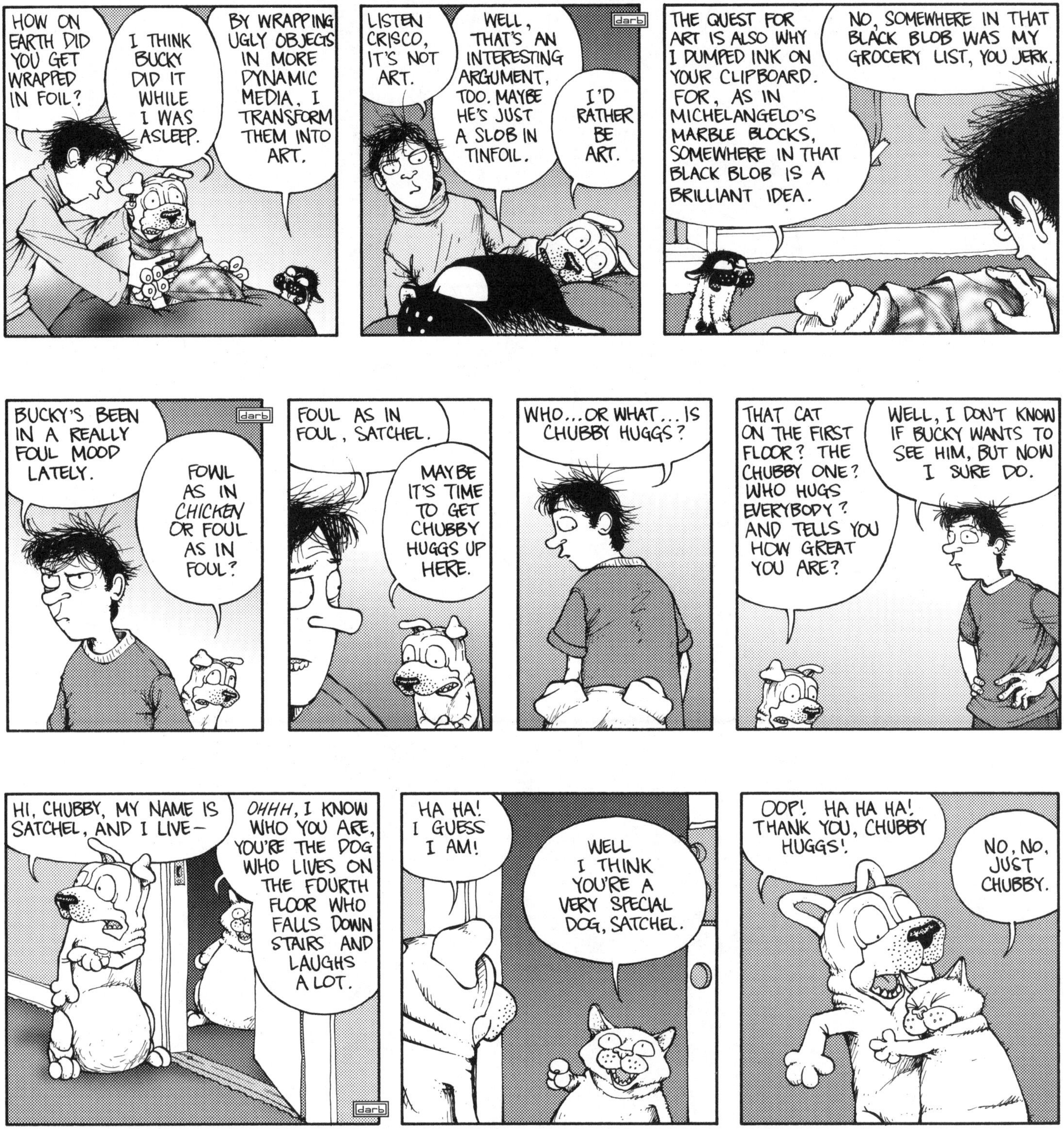
HOW ON EARTH DID YOU GET WRAPPED IN FOIL?
I THINK BUCKY DID IT WHILE I WAS ASLEEP.
BY WRAPPING UGLY OBJECTS IN MORE DYNAMIC MEDIA, I TRANSFORM THEM INTO ART.
darb
LISTEN CRISCO, IT'S NOT ART.
WELL, THAT'S AN INTERESTING ARGUMENT, TOO. MAYBE HE'S JUST A SLOB IN TINFOIL.
I'D RATHER BE ART.
THE QUEST FOR ART IS ALSO WHY I DUMPED INK ON YOUR CLIPBOARD. FOR, AS IN MICHELANGELO'S MARBLE BLOCKS, SOMEWHERE IN THAT BLACK BLOB IS A BRILLIANT IDEA.
NO, SOMEWHERE IN THAT BLACK BLOB WAS MY GROCERY LIST, YOU JERK.
darb
BUCKY'S BEEN IN A REALLY FOUL MOOD LATELY.
FOWL AS IN CHICKEN OR FOUL AS IN FOUL?
FOUL AS IN FOUL, SATCHEL.
MAYBE IT'S TIME TO GET CHUBBY HUGGS UP HERE.
WHO... OR WHAT... IS CHUBBY HUGGS?
THAT CAT ON THE FIRST FLOOR? THE CHUBBY ONE? WHO HUGS EVERYBODY? AND TELLS YOU HOW GREAT YOU ARE?
WELL, I DON'T KNOW IF BUCKY WANTS TO SEE HIM, BUT NOW I SURE DO.
HI, CHUBBY, MY NAME IS SATCHEL, AND I LIVE—
OHHH, I KNOW WHO YOU ARE, YOU'RE THE DOG WHO LIVES ON THE FOURTH FLOOR WHO FALLS DOWN STAIRS AND LAUGHS A LOT.
darb
HA HA! I GUESS I AM!
WELL I THINK YOU'RE A VERY SPECIAL DOG, SATCHEL.
OOP! HA HA HA! THANK YOU, CHUBBY HUGGS!
NO, NO, JUST CHUBBY.

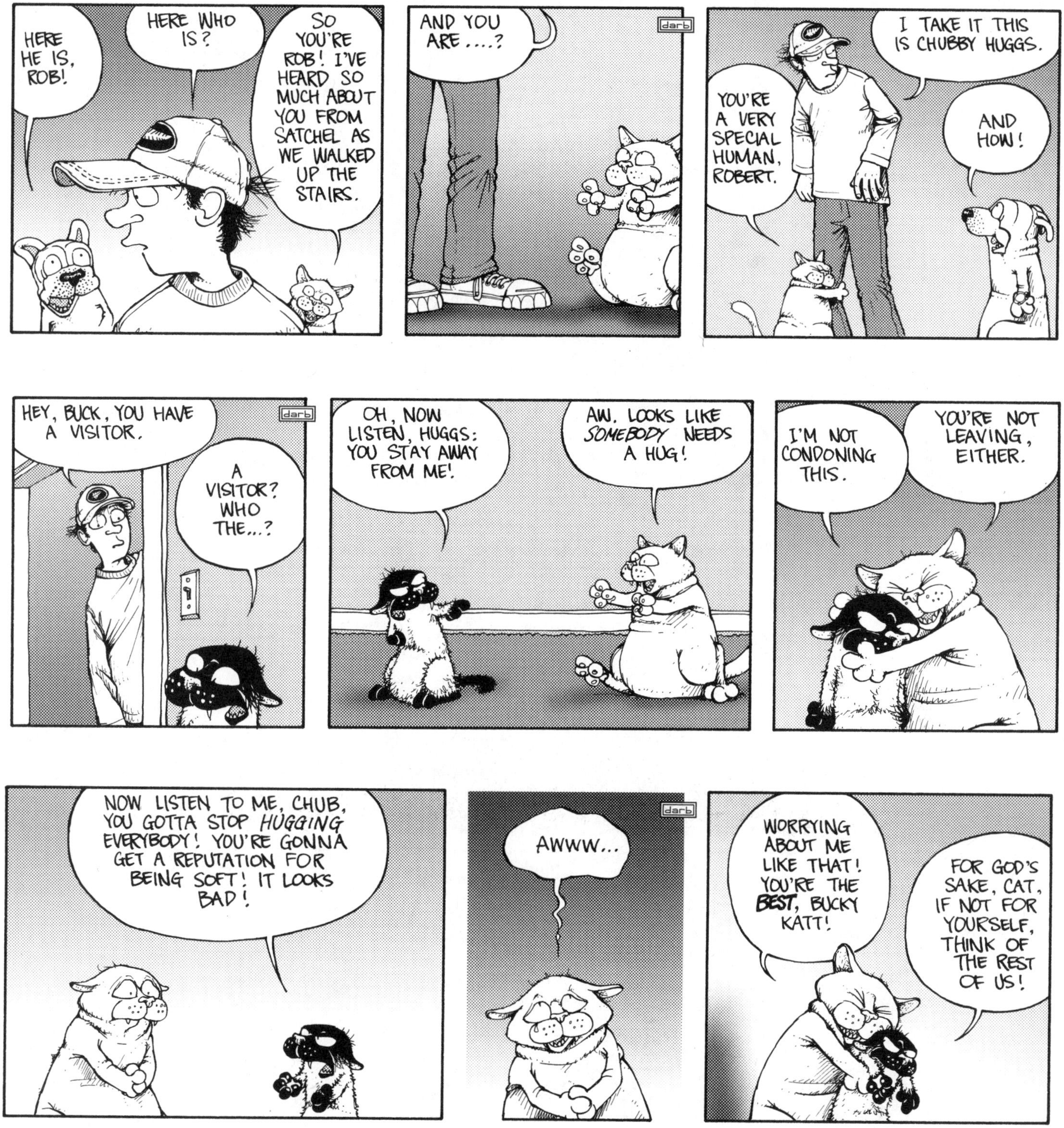
HERE HE IS, ROB!
HERE WHO IS?
SO YOU'RE ROB! I'VE HEARD SO MUCH ABOUT YOU FROM SATCHEL AS WE WALKED UP THE STAIRS.
darb
AND YOU ARE....?
I TAKE IT THIS IS CHUBBY HUGGS.
YOU'RE A VERY SPECIAL HUMAN, ROBERT.
AND HOW!
darb
HEY, BUCK, YOU HAVE A VISITOR.
A VISITOR? WHO THE...?
OH, NOW LISTEN, HUGGS: YOU STAY AWAY FROM ME!
AW. LOOKS LIKE SOMEBODY NEEDS A HUG!
I'M NOT CONDONING THIS.
YOU'RE NOT LEAVING, EITHER.
NOW LISTEN TO ME, CHUB, YOU GOTTA STOP HUGGING EVERYBODY! YOU'RE GONNA GET A REPUTATION FOR BEING SOFT! IT LOOKS BAD!
darb
AWWW...
WORRYING ABOUT ME LIKE THAT! YOU'RE THE BEST, BUCKY KATT!
FOR GOD'S SAKE, CAT, IF NOT FOR YOURSELF, THINK OF THE REST OF US!

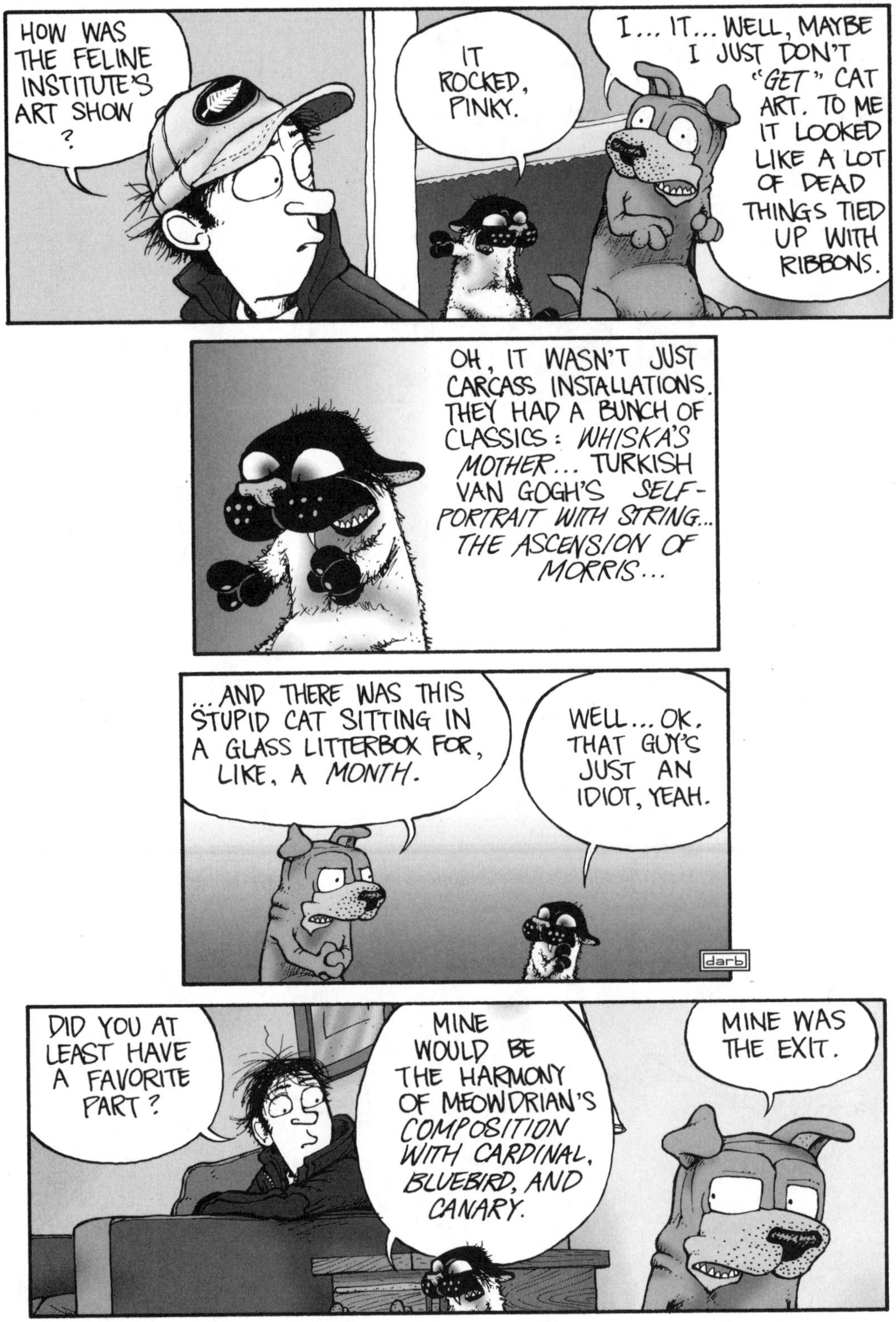
HOW WAS THE FELINE INSTITUTE'S ART SHOW ?
IT ROCKED, PINKY.
I... IT... WELL, MAYBE I JUST DON'T "GET" CAT ART. TO ME IT LOOKED LIKE A LOT OF DEAD THINGS TIED UP WITH RIBBONS.
OH, IT WASN'T JUST CARCASS INSTALLATIONS. THEY HAD A BUNCH OF CLASSICS: WHISKA'S MOTHER... TURKISH VAN GOGH'S SELF-PORTRAIT WITH STRING... THE ASCENSION OF MORRIS...
...AND THERE WAS THIS STUPID CAT SITTING IN A GLASS LITTERBOX FOR, LIKE, A MONTH.
WELL... OK. THAT GUY'S JUST AN IDIOT, YEAH.
darb
DID YOU AT LEAST HAVE A FAVORITE PART ?
MINE WOULD BE THE HARMONY OF MEOWDRIAN'S COMPOSITION WITH CARDINAL, BLUEBIRD, AND CANARY.
MINE WAS THE EXIT.

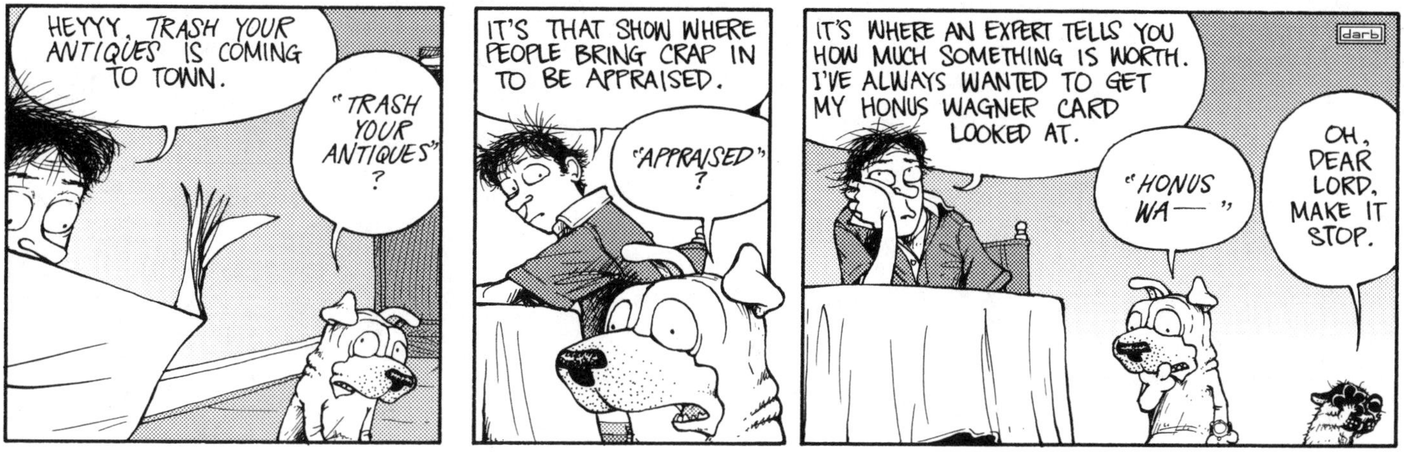
HEYYY, TRASH YOUR ANTIQUES IS COMING TO TOWN.
"TRASH YOUR ANTIQUES"?
IT'S THAT SHOW WHERE PEOPLE BRING CRAP IN TO BE APPRAISED.
"APPRAISED"?
IT'S WHERE AN EXPERT TELLS YOU HOW MUCH SOMETHING IS WORTH. I'VE ALWAYS WANTED TO GET MY HONUS WAGNER CARD LOOKED AT.
"HONUS WA—"
OH, DEAR LORD, MAKE IT STOP.
darb

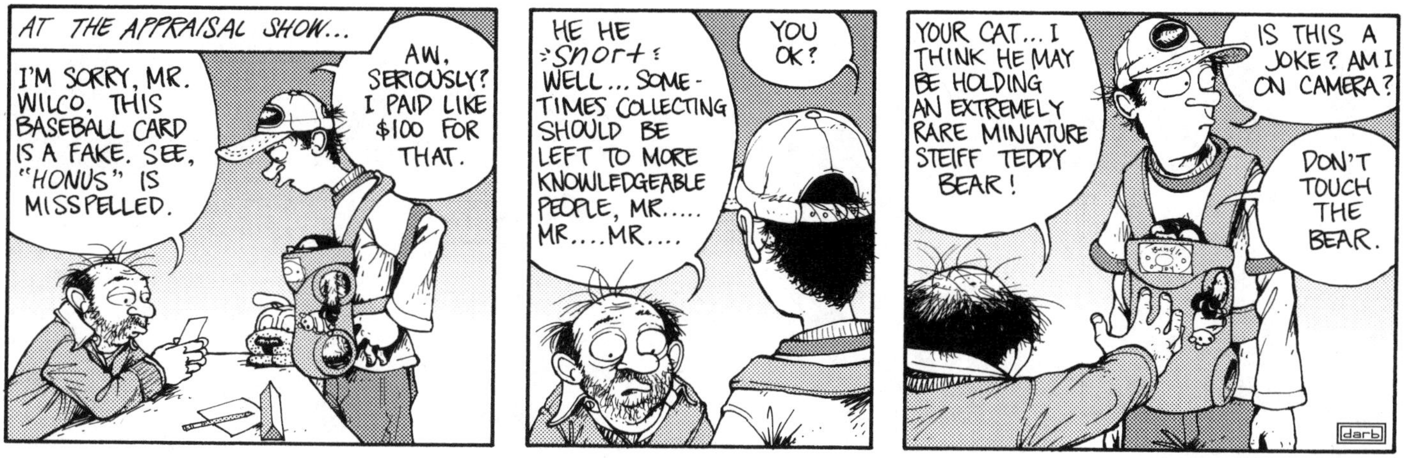
AT THE APPRAISAL SHOW...
I'M SORRY, MR. WILCO, THIS BASEBALL CARD IS A FAKE. SEE, "HONUS" IS MISSPELLED.
AW, SERIOUSLY? I PAID LIKE $100 FOR THAT.
HE HE :SNORT: WELL... SOMETIMES COLLECTING SHOULD BE LEFT TO MORE KNOWLEDGEABLE PEOPLE, MR..... MR....MR....
YOU OK?
YOUR CAT... I THINK HE MAY BE HOLDING AN EXTREMELY RARE MINIATURE STEIFF TEDDY BEAR!
IS THIS A JOKE? AM I ON CAMERA?
DON'T TOUCH THE BEAR.
darb

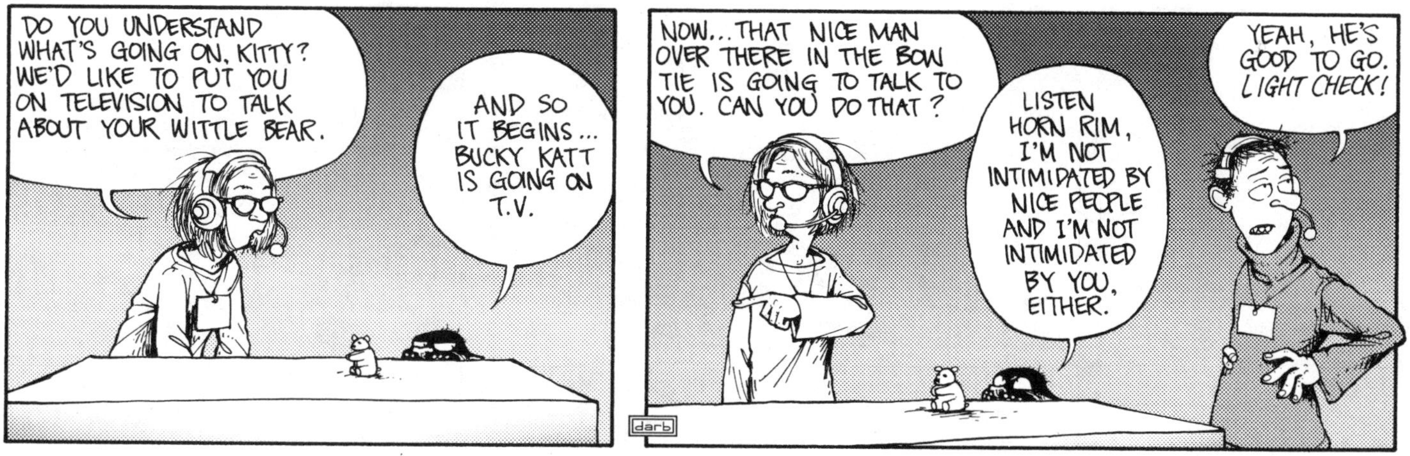
DO YOU UNDERSTAND WHAT'S GOING ON, KITTY? WE'D LIKE TO PUT YOU ON TELEVISION TO TALK ABOUT YOUR WITTLE BEAR.
AND SO IT BEGINS... BUCKY KATT IS GOING ON T.V.
darb
NOW... THAT NICE MAN OVER THERE IN THE BOW TIE IS GOING TO TALK TO YOU. CAN YOU DO THAT?
LISTEN HORN RIM, I'M NOT INTIMIDATED BY NICE PEOPLE AND I'M NOT INTIMIDATED BY YOU, EITHER.
YEAH, HE'S GOOD TO GO. LIGHT CHECK!

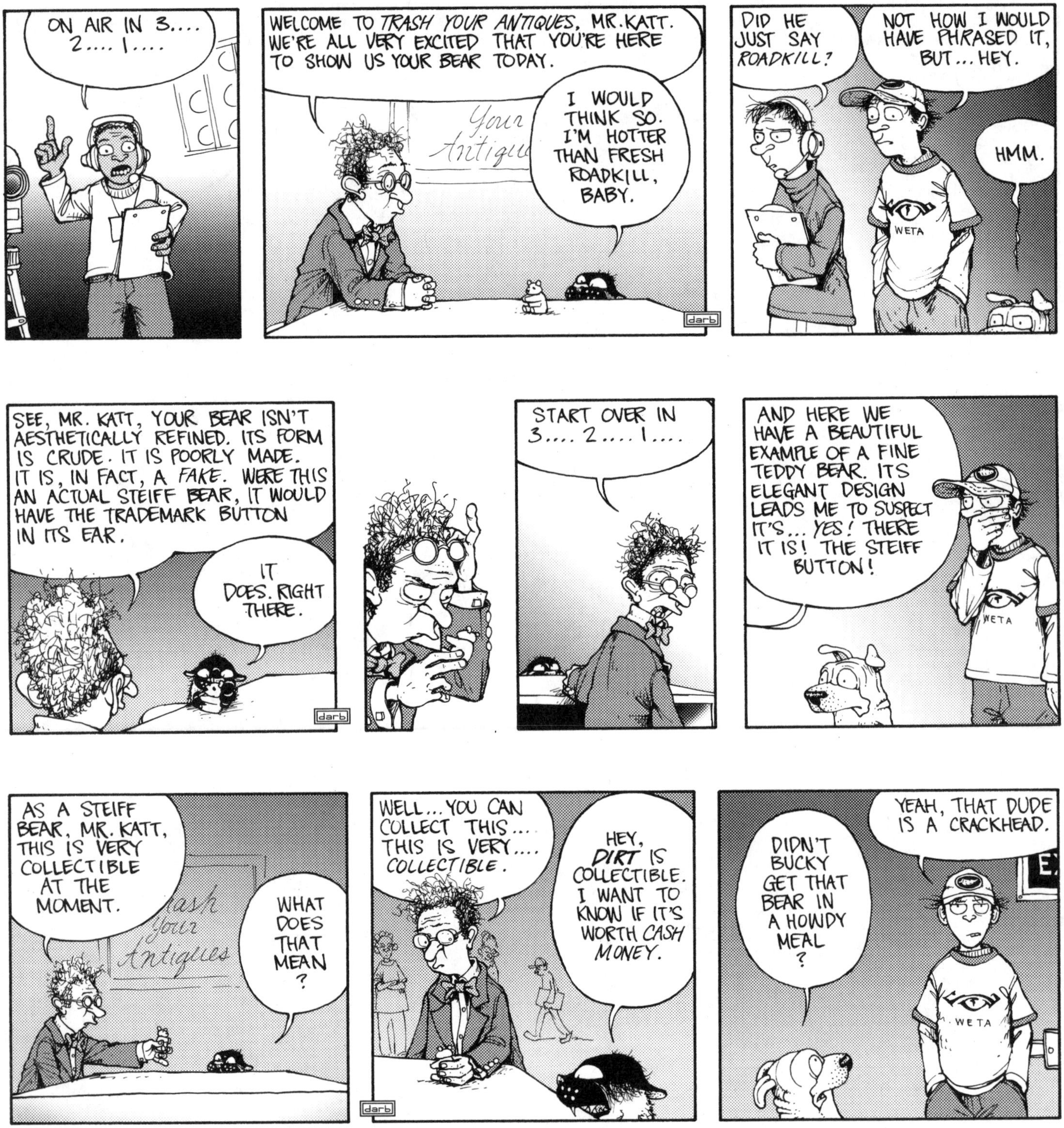

ON AIR IN 3.... 2.... 1....
WELCOME TO TRASH YOUR ANTIQUES, MR. KATT. WE'RE ALL VERY EXCITED THAT YOU'RE HERE TO SHOW US YOUR BEAR TODAY.
I WOULD THINK SO. I'M HOTTER THAN FRESH ROADKILL, BABY.
DID HE JUST SAY ROADKILL?
NOT HOW I WOULD HAVE PHRASED IT, BUT... HEY.
HMM.
WETA
SEE, MR. KATT, YOUR BEAR ISN'T AESTHETICALLY REFINED. ITS FORM IS CRUDE. IT IS POORLY MADE. IT IS, IN FACT, A FAKE. WERE THIS AN ACTUAL STEIFF BEAR, IT WOULD HAVE THE TRADEMARK BUTTON IN ITS EAR.
IT DOES. RIGHT THERE.
START OVER IN 3.... 2.... 1....
AND HERE WE HAVE A BEAUTIFUL EXAMPLE OF A FINE TEDDY BEAR. ITS ELEGANT DESIGN LEADS ME TO SUSPECT IT'S... YES! THERE IT IS! THE STEIFF BUTTON!
WETA
AS A STEIFF BEAR, MR. KATT, THIS IS VERY COLLECTIBLE AT THE MOMENT.
WHAT DOES THAT MEAN?
WELL... YOU CAN COLLECT THIS... THIS IS VERY.... COLLECTIBLE.
HEY, DIRT IS COLLECTIBLE. I WANT TO KNOW IF IT'S WORTH CASH MONEY.
YEAH, THAT DUDE IS A CRACKHEAD.
DIDN'T BUCKY GET THAT BEAR IN A HOWDY MEAL?
WETA

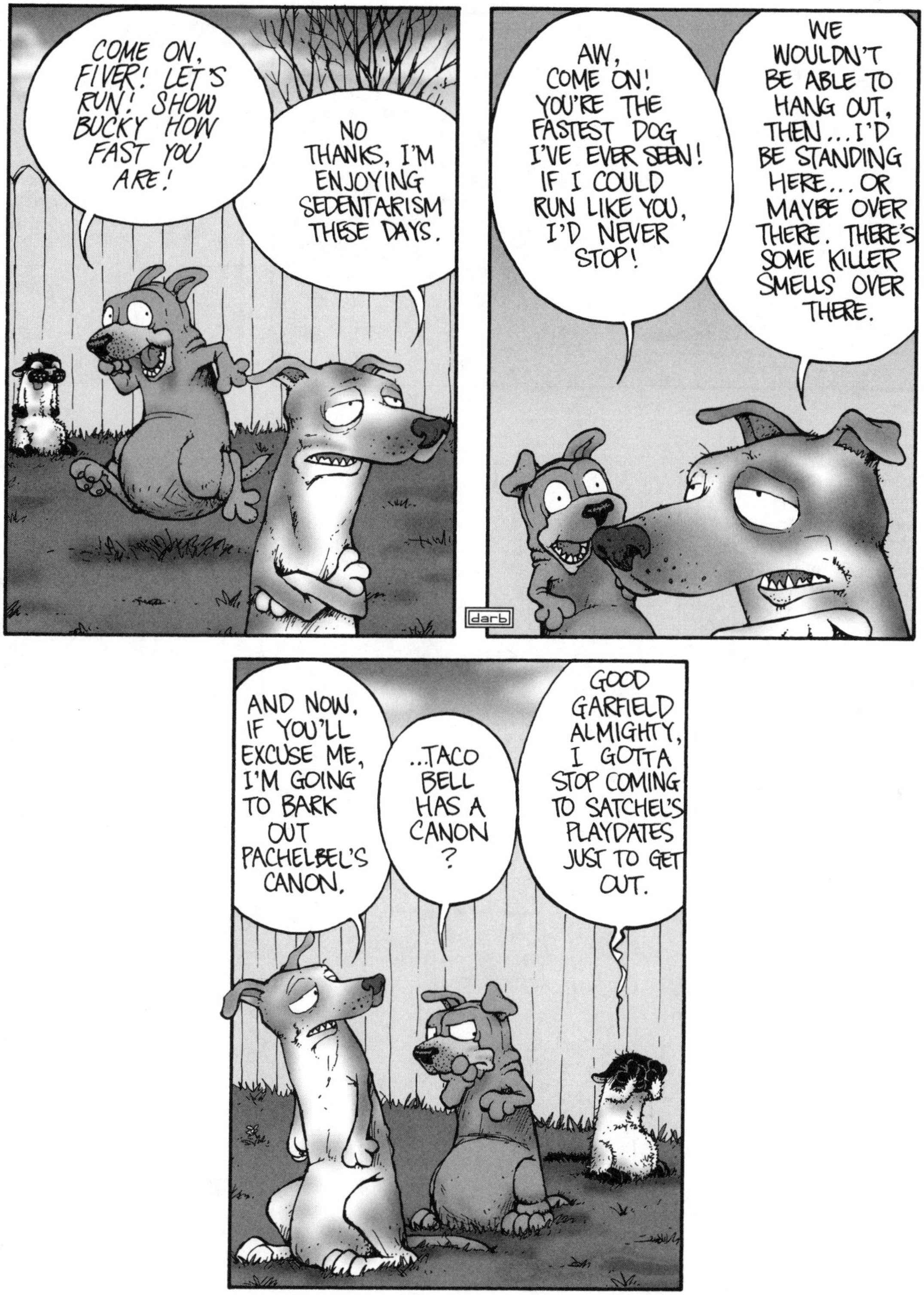
COME ON, FIVER! LET'S RUN! SHOW BUCKY HOW FAST YOU ARE!
NO THANKS, I'M ENJOYING SEDENTARISM THESE DAYS.
AW, COME ON! YOU'RE THE FASTEST DOG I'VE EVER SEEN! IF I COULD RUN LIKE YOU, I'D NEVER STOP!
WE WOULDN'T BE ABLE TO HANG OUT, THEN... I'D BE STANDING HERE... OR MAYBE OVER THERE. THERE'S SOME KILLER SMELLS OVER THERE.
darb
AND NOW, IF YOU'LL EXCUSE ME, I'M GOING TO BARK OUT PACHELBEL'S CANON.
...TACO BELL HAS A CANON?
GOOD GARFIELD ALMIGHTY, I GOTTA STOP COMING TO SATCHEL'S PLAYDATES JUST TO GET OUT.

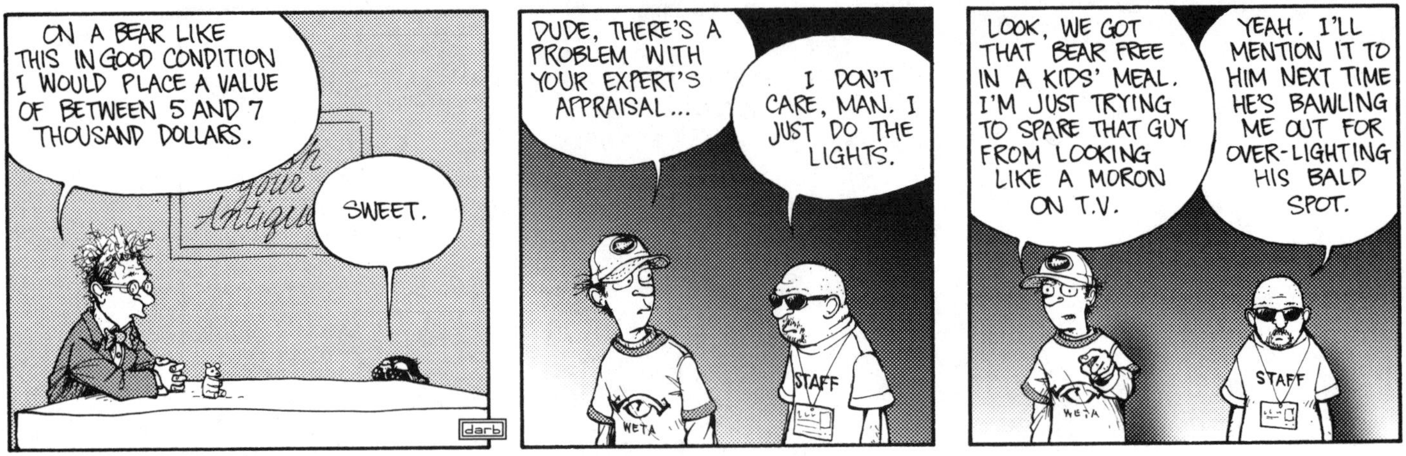
ON A BEAR LIKE THIS IN GOOD CONDITION I WOULD PLACE A VALUE OF BETWEEN 5 AND 7 THOUSAND DOLLARS.
SWEET.
DUDE, THERE'S A PROBLEM WITH YOUR EXPERT'S APPRAISAL...
I DON'T CARE, MAN. I JUST DO THE LIGHTS.
STAFF
WETA
LOOK, WE GOT THAT BEAR FREE IN A KIDS' MEAL. I'M JUST TRYING TO SPARE THAT GUY FROM LOOKING LIKE A MORON ON T.V.
YEAH. I'LL MENTION IT TO HIM NEXT TIME HE'S BAWLING ME OUT FOR OVER-LIGHTING HIS BALD SPOT.
STAFF
WETA

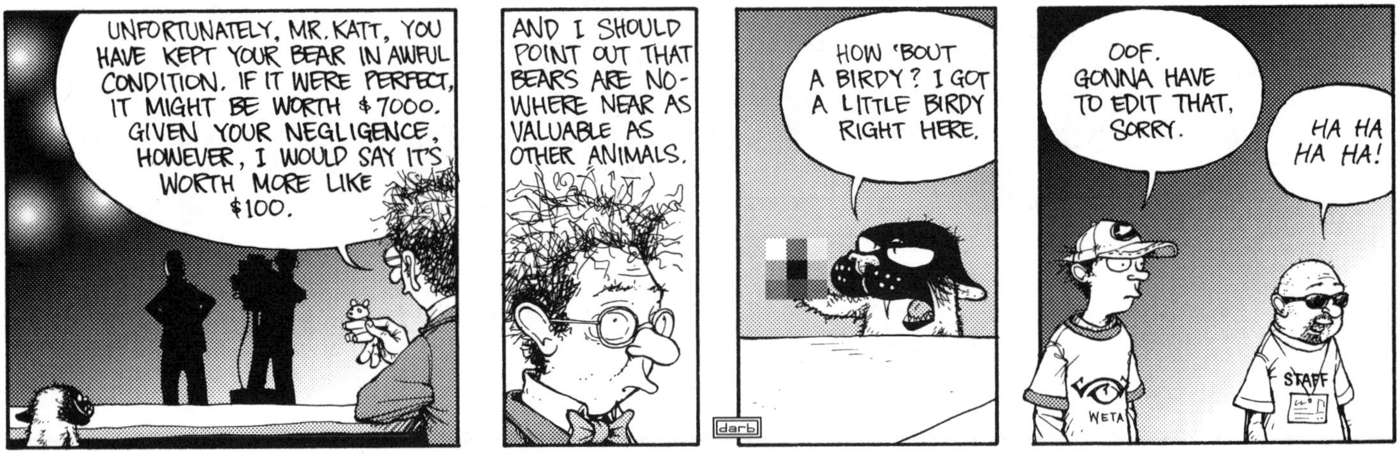
UNFORTUNATELY, MR. KATT, YOU HAVE KEPT YOUR BEAR IN AWFUL CONDITION. IF IT WERE PERFECT, IT MIGHT BE WORTH $7000. GIVEN YOUR NEGLIGENCE, HOWEVER, I WOULD SAY IT'S WORTH MORE LIKE $100.
AND I SHOULD POINT OUT THAT BEARS ARE NOWHERE NEAR AS VALUABLE AS OTHER ANIMALS.
HOW 'BOUT A BIRDY? I GOT A LITTLE BIRDY RIGHT HERE.
OOF. GONNA HAVE TO EDIT THAT, SORRY.
HA HA HA HA!
WETA
STAFF

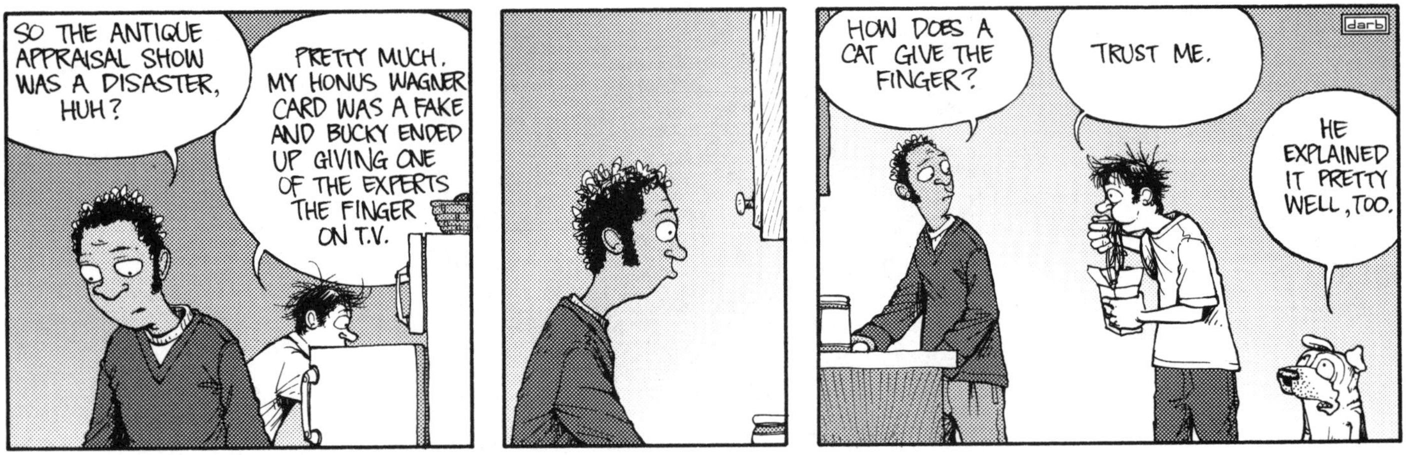
SO THE ANTIQUE APPRAISAL SHOW WAS A DISASTER, HUH?
PRETTY MUCH. MY HONUS WAGNER CARD WAS A FAKE AND BUCKY ENDED UP GIVING ONE OF THE EXPERTS THE FINGER ON T.V.
HOW DOES A CAT GIVE THE FINGER?
TRUST ME.
HE EXPLAINED IT PRETTY WELL, TOO.

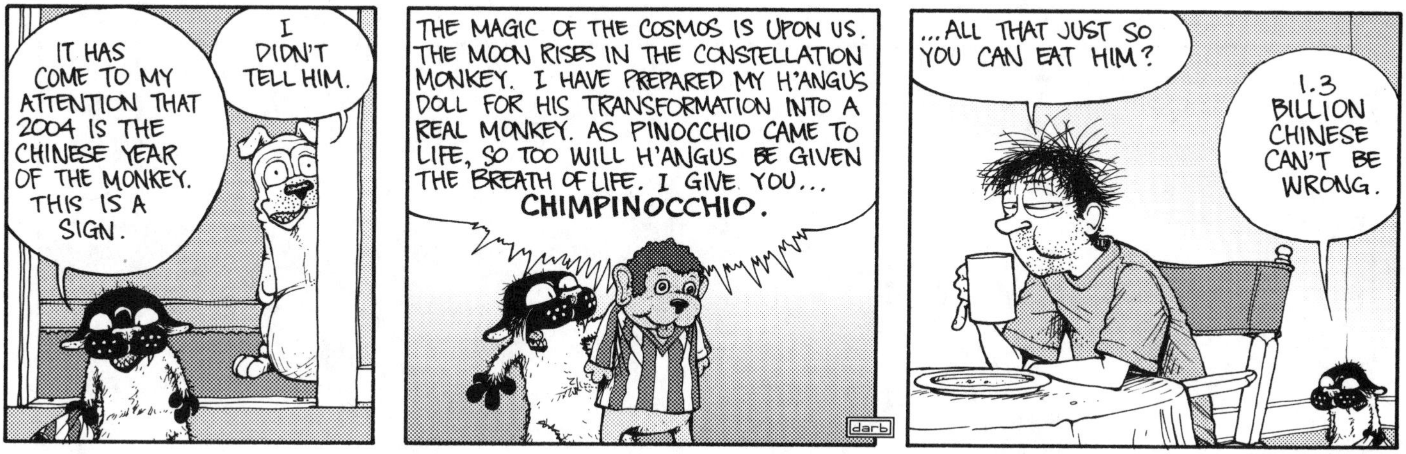
IT HAS COME TO MY ATTENTION THAT 2004 IS THE CHINESE YEAR OF THE MONKEY. THIS IS A SIGN.
I DIDN'T TELL HIM.
THE MAGIC OF THE COSMOS IS UPON US. THE MOON RISES IN THE CONSTELLATION MONKEY. I HAVE PREPARED MY H'ANGUS DOLL FOR HIS TRANSFORMATION INTO A REAL MONKEY. AS PINOCCHIO CAME TO LIFE, SO TOO WILL H'ANGUS BE GIVEN THE BREATH OF LIFE. I GIVE YOU... CHIMPINOCCHIO.
darb
...ALL THAT JUST SO YOU CAN EAT HIM?
1.3 BILLION CHINESE CAN'T BE WRONG.

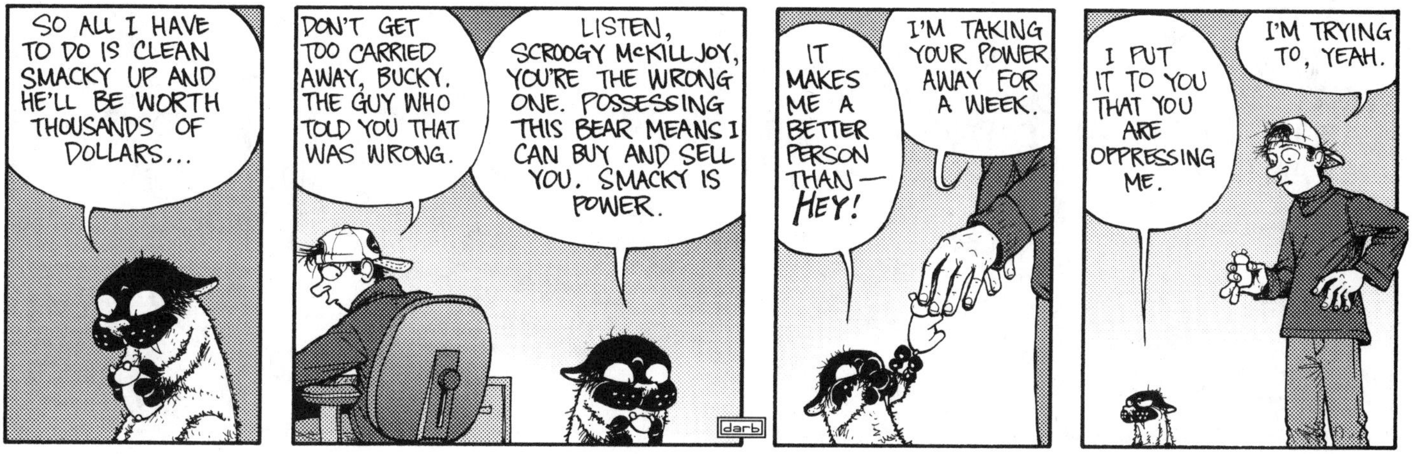
SO ALL I HAVE TO DO IS CLEAN SMACKY UP AND HE'LL BE WORTH THOUSANDS OF DOLLARS...
DON'T GET TOO CARRIED AWAY, BUCKY. THE GUY WHO TOLD YOU THAT WAS WRONG.
LISTEN, SCROOGY McKILLJOY, YOU'RE THE WRONG ONE. POSSESSING THIS BEAR MEANS I CAN BUY AND SELL YOU. SMACKY IS POWER.
darb
IT MAKES ME A BETTER PERSON THAN— HEY!
I'M TAKING YOUR POWER AWAY FOR A WEEK.
I PUT IT TO YOU THAT YOU ARE OPPRESSING ME.
I'M TRYING TO, YEAH.

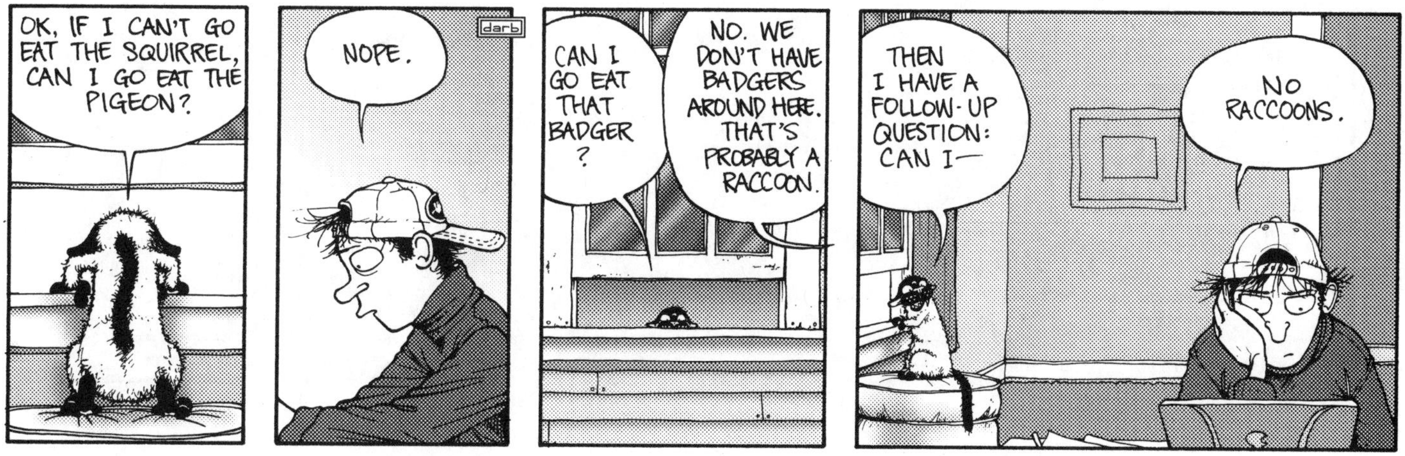
OK, IF I CAN'T GO EAT THE SQUIRREL, CAN I GO EAT THE PIGEON?
darb
NOPE.
CAN I GO EAT THAT BADGER?
NO. WE DON'T HAVE BADGERS AROUND HERE. THAT'S PROBABLY A RACCOON.
THEN I HAVE A FOLLOW-UP QUESTION: CAN I—
NO RACCOONS.

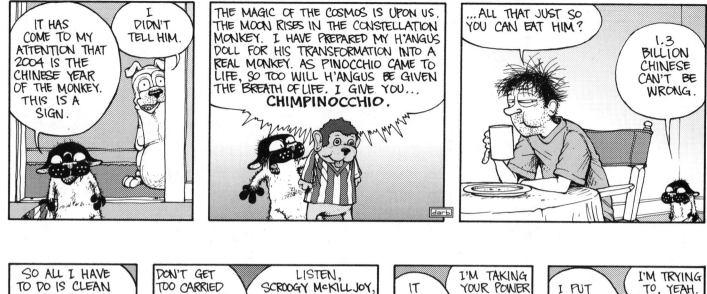

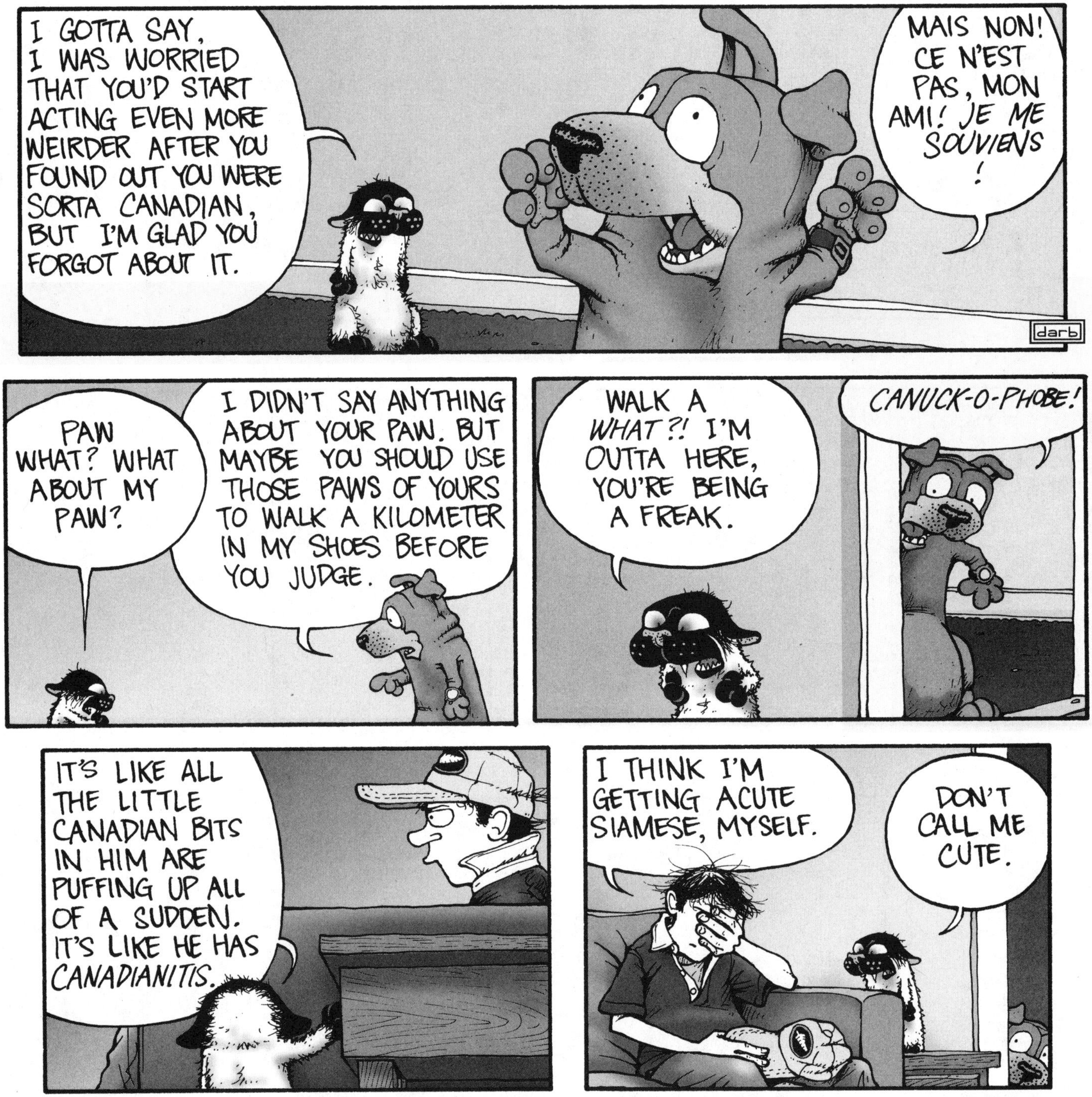
I GOTTA SAY, I WAS WORRIED THAT YOU'D START ACTING EVEN MORE WEIRDER AFTER YOU FOUND OUT YOU WERE SORTA CANADIAN, BUT I'M GLAD YOU FORGOT ABOUT IT.
MAIS NON! CE N'EST PAS, MON AMI! JE ME SOUVIENS!
darb
PAW WHAT? WHAT ABOUT MY PAW?
I DIDN'T SAY ANYTHING ABOUT YOUR PAW. BUT MAYBE YOU SHOULD USE THOSE PAWS OF YOURS TO WALK A KILOMETER IN MY SHOES BEFORE YOU JUDGE.
WALK A WHAT?! I'M OUTTA HERE, YOU'RE BEING A FREAK.
CANUCK-O-PHOBE!
IT'S LIKE ALL THE LITTLE CANADIAN BITS IN HIM ARE PUFFING UP ALL OF A SUDDEN. IT'S LIKE HE HAS CANADIANITIS.
I THINK I'M GETTING ACUTE SIAMESE, MYSELF.
DON'T CALL ME CUTE.

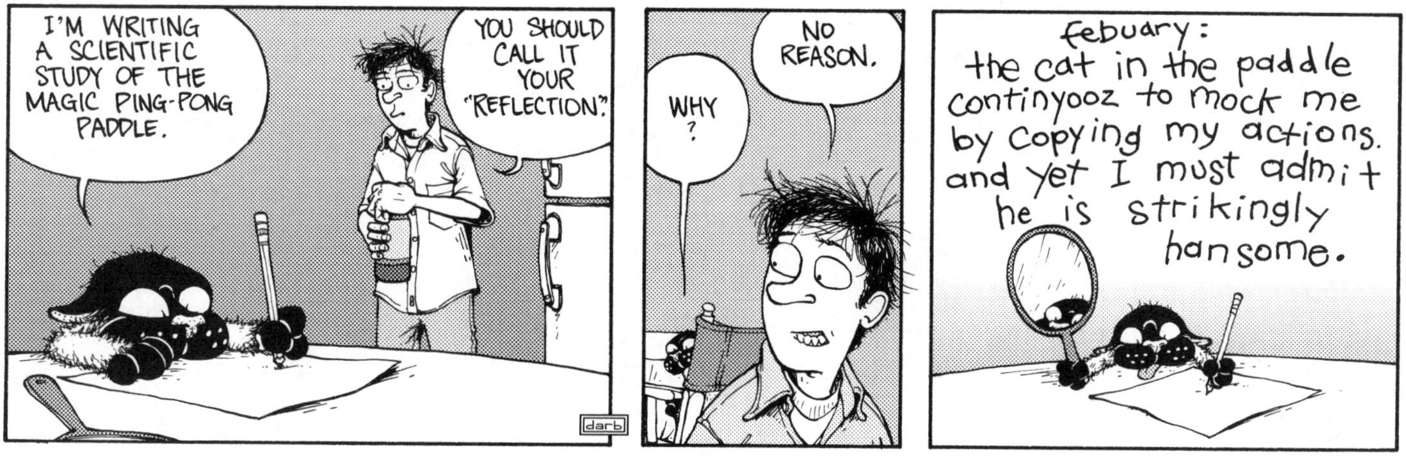

I'M WRITING A SCIENTIFIC STUDY OF THE MAGIC PING-PONG PADDLE.
YOU SHOULD CALL IT YOUR "REFLECTION."
darb
WHY?
NO REASON.
febuary: the cat in the paddle continyooz to mock me by copying my actions. and yet I must admit he is strikingly hansome.

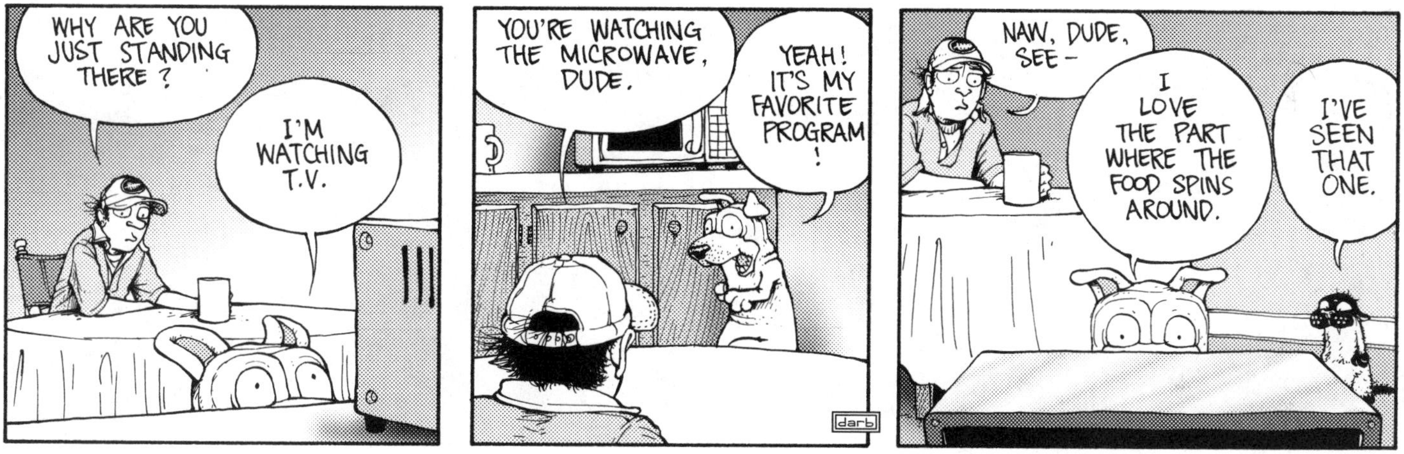

WHY ARE YOU JUST STANDING THERE?
I'M WATCHING T.V.
YOU'RE WATCHING THE MICROWAVE, DUDE.
YEAH! IT'S MY FAVORITE PROGRAM!
darb
NAW, DUDE, SEE-
I LOVE THE PART WHERE THE FOOD SPINS AROUND.
I'VE SEEN THAT ONE.

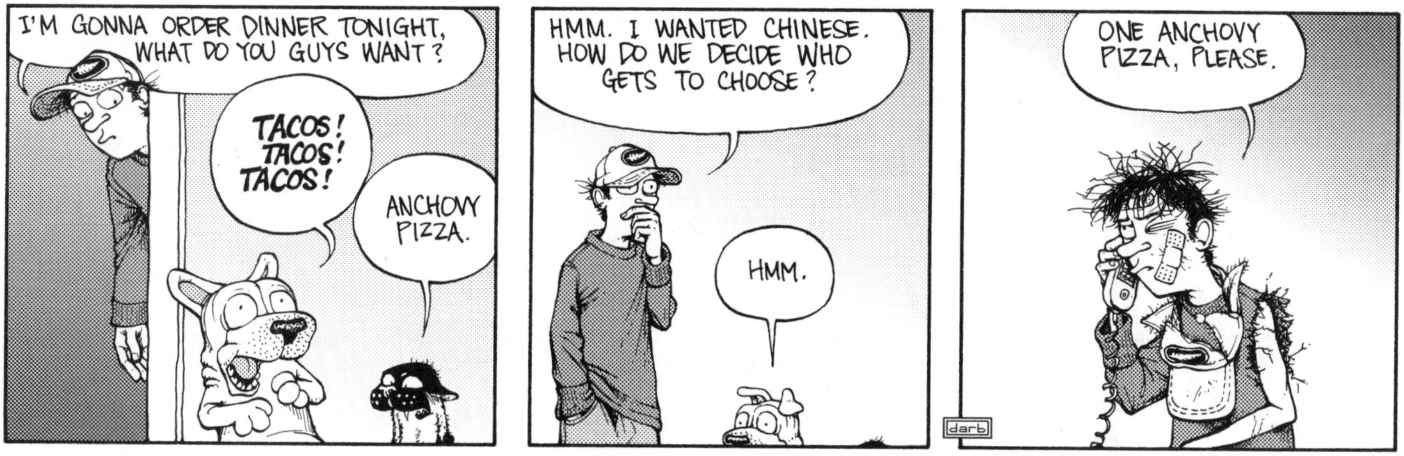

I'M GONNA ORDER DINNER TONIGHT, WHAT DO YOU GUYS WANT?
TACOS! TACOS! TACOS!
ANCHOVY PIZZA.
HMM. I WANTED CHINESE. HOW DO WE DECIDE WHO GETS TO CHOOSE?
HMM.
darb
ONE ANCHOVY PIZZA, PLEASE.

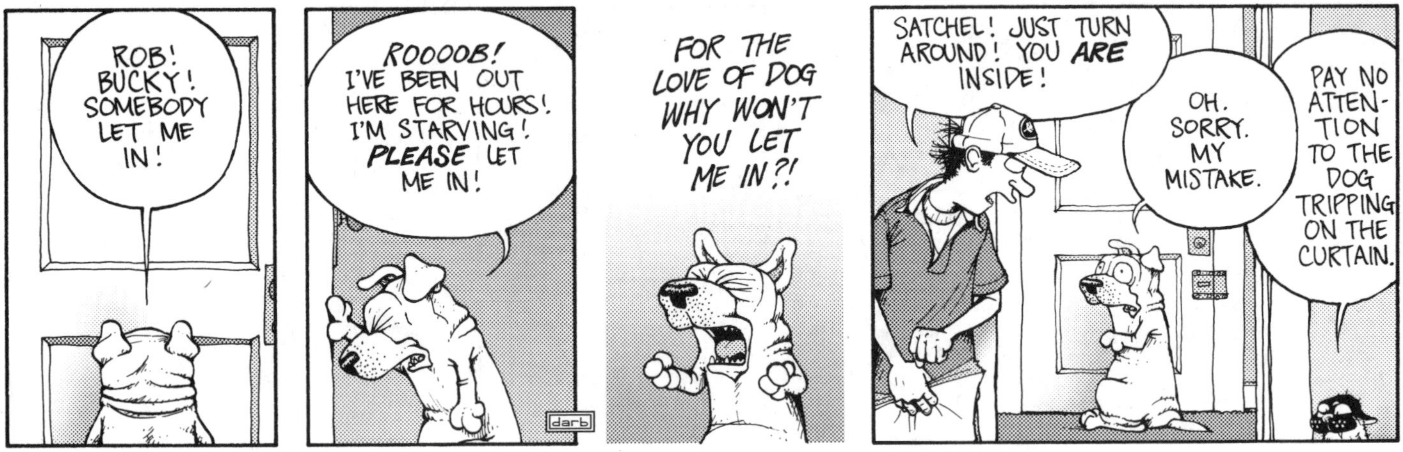
ROB! BUCKY! SOMEBODY LET ME IN!
ROOOOB! I'VE BEEN OUT HERE FOR HOURS! I'M STARVING! PLEASE LET ME IN!
FOR THE LOVE OF DOG WHY WON'T YOU LET ME IN?!
SATCHEL! JUST TURN AROUND! YOU ARE INSIDE!
OH. SORRY. MY MISTAKE.
PAY NO ATTEN-TION TO THE DOG TRIPPING ON THE CURTAIN.
darb

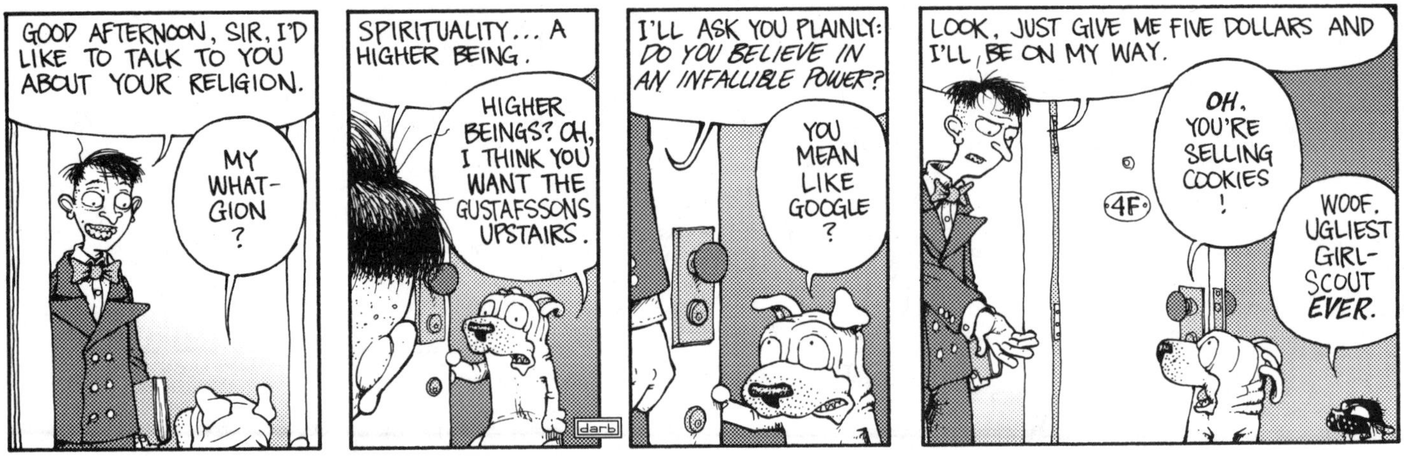
GOOD AFTERNOON, SIR, I'D LIKE TO TALK TO YOU ABOUT YOUR RELIGION.
MY WHAT-GION?
SPIRITUALITY... A HIGHER BEING.
HIGHER BEINGS? OH, I THINK YOU WANT THE GUSTAFSSONS UPSTAIRS.
I'LL ASK YOU PLAINLY: DO YOU BELIEVE IN AN INFALLIBLE POWER?
YOU MEAN LIKE GOOGLE?
LOOK, JUST GIVE ME FIVE DOLLARS AND I'LL BE ON MY WAY.
OH. YOU'RE SELLING COOKIES!
4F
WOOF. UGLIEST GIRL-SCOUT EVER.
darb

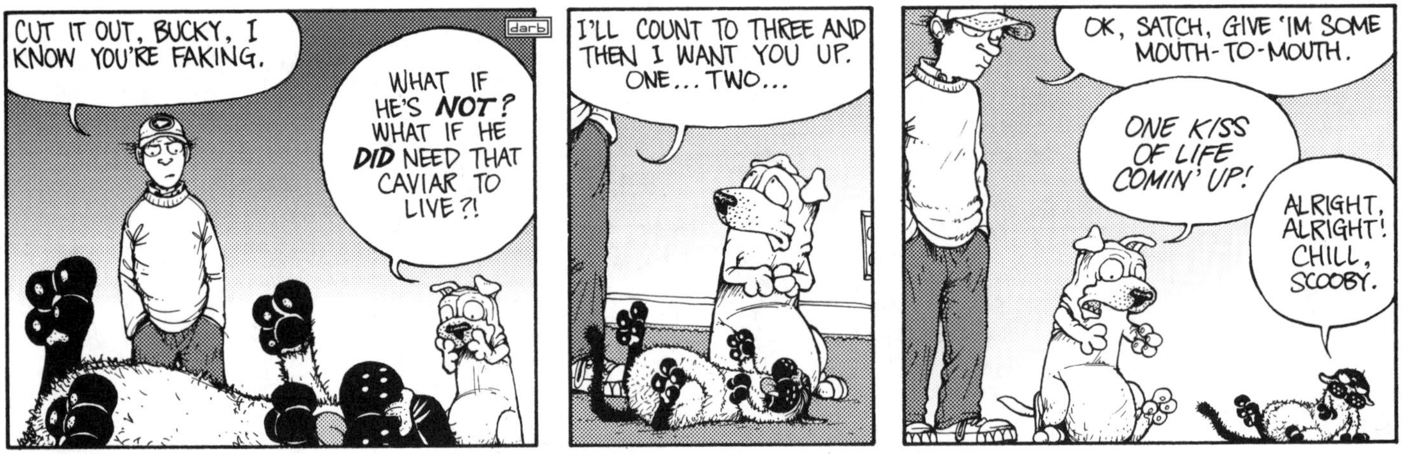
CUT IT OUT, BUCKY, I KNOW YOU'RE FAKING.
WHAT IF HE'S NOT? WHAT IF HE DID NEED THAT CAVIAR TO LIVE?!
I'LL COUNT TO THREE AND THEN I WANT YOU UP. ONE... TWO...
OK, SATCH, GIVE 'IM SOME MOUTH-TO-MOUTH.
ONE KISS OF LIFE COMIN' UP!
ALRIGHT, ALRIGHT! CHILL, SCOOBY.
darb

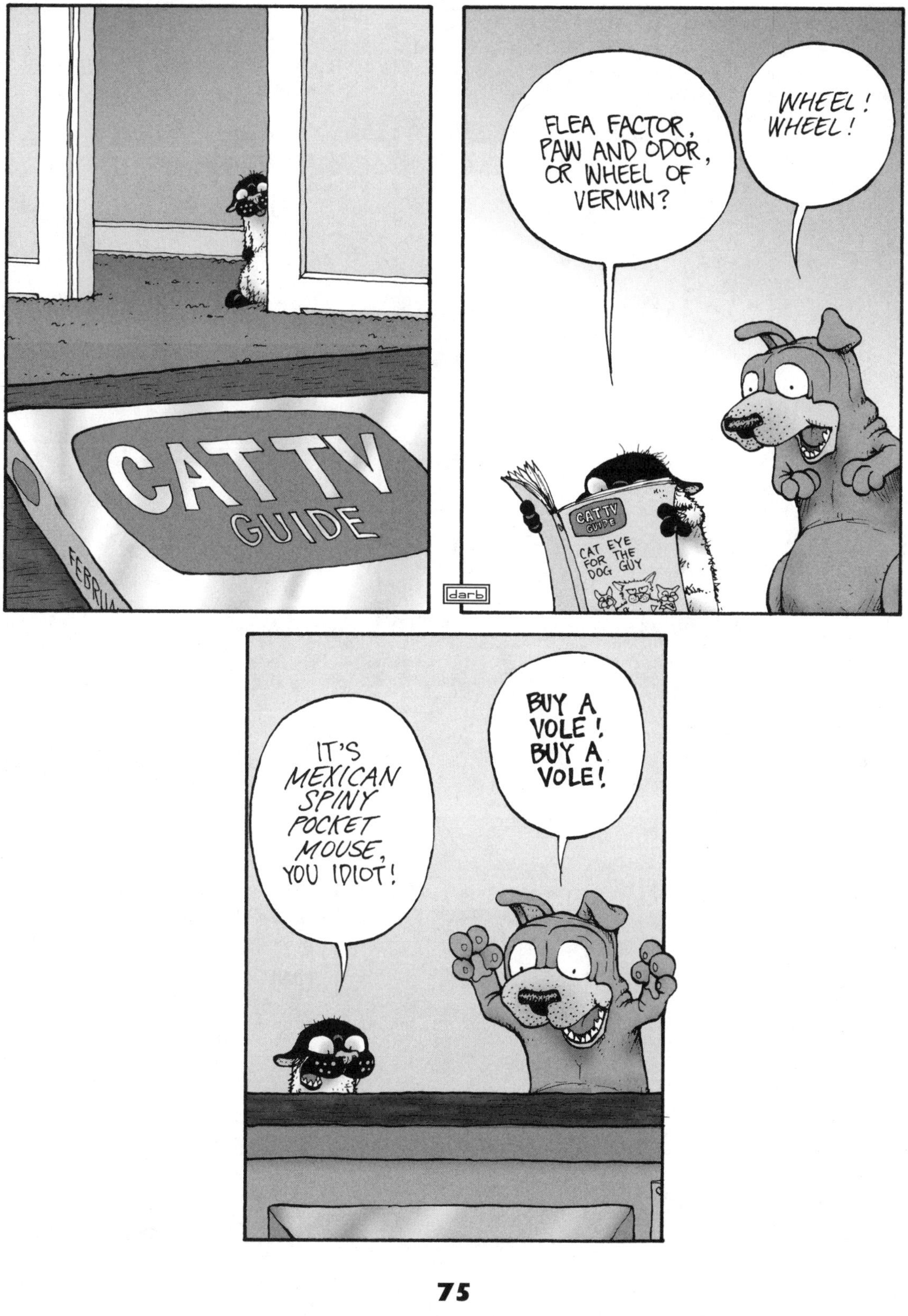
CAT TV
GUIDE
FEBRU
FLEA FACTOR, PAW AND ODOR, OR WHEEL OF VERMIN?
WHEEL! WHEEL!
CAT TV GUIDE
CAT EYE FOR THE DOG GUY
darb
IT'S MEXICAN SPINY POCKET MOUSE, YOU IDIOT!
BUY A VOLE! BUY A VOLE!

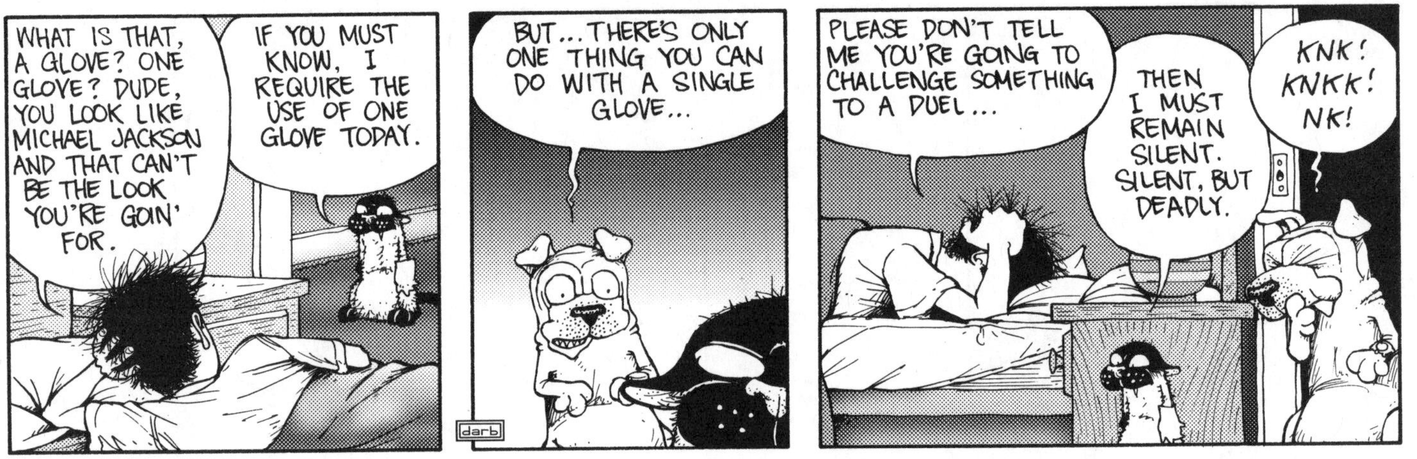
WHAT IS THAT, A GLOVE? ONE GLOVE? DUDE, YOU LOOK LIKE MICHAEL JACKSON AND THAT CAN'T BE THE LOOK YOU'RE GOIN' FOR.
IF YOU MUST KNOW, I REQUIRE THE USE OF ONE GLOVE TODAY.
BUT... THERE'S ONLY ONE THING YOU CAN DO WITH A SINGLE GLOVE...
darb
PLEASE DON'T TELL ME YOU'RE GOING TO CHALLENGE SOMETHING TO A DUEL...
THEN I MUST REMAIN SILENT. SILENT, BUT DEADLY.
KNK! KNKK! NK!

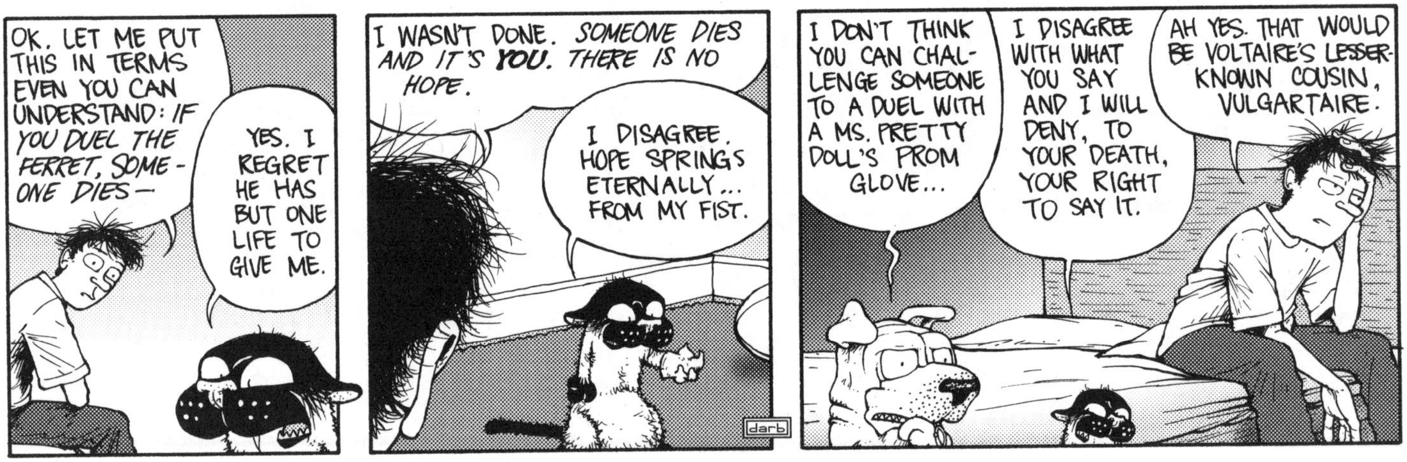
OK. LET ME PUT THIS IN TERMS EVEN YOU CAN UNDERSTAND: *IF YOU DUEL THE FERRET, SOMEONE DIES*—
YES. I REGRET HE HAS BUT ONE LIFE TO GIVE ME.
I WASN'T DONE. *SOMEONE DIES AND IT'S* ***YOU****. THERE IS NO HOPE.*
I DISAGREE. HOPE SPRINGS ETERNALLY... FROM MY FIST.
darb
I DON'T THINK YOU CAN CHALLENGE SOMEONE TO A DUEL WITH A MS. PRETTY DOLL'S PROM GLOVE...
I DISAGREE WITH WHAT YOU SAY AND I WILL DENY, TO YOUR DEATH, YOUR RIGHT TO SAY IT.
AH YES. THAT WOULD BE VOLTAIRE'S LESSER-KNOWN COUSIN, VULGARTAIRE.

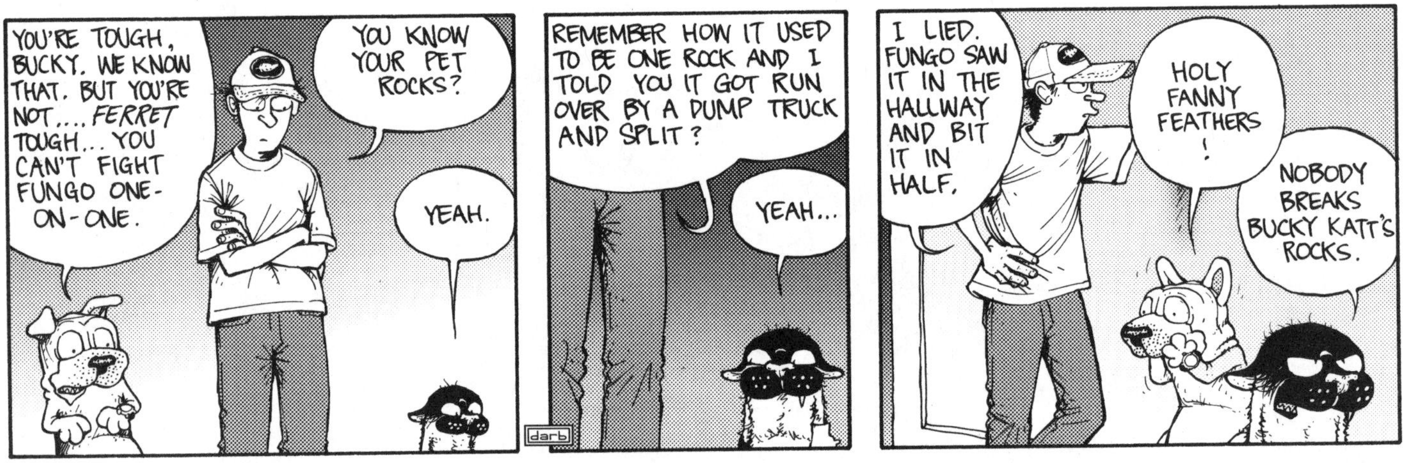
YOU'RE TOUGH, BUCKY. WE KNOW THAT. BUT YOU'RE NOT.... *FERRET* TOUGH... YOU CAN'T FIGHT FUNGO ONE-ON-ONE.
YOU KNOW YOUR PET ROCKS?
YEAH.
REMEMBER HOW IT USED TO BE ONE ROCK AND I TOLD YOU IT GOT RUN OVER BY A DUMP TRUCK AND SPLIT?
YEAH...
darb
I LIED. FUNGO SAW IT IN THE HALLWAY AND BIT IT IN HALF.
HOLY FANNY FEATHERS!
NOBODY BREAKS BUCKY KATT'S ROCKS.

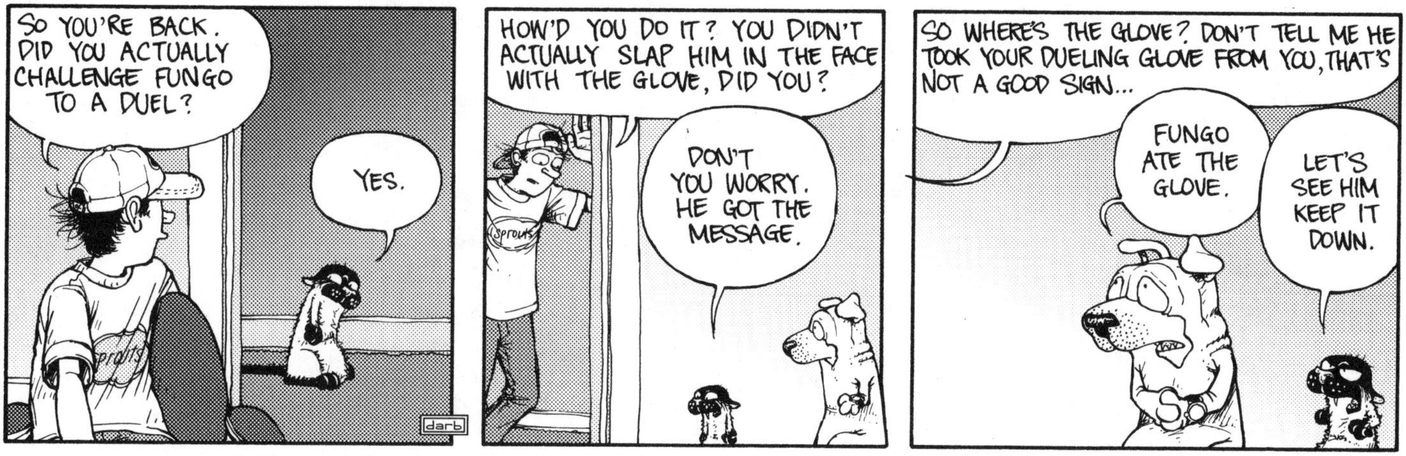
SO YOU'RE BACK. DID YOU ACTUALLY CHALLENGE FUNGO TO A DUEL?
YES.
HOW'D YOU DO IT? YOU DIDN'T ACTUALLY SLAP HIM IN THE FACE WITH THE GLOVE, DID YOU?
DON'T YOU WORRY. HE GOT THE MESSAGE.
SO WHERE'S THE GLOVE? DON'T TELL ME HE TOOK YOUR DUELING GLOVE FROM YOU, THAT'S NOT A GOOD SIGN...
FUNGO ATE THE GLOVE.
LET'S SEE HIM KEEP IT DOWN.

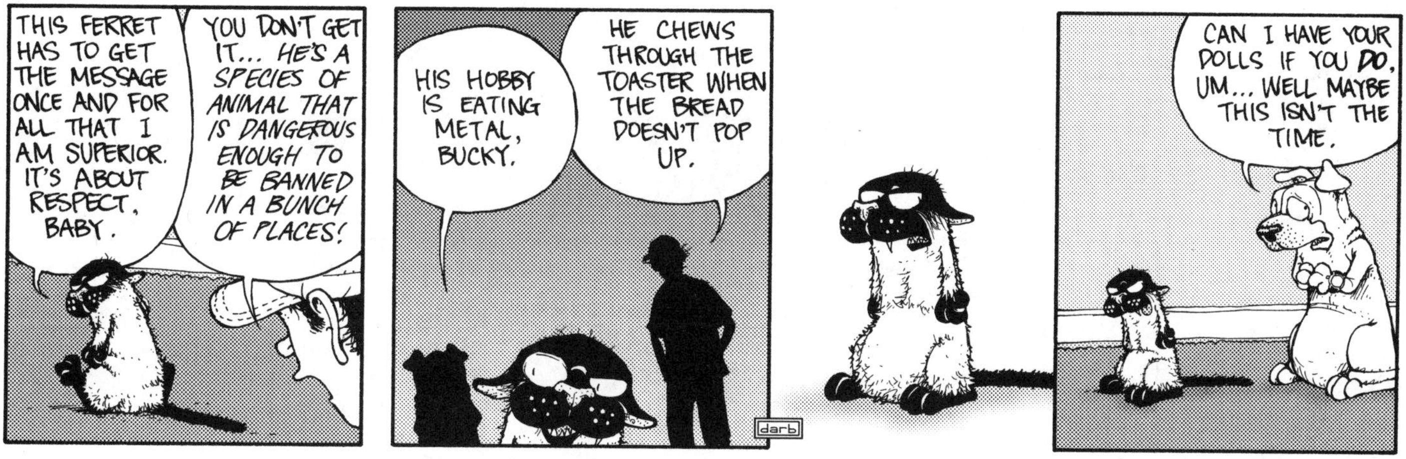
THIS FERRET HAS TO GET THE MESSAGE ONCE AND FOR ALL THAT I AM SUPERIOR. IT'S ABOUT RESPECT, BABY.
YOU DON'T GET IT... HE'S A SPECIES OF ANIMAL THAT IS DANGEROUS ENOUGH TO BE BANNED IN A BUNCH OF PLACES!
HIS HOBBY IS EATING METAL, BUCKY.
HE CHEWS THROUGH THE TOASTER WHEN THE BREAD DOESN'T POP UP.
CAN I HAVE YOUR DOLLS IF YOU DO, UM... WELL MAYBE THIS ISN'T THE TIME.

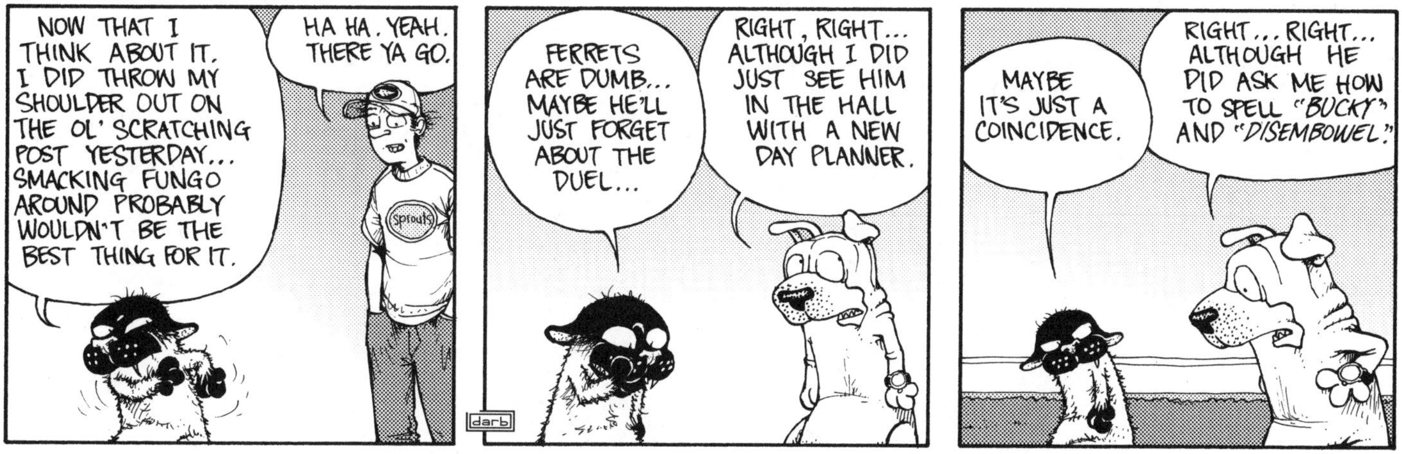
NOW THAT I THINK ABOUT IT, I DID THROW MY SHOULDER OUT ON THE OL' SCRATCHING POST YESTERDAY... SMACKING FUNGO AROUND PROBABLY WOULDN'T BE THE BEST THING FOR IT.
HA HA. YEAH. THERE YA GO.
FERRETS ARE DUMB... MAYBE HE'LL JUST FORGET ABOUT THE DUEL...
RIGHT, RIGHT... ALTHOUGH I DID JUST SEE HIM IN THE HALL WITH A NEW DAY PLANNER.
MAYBE IT'S JUST A COINCIDENCE.
RIGHT... RIGHT... ALTHOUGH HE DID ASK ME HOW TO SPELL "BUCKY" AND "DISEMBOWEL."

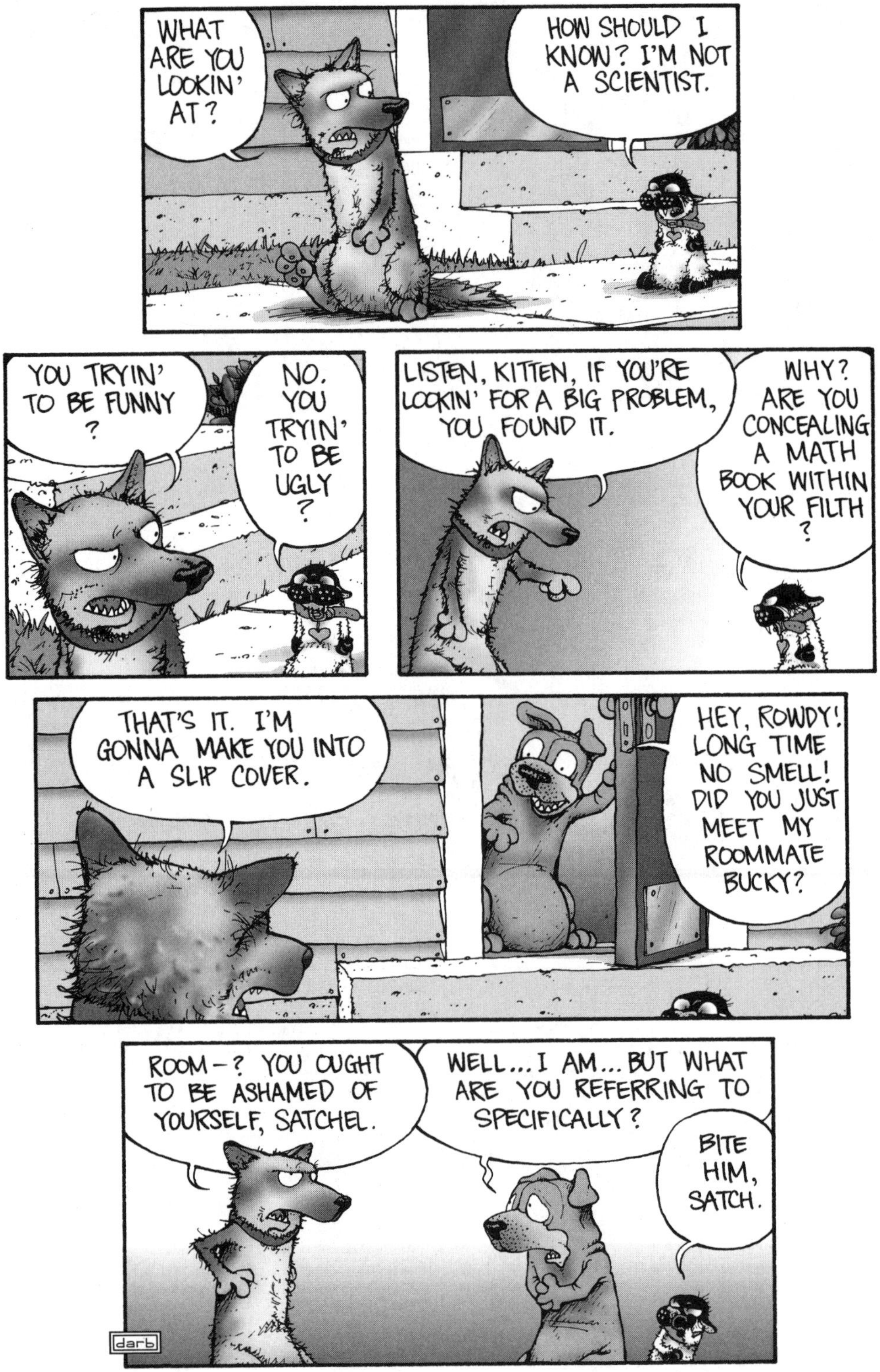
WHAT ARE YOU LOOKIN' AT?
HOW SHOULD I KNOW? I'M NOT A SCIENTIST.
YOU TRYIN' TO BE FUNNY?
NO. YOU TRYIN' TO BE UGLY?
LISTEN, KITTEN, IF YOU'RE LOOKIN' FOR A BIG PROBLEM, YOU FOUND IT.
WHY? ARE YOU CONCEALING A MATH BOOK WITHIN YOUR FILTH?
THAT'S IT. I'M GONNA MAKE YOU INTO A SLIP COVER.
HEY, ROWDY! LONG TIME NO SMELL! DID YOU JUST MEET MY ROOMMATE BUCKY?
ROOM-? YOU OUGHT TO BE ASHAMED OF YOURSELF, SATCHEL.
WELL... I AM... BUT WHAT ARE YOU REFERRING TO SPECIFICALLY?
BITE HIM, SATCH.
darb

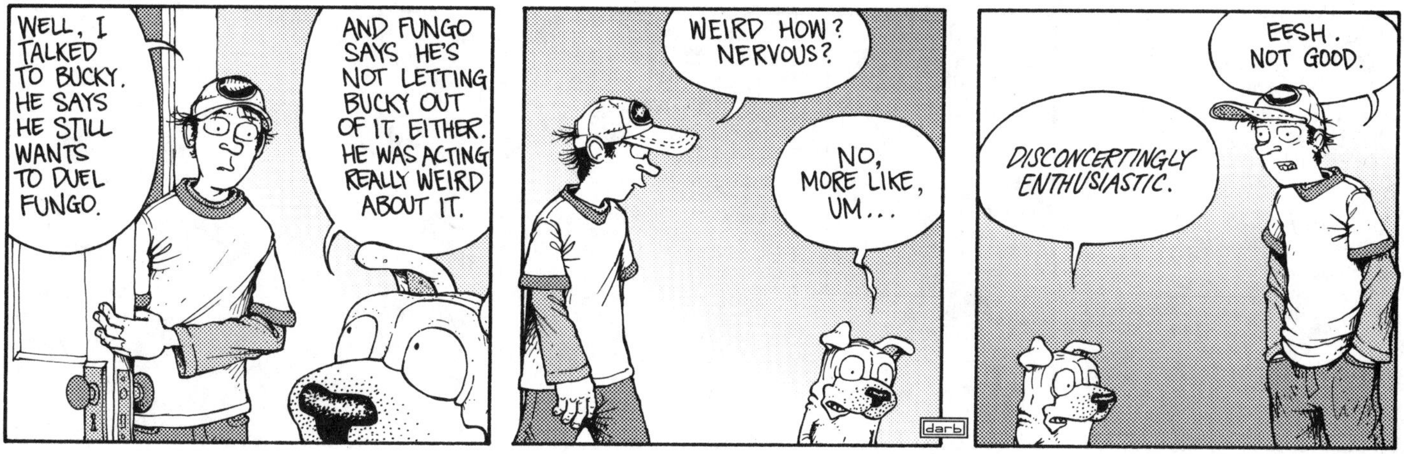
WELL, I TALKED TO BUCKY. HE SAYS HE STILL WANTS TO DUEL FUNGO.
AND FUNGO SAYS HE'S NOT LETTING BUCKY OUT OF IT, EITHER. HE WAS ACTING REALLY WEIRD ABOUT IT.
WEIRD HOW? NERVOUS?
NO, MORE LIKE, UM...
DISCONCERTINGLY ENTHUSIASTIC.
EESH. NOT GOOD.
darb

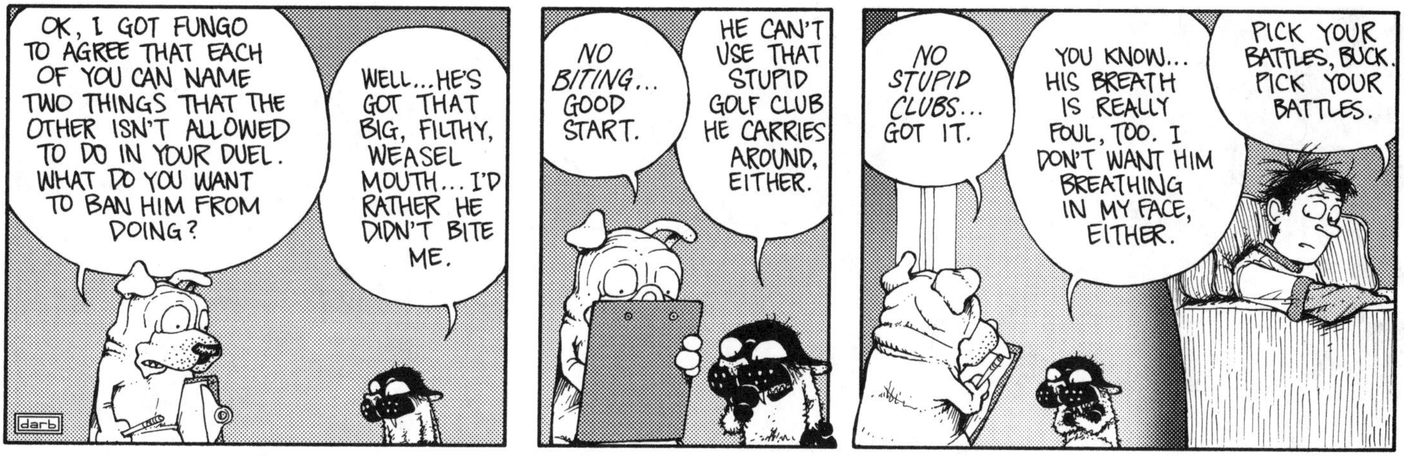
OK, I GOT FUNGO TO AGREE THAT EACH OF YOU CAN NAME TWO THINGS THAT THE OTHER ISN'T ALLOWED TO DO IN YOUR DUEL. WHAT DO YOU WANT TO BAN HIM FROM DOING?
WELL... HE'S GOT THAT BIG, FILTHY, WEASEL MOUTH... I'D RATHER HE DIDN'T BITE ME.
darb
NO BITING... GOOD START.
HE CAN'T USE THAT STUPID GOLF CLUB HE CARRIES AROUND, EITHER.
NO STUPID CLUBS... GOT IT.
YOU KNOW... HIS BREATH IS REALLY FOUL, TOO. I DON'T WANT HIM BREATHING IN MY FACE, EITHER.
PICK YOUR BATTLES, BUCK. PICK YOUR BATTLES.

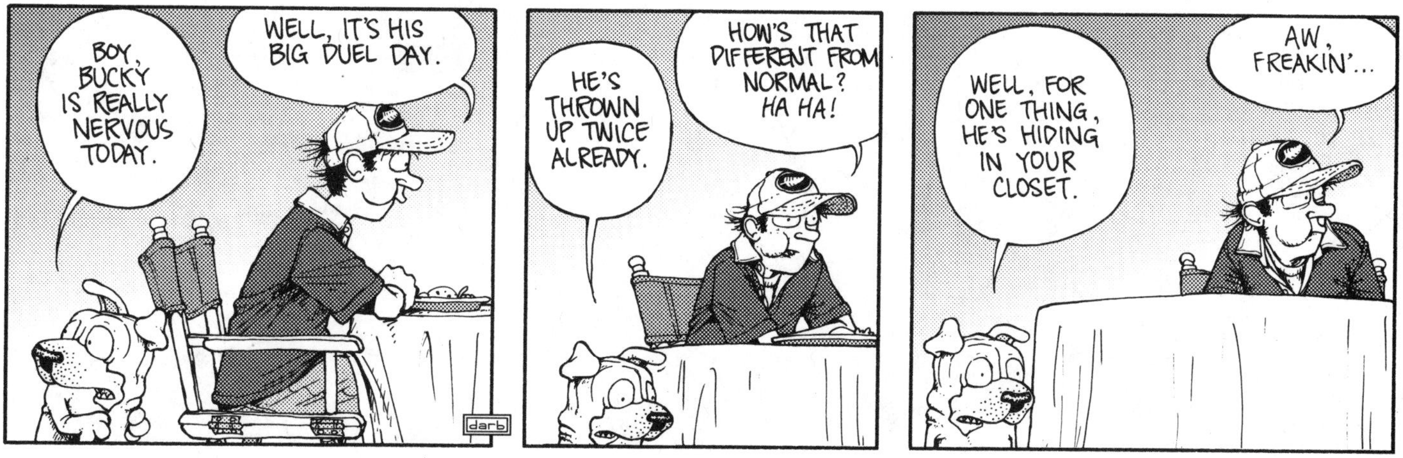
BOY, BUCKY IS REALLY NERVOUS TODAY.
WELL, IT'S HIS BIG DUEL DAY.
darb
HE'S THROWN UP TWICE ALREADY.
HOW'S THAT DIFFERENT FROM NORMAL? HA HA!
WELL, FOR ONE THING, HE'S HIDING IN YOUR CLOSET.
AW, FREAKIN'...

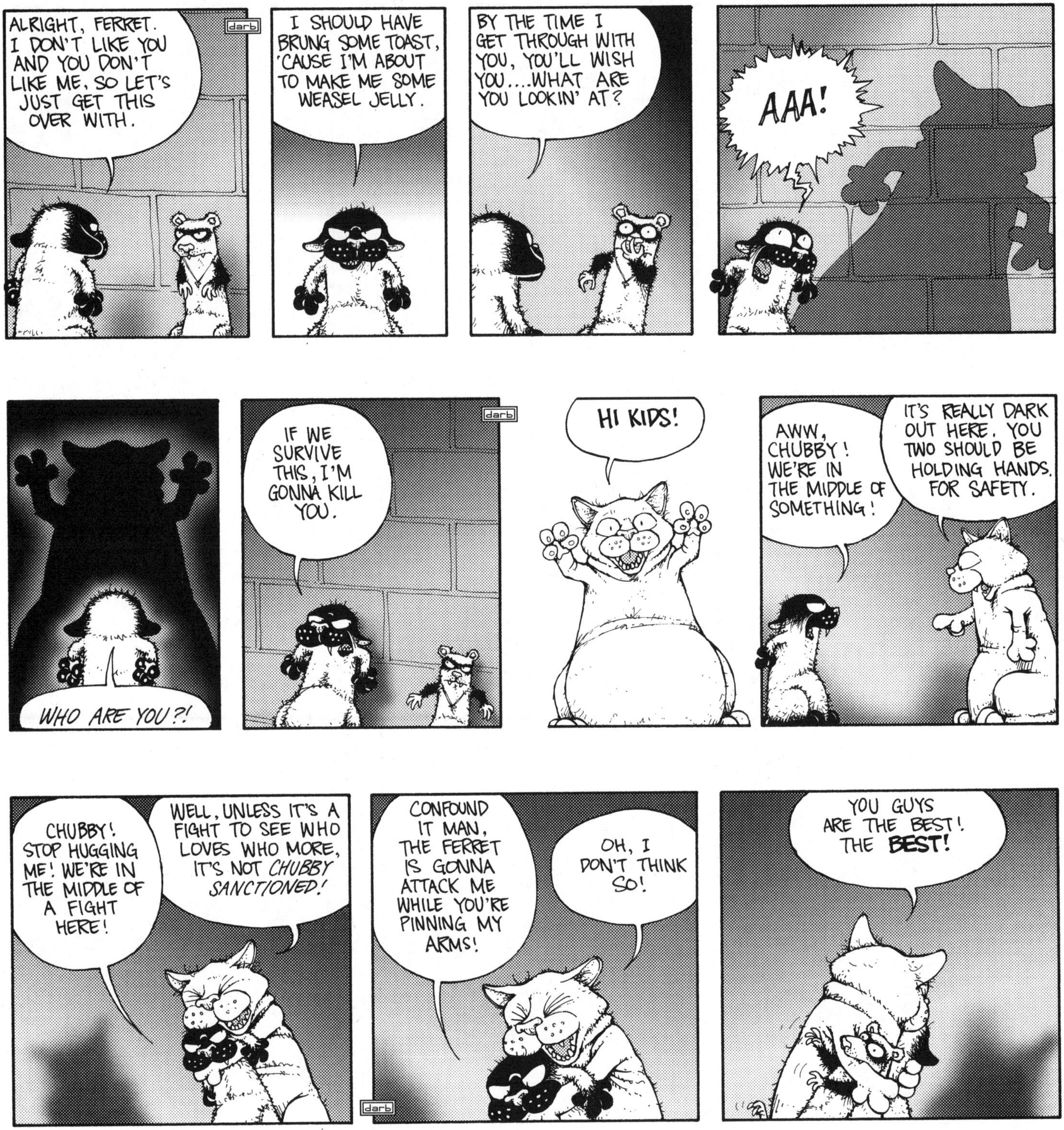
darb
ALRIGHT, FERRET. I DON'T LIKE YOU AND YOU DON'T LIKE ME, SO LET'S JUST GET THIS OVER WITH.
I SHOULD HAVE BRUNG SOME TOAST, 'CAUSE I'M ABOUT TO MAKE ME SOME WEASEL JELLY.
BY THE TIME I GET THROUGH WITH YOU, YOU'LL WISH YOU....WHAT ARE YOU LOOKIN' AT?
AAA!
WHO ARE YOU?!
darb
IF WE SURVIVE THIS, I'M GONNA KILL YOU.
HI KIDS!
AWW, CHUBBY! WE'RE IN THE MIDDLE OF SOMETHING!
IT'S REALLY DARK OUT HERE. YOU TWO SHOULD BE HOLDING HANDS. FOR SAFETY.
CHUBBY! STOP HUGGING ME! WE'RE IN THE MIDDLE OF A FIGHT HERE!
WELL, UNLESS IT'S A FIGHT TO SEE WHO LOVES WHO MORE, IT'S NOT CHUBBY SANCTIONED!
darb
CONFOUND IT MAN, THE FERRET IS GONNA ATTACK ME WHILE YOU'RE PINNING MY ARMS!
OH, I DON'T THINK SO!
YOU GUYS ARE THE BEST! THE BEST!

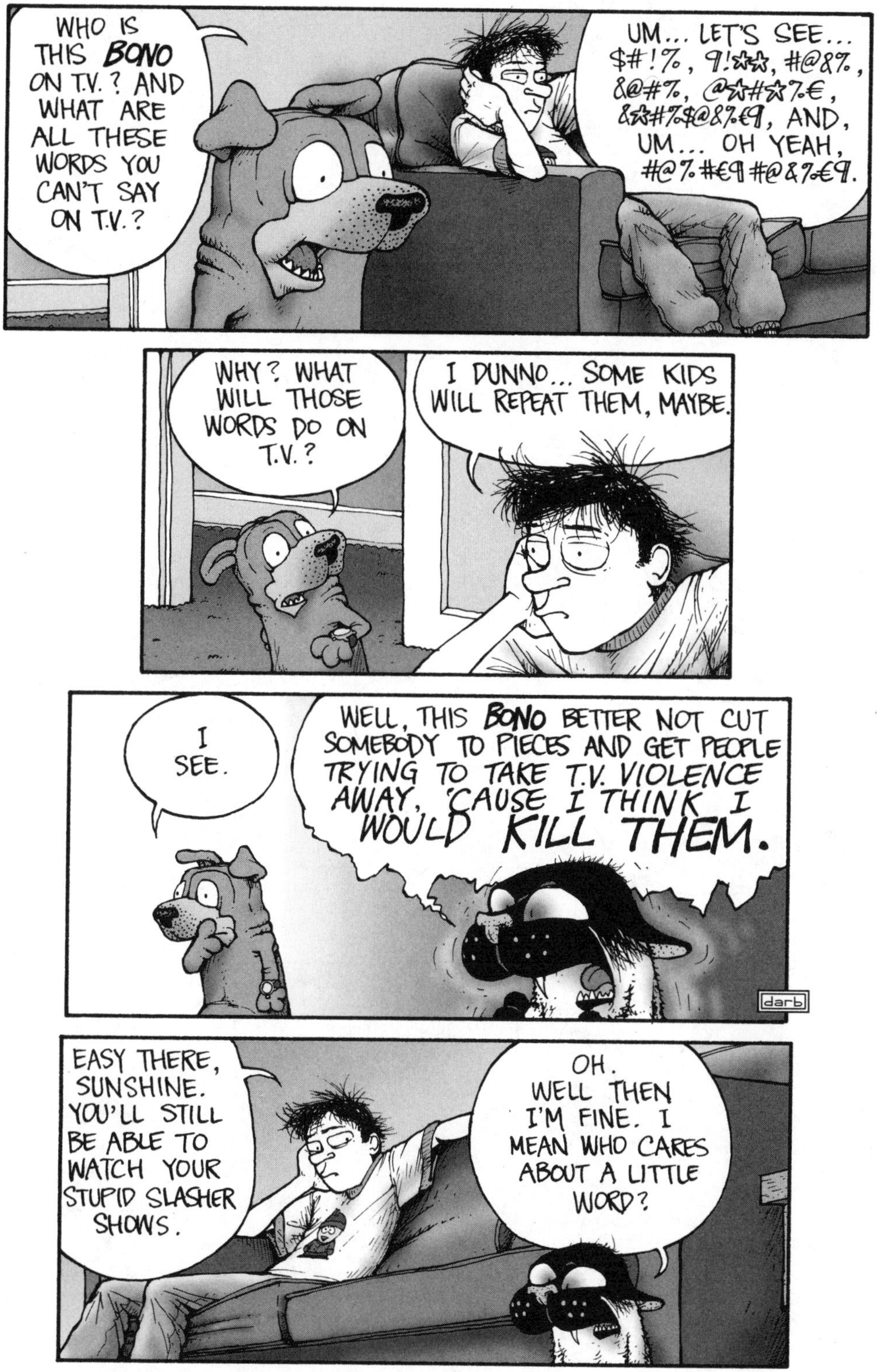
WHO IS THIS BONO ON T.V.? AND WHAT ARE ALL THESE WORDS YOU CAN'T SAY ON T.V.?
UM... LET'S SEE... $#!%, 9!☆☆, #@&%, &@#%, @☆#☆%€, &☆#%$@&%€9, AND, UM... OH YEAH, #@%#€9 #@&%€9.
WHY? WHAT WILL THOSE WORDS DO ON T.V.?
I DUNNO... SOME KIDS WILL REPEAT THEM, MAYBE.
I SEE.
WELL, THIS BONO BETTER NOT CUT SOMEBODY TO PIECES AND GET PEOPLE TRYING TO TAKE T.V. VIOLENCE AWAY, 'CAUSE I THINK I WOULD KILL THEM.
darb
EASY THERE, SUNSHINE. YOU'LL STILL BE ABLE TO WATCH YOUR STUPID SLASHER SHOWS.
OH. WELL THEN I'M FINE. I MEAN WHO CARES ABOUT A LITTLE WORD?

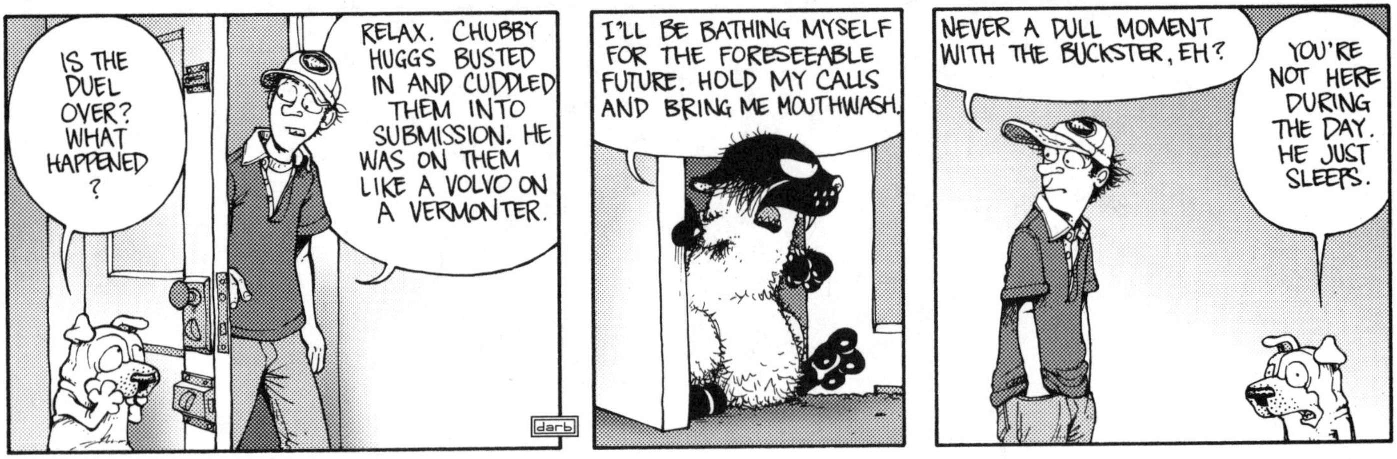
IS THE DUEL OVER? WHAT HAPPENED?
RELAX. CHUBBY HUGGS BUSTED IN AND CUDDLED THEM INTO SUBMISSION. HE WAS ON THEM LIKE A VOLVO ON A VERMONTER.
darb
I'LL BE BATHING MYSELF FOR THE FORESEEABLE FUTURE. HOLD MY CALLS AND BRING ME MOUTHWASH.
NEVER A DULL MOMENT WITH THE BUCKSTER, EH?
YOU'RE NOT HERE DURING THE DAY. HE JUST SLEEPS.

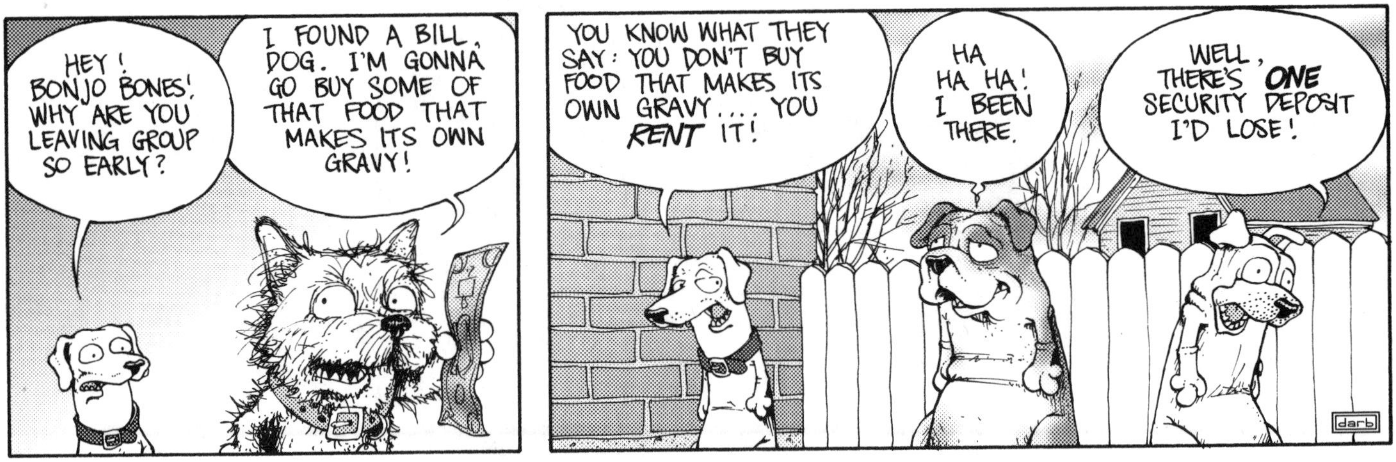
HEY! BONJO BONES! WHY ARE YOU LEAVING GROUP SO EARLY?
I FOUND A BILL, DOG. I'M GONNA GO BUY SOME OF THAT FOOD THAT MAKES ITS OWN GRAVY!
YOU KNOW WHAT THEY SAY: YOU DON'T BUY FOOD THAT MAKES ITS OWN GRAVY.... YOU *RENT* IT!
HA HA HA! I BEEN THERE.
WELL, THERE'S **ONE** SECURITY DEPOSIT I'D LOSE!
darb

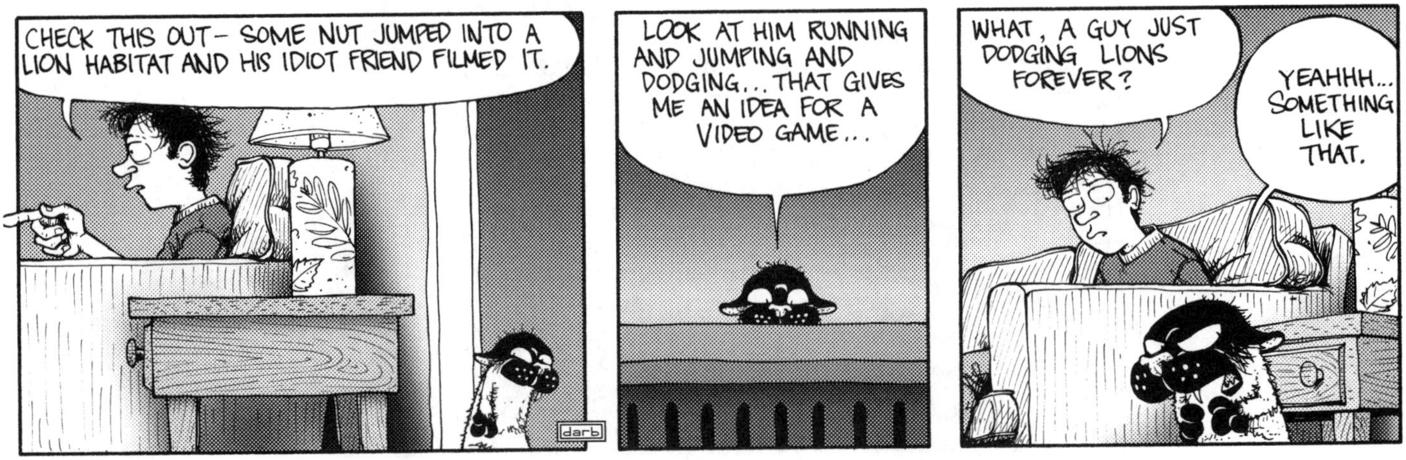
CHECK THIS OUT– SOME NUT JUMPED INTO A LION HABITAT AND HIS IDIOT FRIEND FILMED IT.
darb
LOOK AT HIM RUNNING AND JUMPING AND DODGING... THAT GIVES ME AN IDEA FOR A VIDEO GAME...
WHAT, A GUY JUST DODGING LIONS FOREVER?
YEAHHH... SOMETHING LIKE THAT.

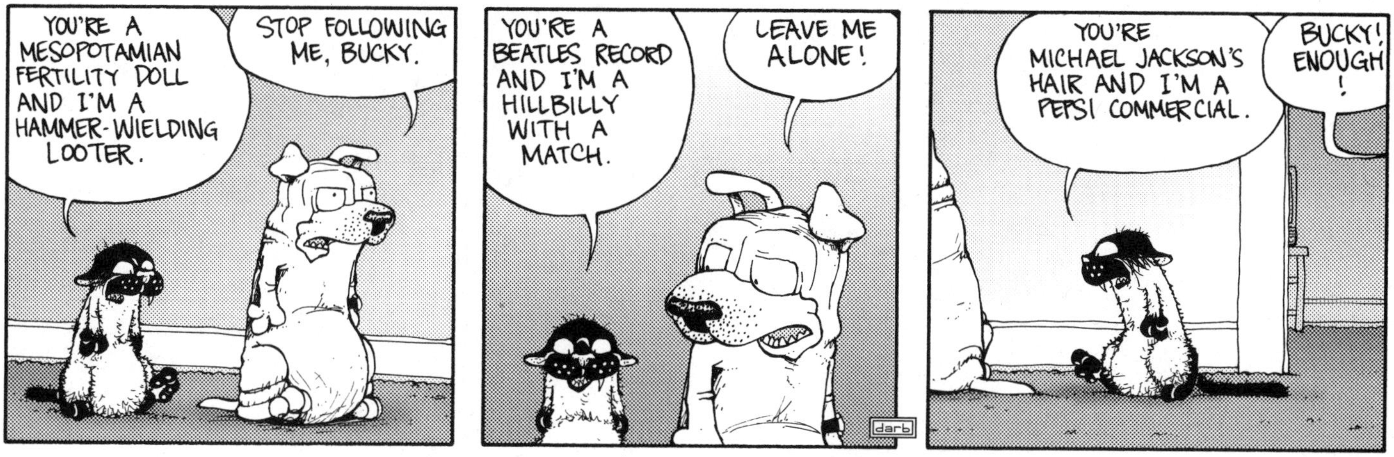
YOU'RE A MESOPOTAMIAN FERTILITY DOLL AND I'M A HAMMER-WIELDING LOOTER.
STOP FOLLOWING ME, BUCKY.
YOU'RE A BEATLES RECORD AND I'M A HILLBILLY WITH A MATCH.
LEAVE ME ALONE!
darb
YOU'RE MICHAEL JACKSON'S HAIR AND I'M A PEPSI COMMERCIAL.
BUCKY! ENOUGH!

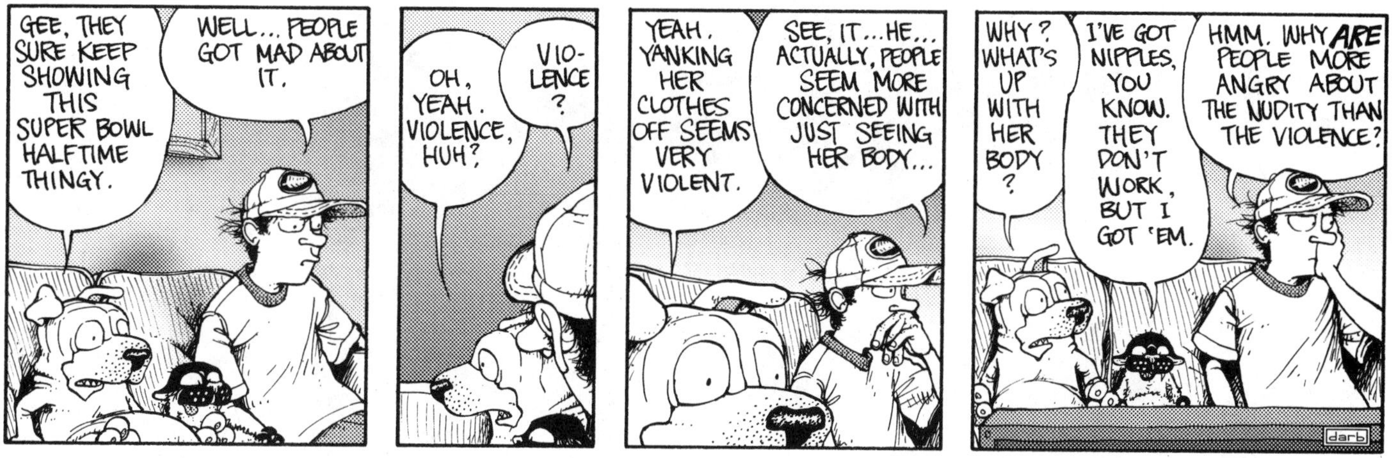
GEE, THEY SURE KEEP SHOWING THIS SUPER BOWL HALFTIME THINGY.
WELL... PEOPLE GOT MAD ABOUT IT.
OH, YEAH. VIOLENCE, HUH?
VIO-LENCE?
YEAH. YANKING HER CLOTHES OFF SEEMS VERY VIOLENT.
SEE, IT... HE... ACTUALLY, PEOPLE SEEM MORE CONCERNED WITH JUST SEEING HER BODY...
WHY? WHAT'S UP WITH HER BODY?
I'VE GOT NIPPLES, YOU KNOW. THEY DON'T WORK, BUT I GOT 'EM.
HMM. WHY ARE PEOPLE MORE ANGRY ABOUT THE NUDITY THAN THE VIOLENCE?
darb

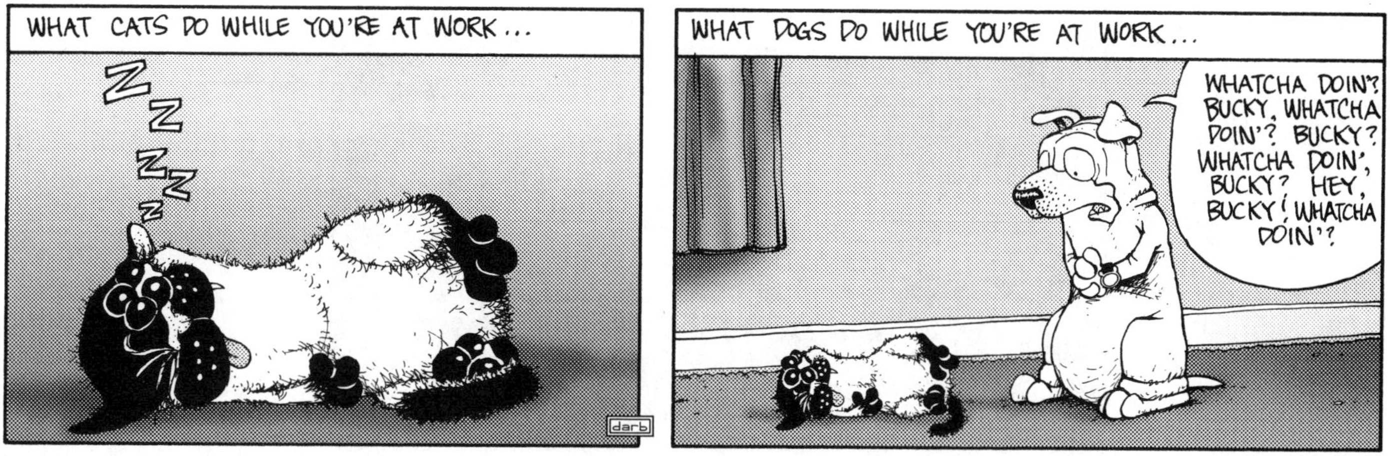
WHAT CATS DO WHILE YOU'RE AT WORK...
Z Z Z Z Z
darb
WHAT DOGS DO WHILE YOU'RE AT WORK...
WHATCHA DOIN'? BUCKY, WHATCHA DOIN'? BUCKY? WHATCHA DOIN', BUCKY? HEY, BUCKY! WHATCHA DOIN'?

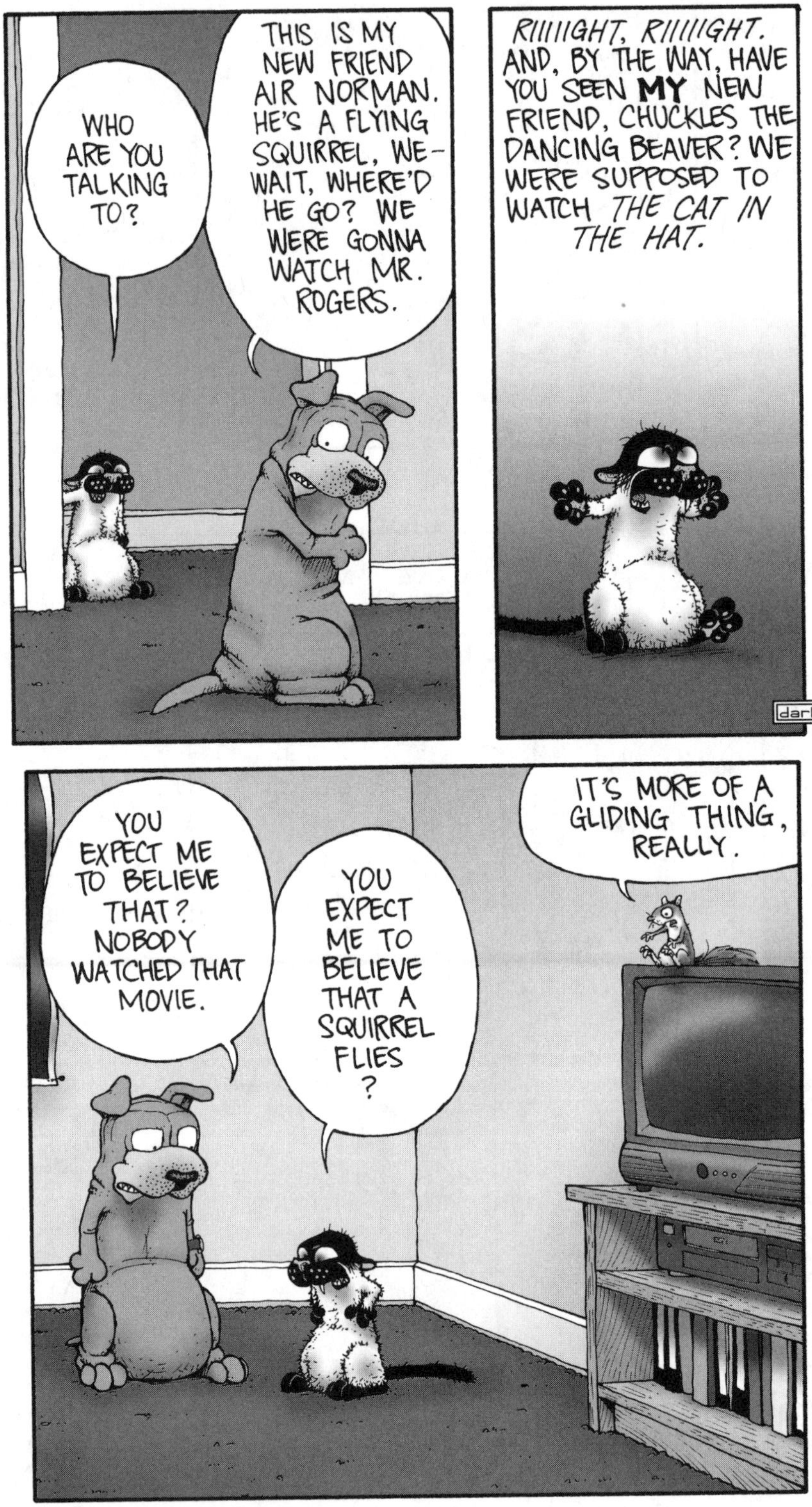
WHO ARE YOU TALKING TO?
THIS IS MY NEW FRIEND AIR NORMAN. HE'S A FLYING SQUIRREL, WE- WAIT, WHERE'D HE GO? WE WERE GONNA WATCH MR. ROGERS.
RIIIIIGHT, RIIIIIGHT. AND, BY THE WAY, HAVE YOU SEEN **MY** NEW FRIEND, CHUCKLES THE DANCING BEAVER? WE WERE SUPPOSED TO WATCH *THE CAT IN THE HAT.*
darb
YOU EXPECT ME TO BELIEVE THAT? NOBODY WATCHED THAT MOVIE.
YOU EXPECT ME TO BELIEVE THAT A SQUIRREL FLIES?
IT'S MORE OF A GLIDING THING, REALLY.

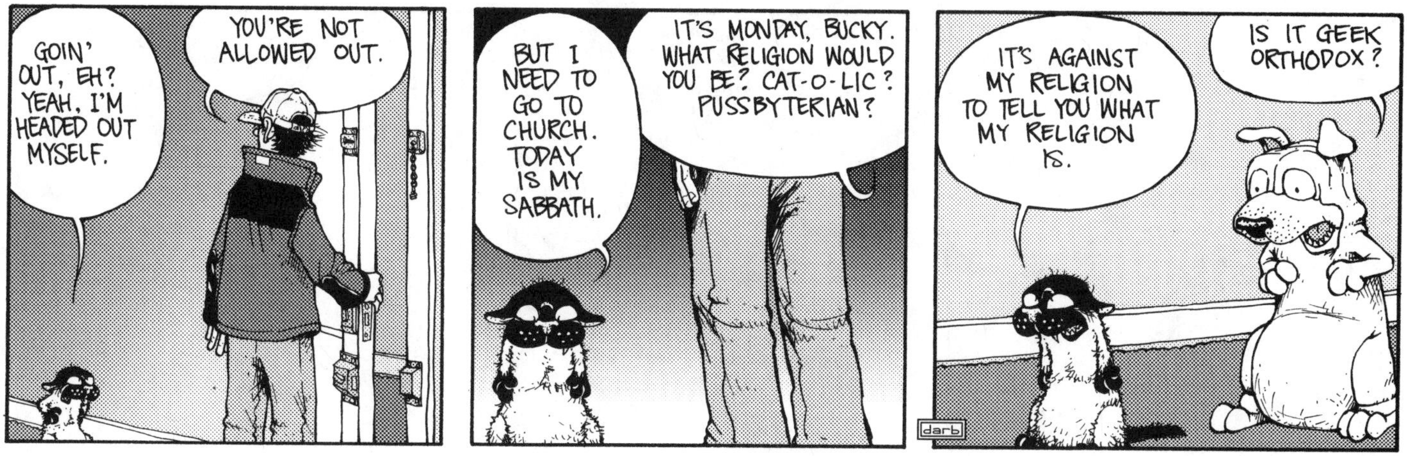
GOIN' OUT, EH? YEAH, I'M HEADED OUT MYSELF.
YOU'RE NOT ALLOWED OUT.
BUT I NEED TO GO TO CHURCH. TODAY IS MY SABBATH.
IT'S MONDAY, BUCKY. WHAT RELIGION WOULD YOU BE? CAT-O-LIC? PUSSBYTERIAN?
IT'S AGAINST MY RELIGION TO TELL YOU WHAT MY RELIGION IS.
IS IT GEEK ORTHODOX?
darb

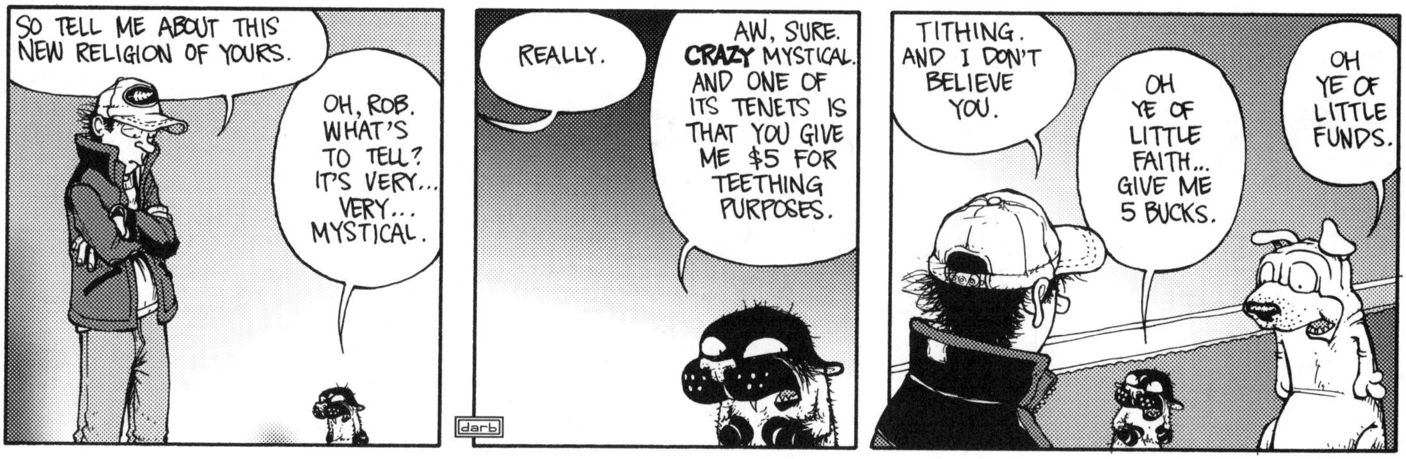
SO TELL ME ABOUT THIS NEW RELIGION OF YOURS.
OH, ROB. WHAT'S TO TELL? IT'S VERY... VERY... MYSTICAL.
REALLY.
AW, SURE. CRAZY MYSTICAL. AND ONE OF ITS TENETS IS THAT YOU GIVE ME $5 FOR TEETHING PURPOSES.
TITHING. AND I DON'T BELIEVE YOU.
OH YE OF LITTLE FAITH... GIVE ME 5 BUCKS.
OH YE OF LITTLE FUNDS.
darb

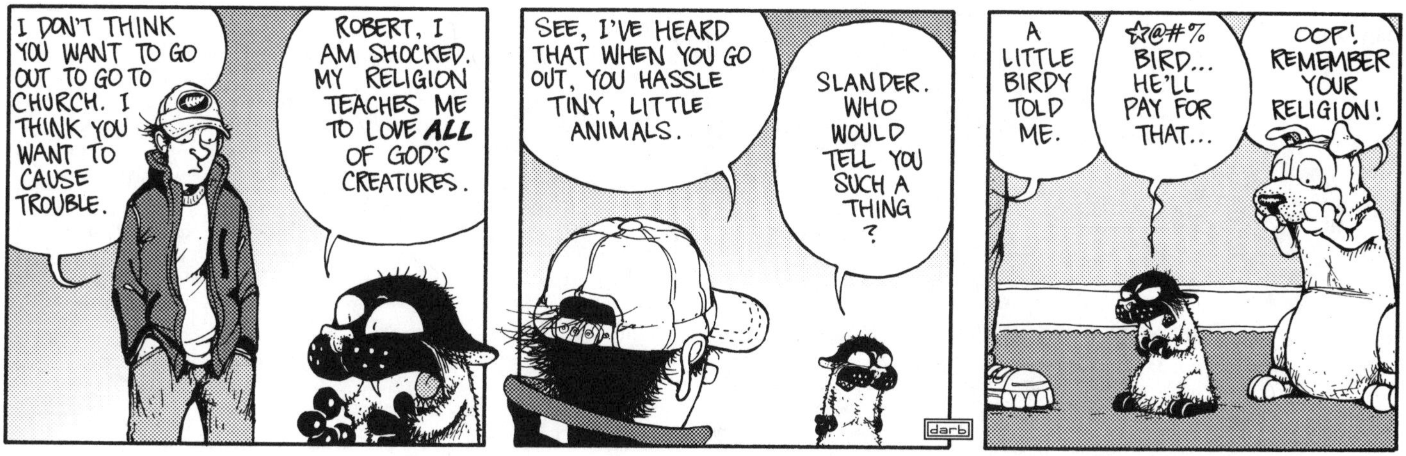
I DON'T THINK YOU WANT TO GO OUT TO GO TO CHURCH. I THINK YOU WANT TO CAUSE TROUBLE.
ROBERT, I AM SHOCKED. MY RELIGION TEACHES ME TO LOVE ALL OF GOD'S CREATURES.
SEE, I'VE HEARD THAT WHEN YOU GO OUT, YOU HASSLE TINY, LITTLE ANIMALS.
SLANDER. WHO WOULD TELL YOU SUCH A THING?
A LITTLE BIRDY TOLD ME.
☆@#% BIRD... HE'LL PAY FOR THAT...
OOP! REMEMBER YOUR RELIGION!
darb

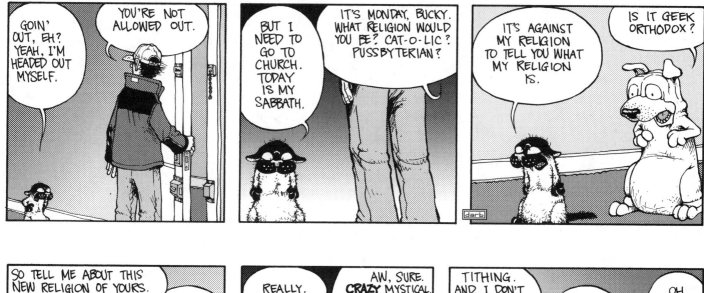

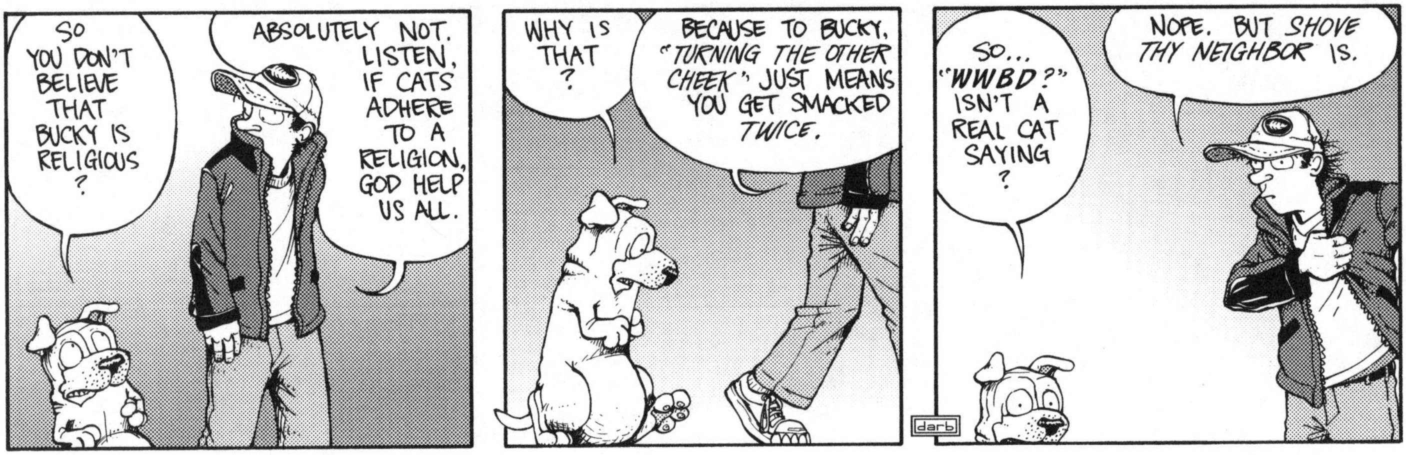
SO YOU DON'T BELIEVE THAT BUCKY IS RELIGIOUS?
ABSOLUTELY NOT. LISTEN, IF CATS ADHERE TO A RELIGION, GOD HELP US ALL.
WHY IS THAT?
BECAUSE TO BUCKY, "*TURNING THE OTHER CHEEK*" JUST MEANS YOU GET SMACKED *TWICE*.
SO... "***WWBD?***" ISN'T A REAL CAT SAYING?
NOPE. BUT *SHOVE THY NEIGHBOR* IS.

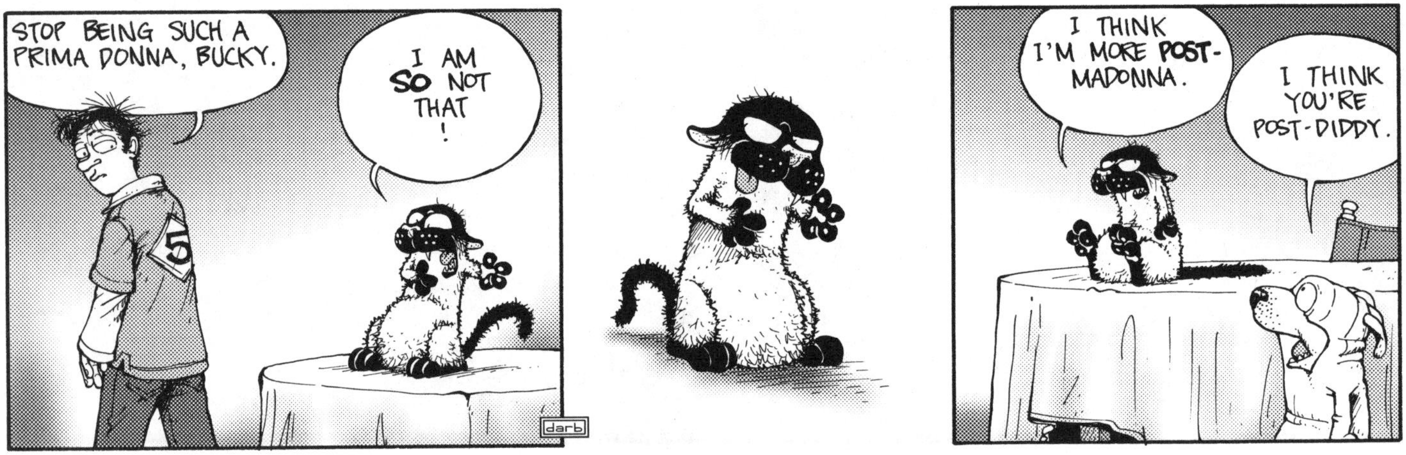
STOP BEING SUCH A PRIMA DONNA, BUCKY.
I AM **SO** NOT THAT!
I THINK I'M MORE **POST**-MADONNA.
I THINK YOU'RE POST-DIDDY.

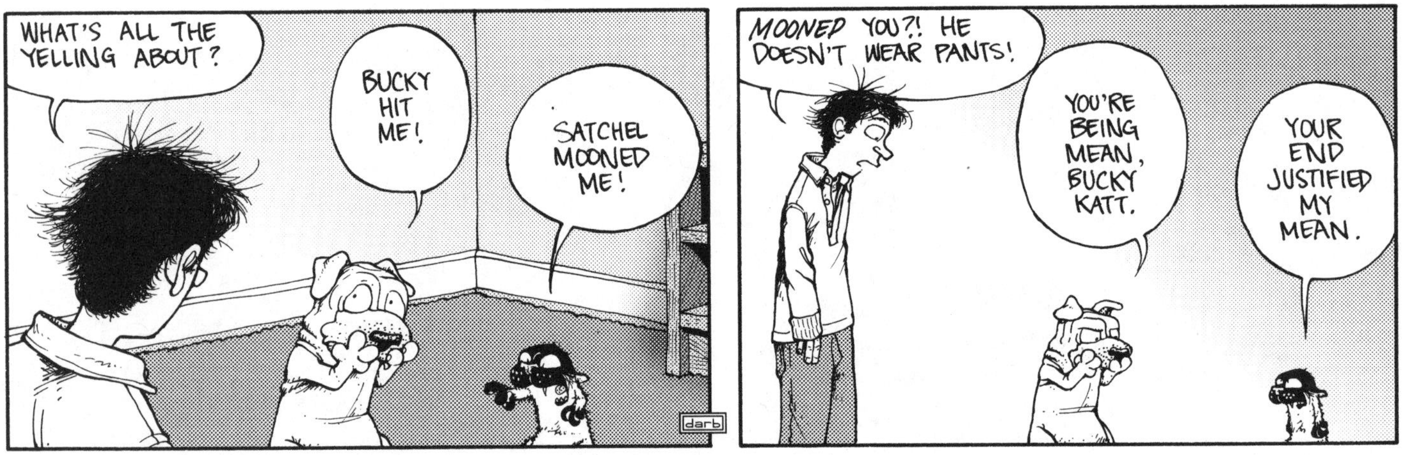
WHAT'S ALL THE YELLING ABOUT?
BUCKY HIT ME!
SATCHEL MOONED ME!
MOONED YOU?! HE DOESN'T WEAR PANTS!
YOU'RE BEING MEAN, BUCKY KATT.
YOUR END JUSTIFIED MY MEAN.

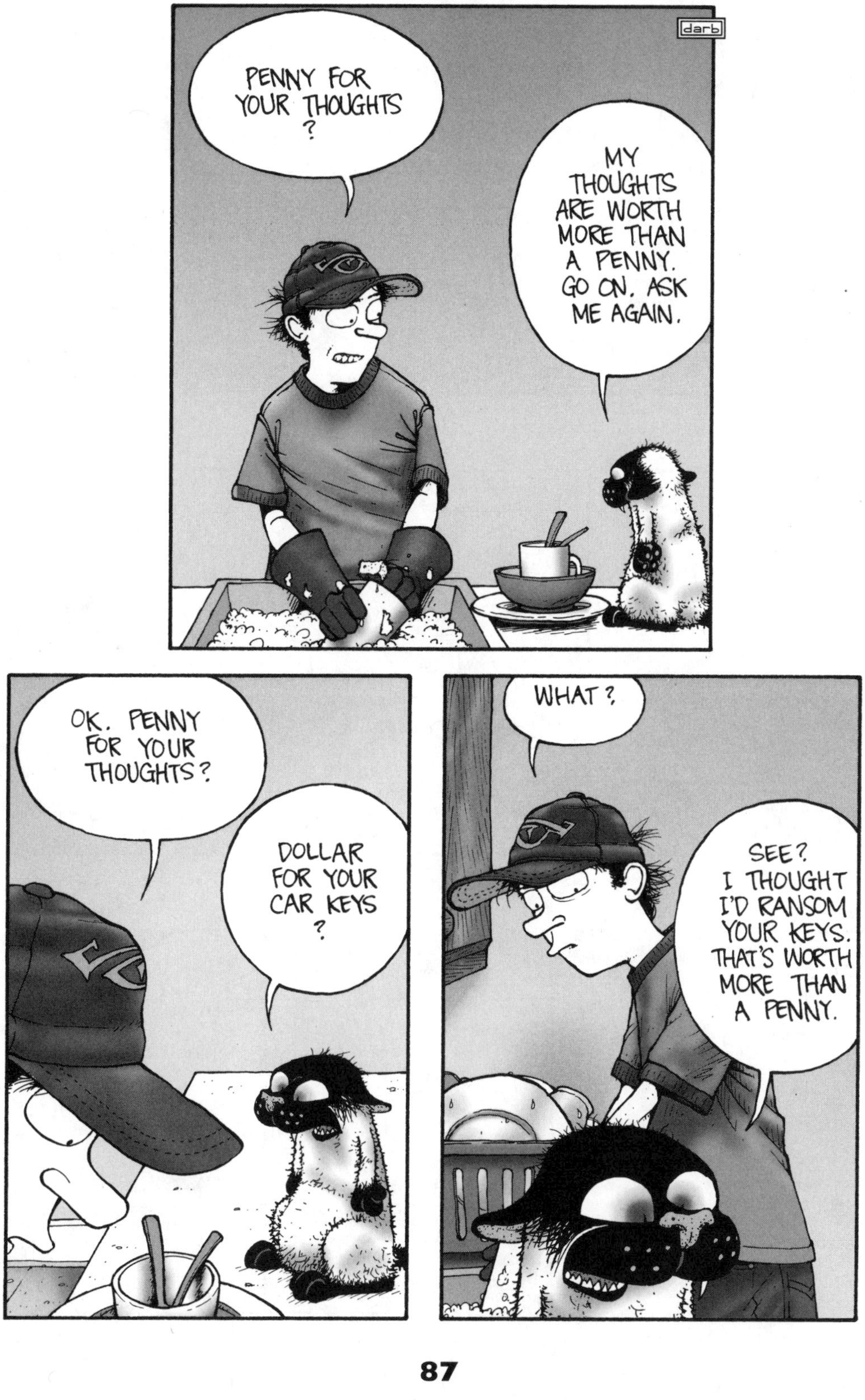
darb
PENNY FOR YOUR THOUGHTS ?
MY THOUGHTS ARE WORTH MORE THAN A PENNY. GO ON, ASK ME AGAIN.
OK. PENNY FOR YOUR THOUGHTS?
DOLLAR FOR YOUR CAR KEYS ?
WHAT?
SEE? I THOUGHT I'D RANSOM YOUR KEYS. THAT'S WORTH MORE THAN A PENNY.

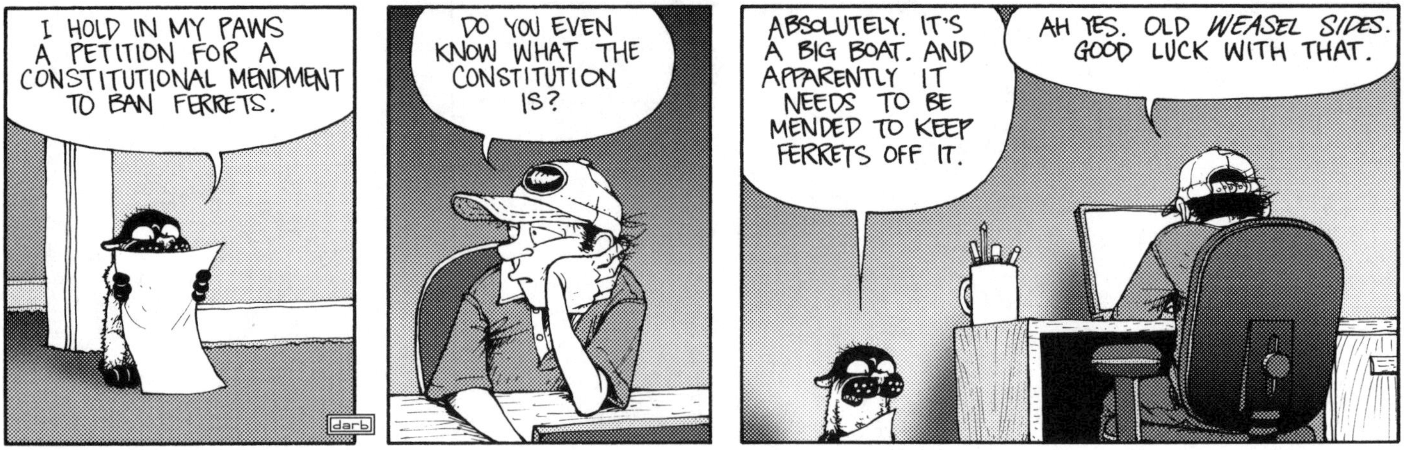
I HOLD IN MY PAWS A PETITION FOR A CONSTITUTIONAL MENDMENT TO BAN FERRETS.
darb
DO YOU EVEN KNOW WHAT THE CONSTITUTION IS?
ABSOLUTELY. IT'S A BIG BOAT. AND APPARENTLY IT NEEDS TO BE MENDED TO KEEP FERRETS OFF IT.
AH YES. OLD *WEASEL SIDES*. GOOD LUCK WITH THAT.

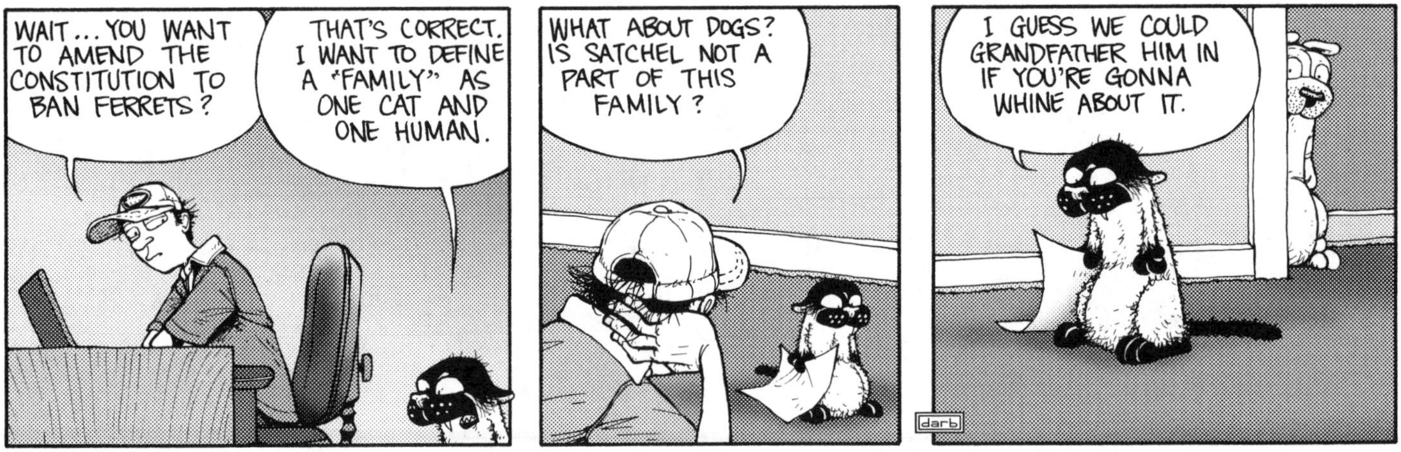
WAIT... YOU WANT TO AMEND THE CONSTITUTION TO BAN FERRETS?
THAT'S CORRECT. I WANT TO DEFINE A "FAMILY" AS ONE CAT AND ONE HUMAN.
WHAT ABOUT DOGS? IS SATCHEL NOT A PART OF THIS FAMILY?
I GUESS WE COULD GRANDFATHER HIM IN IF YOU'RE GONNA WHINE ABOUT IT.
darb

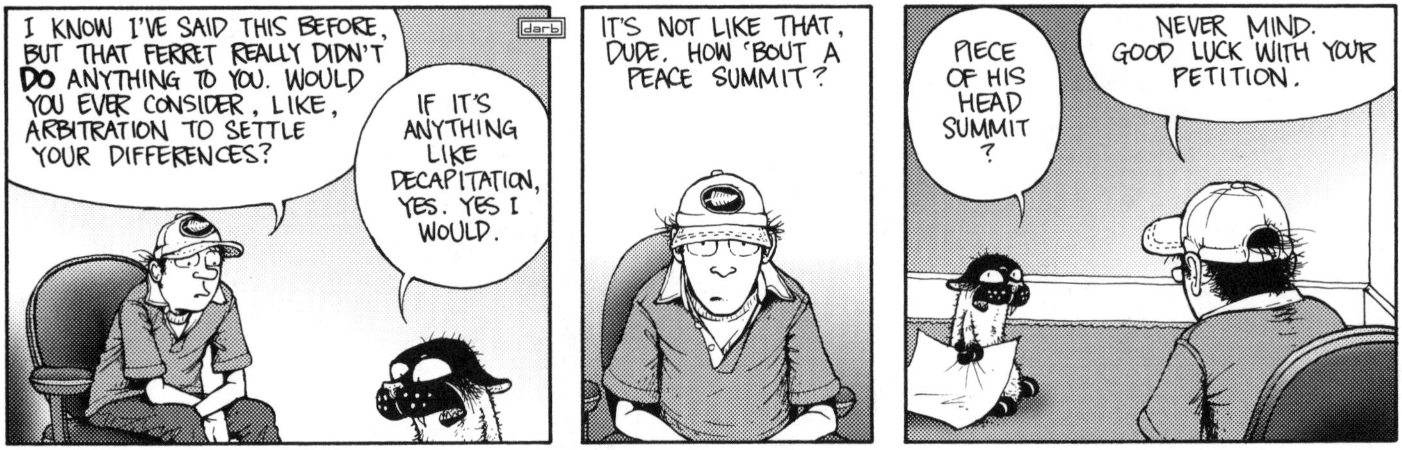
darb
I KNOW I'VE SAID THIS BEFORE, BUT THAT FERRET REALLY DIDN'T **DO** ANYTHING TO YOU. WOULD YOU EVER CONSIDER, LIKE, ARBITRATION TO SETTLE YOUR DIFFERENCES?
IF IT'S ANYTHING LIKE DECAPITATION, YES. YES I WOULD.
IT'S NOT LIKE THAT, DUDE. HOW 'BOUT A PEACE SUMMIT?
PIECE OF HIS HEAD SUMMIT?
NEVER MIND. GOOD LUCK WITH YOUR PETITION.

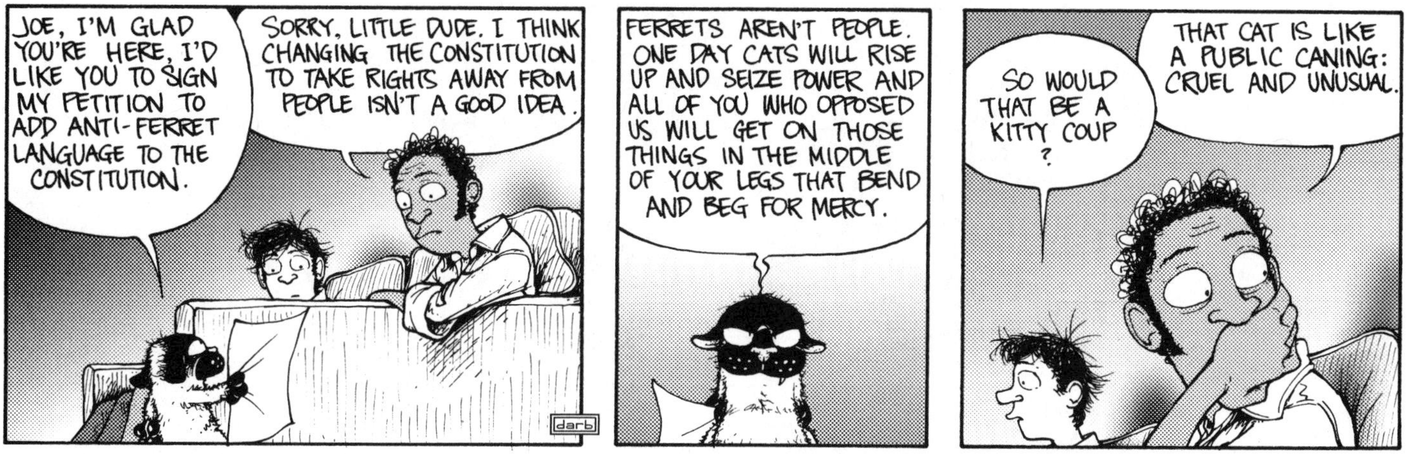
JOE, I'M GLAD YOU'RE HERE, I'D LIKE YOU TO SIGN MY PETITION TO ADD ANTI-FERRET LANGUAGE TO THE CONSTITUTION.
SORRY, LITTLE DUDE. I THINK CHANGING THE CONSTITUTION TO TAKE RIGHTS AWAY FROM PEOPLE ISN'T A GOOD IDEA.
darb
FERRETS AREN'T PEOPLE. ONE DAY CATS WILL RISE UP AND SEIZE POWER AND ALL OF YOU WHO OPPOSED US WILL GET ON THOSE THINGS IN THE MIDDLE OF YOUR LEGS THAT BEND AND BEG FOR MERCY.
SO WOULD THAT BE A KITTY COUP?
THAT CAT IS LIKE A PUBLIC CANING: CRUEL AND UNUSUAL.

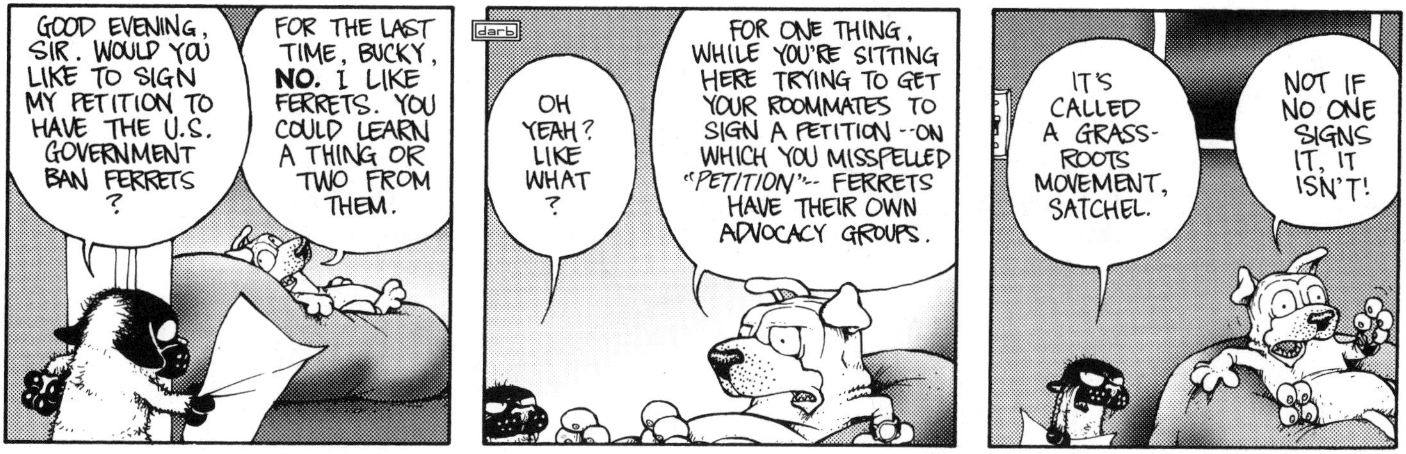
GOOD EVENING, SIR. WOULD YOU LIKE TO SIGN MY PETITION TO HAVE THE U.S. GOVERNMENT BAN FERRETS?
FOR THE LAST TIME, BUCKY, NO. I LIKE FERRETS. YOU COULD LEARN A THING OR TWO FROM THEM.
darb
OH YEAH? LIKE WHAT?
FOR ONE THING, WHILE YOU'RE SITTING HERE TRYING TO GET YOUR ROOMMATES TO SIGN A PETITION--ON WHICH YOU MISSPELLED "PETITION"--FERRETS HAVE THEIR OWN ADVOCACY GROUPS.
IT'S CALLED A GRASS-ROOTS MOVEMENT, SATCHEL.
NOT IF NO ONE SIGNS IT, IT ISN'T!

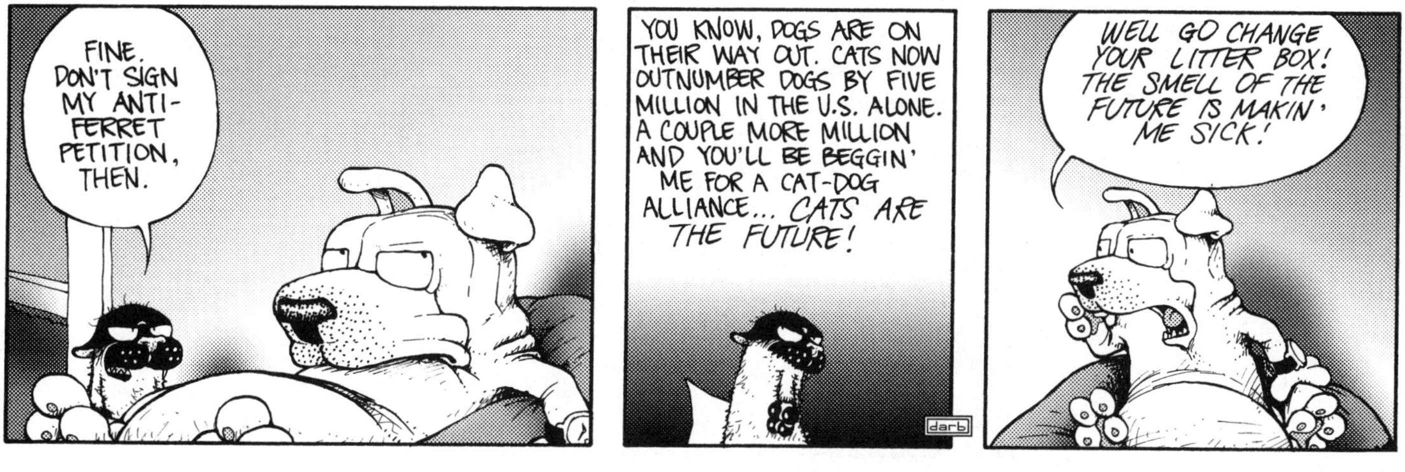
FINE. DON'T SIGN MY ANTI-FERRET PETITION, THEN.
YOU KNOW, DOGS ARE ON THEIR WAY OUT. CATS NOW OUTNUMBER DOGS BY FIVE MILLION IN THE U.S. ALONE. A COUPLE MORE MILLION AND YOU'LL BE BEGGIN' ME FOR A CAT-DOG ALLIANCE... CATS ARE THE FUTURE!
darb
WELL GO CHANGE YOUR LITTER BOX! THE SMELL OF THE FUTURE IS MAKIN' ME SICK!

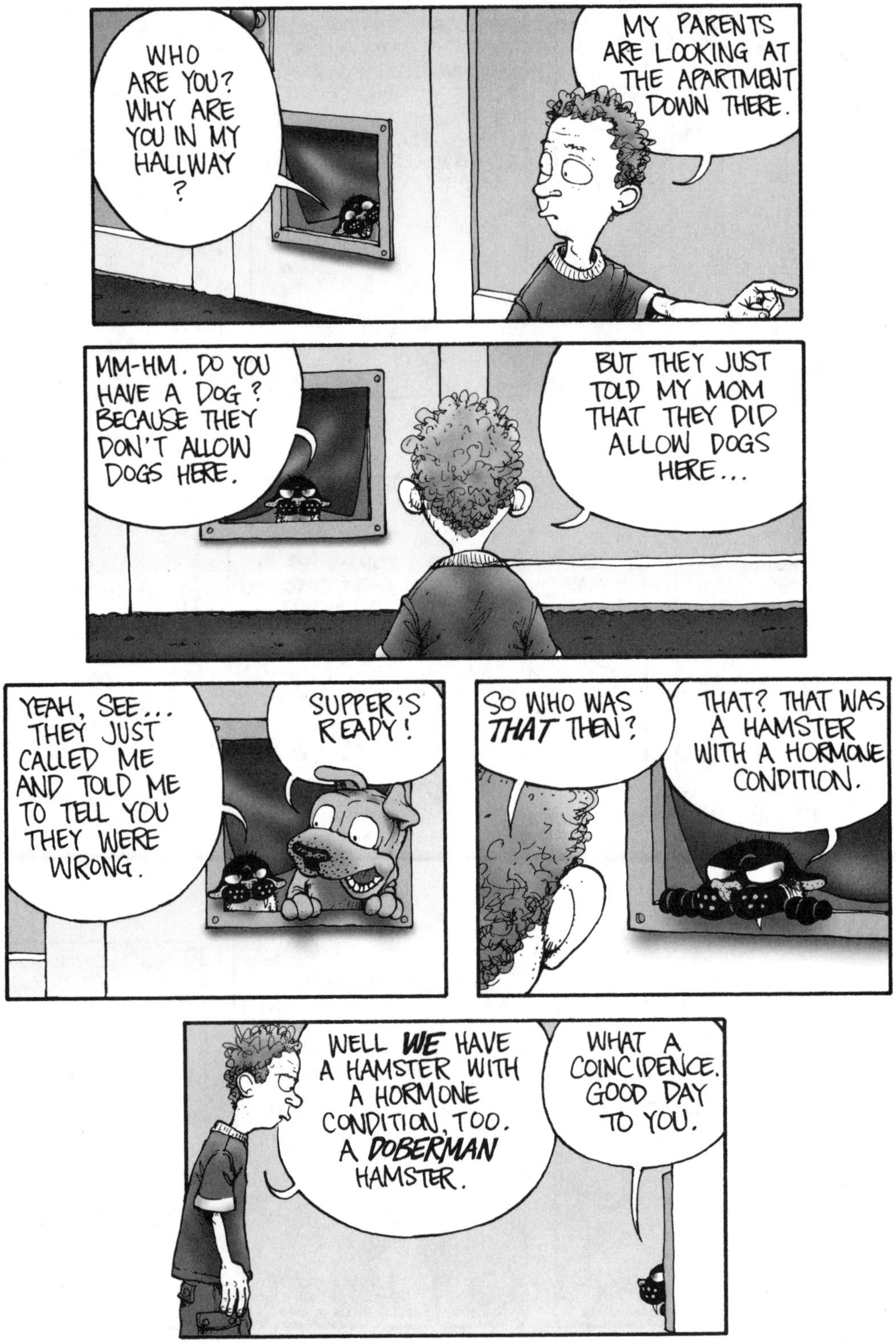
WHO ARE YOU? WHY ARE YOU IN MY HALLWAY ?
MY PARENTS ARE LOOKING AT THE APARTMENT DOWN THERE.
MM-HM. DO YOU HAVE A DOG? BECAUSE THEY DON'T ALLOW DOGS HERE.
BUT THEY JUST TOLD MY MOM THAT THEY DID ALLOW DOGS HERE...
YEAH, SEE... THEY JUST CALLED ME AND TOLD ME TO TELL YOU THEY WERE WRONG.
SUPPER'S READY!
SO WHO WAS **THAT** THEN?
THAT? THAT WAS A HAMSTER WITH A HORMONE CONDITION.
WELL **WE** HAVE A HAMSTER WITH A HORMONE CONDITION, TOO. A **DOBERMAN** HAMSTER.
WHAT A COINCIDENCE. GOOD DAY TO YOU.

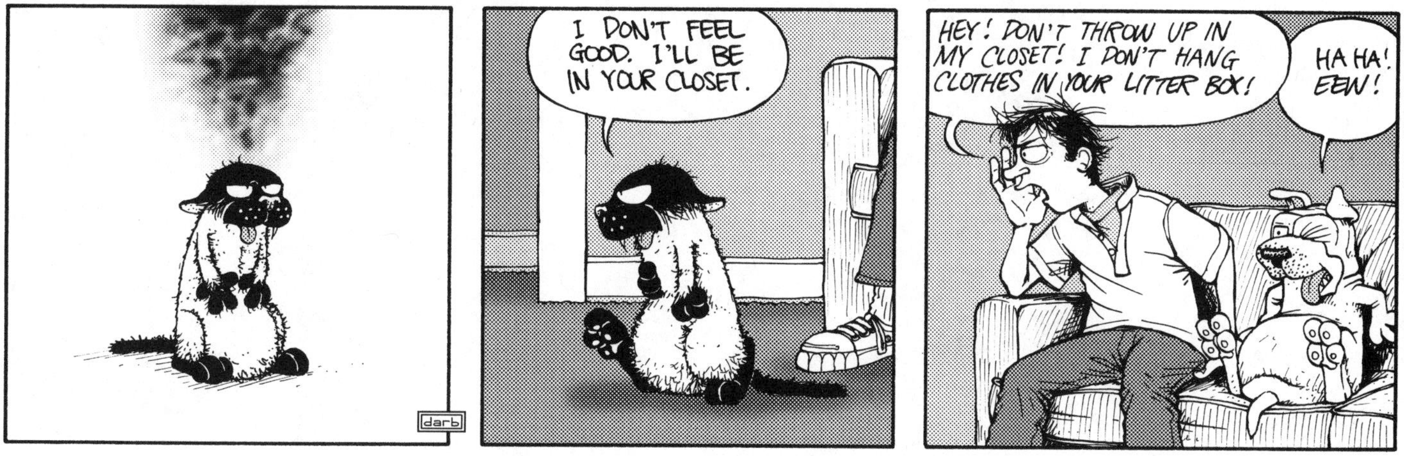
I DON'T FEEL GOOD. I'LL BE IN YOUR CLOSET.
HEY! DON'T THROW UP IN MY CLOSET! I DON'T HANG CLOTHES IN YOUR LITTER BOX!
HA HA! EEW!
darb

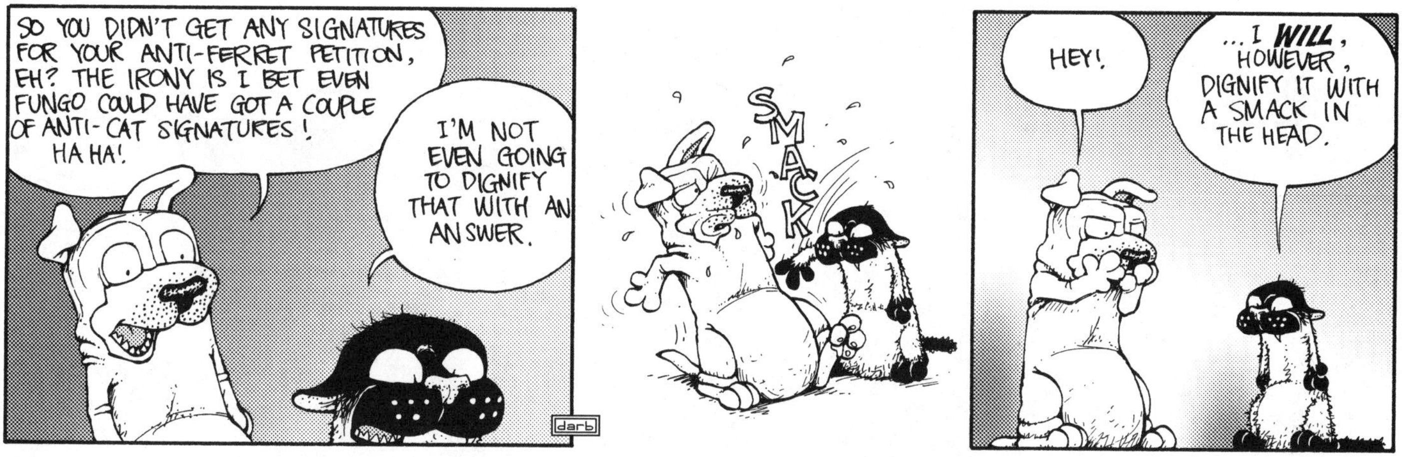
SO YOU DIDN'T GET ANY SIGNATURES FOR YOUR ANTI-FERRET PETITION, EH? THE IRONY IS I BET EVEN FUNGO COULD HAVE GOT A COUPLE OF ANTI-CAT SIGNATURES! HA HA!
I'M NOT EVEN GOING TO DIGNIFY THAT WITH AN ANSWER.
darb
SMACK
HEY!
...I WILL, HOWEVER, DIGNIFY IT WITH A SMACK IN THE HEAD.

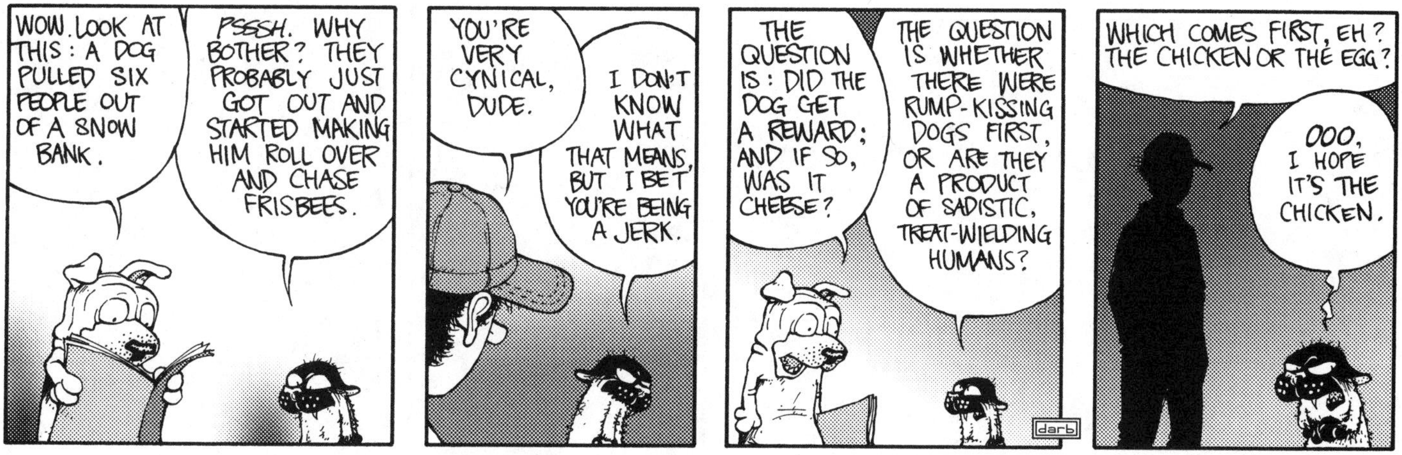
WOW. LOOK AT THIS: A DOG PULLED SIX PEOPLE OUT OF A SNOW BANK.
PSSSH. WHY BOTHER? THEY PROBABLY JUST GOT OUT AND STARTED MAKING HIM ROLL OVER AND CHASE FRISBEES.
YOU'RE VERY CYNICAL, DUDE.
I DON'T KNOW WHAT THAT MEANS, BUT I BET YOU'RE BEING A JERK.
THE QUESTION IS: DID THE DOG GET A REWARD; AND IF SO, WAS IT CHEESE?
THE QUESTION IS WHETHER THERE WERE RUMP-KISSING DOGS FIRST, OR ARE THEY A PRODUCT OF SADISTIC, TREAT-WIELDING HUMANS?
darb
WHICH COMES FIRST, EH? THE CHICKEN OR THE EGG?
OOO, I HOPE IT'S THE CHICKEN.

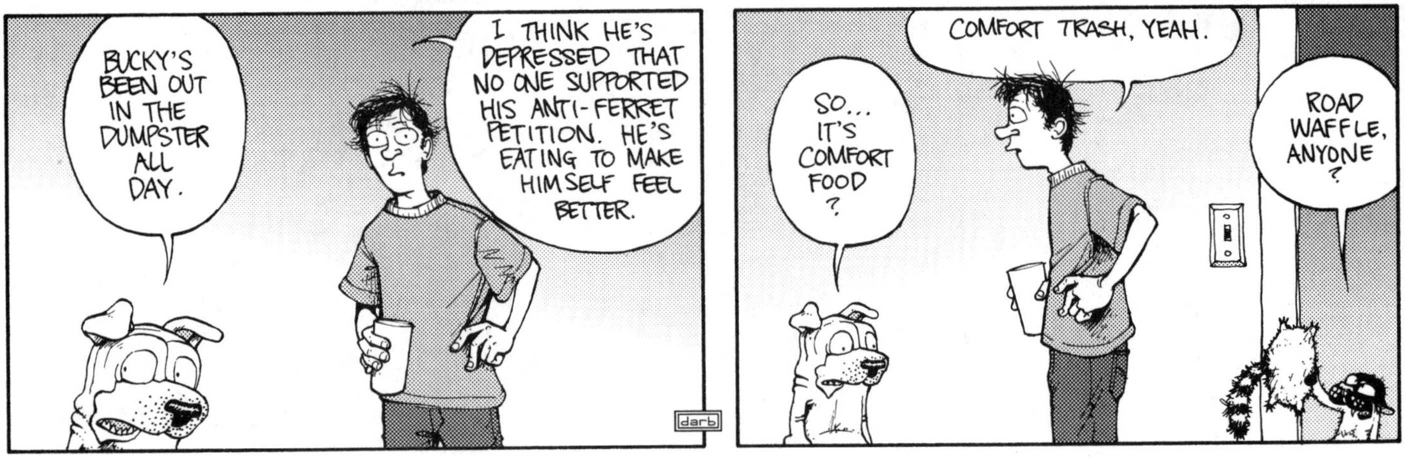
BUCKY'S BEEN OUT IN THE DUMPSTER ALL DAY.
I THINK HE'S DEPRESSED THAT NO ONE SUPPORTED HIS ANTI-FERRET PETITION. HE'S EATING TO MAKE HIMSELF FEEL BETTER.
darb
SO... IT'S COMFORT FOOD?
COMFORT TRASH, YEAH.
ROAD WAFFLE, ANYONE?

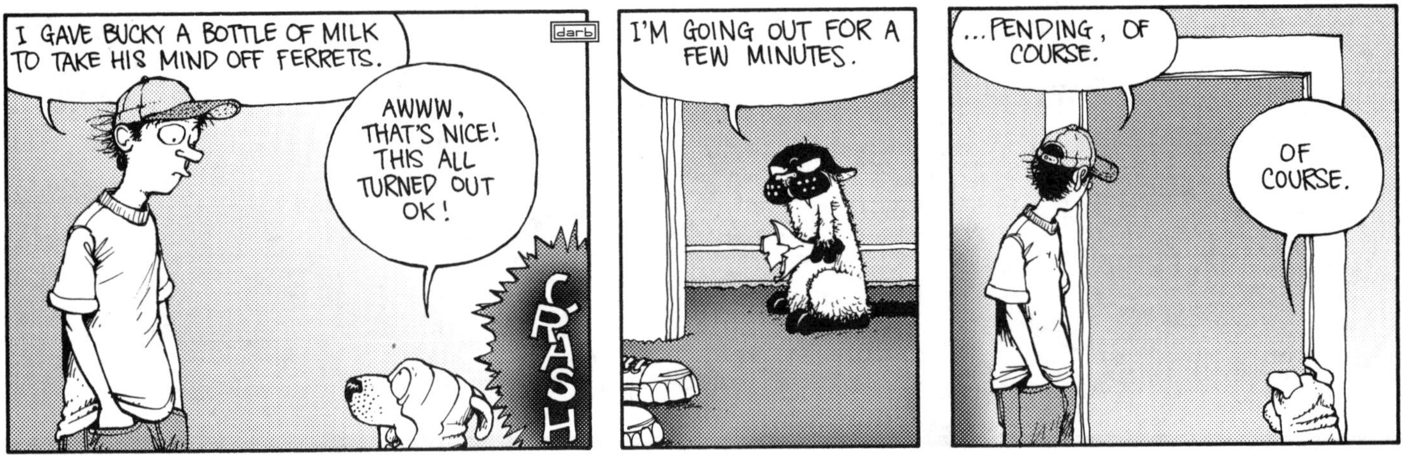
I GAVE BUCKY A BOTTLE OF MILK TO TAKE HIS MIND OFF FERRETS.
darb
AWWW, THAT'S NICE! THIS ALL TURNED OUT OK!
CRASH
I'M GOING OUT FOR A FEW MINUTES.
...PENDING, OF COURSE.
OF COURSE.

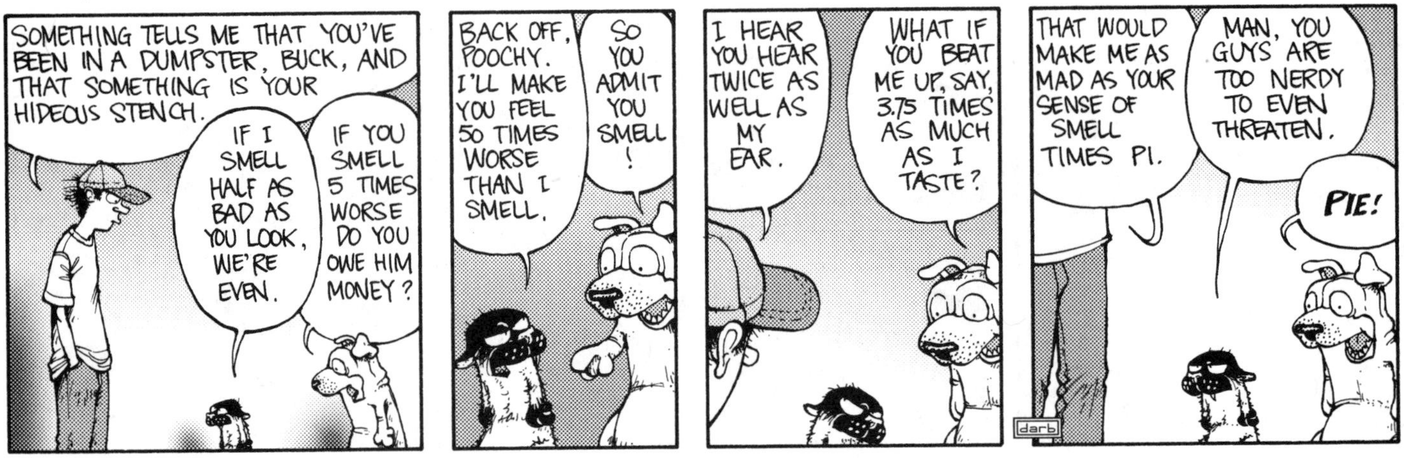
SOMETHING TELLS ME THAT YOU'VE BEEN IN A DUMPSTER, BUCK, AND THAT SOMETHING IS YOUR HIDEOUS STENCH.
IF I SMELL HALF AS BAD AS YOU LOOK, WE'RE EVEN.
IF YOU SMELL 5 TIMES WORSE DO YOU OWE HIM MONEY?
BACK OFF, POOCHY. I'LL MAKE YOU FEEL 50 TIMES WORSE THAN I SMELL.
SO YOU ADMIT YOU SMELL!
I HEAR YOU HEAR TWICE AS WELL AS MY EAR.
WHAT IF YOU BEAT ME UP, SAY, 3.75 TIMES AS MUCH AS I TASTE?
darb
THAT WOULD MAKE ME AS MAD AS YOUR SENSE OF SMELL TIMES PI.
MAN, YOU GUYS ARE TOO NERDY TO EVEN THREATEN.
PIE!

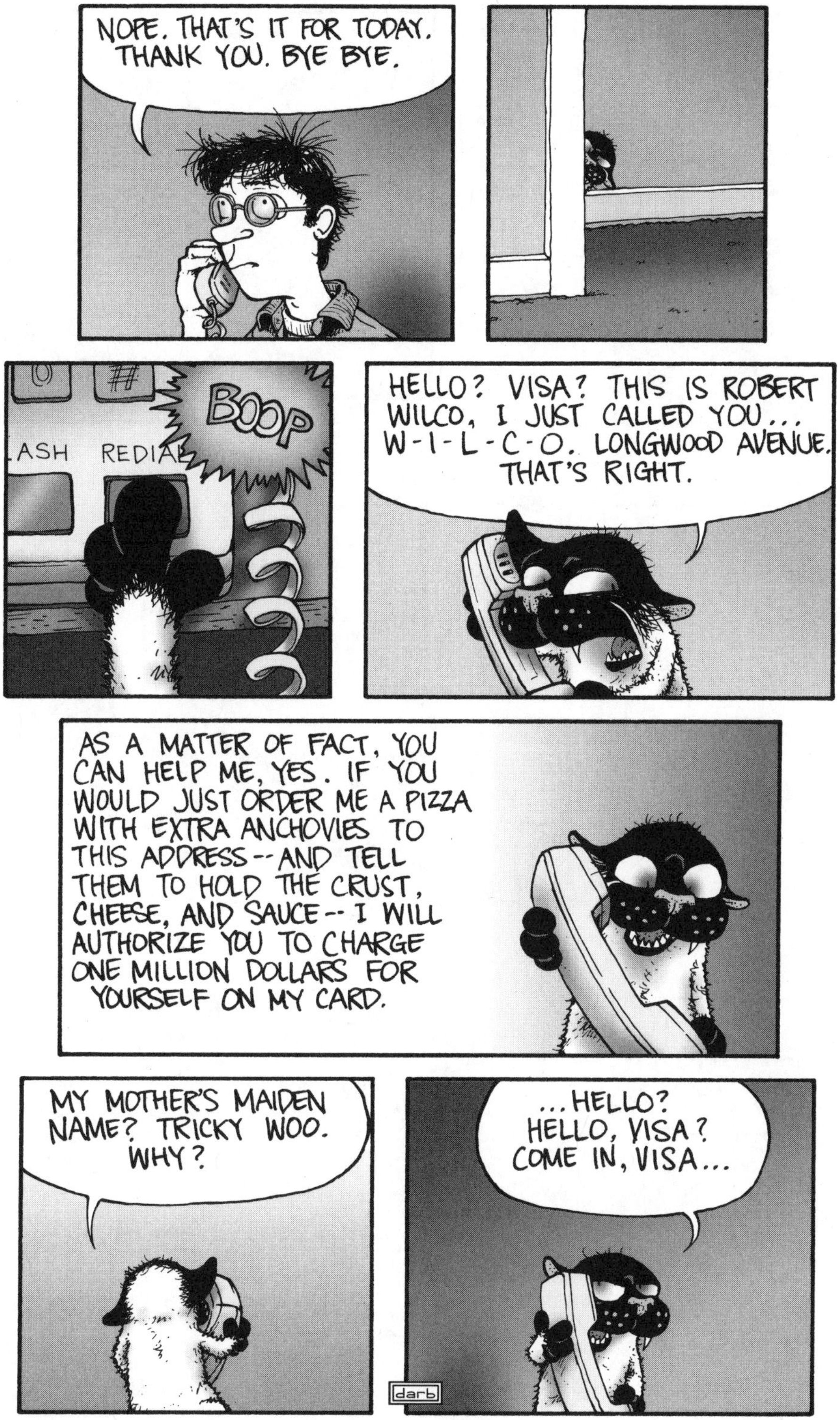
NOPE. THAT'S IT FOR TODAY. THANK YOU. BYE BYE.
FLASH
REDIAL
BOOP
HELLO? VISA? THIS IS ROBERT WILCO, I JUST CALLED YOU... W-I-L-C-O. LONGWOOD AVENUE. THAT'S RIGHT.
AS A MATTER OF FACT, YOU CAN HELP ME, YES. IF YOU WOULD JUST ORDER ME A PIZZA WITH EXTRA ANCHOVIES TO THIS ADDRESS--AND TELL THEM TO HOLD THE CRUST, CHEESE, AND SAUCE-- I WILL AUTHORIZE YOU TO CHARGE ONE MILLION DOLLARS FOR YOURSELF ON MY CARD.
MY MOTHER'S MAIDEN NAME? TRICKY WOO. WHY?
darb
...HELLO? HELLO, VISA? COME IN, VISA...

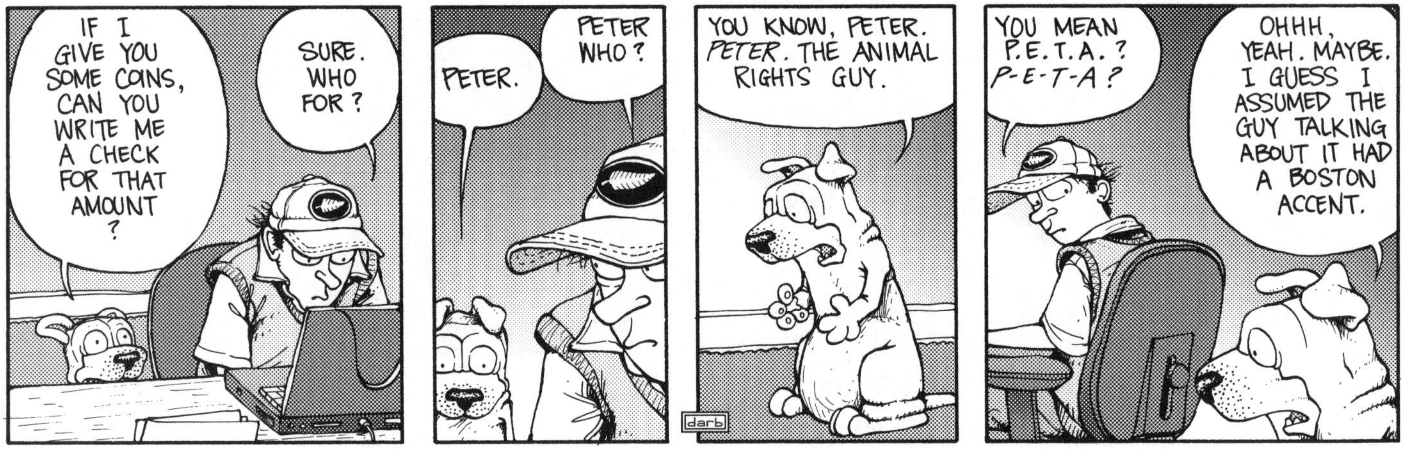
IF I GIVE YOU SOME COINS, CAN YOU WRITE ME A CHECK FOR THAT AMOUNT ?
SURE. WHO FOR ?
PETER.
PETER WHO ?
YOU KNOW, PETER. *PETER*. THE ANIMAL RIGHTS GUY.
YOU MEAN P.E.T.A. ? *P-E-T-A ?*
OHHH, YEAH. MAYBE. I GUESS I ASSUMED THE GUY TALKING ABOUT IT HAD A BOSTON ACCENT.
darb

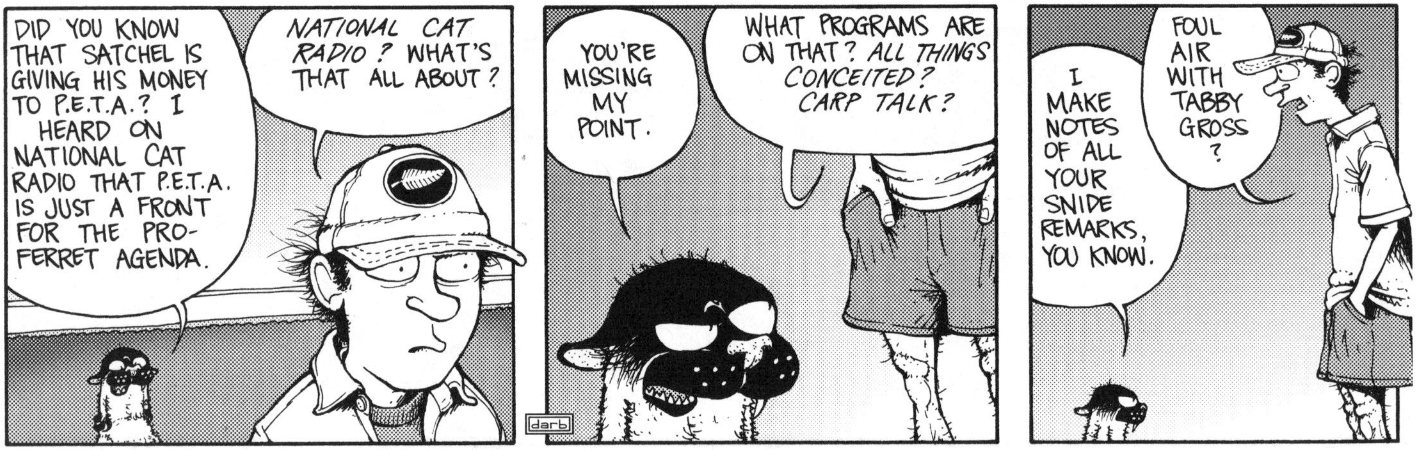
DID YOU KNOW THAT SATCHEL IS GIVING HIS MONEY TO P.E.T.A.? I HEARD ON NATIONAL CAT RADIO THAT P.E.T.A. IS JUST A FRONT FOR THE PRO-FERRET AGENDA.
NATIONAL CAT RADIO? WHAT'S THAT ALL ABOUT?
YOU'RE MISSING MY POINT.
WHAT PROGRAMS ARE ON THAT? *ALL THINGS CONCEITED? CARP TALK?*
I MAKE NOTES OF ALL YOUR SNIDE REMARKS, YOU KNOW.
FOUL AIR WITH TABBY GROSS ?
darb

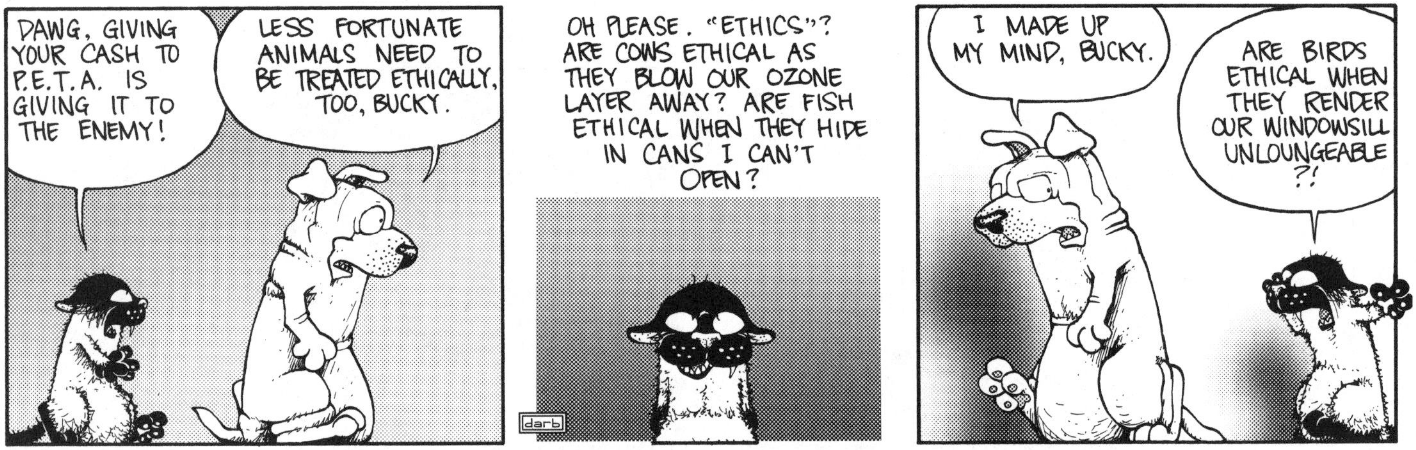
DAWG, GIVING YOUR CASH TO P.E.T.A. IS GIVING IT TO THE ENEMY!
LESS FORTUNATE ANIMALS NEED TO BE TREATED ETHICALLY, TOO, BUCKY.
OH PLEASE. "ETHICS"? ARE COWS ETHICAL AS THEY BLOW OUR OZONE LAYER AWAY? ARE FISH ETHICAL WHEN THEY HIDE IN CANS I CAN'T OPEN?
I MADE UP MY MIND, BUCKY.
ARE BIRDS ETHICAL WHEN THEY RENDER OUR WINDOWSILL UNLOUNGEABLE ?!
darb

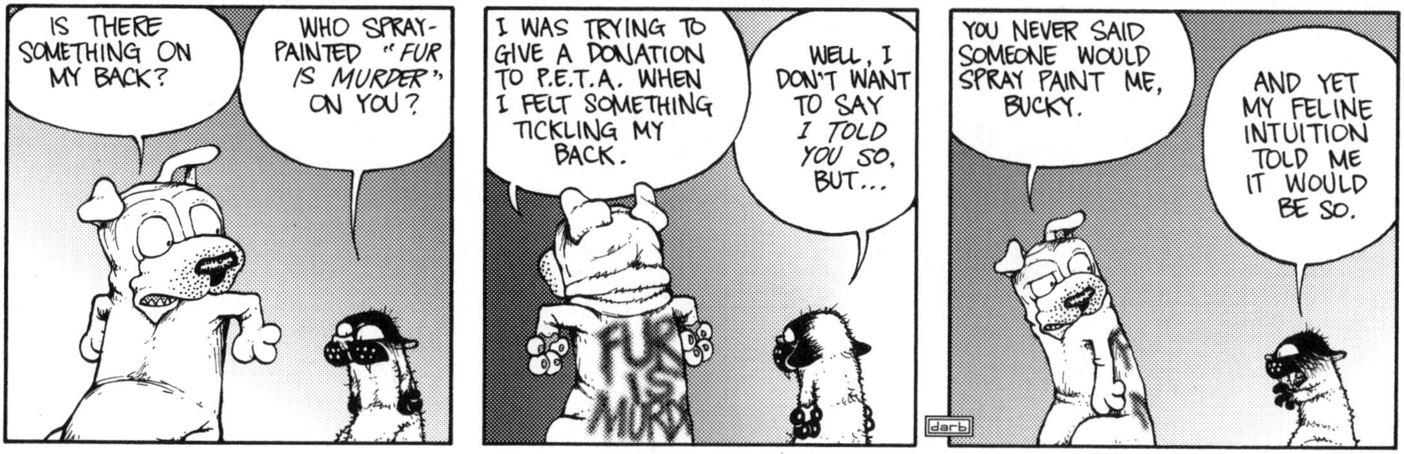
IS THERE SOMETHING ON MY BACK?
WHO SPRAY-PAINTED "FUR IS MURDER" ON YOU?
I WAS TRYING TO GIVE A DONATION TO P.E.T.A. WHEN I FELT SOMETHING TICKLING MY BACK.
WELL, I DON'T WANT TO SAY I TOLD YOU SO, BUT...
FUR IS MURD
YOU NEVER SAID SOMEONE WOULD SPRAY PAINT ME, BUCKY.
AND YET MY FELINE INTUITION TOLD ME IT WOULD BE SO.
darb

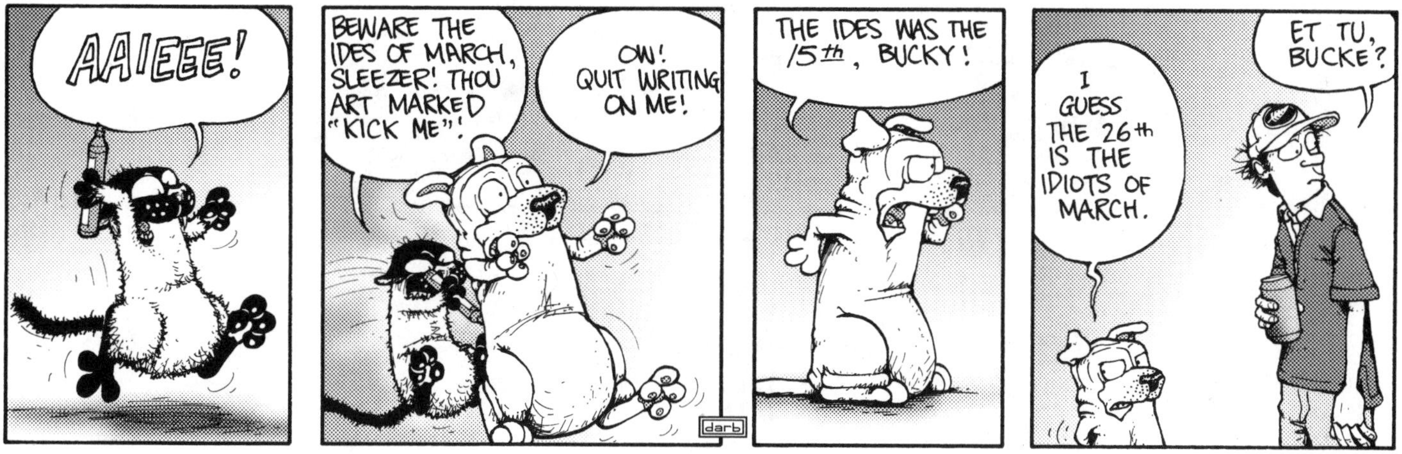
AAIEEE!
BEWARE THE IDES OF MARCH, SLEEZER! THOU ART MARKED "KICK ME"!
OW! QUIT WRITING ON ME!
darb
THE IDES WAS THE 15th, BUCKY!
I GUESS THE 26th IS THE IDIOTS OF MARCH.
ET TU, BUCKE?

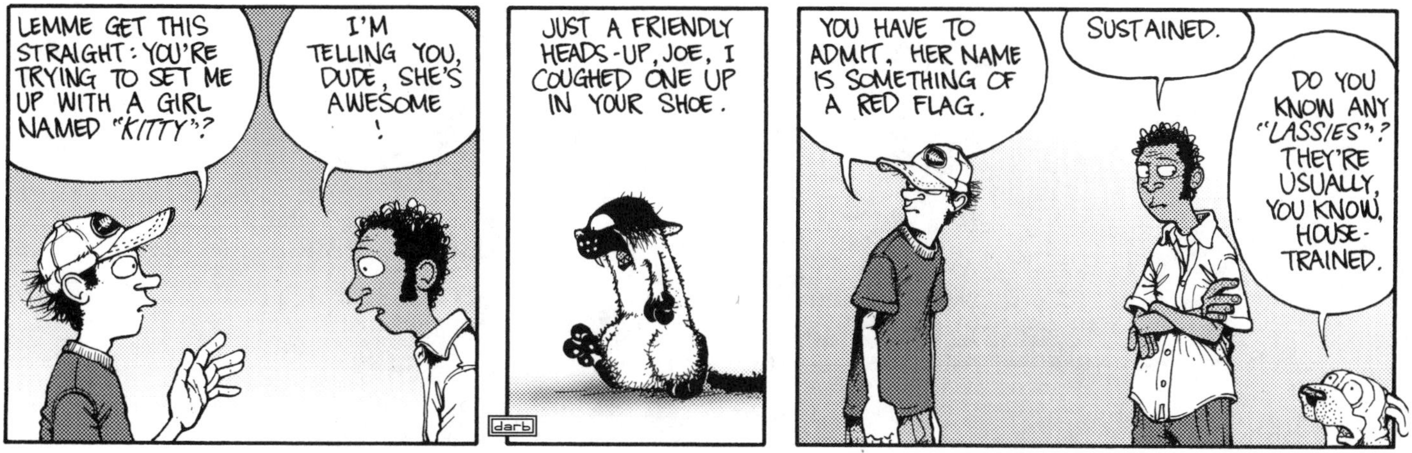
LEMME GET THIS STRAIGHT: YOU'RE TRYING TO SET ME UP WITH A GIRL NAMED "KITTY"?
I'M TELLING YOU, DUDE, SHE'S AWESOME!
darb
JUST A FRIENDLY HEADS-UP, JOE, I COUGHED ONE UP IN YOUR SHOE.
YOU HAVE TO ADMIT, HER NAME IS SOMETHING OF A RED FLAG.
SUSTAINED.
DO YOU KNOW ANY "LASSIES"? THEY'RE USUALLY, YOU KNOW, HOUSE-TRAINED.

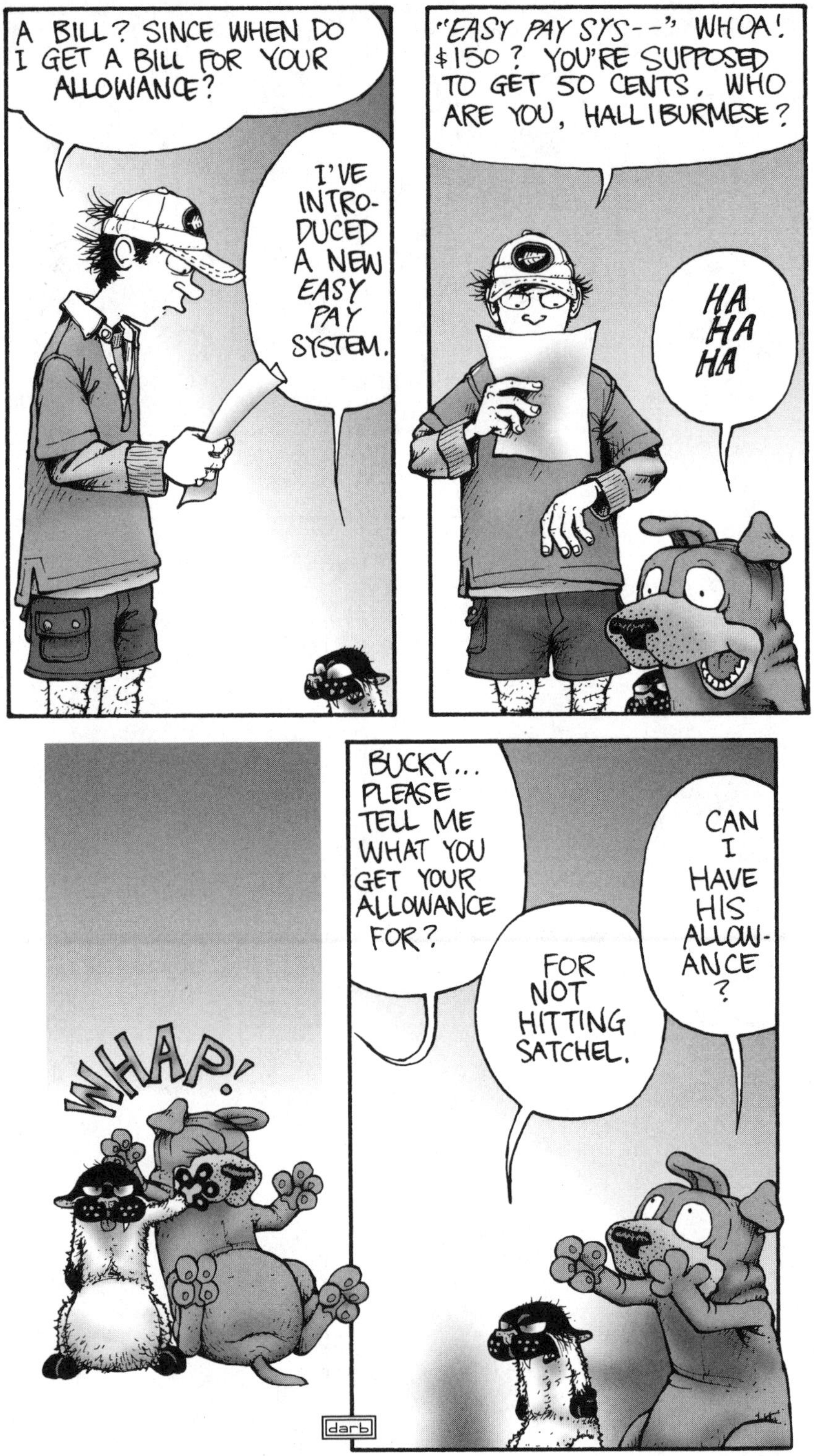
A BILL? SINCE WHEN DO I GET A BILL FOR YOUR ALLOWANCE?
I'VE INTRODUCED A NEW EASY PAY SYSTEM.
"EASY PAY SYS--" WHOA! $150? YOU'RE SUPPOSED TO GET 50 CENTS, WHO ARE YOU, HALLIBURMESE?
HA HA HA
BUCKY... PLEASE TELL ME WHAT YOU GET YOUR ALLOWANCE FOR?
FOR NOT HITTING SATCHEL.
CAN I HAVE HIS ALLOWANCE?
WHAP!
darb

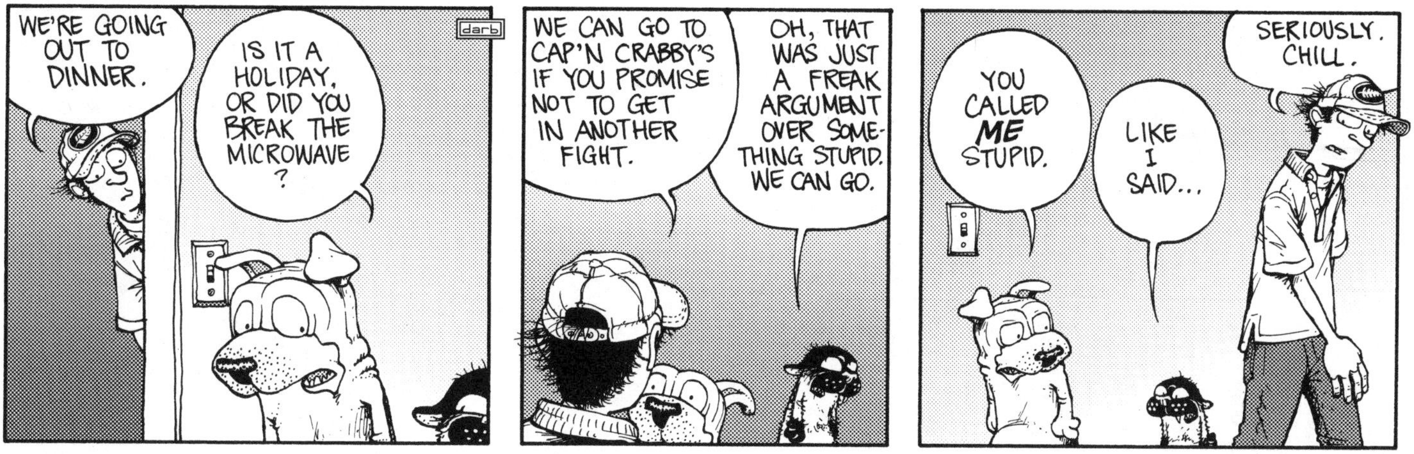
WE'RE GOING OUT TO DINNER.
IS IT A HOLIDAY, OR DID YOU BREAK THE MICROWAVE ?
WE CAN GO TO CAP'N CRABBY'S IF YOU PROMISE NOT TO GET IN ANOTHER FIGHT.
OH, THAT WAS JUST A FREAK ARGUMENT OVER SOME-THING STUPID. WE CAN GO.
SERIOUSLY. CHILL.
YOU CALLED ME STUPID.
LIKE I SAID...

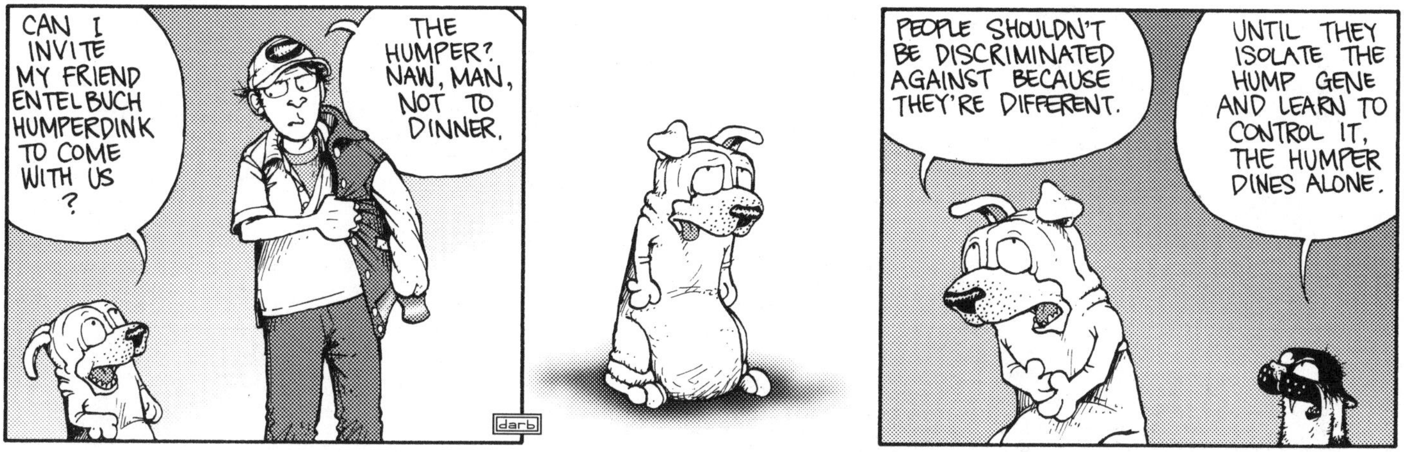
CAN I INVITE MY FRIEND ENTELBUCH HUMPERDINK TO COME WITH US ?
THE HUMPER? NAW, MAN, NOT TO DINNER.
PEOPLE SHOULDN'T BE DISCRIMINATED AGAINST BECAUSE THEY'RE DIFFERENT.
UNTIL THEY ISOLATE THE HUMP GENE AND LEARN TO CONTROL IT, THE HUMPER DINES ALONE.

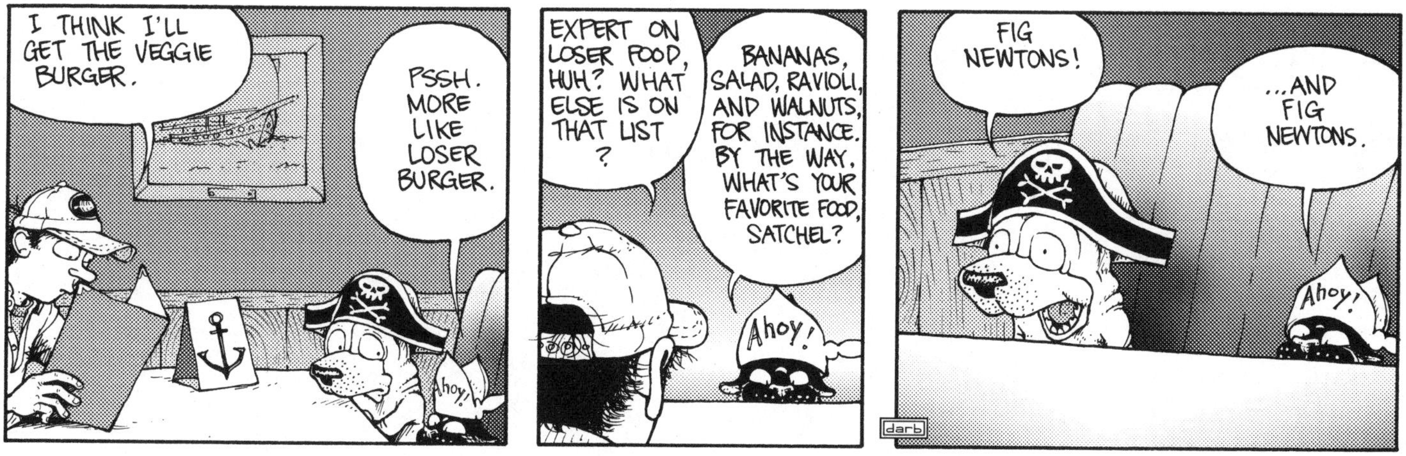
I THINK I'LL GET THE VEGGIE BURGER.
PSSH. MORE LIKE LOSER BURGER.
Ahoy!
EXPERT ON LOSER FOOD, HUH? WHAT ELSE IS ON THAT LIST ?
BANANAS, SALAD, RAVIOLI, AND WALNUTS, FOR INSTANCE. BY THE WAY, WHAT'S YOUR FAVORITE FOOD, SATCHEL?
Ahoy!
FIG NEWTONS!
...AND FIG NEWTONS.
Ahoy!

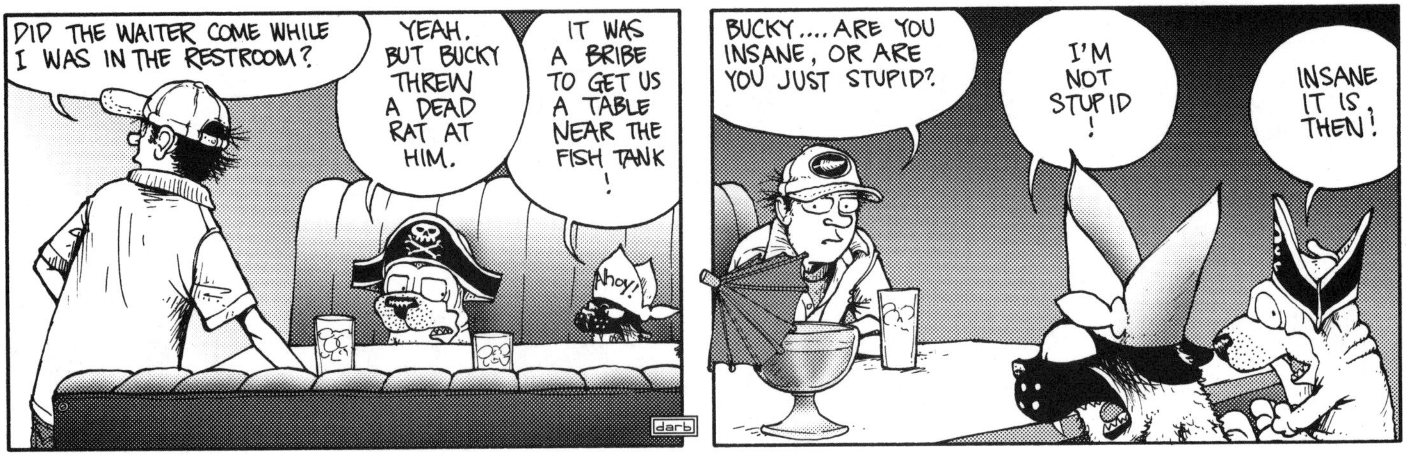
DID THE WAITER COME WHILE I WAS IN THE RESTROOM?
YEAH. BUT BUCKY THREW A DEAD RAT AT HIM.
IT WAS A BRIBE TO GET US A TABLE NEAR THE FISH TANK!
Ahoy!
darb
BUCKY.... ARE YOU INSANE, OR ARE YOU JUST STUPID?
I'M NOT STUPID!
INSANE IT IS, THEN!

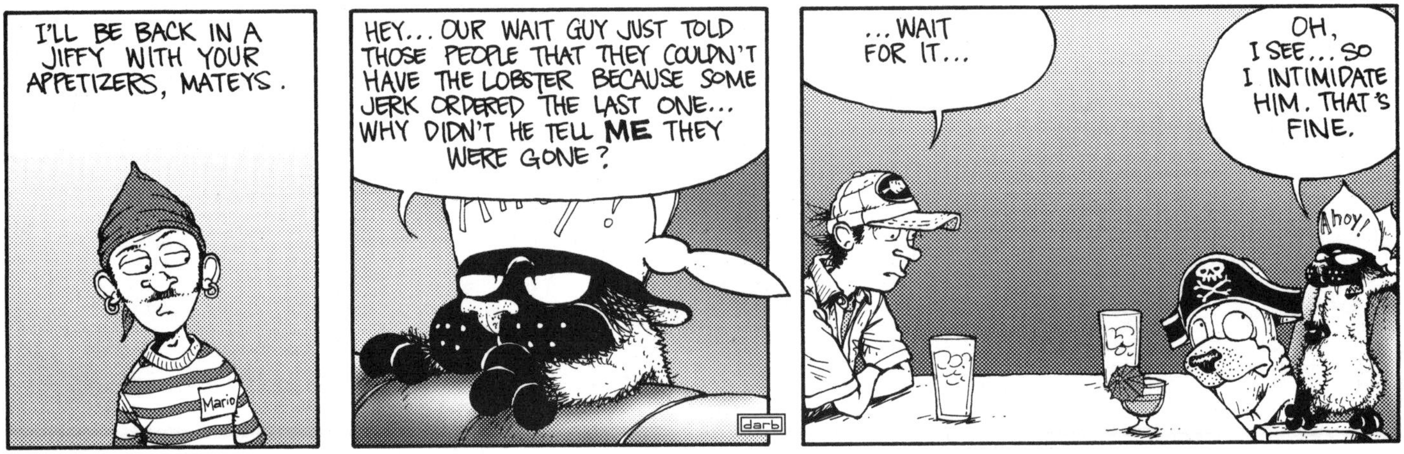
I'LL BE BACK IN A JIFFY WITH YOUR APPETIZERS, MATEYS.
Mario
HEY... OUR WAIT GUY JUST TOLD THOSE PEOPLE THAT THEY COULDN'T HAVE THE LOBSTER BECAUSE SOME JERK ORDERED THE LAST ONE... WHY DIDN'T HE TELL **ME** THEY WERE GONE?
darb
...WAIT FOR IT...
OH, I SEE... SO I INTIMIDATE HIM. THAT'S FINE.
Ahoy!

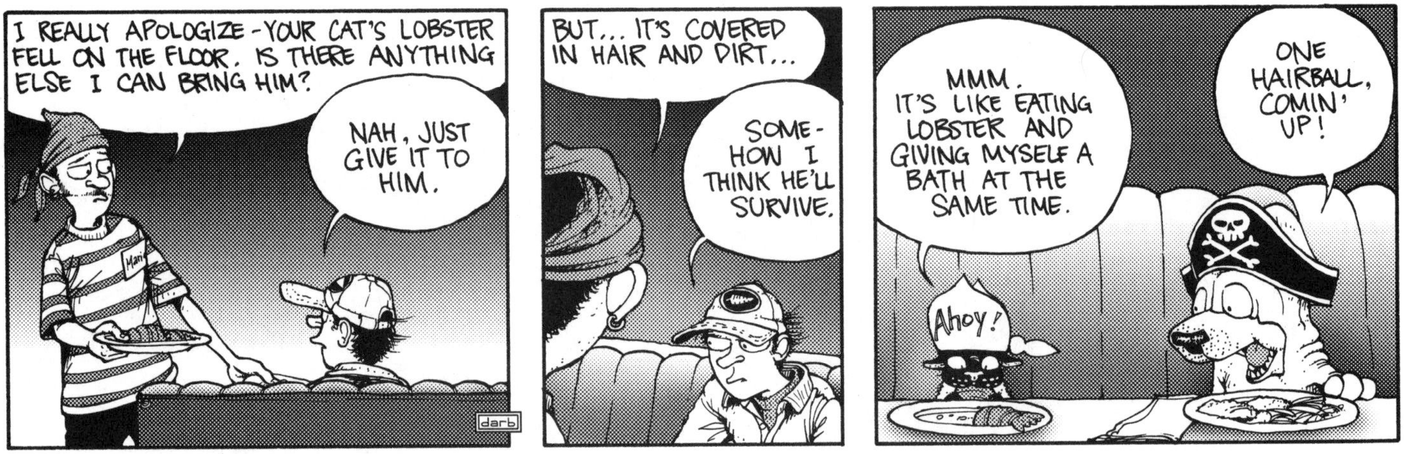
I REALLY APOLOGIZE - YOUR CAT'S LOBSTER FELL ON THE FLOOR. IS THERE ANYTHING ELSE I CAN BRING HIM?
NAH, JUST GIVE IT TO HIM.
darb
BUT... IT'S COVERED IN HAIR AND DIRT...
SOME-HOW I THINK HE'LL SURVIVE.
MMM. IT'S LIKE EATING LOBSTER AND GIVING MYSELF A BATH AT THE SAME TIME.
ONE HAIRBALL, COMIN' UP!
Ahoy!

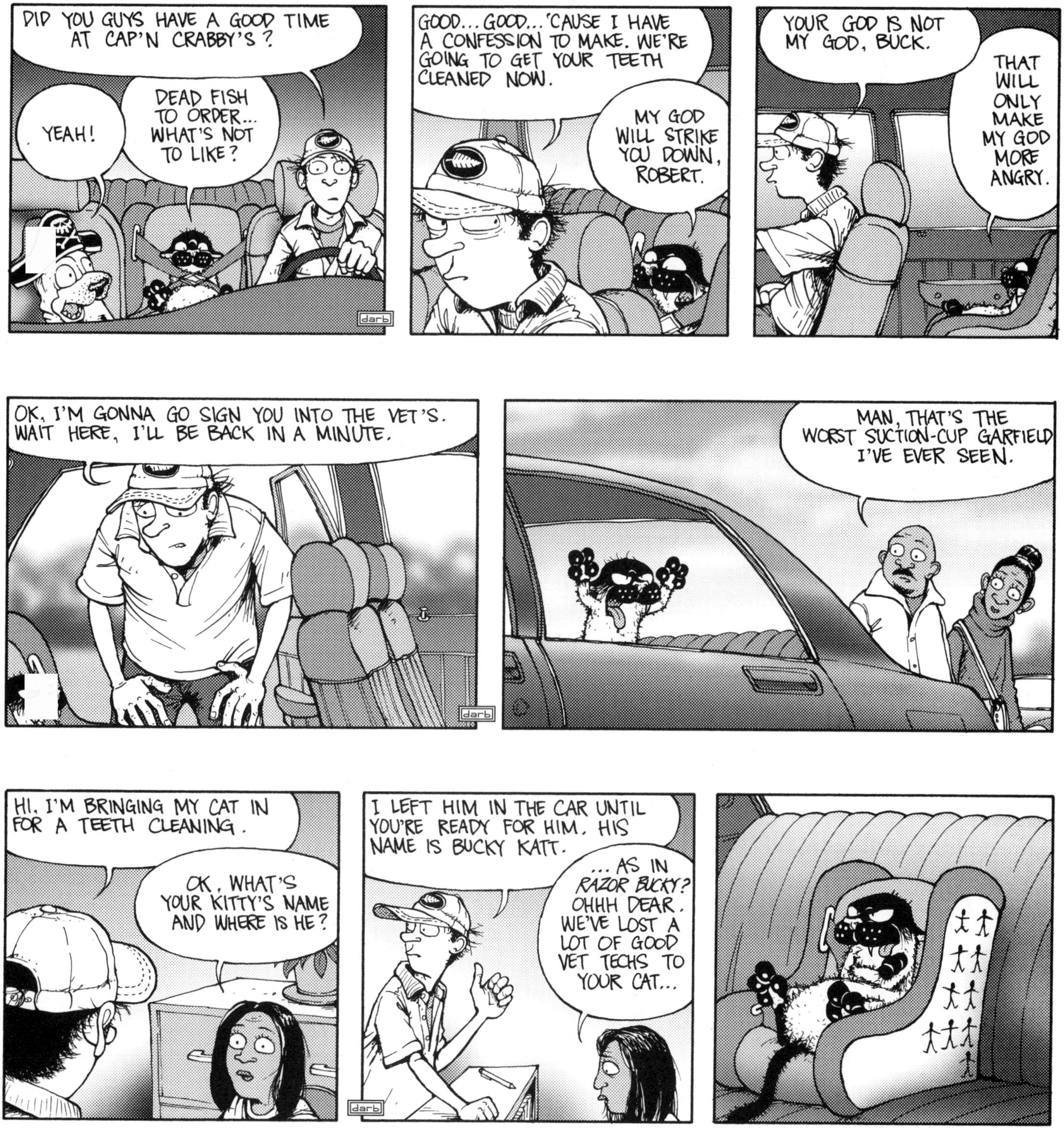
DID YOU GUYS HAVE A GOOD TIME AT CAP'N CRABBY'S?
YEAH!
DEAD FISH TO ORDER... WHAT'S NOT TO LIKE?
GOOD... GOOD... 'CAUSE I HAVE A CONFESSION TO MAKE. WE'RE GOING TO GET YOUR TEETH CLEANED NOW.
MY GOD WILL STRIKE YOU DOWN, ROBERT.
YOUR GOD IS NOT MY GOD, BUCK.
THAT WILL ONLY MAKE MY GOD MORE ANGRY.
OK, I'M GONNA GO SIGN YOU INTO THE VET'S. WAIT HERE, I'LL BE BACK IN A MINUTE.
MAN, THAT'S THE WORST SUCTION-CUP GARFIELD I'VE EVER SEEN.
HI, I'M BRINGING MY CAT IN FOR A TEETH CLEANING.
OK, WHAT'S YOUR KITTY'S NAME AND WHERE IS HE?
I LEFT HIM IN THE CAR UNTIL YOU'RE READY FOR HIM. HIS NAME IS BUCKY KATT.
... AS IN *RAZOR BUCKY?* OHHH DEAR. WE'VE LOST A LOT OF GOOD VET TECHS TO YOUR CAT...

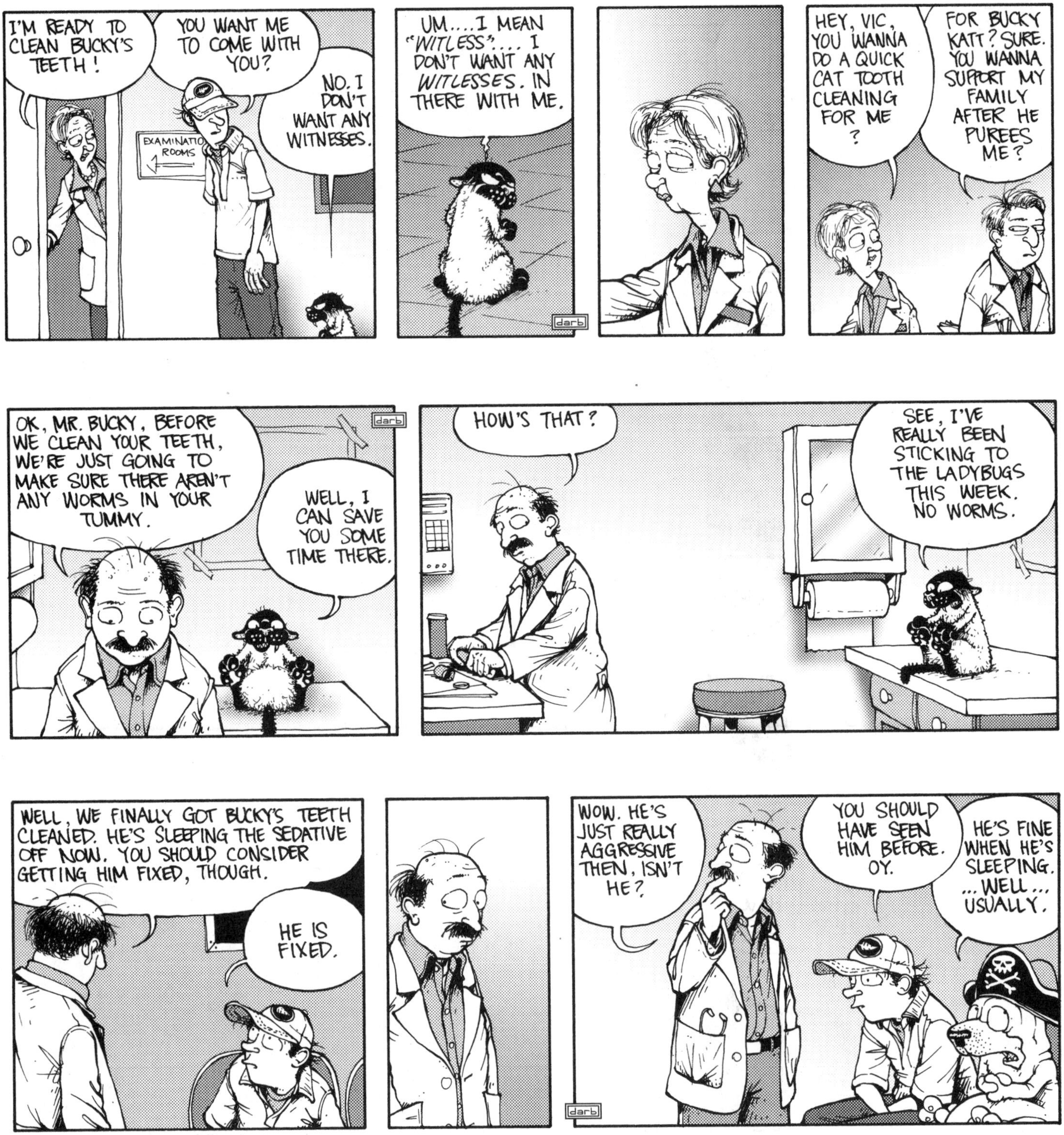
I'M READY TO CLEAN BUCKY'S TEETH!
YOU WANT ME TO COME WITH YOU?
NO. I DON'T WANT ANY WITNESSES.
EXAMINATIO ROOMS
UM.... I MEAN "WITLESS".... I DON'T WANT ANY WITLESSES. IN THERE WITH ME.
darb
HEY, VIC, YOU WANNA DO A QUICK CAT TOOTH CLEANING FOR ME?
FOR BUCKY KATT? SURE. YOU WANNA SUPPORT MY FAMILY AFTER HE PUREES ME?
darb
OK, MR. BUCKY, BEFORE WE CLEAN YOUR TEETH, WE'RE JUST GOING TO MAKE SURE THERE AREN'T ANY WORMS IN YOUR TUMMY.
WELL, I CAN SAVE YOU SOME TIME THERE.
HOW'S THAT?
SEE, I'VE REALLY BEEN STICKING TO THE LADYBUGS THIS WEEK. NO WORMS.
WELL, WE FINALLY GOT BUCKY'S TEETH CLEANED. HE'S SLEEPING THE SEDATIVE OFF NOW. YOU SHOULD CONSIDER GETTING HIM FIXED, THOUGH.
HE IS FIXED.
WOW. HE'S JUST REALLY AGGRESSIVE THEN, ISN'T HE?
YOU SHOULD HAVE SEEN HIM BEFORE. OY.
HE'S FINE WHEN HE'S SLEEPING. ...WELL... USUALLY.
darb

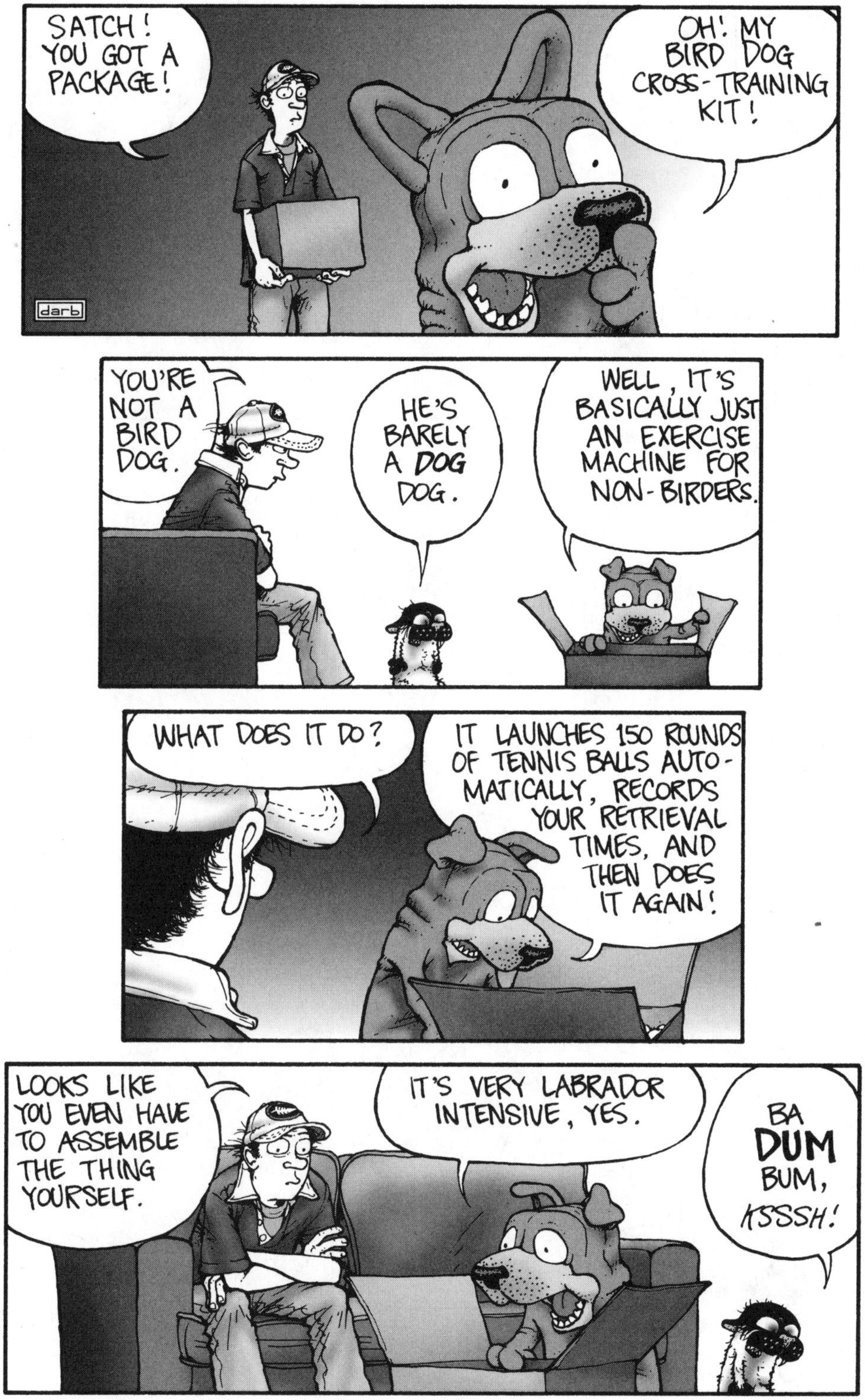

SATCH! YOU GOT A PACKAGE!
OH! MY BIRD DOG CROSS-TRAINING KIT!
darb
YOU'RE NOT A BIRD DOG.
HE'S BARELY A **DOG** DOG.
WELL, IT'S BASICALLY JUST AN EXERCISE MACHINE FOR NON-BIRDERS.
WHAT DOES IT DO?
IT LAUNCHES 150 ROUNDS OF TENNIS BALLS AUTO-MATICALLY, RECORDS YOUR RETRIEVAL TIMES, AND THEN DOES IT AGAIN!
LOOKS LIKE YOU EVEN HAVE TO ASSEMBLE THE THING YOURSELF.
IT'S VERY LABRADOR INTENSIVE, YES.
BA **DUM** BUM, *KSSSH!*

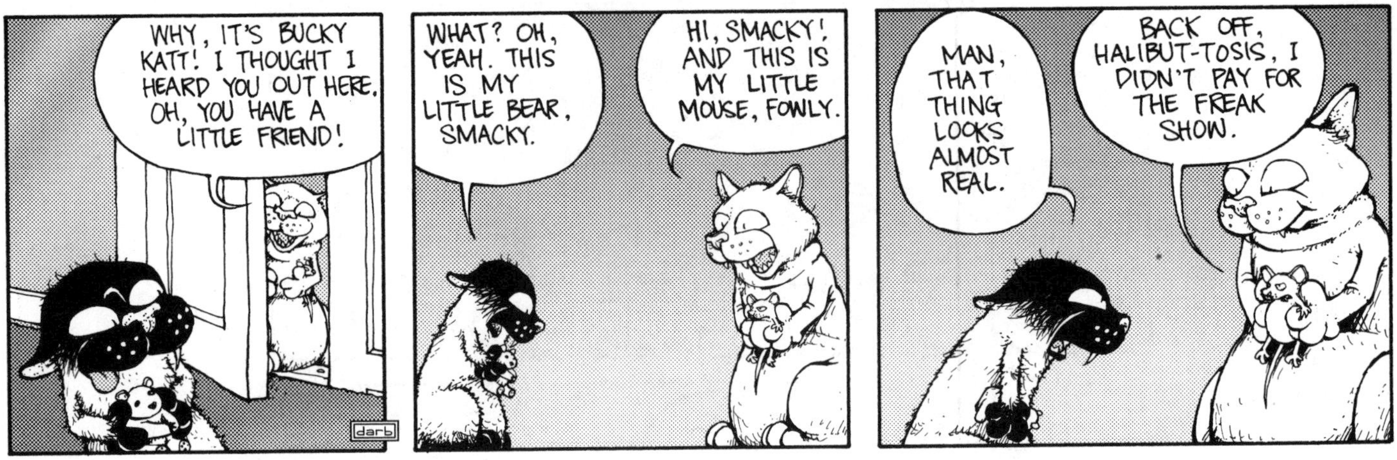
WHY, IT'S BUCKY KATT! I THOUGHT I HEARD YOU OUT HERE. OH, YOU HAVE A LITTLE FRIEND!
WHAT? OH, YEAH. THIS IS MY LITTLE BEAR, SMACKY.
HI, SMACKY! AND THIS IS MY LITTLE MOUSE, FOWLY.
MAN, THAT THING LOOKS ALMOST REAL.
BACK OFF, HALIBUT-TOSIS, I DIDN'T PAY FOR THE FREAK SHOW.

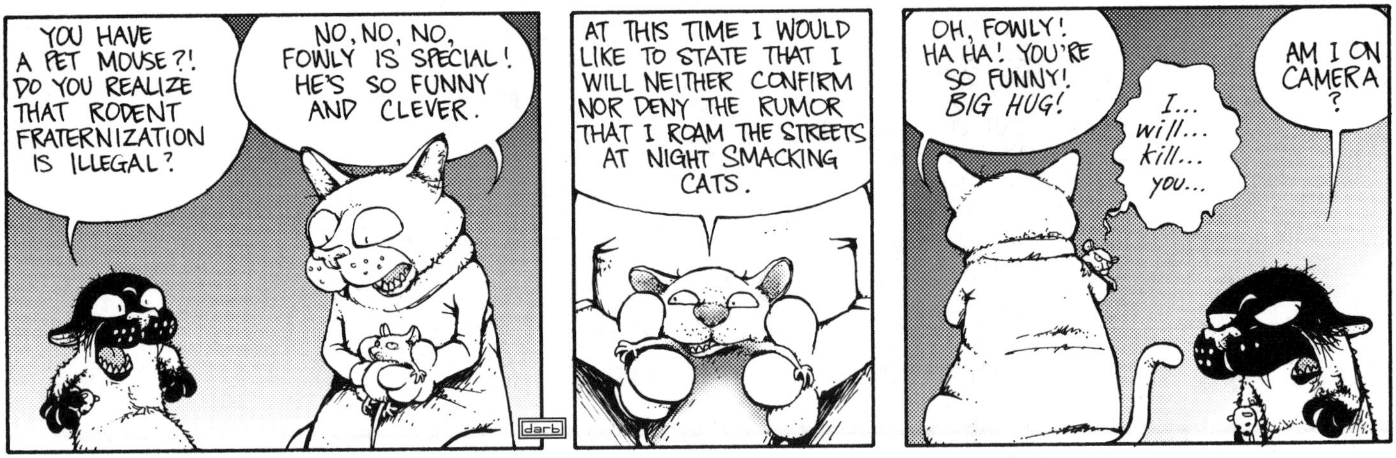
YOU HAVE A PET MOUSE?! DO YOU REALIZE THAT RODENT FRATERNIZATION IS ILLEGAL?
NO, NO, NO, FOWLY IS SPECIAL! HE'S SO FUNNY AND CLEVER.
AT THIS TIME I WOULD LIKE TO STATE THAT I WILL NEITHER CONFIRM NOR DENY THE RUMOR THAT I ROAM THE STREETS AT NIGHT SMACKING CATS.
OH, FOWLY! HA HA! YOU'RE SO FUNNY! BIG HUG!
I... will... kill... you...
AM I ON CAMERA?

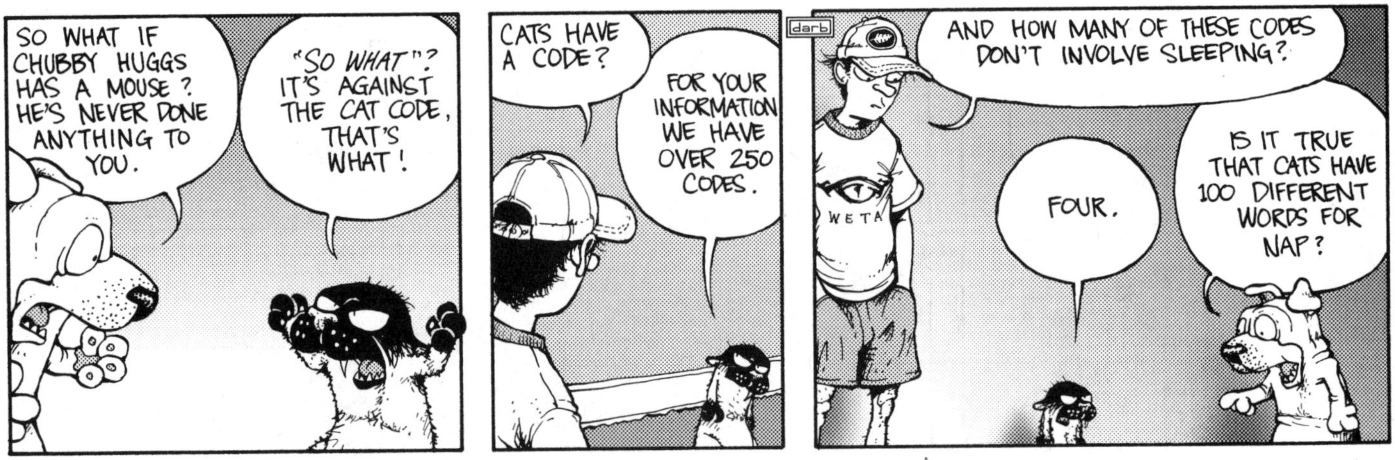
SO WHAT IF CHUBBY HUGGS HAS A MOUSE? HE'S NEVER DONE ANYTHING TO YOU.
"SO WHAT"? IT'S AGAINST THE CAT CODE, THAT'S WHAT!
CATS HAVE A CODE?
FOR YOUR INFORMATION WE HAVE OVER 250 CODES.
AND HOW MANY OF THESE CODES DON'T INVOLVE SLEEPING?
FOUR.
IS IT TRUE THAT CATS HAVE 100 DIFFERENT WORDS FOR NAP?

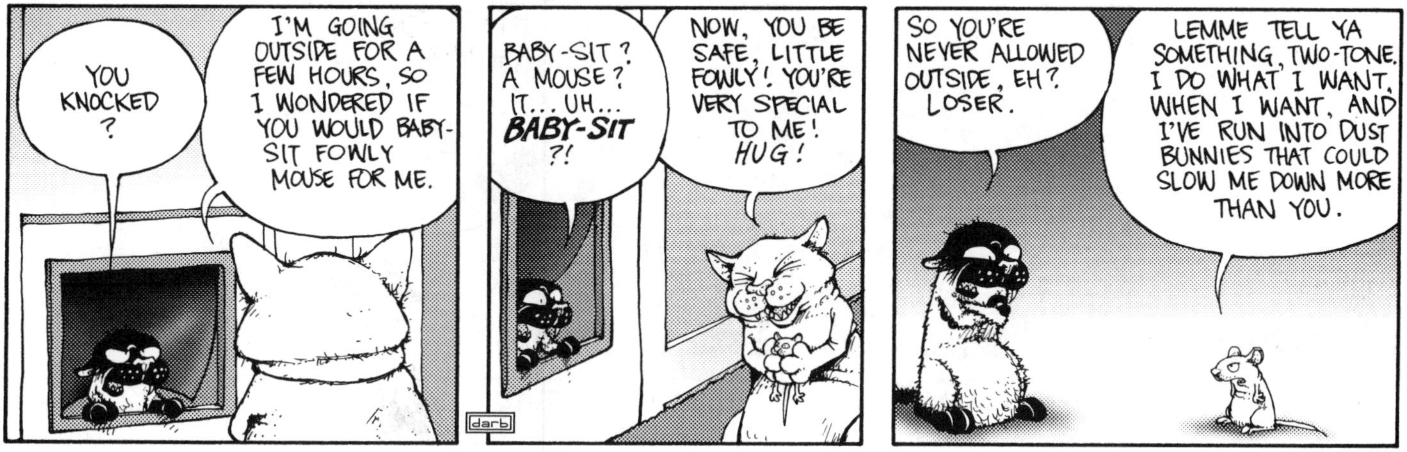
YOU KNOCKED ?
I'M GOING OUTSIDE FOR A FEW HOURS, SO I WONDERED IF YOU WOULD BABY-SIT FOWLY MOUSE FOR ME.
BABY-SIT ? A MOUSE ? IT... UH... BABY-SIT ?!
NOW, YOU BE SAFE, LITTLE FOWLY! YOU'RE VERY SPECIAL TO ME! HUG!
darb
SO YOU'RE NEVER ALLOWED OUTSIDE, EH? LOSER.
LEMME TELL YA SOMETHING, TWO-TONE. I DO WHAT I WANT, WHEN I WANT, AND I'VE RUN INTO DUST BUNNIES THAT COULD SLOW ME DOWN MORE THAN YOU.

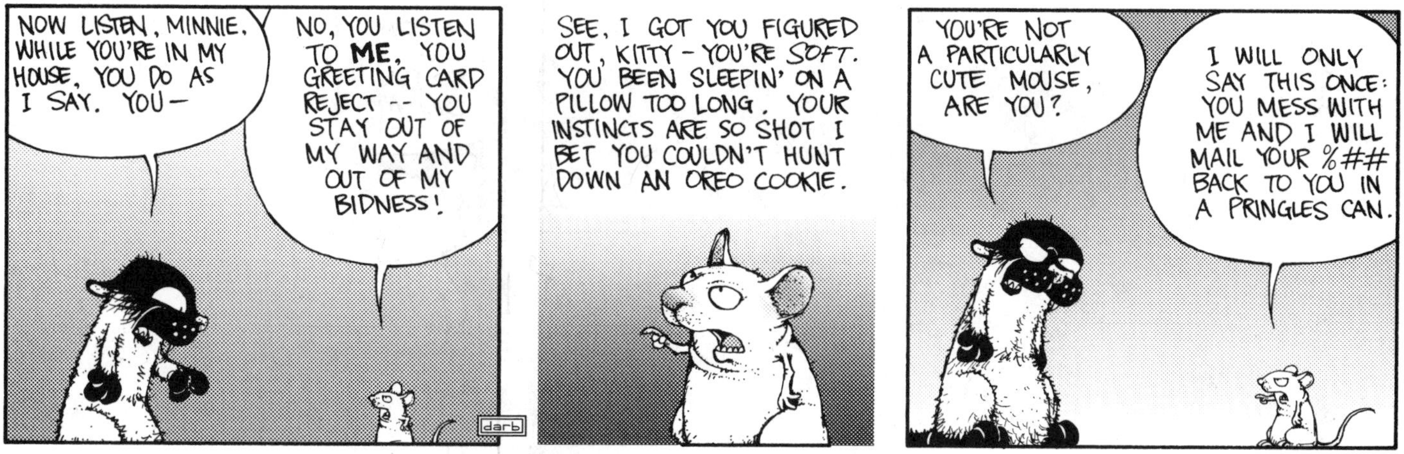
NOW LISTEN, MINNIE. WHILE YOU'RE IN MY HOUSE, YOU DO AS I SAY. YOU—
NO, YOU LISTEN TO ME, YOU GREETING CARD REJECT -- YOU STAY OUT OF MY WAY AND OUT OF MY BIDNESS!
darb
SEE, I GOT YOU FIGURED OUT, KITTY - YOU'RE SOFT. YOU BEEN SLEEPIN' ON A PILLOW TOO LONG. YOUR INSTINCTS ARE SO SHOT I BET YOU COULDN'T HUNT DOWN AN OREO COOKIE.
YOU'RE NOT A PARTICULARLY CUTE MOUSE, ARE YOU?
I WILL ONLY SAY THIS ONCE: YOU MESS WITH ME AND I WILL MAIL YOUR %## BACK TO YOU IN A PRINGLES CAN.

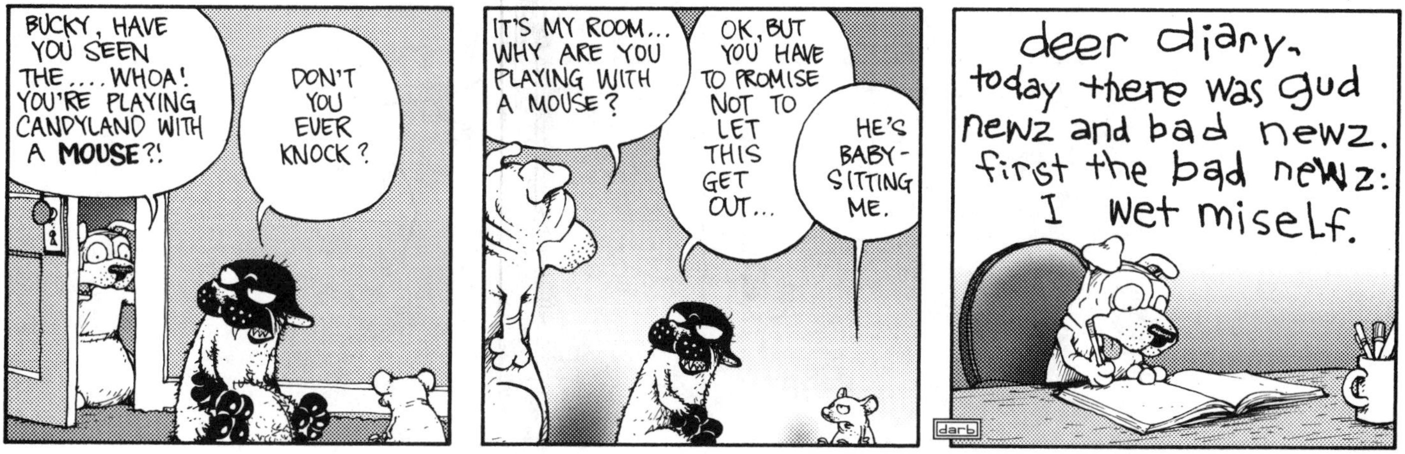
BUCKY, HAVE YOU SEEN THE.... WHOA! YOU'RE PLAYING CANDYLAND WITH A MOUSE?!
DON'T YOU EVER KNOCK ?
IT'S MY ROOM... WHY ARE YOU PLAYING WITH A MOUSE?
OK, BUT YOU HAVE TO PROMISE NOT TO LET THIS GET OUT...
HE'S BABY-SITTING ME.
deer diary, today there was gud newz and bad newz. first the bad newz: I wet miself.
darb

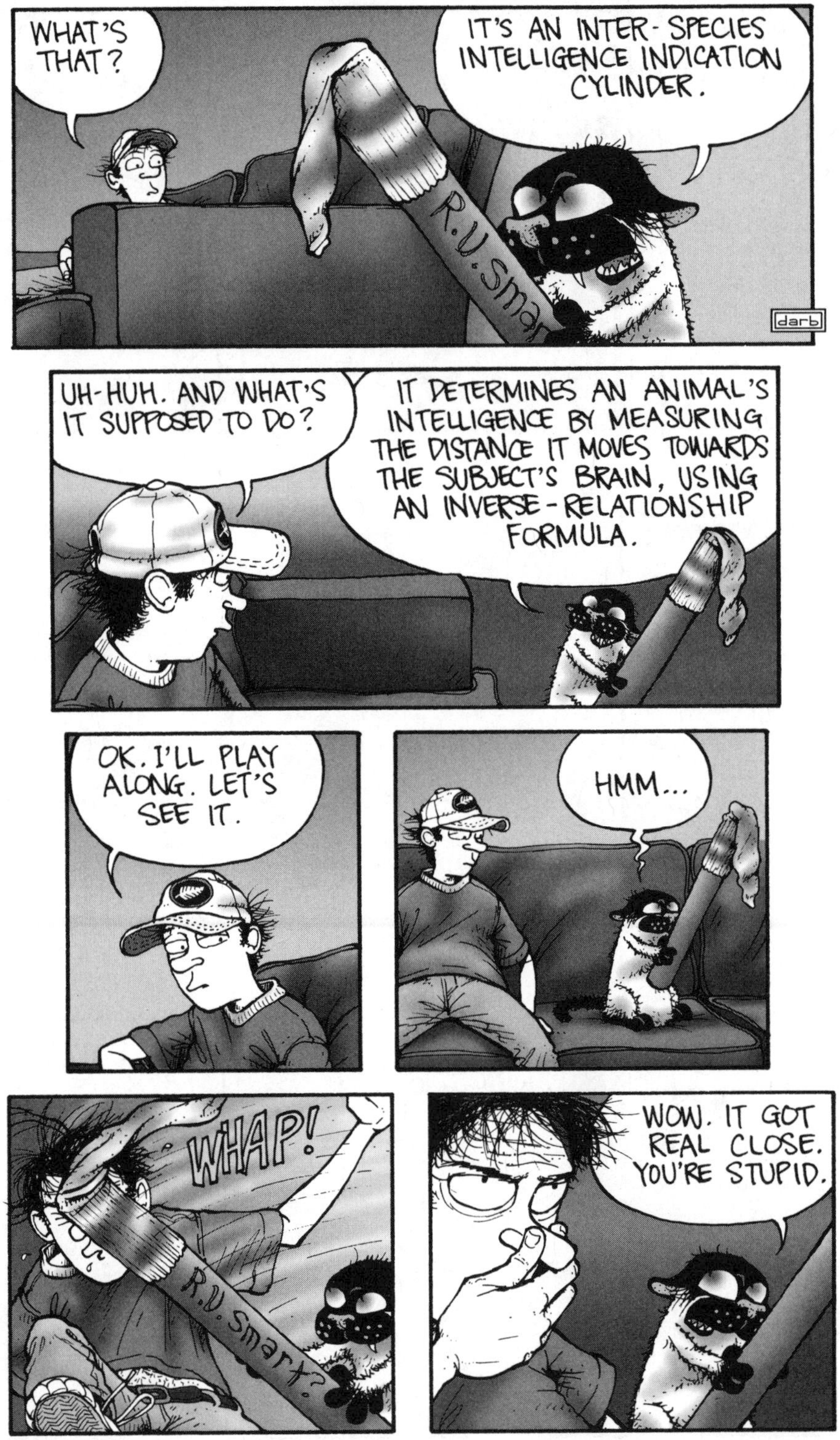
WHAT'S THAT?
IT'S AN INTER-SPECIES INTELLIGENCE INDICATION CYLINDER.
R.U. Smart
darb
UH-HUH. AND WHAT'S IT SUPPOSED TO DO?
IT DETERMINES AN ANIMAL'S INTELLIGENCE BY MEASURING THE DISTANCE IT MOVES TOWARDS THE SUBJECT'S BRAIN, USING AN INVERSE-RELATIONSHIP FORMULA.
OK. I'LL PLAY ALONG. LET'S SEE IT.
HMM...
WHAP!
R.U. Smart?
WOW. IT GOT REAL CLOSE. YOU'RE STUPID.

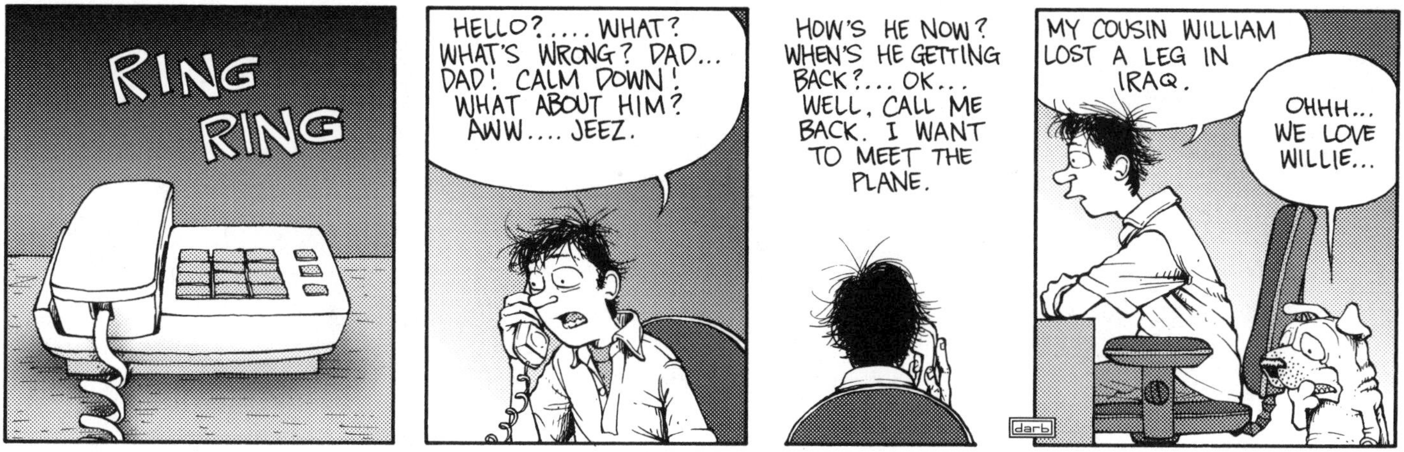
RING
RING
HELLO?.... WHAT? WHAT'S WRONG? DAD... DAD! CALM DOWN! WHAT ABOUT HIM? AWW.... JEEZ.
HOW'S HE NOW? WHEN'S HE GETTING BACK?... OK... WELL, CALL ME BACK. I WANT TO MEET THE PLANE.
MY COUSIN WILLIAM LOST A LEG IN IRAQ.
OHHH... WE LOVE WILLIE...
darb

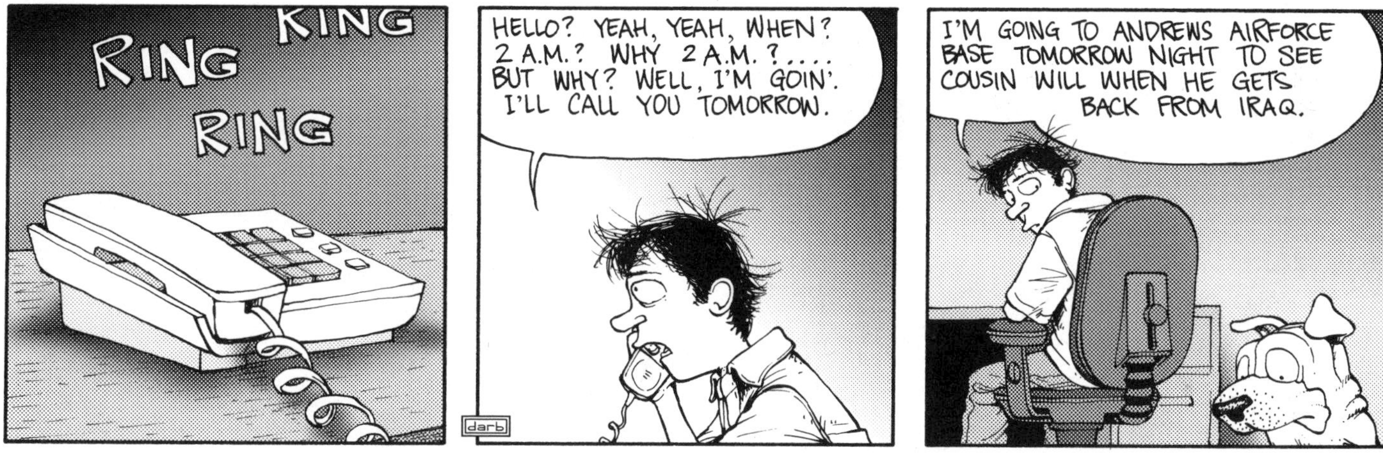
RING
RING
RING
darb
HELLO? YEAH, YEAH, WHEN? 2 A.M.? WHY 2 A.M.?.... BUT WHY? WELL, I'M GOIN'. I'LL CALL YOU TOMORROW.
I'M GOING TO ANDREWS AIRFORCE BASE TOMORROW NIGHT TO SEE COUSIN WILL WHEN HE GETS BACK FROM IRAQ.

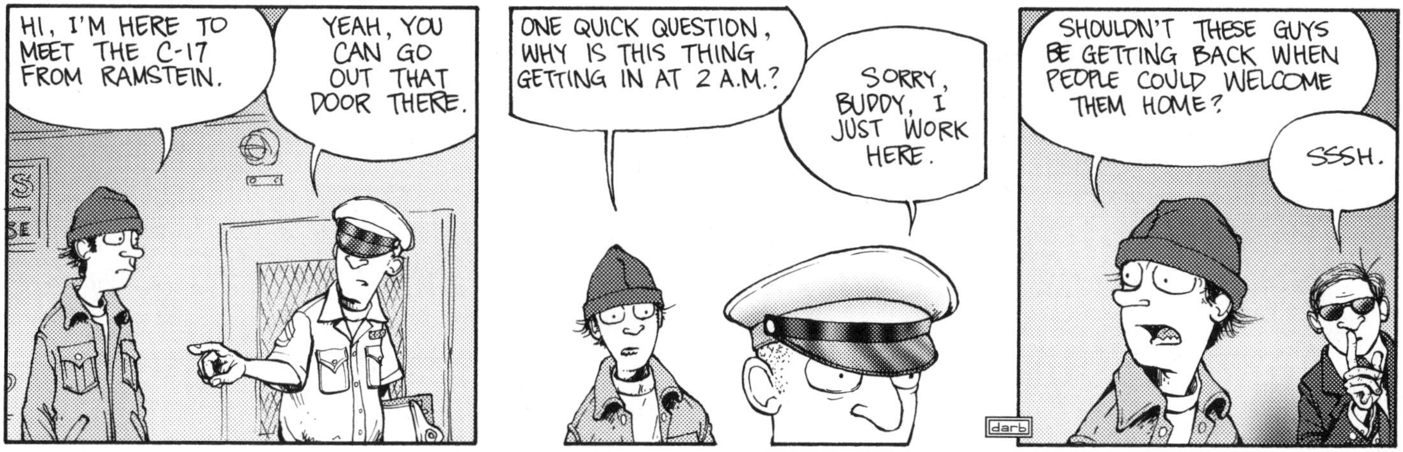
HI, I'M HERE TO MEET THE C-17 FROM RAMSTEIN.
YEAH, YOU CAN GO OUT THAT DOOR THERE.
ONE QUICK QUESTION, WHY IS THIS THING GETTING IN AT 2 A.M.?
SORRY, BUDDY, I JUST WORK HERE.
darb
SHOULDN'T THESE GUYS BE GETTING BACK WHEN PEOPLE COULD WELCOME THEM HOME?
SSSH.

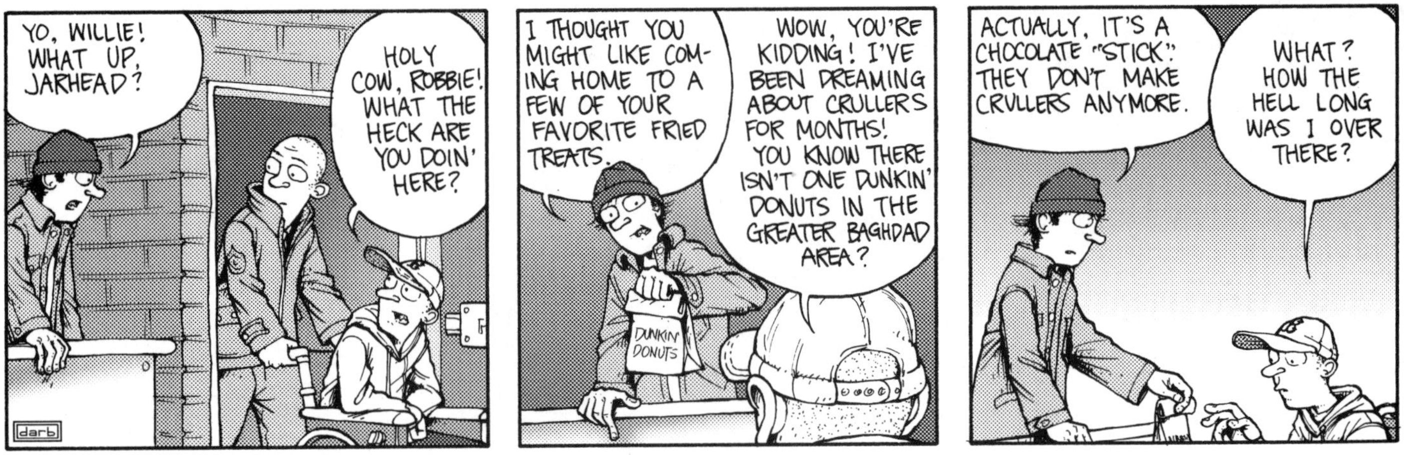

YO, WILLIE! WHAT UP, JARHEAD?
HOLY COW, ROBBIE! WHAT THE HECK ARE YOU DOIN' HERE?
darb
I THOUGHT YOU MIGHT LIKE COMING HOME TO A FEW OF YOUR FAVORITE FRIED TREATS.
WOW, YOU'RE KIDDING! I'VE BEEN DREAMING ABOUT CRULLERS FOR MONTHS! YOU KNOW THERE ISN'T ONE DUNKIN' DONUTS IN THE GREATER BAGHDAD AREA?
DUNKIN' DONUTS
ACTUALLY, IT'S A CHOCOLATE "STICK." THEY DON'T MAKE CRULLERS ANYMORE.
WHAT? HOW THE HELL LONG WAS I OVER THERE?

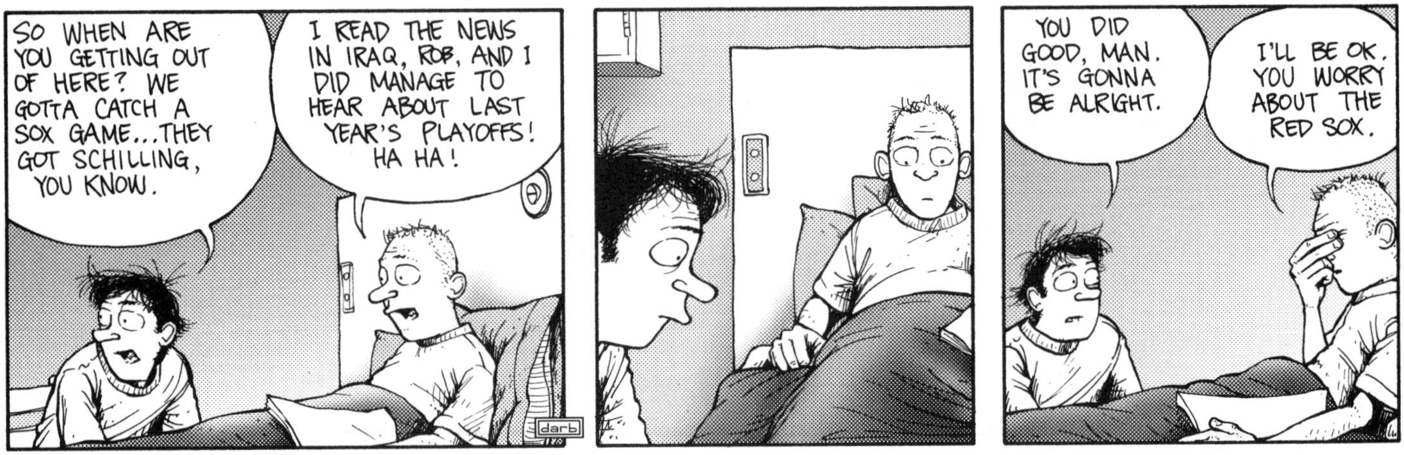

SO WHEN ARE YOU GETTING OUT OF HERE? WE GOTTA CATCH A SOX GAME...THEY GOT SCHILLING, YOU KNOW.
I READ THE NEWS IN IRAQ, ROB, AND I DID MANAGE TO HEAR ABOUT LAST YEAR'S PLAYOFFS! HA HA!
darb
YOU DID GOOD, MAN. IT'S GONNA BE ALRIGHT.
I'LL BE OK. YOU WORRY ABOUT THE RED SOX.

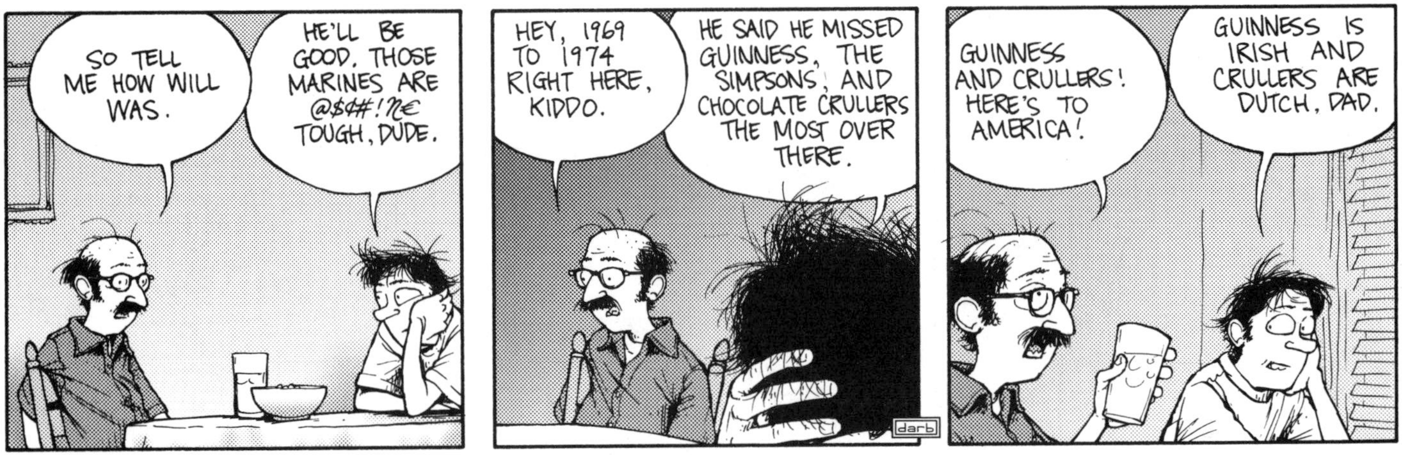

SO TELL ME HOW WILL WAS.
HE'LL BE GOOD. THOSE MARINES ARE @$¢#!?€ TOUGH, DUDE.
HEY, 1969 TO 1974 RIGHT HERE, KIDDO.
HE SAID HE MISSED GUINNESS, THE SIMPSONS, AND CHOCOLATE CRULLERS THE MOST OVER THERE.
darb
GUINNESS AND CRULLERS! HERE'S TO AMERICA!
GUINNESS IS IRISH AND CRULLERS ARE DUTCH, DAD.

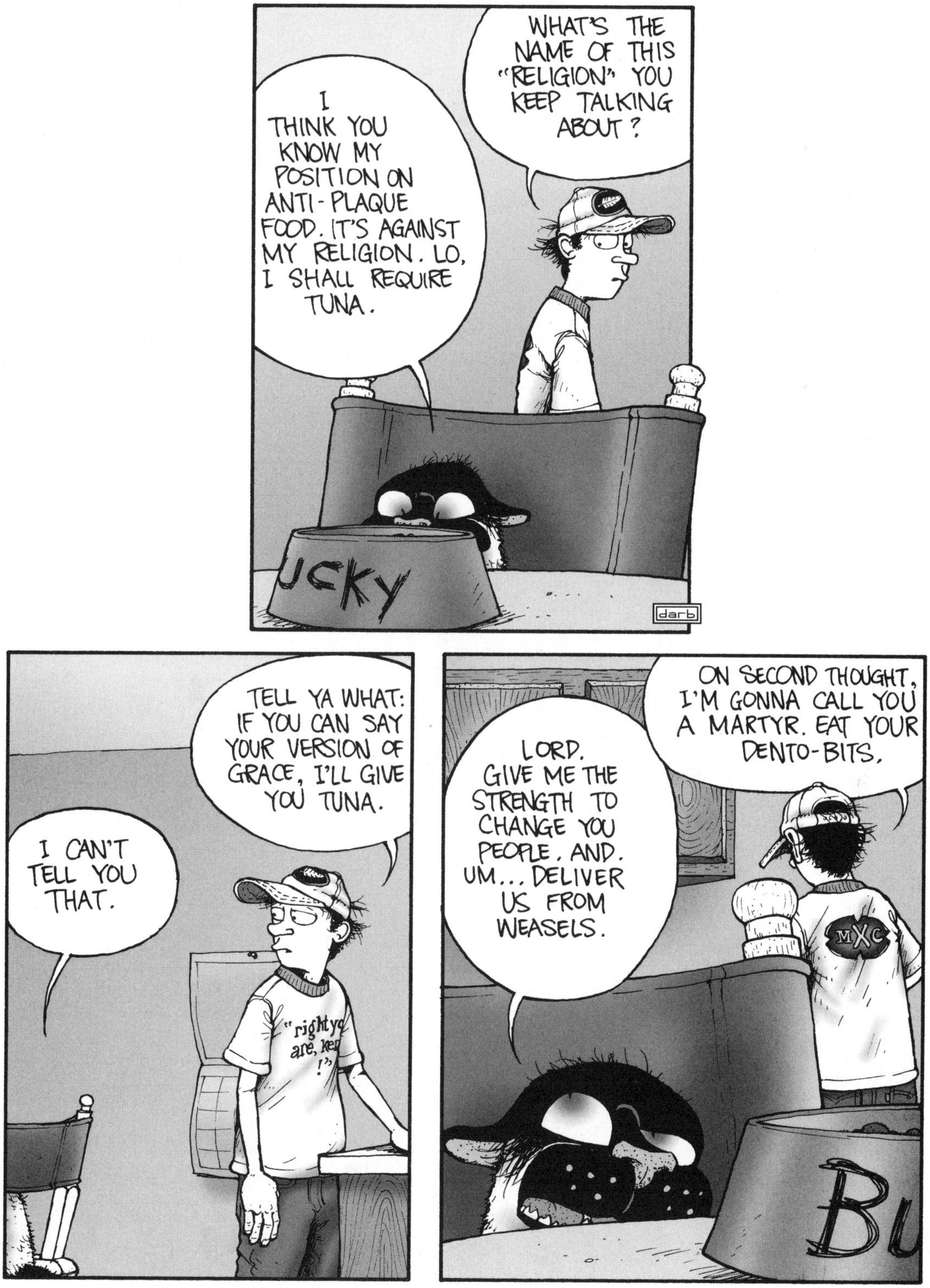
WHAT'S THE NAME OF THIS "RELIGION" YOU KEEP TALKING ABOUT?
I THINK YOU KNOW MY POSITION ON ANTI-PLAQUE FOOD. IT'S AGAINST MY RELIGION. LO, I SHALL REQUIRE TUNA.
UCKY
darb
TELL YA WHAT: IF YOU CAN SAY YOUR VERSION OF GRACE, I'LL GIVE YOU TUNA.
I CAN'T TELL YOU THAT.
LORD. GIVE ME THE STRENGTH TO CHANGE YOU PEOPLE. AND. UM... DELIVER US FROM WEASELS.
ON SECOND THOUGHT, I'M GONNA CALL YOU A MARTYR. EAT YOUR DENTO-BITS.
MXC
BU

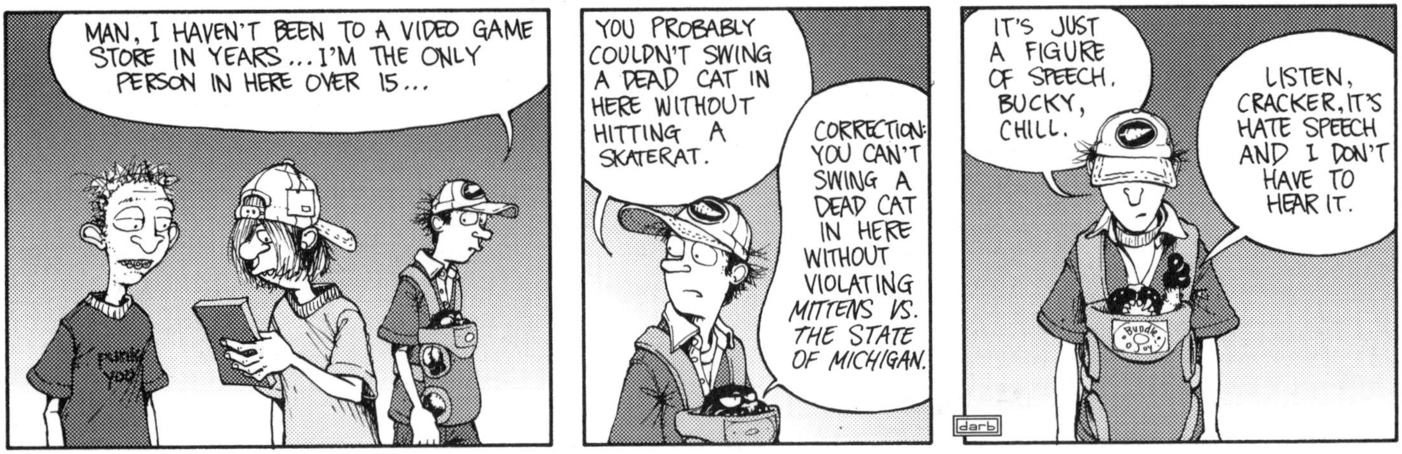
MAN, I HAVEN'T BEEN TO A VIDEO GAME STORE IN YEARS... I'M THE ONLY PERSON IN HERE OVER 15...
YOU PROBABLY COULDN'T SWING A DEAD CAT IN HERE WITHOUT HITTING A SKATERAT.
CORRECTION: YOU CAN'T SWING A DEAD CAT IN HERE WITHOUT VIOLATING *MITTENS VS. THE STATE OF MICHIGAN.*
IT'S JUST A FIGURE OF SPEECH. BUCKY, CHILL.
LISTEN, CRACKER, IT'S HATE SPEECH AND I DON'T HAVE TO HEAR IT.

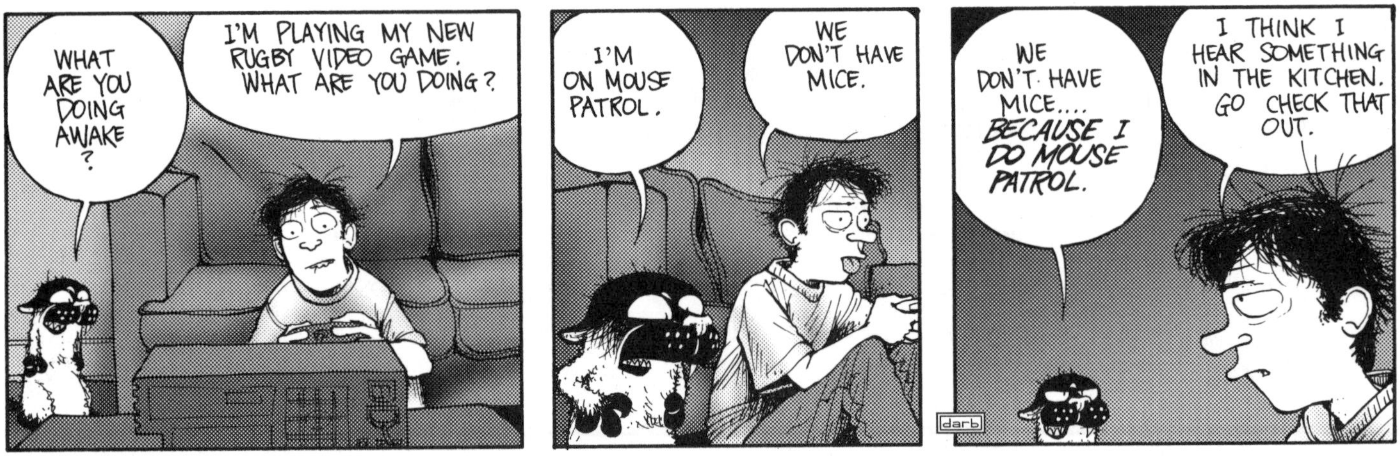
WHAT ARE YOU DOING AWAKE ?
I'M PLAYING MY NEW RUGBY VIDEO GAME. WHAT ARE YOU DOING?
I'M ON MOUSE PATROL.
WE DON'T HAVE MICE.
WE DON'T HAVE MICE.... ***BECAUSE I DO MOUSE PATROL.***
I THINK I HEAR SOMETHING IN THE KITCHEN. GO CHECK THAT OUT.

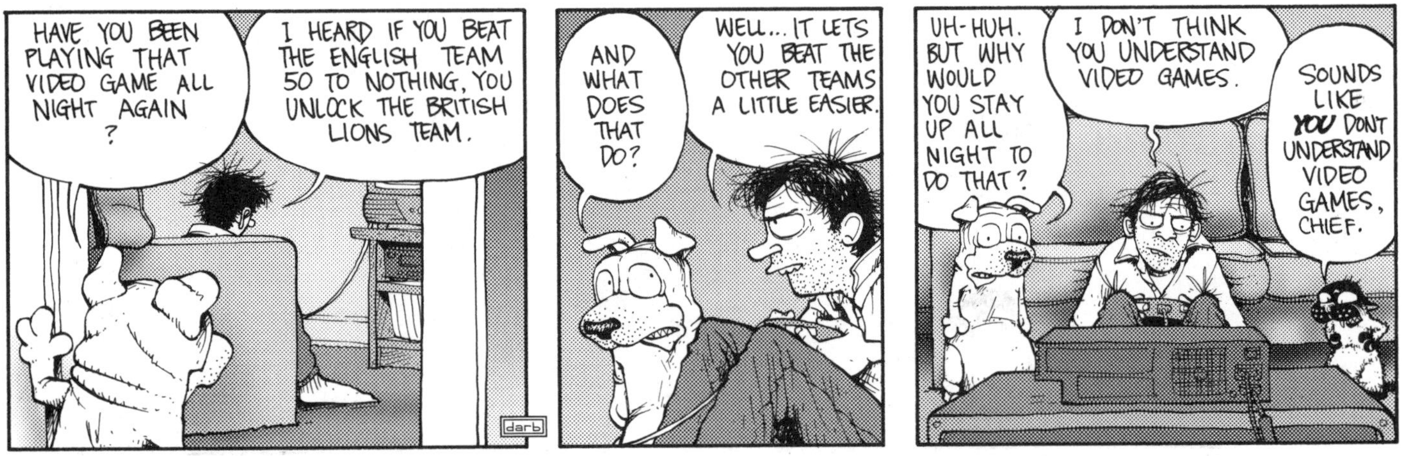
HAVE YOU BEEN PLAYING THAT VIDEO GAME ALL NIGHT AGAIN ?
I HEARD IF YOU BEAT THE ENGLISH TEAM 50 TO NOTHING, YOU UNLOCK THE BRITISH LIONS TEAM.
AND WHAT DOES THAT DO?
WELL... IT LETS YOU BEAT THE OTHER TEAMS A LITTLE EASIER.
UH-HUH. BUT WHY WOULD YOU STAY UP ALL NIGHT TO DO THAT?
I DON'T THINK YOU UNDERSTAND VIDEO GAMES.
SOUNDS LIKE ***YOU*** DON'T UNDERSTAND VIDEO GAMES, CHIEF.

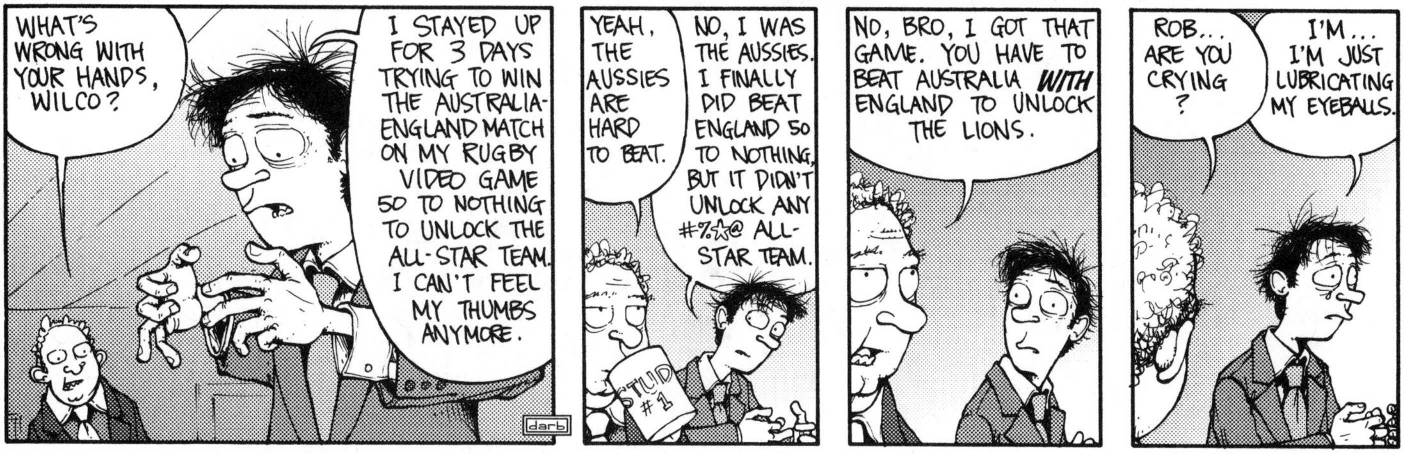
WHAT'S WRONG WITH YOUR HANDS, WILCO?
I STAYED UP FOR 3 DAYS TRYING TO WIN THE AUSTRALIA-ENGLAND MATCH ON MY RUGBY VIDEO GAME 50 TO NOTHING TO UNLOCK THE ALL-STAR TEAM. I CAN'T FEEL MY THUMBS ANYMORE.
darb
YEAH, THE AUSSIES ARE HARD TO BEAT.
NO, I WAS THE AUSSIES. I FINALLY DID BEAT ENGLAND 50 TO NOTHING, BUT IT DIDN'T UNLOCK ANY #%☆@ ALL-STAR TEAM.
STUD #1
NO, BRO, I GOT THAT GAME. YOU HAVE TO BEAT AUSTRALIA **WITH** ENGLAND TO UNLOCK THE LIONS.
ROB... ARE YOU CRYING?
I'M... I'M JUST LUBRICATING MY EYEBALLS.

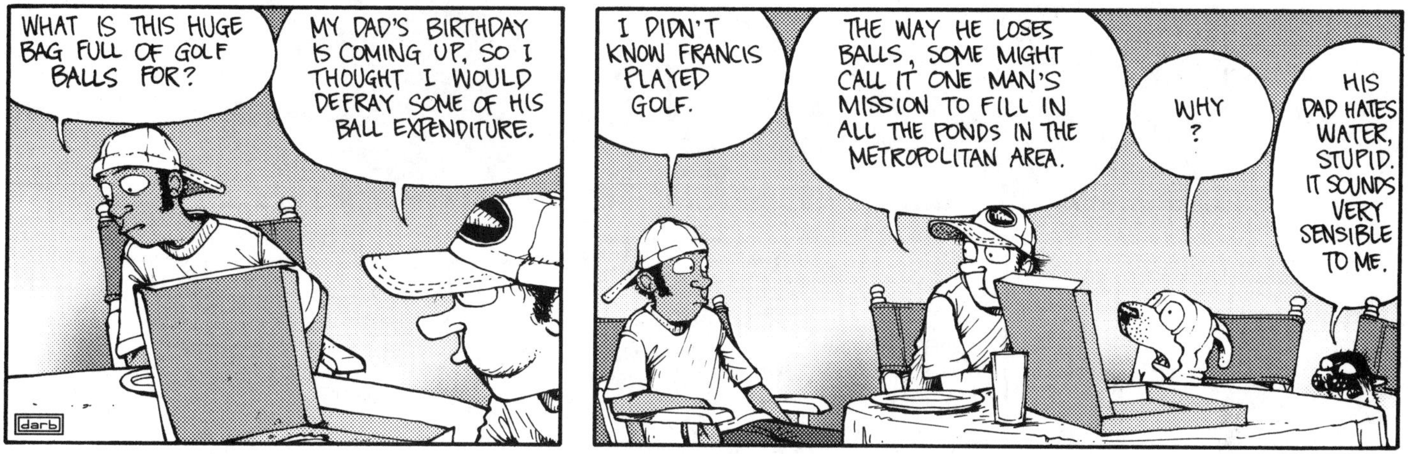
WHAT IS THIS HUGE BAG FULL OF GOLF BALLS FOR?
MY DAD'S BIRTHDAY IS COMING UP, SO I THOUGHT I WOULD DEFRAY SOME OF HIS BALL EXPENDITURE.
darb
I DIDN'T KNOW FRANCIS PLAYED GOLF.
THE WAY HE LOSES BALLS, SOME MIGHT CALL IT ONE MAN'S MISSION TO FILL IN ALL THE PONDS IN THE METROPOLITAN AREA.
WHY?
HIS DAD HATES WATER, STUPID. IT SOUNDS VERY SENSIBLE TO ME.

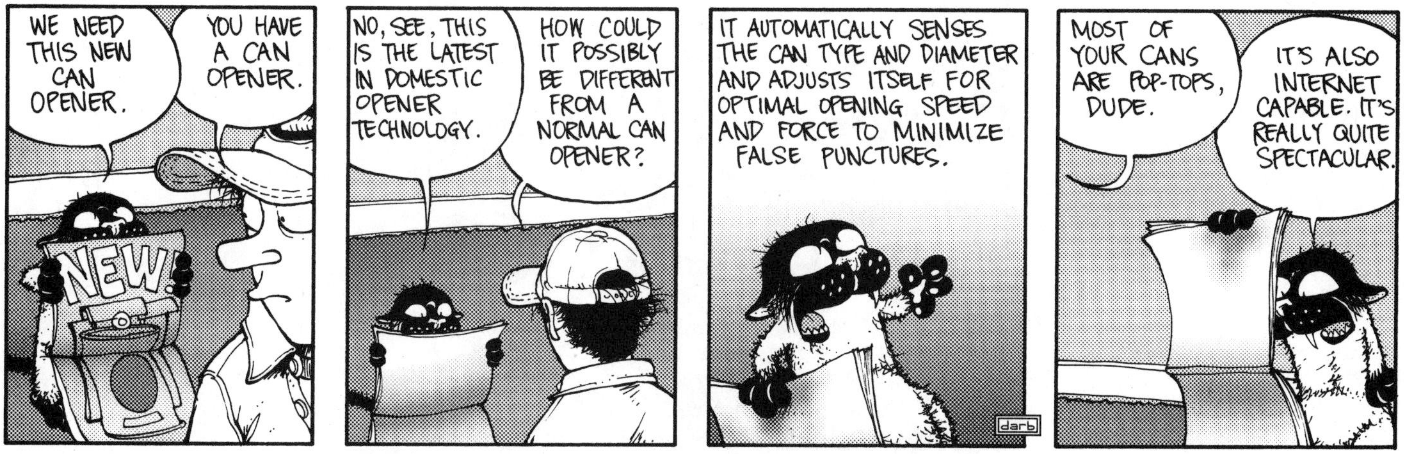
WE NEED THIS NEW CAN OPENER.
YOU HAVE A CAN OPENER.
NEW!
NO, SEE, THIS IS THE LATEST IN DOMESTIC OPENER TECHNOLOGY.
HOW COULD IT POSSIBLY BE DIFFERENT FROM A NORMAL CAN OPENER?
IT AUTOMATICALLY SENSES THE CAN TYPE AND DIAMETER AND ADJUSTS ITSELF FOR OPTIMAL OPENING SPEED AND FORCE TO MINIMIZE FALSE PUNCTURES.
darb
MOST OF YOUR CANS ARE POP-TOPS, DUDE.
IT'S ALSO INTERNET CAPABLE. IT'S REALLY QUITE SPECTACULAR.

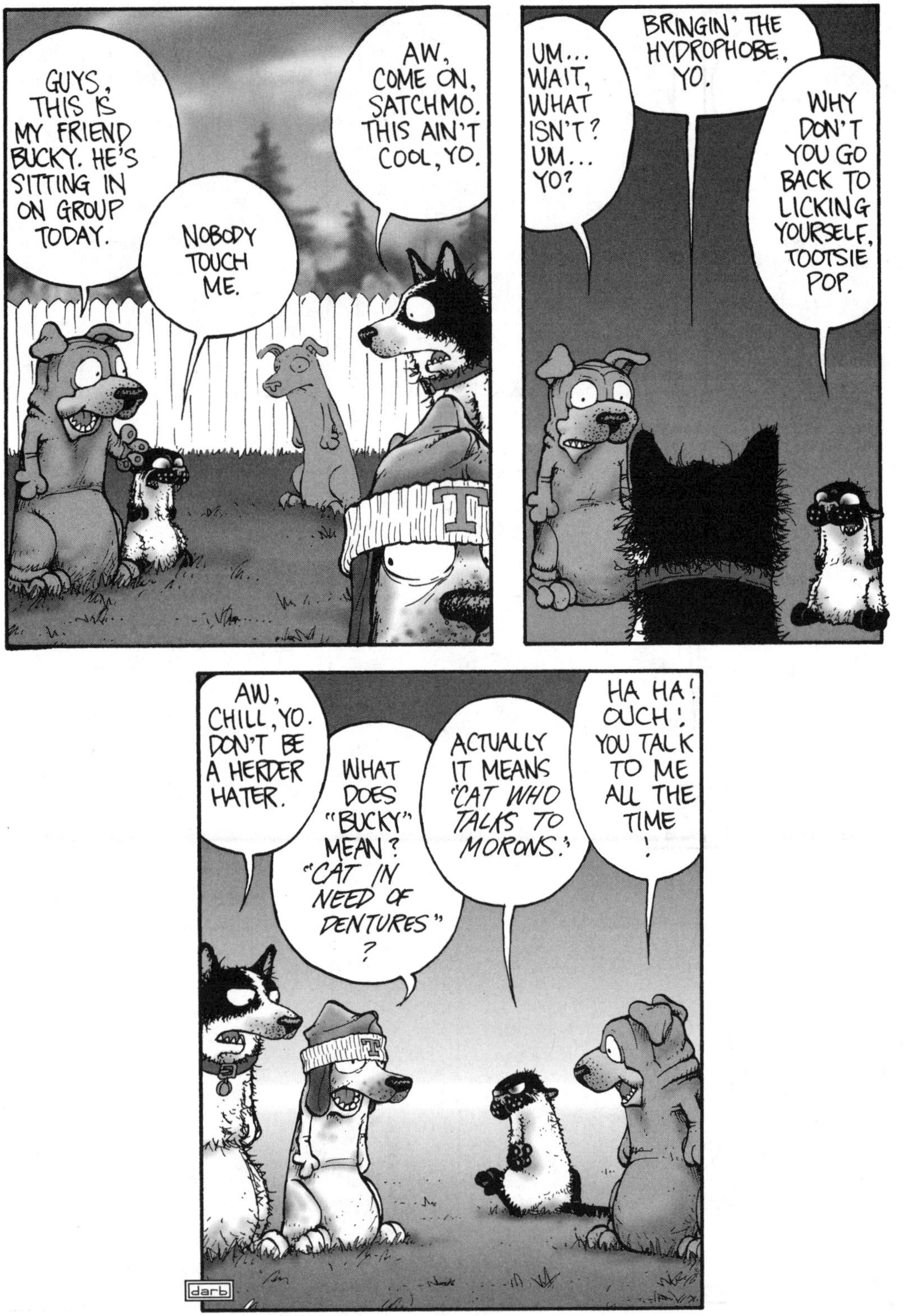
GUYS, THIS IS MY FRIEND BUCKY. HE'S SITTING IN ON GROUP TODAY.
NOBODY TOUCH ME.
AW, COME ON, SATCHMO. THIS AIN'T COOL, YO.
UM... WAIT, WHAT ISN'T? UM... YO?
BRINGIN' THE HYDROPHOBE, YO.
WHY DON'T YOU GO BACK TO LICKING YOURSELF, TOOTSIE POP.
AW, CHILL, YO. DON'T BE A HERDER HATER.
WHAT DOES "BUCKY" MEAN? "CAT IN NEED OF DENTURES"?
ACTUALLY IT MEANS "CAT WHO TALKS TO MORONS."
HA HA! OUCH! YOU TALK TO ME ALL THE TIME!
darb

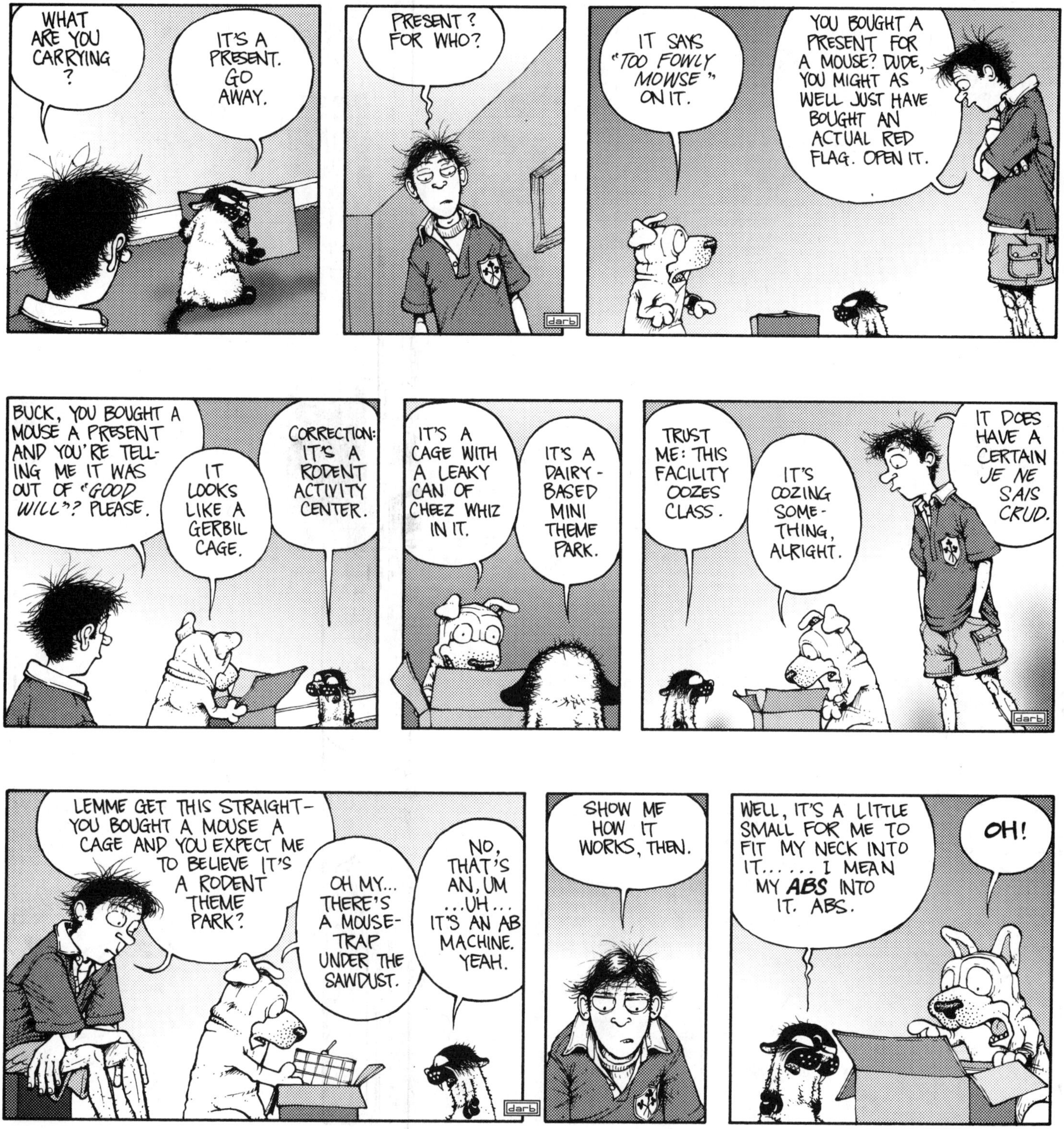
WHAT ARE YOU CARRYING?
IT'S A PRESENT. GO AWAY.
PRESENT? FOR WHO?
IT SAYS "*TOO FOWLY MOWSE*" ON IT.
YOU BOUGHT A PRESENT FOR A MOUSE? DUDE, YOU MIGHT AS WELL JUST HAVE BOUGHT AN ACTUAL RED FLAG. OPEN IT.
BUCK, YOU BOUGHT A MOUSE A PRESENT AND YOU'RE TELLING ME IT WAS OUT OF "*GOOD WILL*"? PLEASE.
IT LOOKS LIKE A GERBIL CAGE.
CORRECTION: IT'S A RODENT ACTIVITY CENTER.
IT'S A CAGE WITH A LEAKY CAN OF CHEEZ WHIZ IN IT.
IT'S A DAIRY-BASED MINI THEME PARK.
TRUST ME: THIS FACILITY OOZES CLASS.
IT'S OOZING SOMETHING, ALRIGHT.
IT DOES HAVE A CERTAIN *JE NE SAIS CRUD*.
LEMME GET THIS STRAIGHT- YOU BOUGHT A MOUSE A CAGE AND YOU EXPECT ME TO BELIEVE IT'S A RODENT THEME PARK?
OH MY... THERE'S A MOUSE-TRAP UNDER THE SAWDUST.
NO, THAT'S AN, UM ...UH... IT'S AN AB MACHINE. YEAH.
SHOW ME HOW IT WORKS, THEN.
WELL, IT'S A LITTLE SMALL FOR ME TO FIT MY NECK INTO IT...... I MEAN MY **ABS** INTO IT. ABS.
OH!

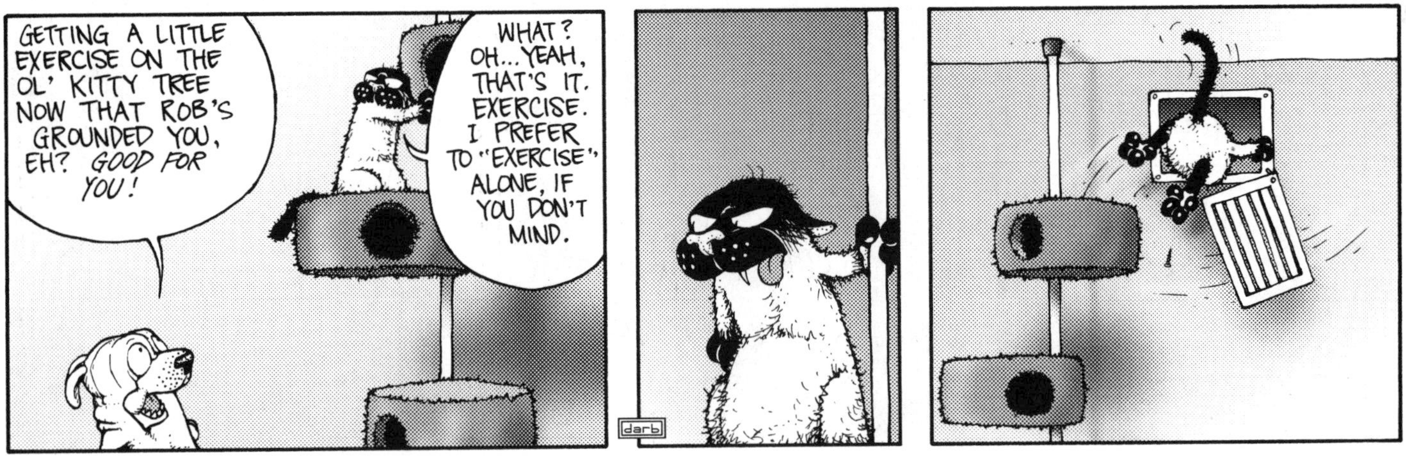
GETTING A LITTLE EXERCISE ON THE OL' KITTY TREE NOW THAT ROB'S GROUNDED YOU, EH? GOOD FOR YOU!
WHAT? OH... YEAH, THAT'S IT. EXERCISE. I PREFER TO "EXERCISE" ALONE, IF YOU DON'T MIND.
darb

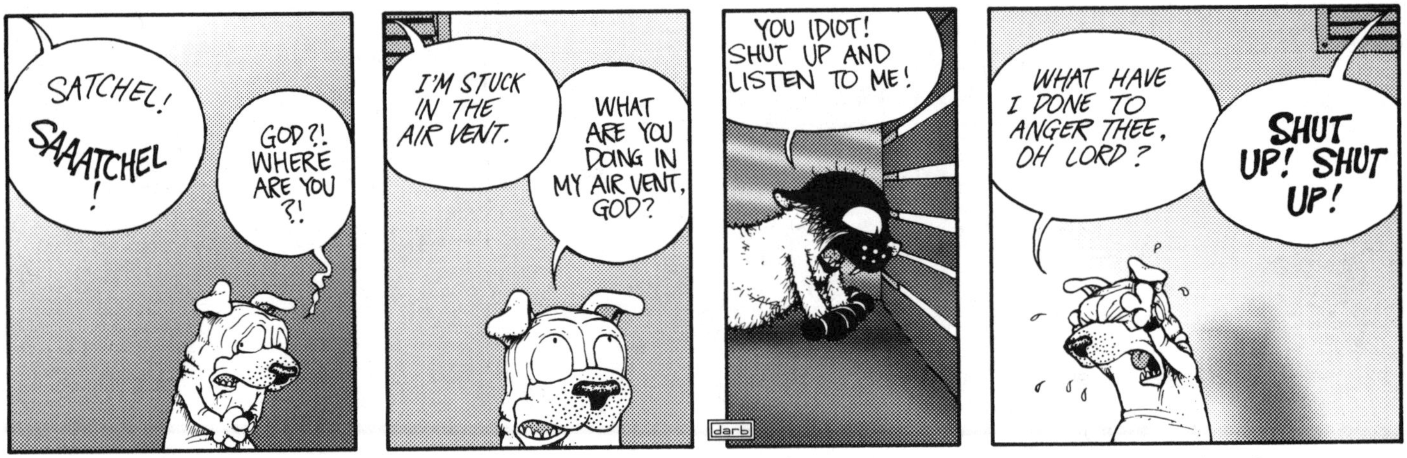
SATCHEL! SAAATCHEL!
GOD?! WHERE ARE YOU?!
I'M STUCK IN THE AIR VENT.
WHAT ARE YOU DOING IN MY AIR VENT, GOD?
YOU IDIOT! SHUT UP AND LISTEN TO ME!
darb
WHAT HAVE I DONE TO ANGER THEE, OH LORD?
SHUT UP! SHUT UP!

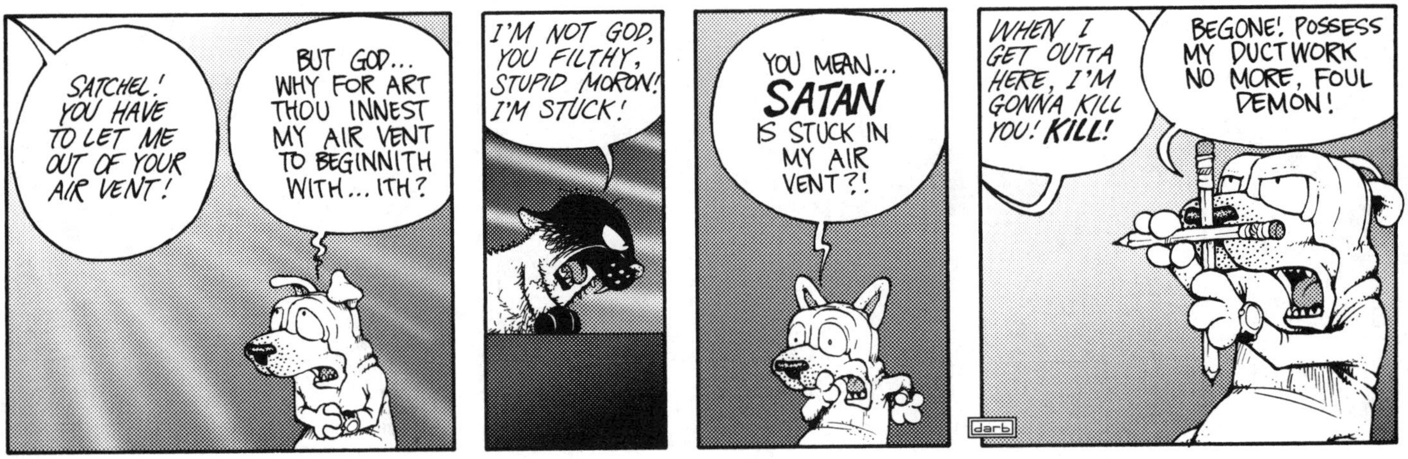
SATCHEL! YOU HAVE TO LET ME OUT OF YOUR AIR VENT!
BUT GOD... WHY FOR ART THOU INNEST MY AIR VENT TO BEGINNITH WITH... ITH?
I'M NOT GOD, YOU FILTHY, STUPID MORON! I'M STUCK!
YOU MEAN... SATAN IS STUCK IN MY AIR VENT?!
WHEN I GET OUTTA HERE, I'M GONNA KILL YOU! KILL!
BEGONE! POSSESS MY DUCTWORK NO MORE, FOUL DEMON!
darb

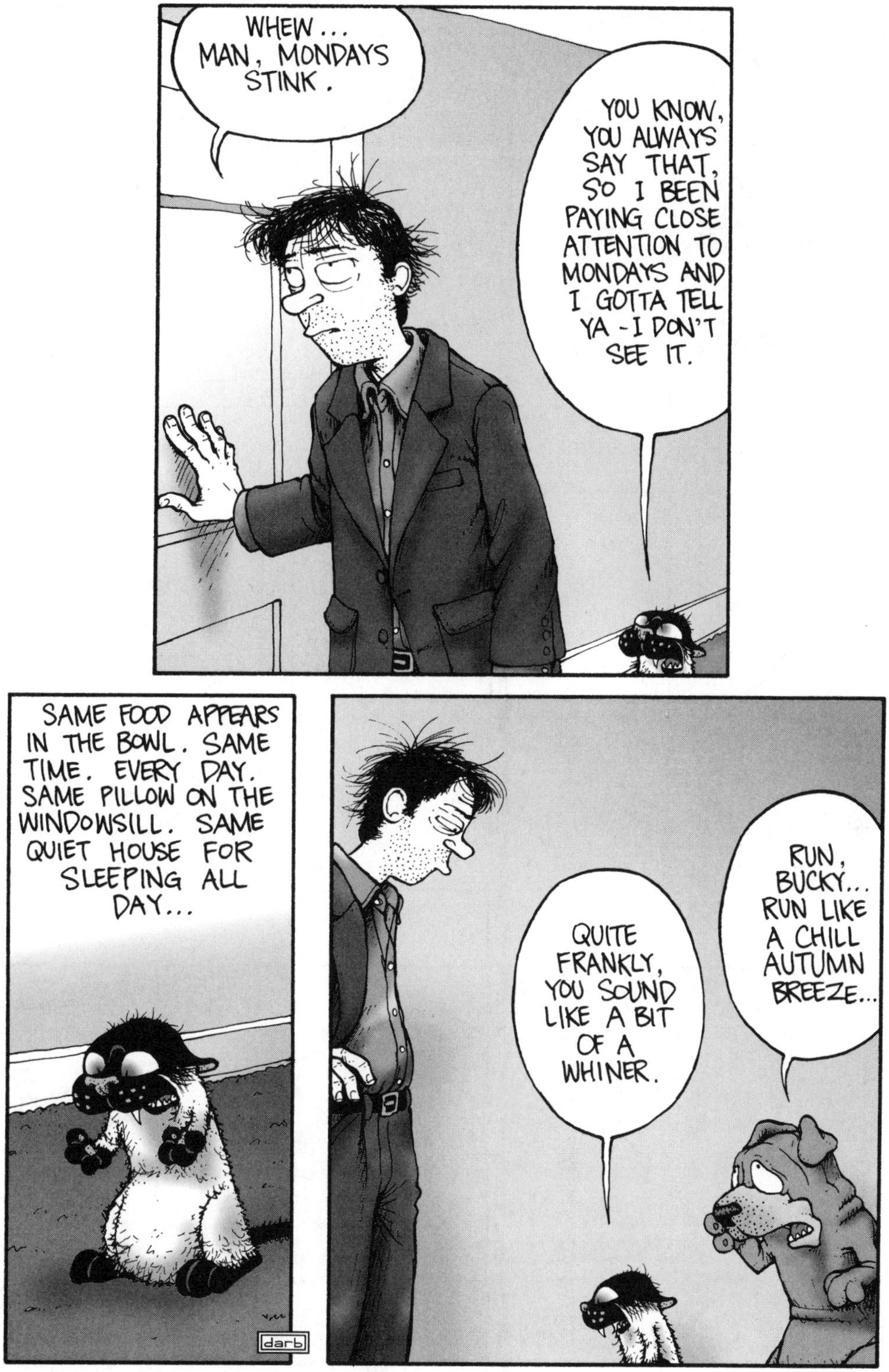
WHEW... MAN, MONDAYS STINK.
YOU KNOW, YOU ALWAYS SAY THAT, SO I BEEN PAYING CLOSE ATTENTION TO MONDAYS AND I GOTTA TELL YA - I DON'T SEE IT.
SAME FOOD APPEARS IN THE BOWL. SAME TIME. EVERY DAY. SAME PILLOW ON THE WINDOWSILL. SAME QUIET HOUSE FOR SLEEPING ALL DAY...
darb
QUITE FRANKLY, YOU SOUND LIKE A BIT OF A WHINER.
RUN, BUCKY... RUN LIKE A CHILL AUTUMN BREEZE...

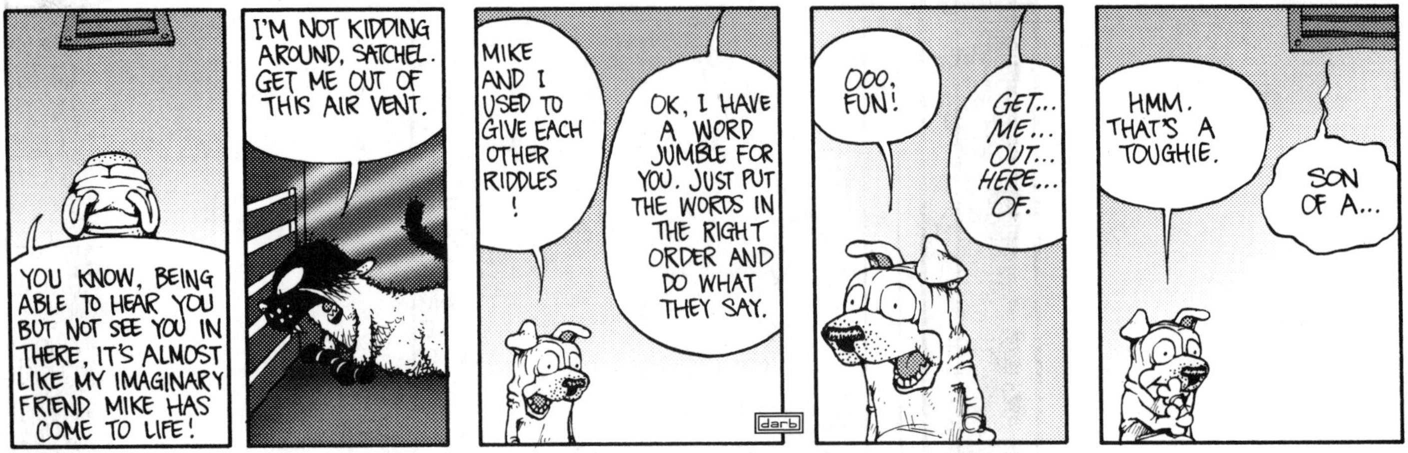
YOU KNOW, BEING ABLE TO HEAR YOU BUT NOT SEE YOU IN THERE, IT'S ALMOST LIKE MY IMAGINARY FRIEND MIKE HAS COME TO LIFE!
I'M NOT KIDDING AROUND, SATCHEL. GET ME OUT OF THIS AIR VENT.
MIKE AND I USED TO GIVE EACH OTHER RIDDLES!
OK, I HAVE A WORD JUMBLE FOR YOU. JUST PUT THE WORDS IN THE RIGHT ORDER AND DO WHAT THEY SAY.
darb
OOO, FUN!
GET... ME... OUT... HERE... OF.
HMM. THAT'S A TOUGHIE.
SON OF A...

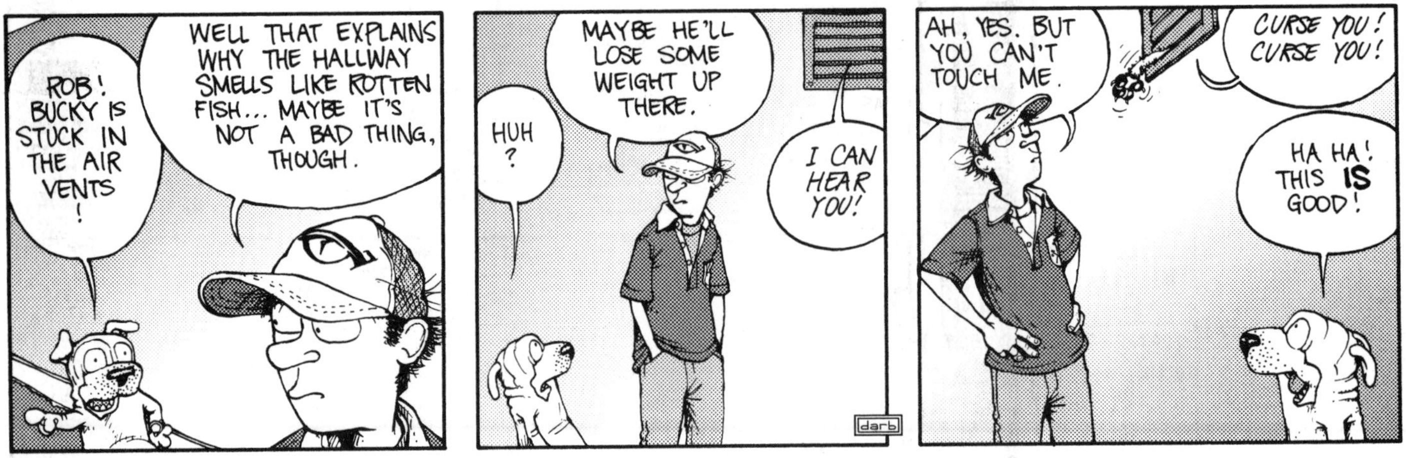
ROB! BUCKY IS STUCK IN THE AIR VENTS!
WELL THAT EXPLAINS WHY THE HALLWAY SMELLS LIKE ROTTEN FISH... MAYBE IT'S NOT A BAD THING, THOUGH.
HUH?
MAYBE HE'LL LOSE SOME WEIGHT UP THERE.
I CAN HEAR YOU!
darb
AH, YES. BUT YOU CAN'T TOUCH ME.
CURSE YOU! CURSE YOU!
HA HA! THIS IS GOOD!

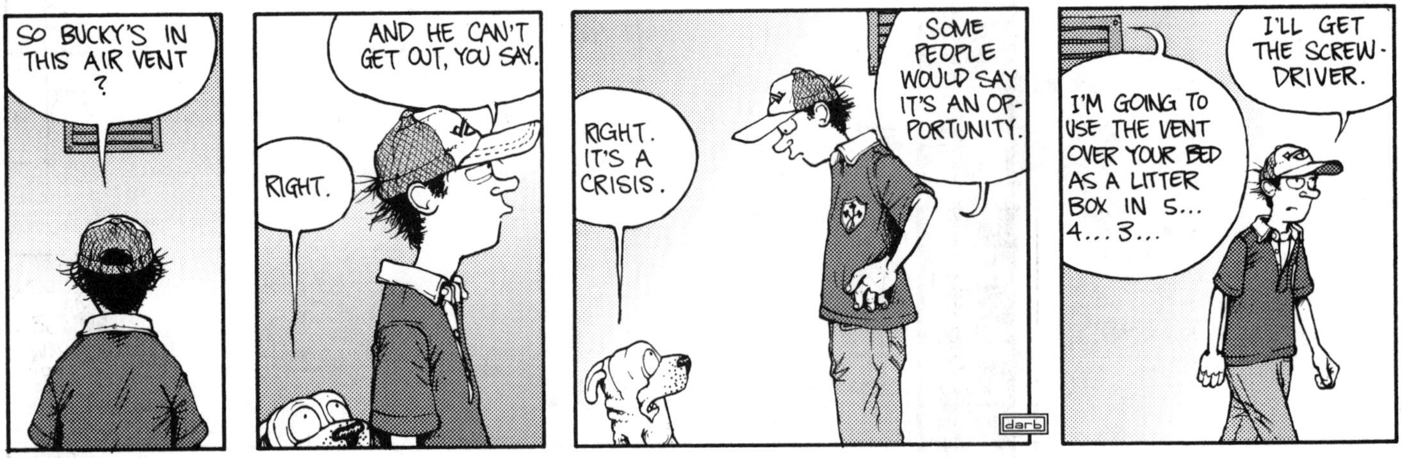
SO BUCKY'S IN THIS AIR VENT?
AND HE CAN'T GET OUT, YOU SAY.
RIGHT.
RIGHT. IT'S A CRISIS.
SOME PEOPLE WOULD SAY IT'S AN OPPORTUNITY.
darb
I'LL GET THE SCREWDRIVER.
I'M GOING TO USE THE VENT OVER YOUR BED AS A LITTER BOX IN 5... 4... 3...

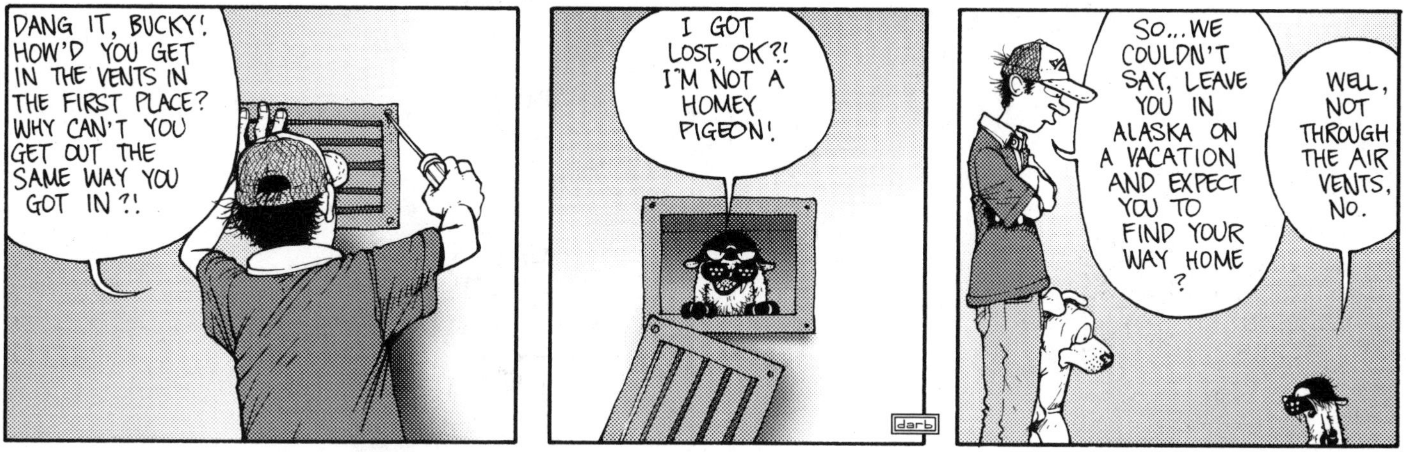
DANG IT, BUCKY! HOW'D YOU GET IN THE VENTS IN THE FIRST PLACE? WHY CAN'T YOU GET OUT THE SAME WAY YOU GOT IN?!
I GOT LOST, OK?! I'M NOT A HOMEY PIGEON!
darb
SO... WE COULDN'T SAY, LEAVE YOU IN ALASKA ON A VACATION AND EXPECT YOU TO FIND YOUR WAY HOME ?
WELL, NOT THROUGH THE AIR VENTS, NO.

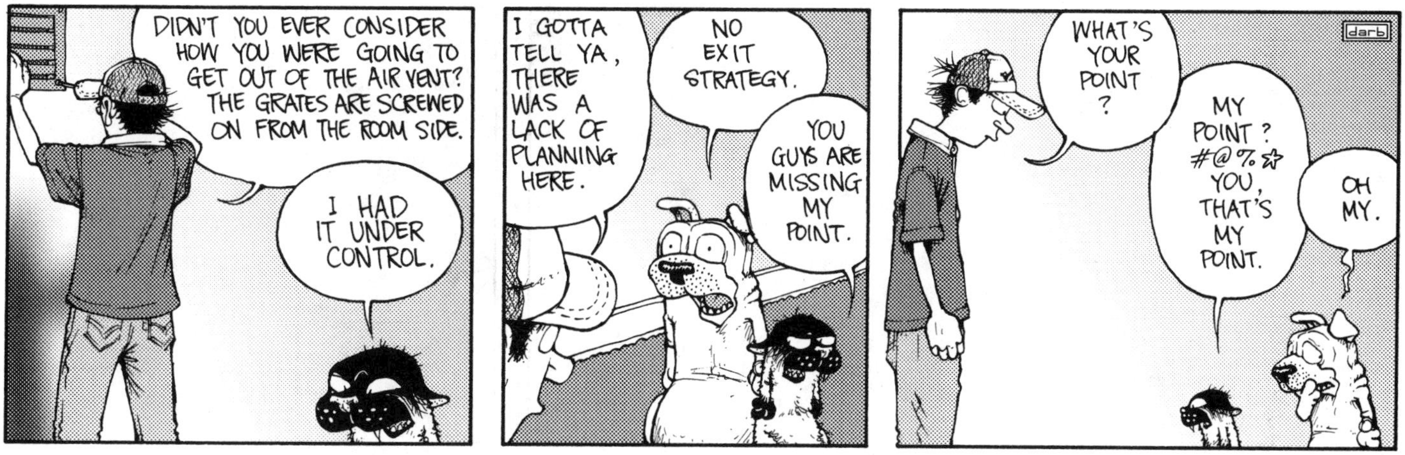
DIDN'T YOU EVER CONSIDER HOW YOU WERE GOING TO GET OUT OF THE AIR VENT? THE GRATES ARE SCREWED ON FROM THE ROOM SIDE.
I HAD IT UNDER CONTROL.
I GOTTA TELL YA, THERE WAS A LACK OF PLANNING HERE.
NO EXIT STRATEGY.
YOU GUYS ARE MISSING MY POINT.
darb
WHAT'S YOUR POINT ?
MY POINT ? #@%☆ YOU, THAT'S MY POINT.
OH MY.

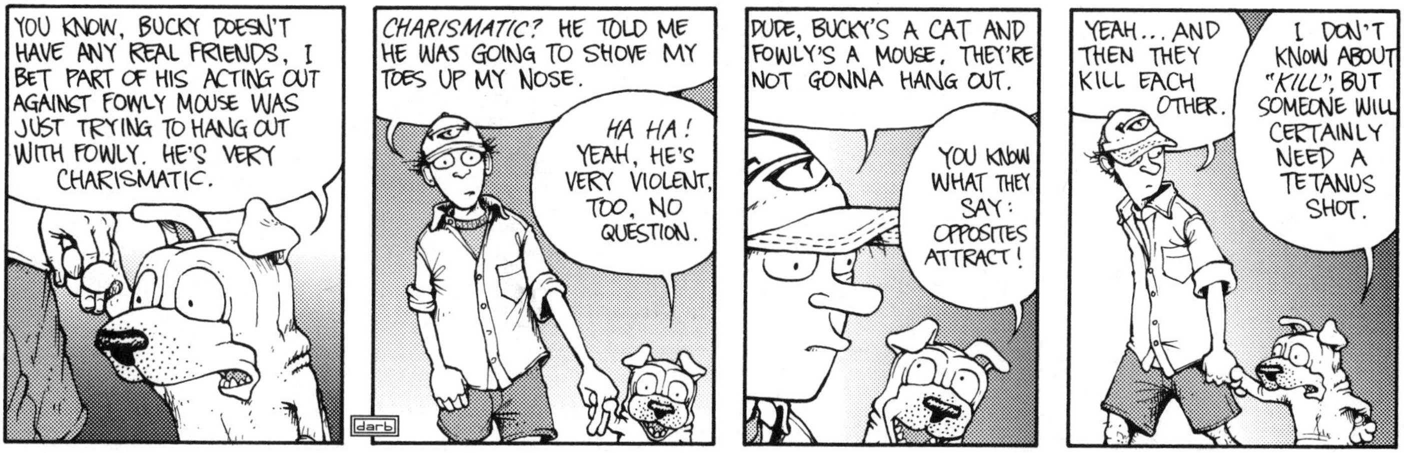
YOU KNOW, BUCKY DOESN'T HAVE ANY REAL FRIENDS, I BET PART OF HIS ACTING OUT AGAINST FOWLY MOUSE WAS JUST TRYING TO HANG OUT WITH FOWLY. HE'S VERY CHARISMATIC.
darb
CHARISMATIC? HE TOLD ME HE WAS GOING TO SHOVE MY TOES UP MY NOSE.
HA HA! YEAH, HE'S VERY VIOLENT, TOO, NO QUESTION.
DUDE, BUCKY'S A CAT AND FOWLY'S A MOUSE, THEY'RE NOT GONNA HANG OUT.
YOU KNOW WHAT THEY SAY: OPPOSITES ATTRACT!
YEAH... AND THEN THEY KILL EACH OTHER.
I DON'T KNOW ABOUT "KILL", BUT SOMEONE WILL CERTAINLY NEED A TETANUS SHOT.

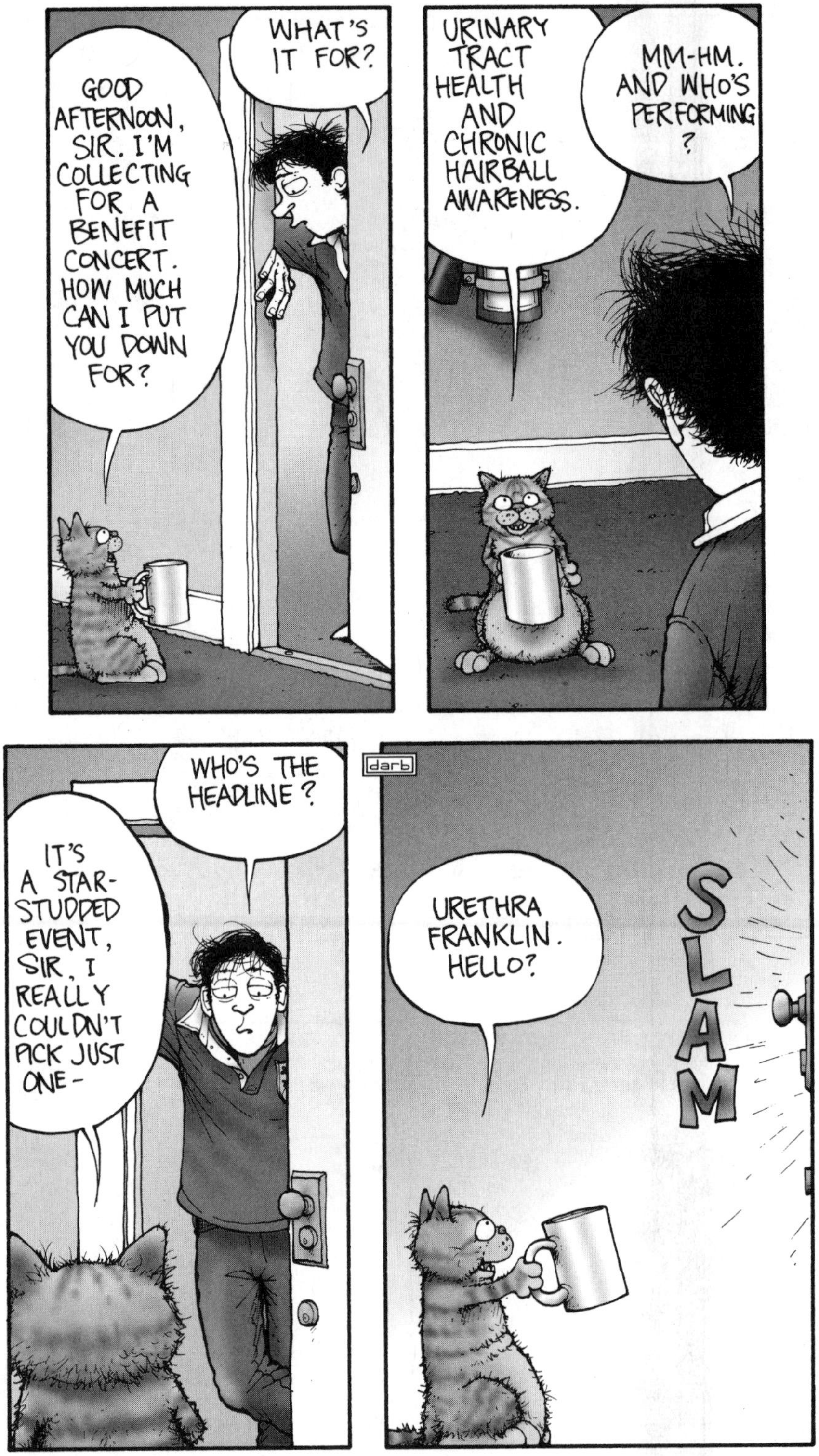
GOOD AFTERNOON, SIR. I'M COLLECTING FOR A BENEFIT CONCERT. HOW MUCH CAN I PUT YOU DOWN FOR?
WHAT'S IT FOR?
URINARY TRACT HEALTH AND CHRONIC HAIRBALL AWARENESS.
MM-HM. AND WHO'S PERFORMING?
WHO'S THE HEADLINE?
IT'S A STAR-STUDDED EVENT, SIR, I REALLY COULDN'T PICK JUST ONE-
URETHRA FRANKLIN. HELLO?
SLAM
darb

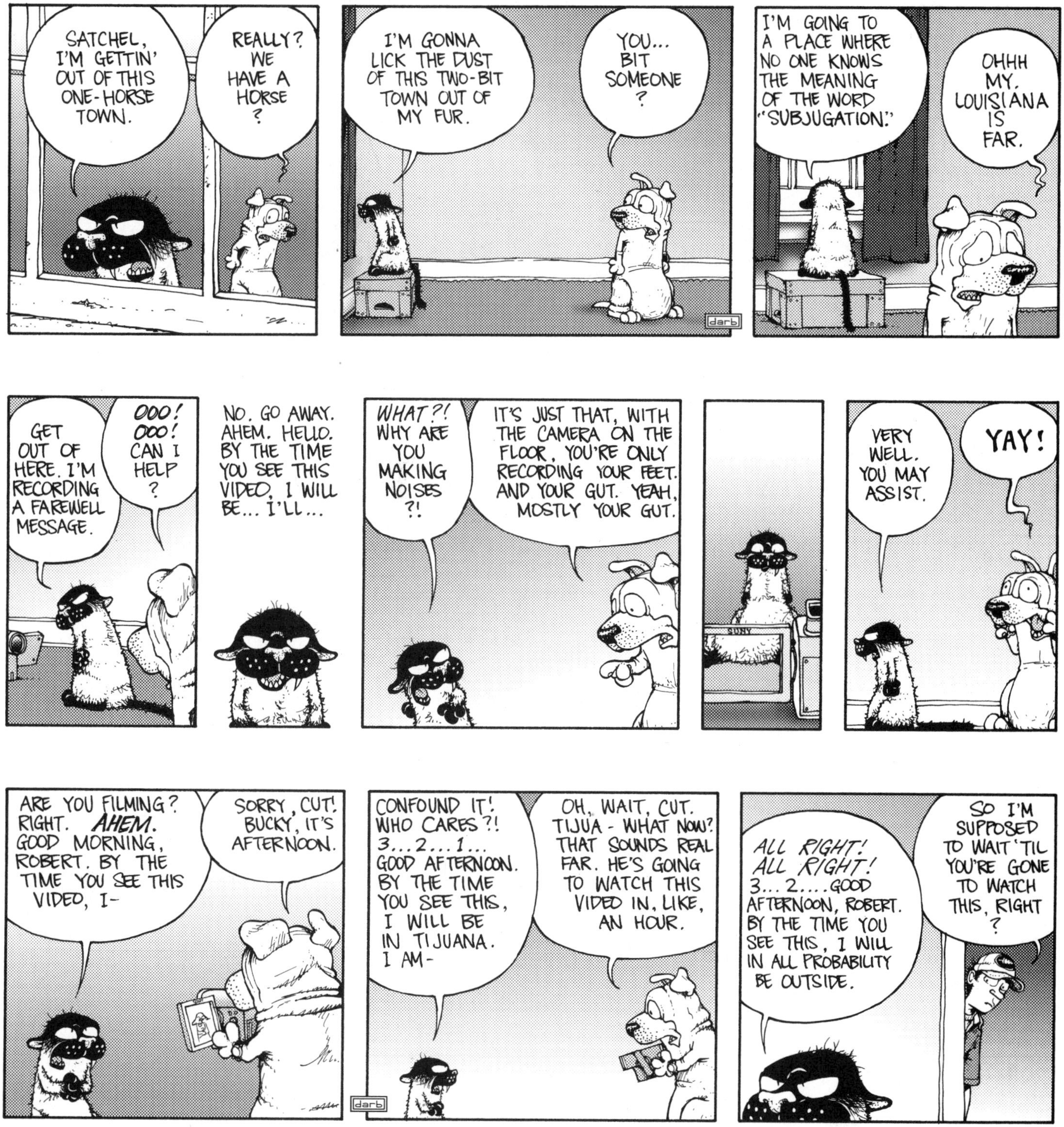
SATCHEL, I'M GETTIN' OUT OF THIS ONE-HORSE TOWN.
REALLY? WE HAVE A HORSE?
I'M GONNA LICK THE DUST OF THIS TWO-BIT TOWN OUT OF MY FUR.
YOU... BIT SOMEONE?
darb
I'M GOING TO A PLACE WHERE NO ONE KNOWS THE MEANING OF THE WORD "SUBJUGATION."
OHHH MY. LOUISIANA IS FAR.
GET OUT OF HERE. I'M RECORDING A FAREWELL MESSAGE.
OOO! OOO! CAN I HELP?
NO. GO AWAY. AHEM. HELLO. BY THE TIME YOU SEE THIS VIDEO, I WILL BE... I'LL...
WHAT?! WHY ARE YOU MAKING NOISES?!
IT'S JUST THAT, WITH THE CAMERA ON THE FLOOR, YOU'RE ONLY RECORDING YOUR FEET. AND YOUR GUT. YEAH, MOSTLY YOUR GUT.
SONY
VERY WELL. YOU MAY ASSIST.
YAY!
ARE YOU FILMING? RIGHT. AHEM. GOOD MORNING, ROBERT. BY THE TIME YOU SEE THIS VIDEO, I-
SORRY, CUT! BUCKY, IT'S AFTERNOON.
darb
CONFOUND IT! WHO CARES?! 3...2...1... GOOD AFTERNOON. BY THE TIME YOU SEE THIS, I WILL BE IN TIJUANA. I AM-
OH, WAIT, CUT. TIJUA- WHAT NOW? THAT SOUNDS REAL FAR. HE'S GOING TO WATCH THIS VIDEO IN, LIKE, AN HOUR.
ALL RIGHT! ALL RIGHT! 3... 2.... GOOD AFTERNOON, ROBERT. BY THE TIME YOU SEE THIS, I WILL IN ALL PROBABILITY BE OUTSIDE.
SO I'M SUPPOSED TO WAIT 'TIL YOU'RE GONE TO WATCH THIS, RIGHT?

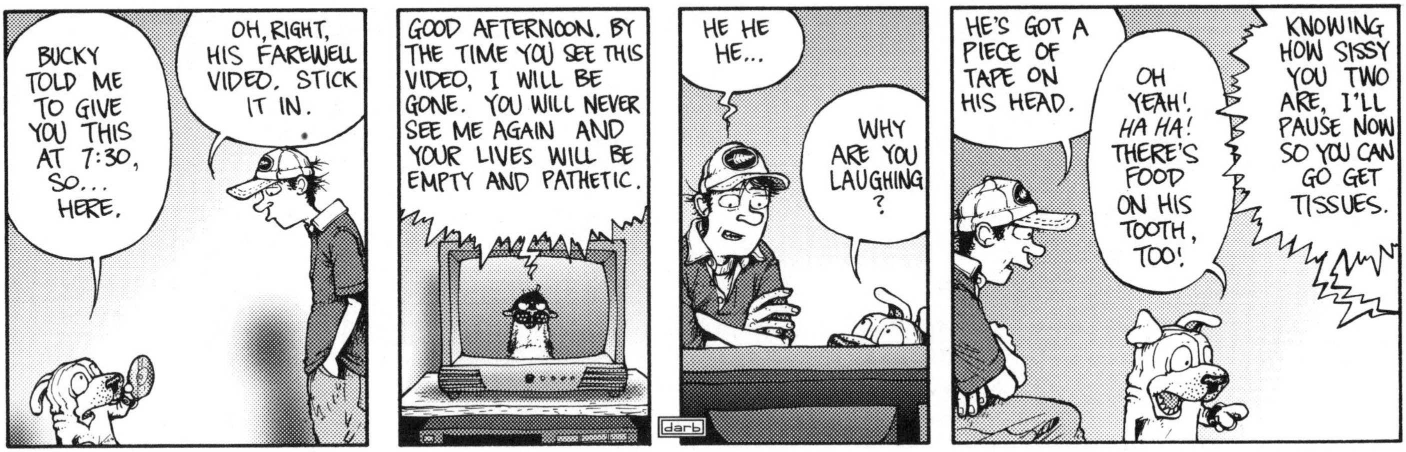
BUCKY TOLD ME TO GIVE YOU THIS AT 7:30, SO... HERE.
OH, RIGHT, HIS FAREWELL VIDEO. STICK IT IN.
GOOD AFTERNOON. BY THE TIME YOU SEE THIS VIDEO, I WILL BE GONE. YOU WILL NEVER SEE ME AGAIN AND YOUR LIVES WILL BE EMPTY AND PATHETIC.
darb
HE HE HE...
WHY ARE YOU LAUGHING?
HE'S GOT A PIECE OF TAPE ON HIS HEAD.
OH YEAH! HA HA! THERE'S FOOD ON HIS TOOTH, TOO!
KNOWING HOW SISSY YOU TWO ARE, I'LL PAUSE NOW SO YOU CAN GO GET TISSUES.

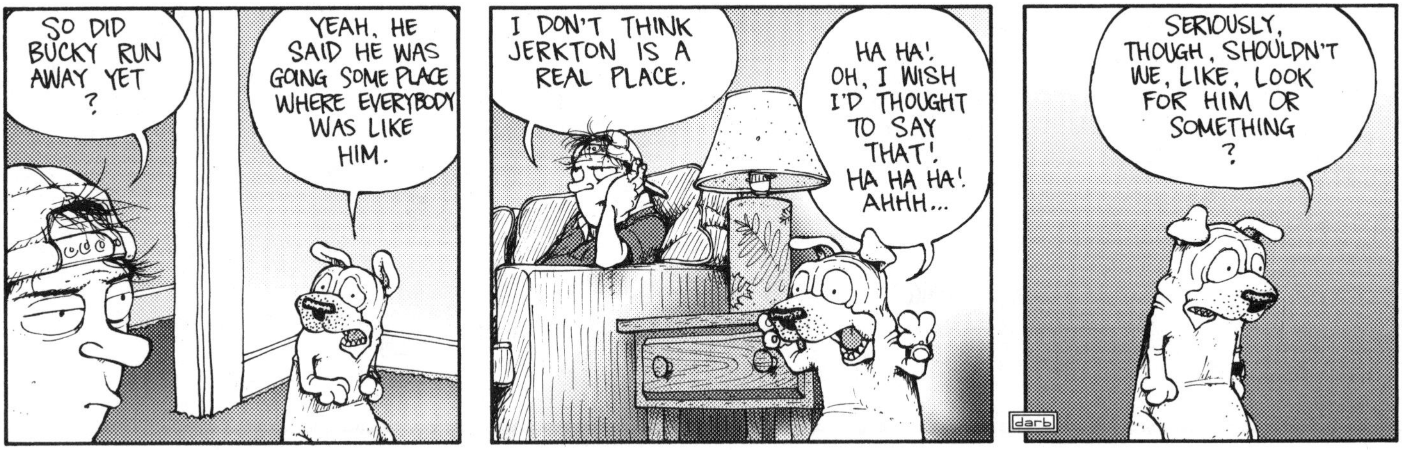
SO DID BUCKY RUN AWAY YET?
YEAH. HE SAID HE WAS GOING SOME PLACE WHERE EVERYBODY WAS LIKE HIM.
I DON'T THINK JERKTON IS A REAL PLACE.
HA HA! OH, I WISH I'D THOUGHT TO SAY THAT! HA HA HA! AHHH...
SERIOUSLY, THOUGH, SHOULDN'T WE, LIKE, LOOK FOR HIM OR SOMETHING?
darb

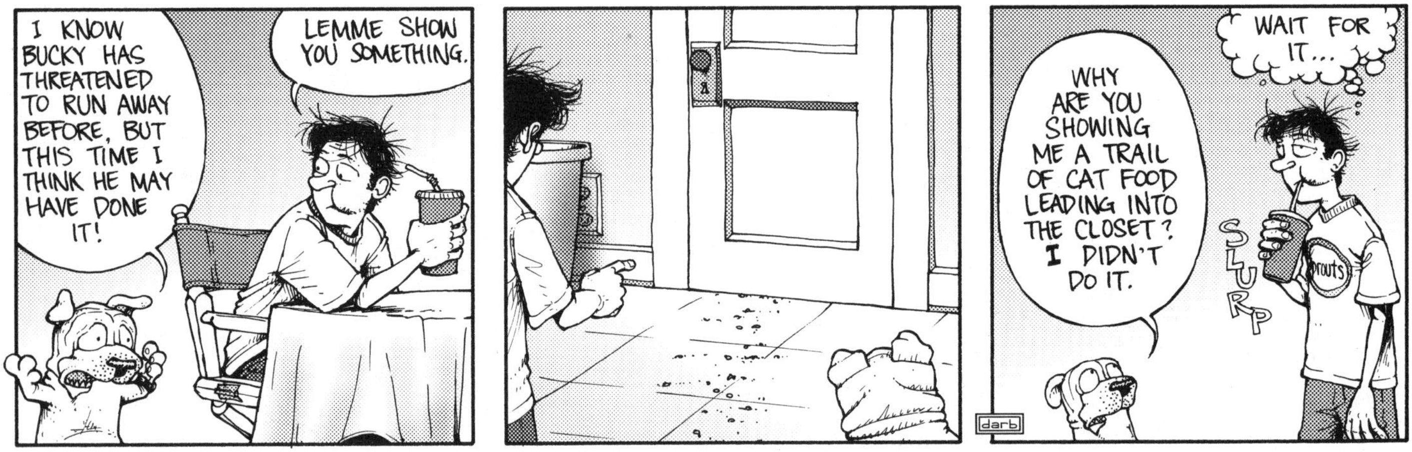
I KNOW BUCKY HAS THREATENED TO RUN AWAY BEFORE, BUT THIS TIME I THINK HE MAY HAVE DONE IT!
LEMME SHOW YOU SOMETHING.
darb
WAIT FOR IT...
WHY ARE YOU SHOWING ME A TRAIL OF CAT FOOD LEADING INTO THE CLOSET? **I** DIDN'T DO IT.
SLURP

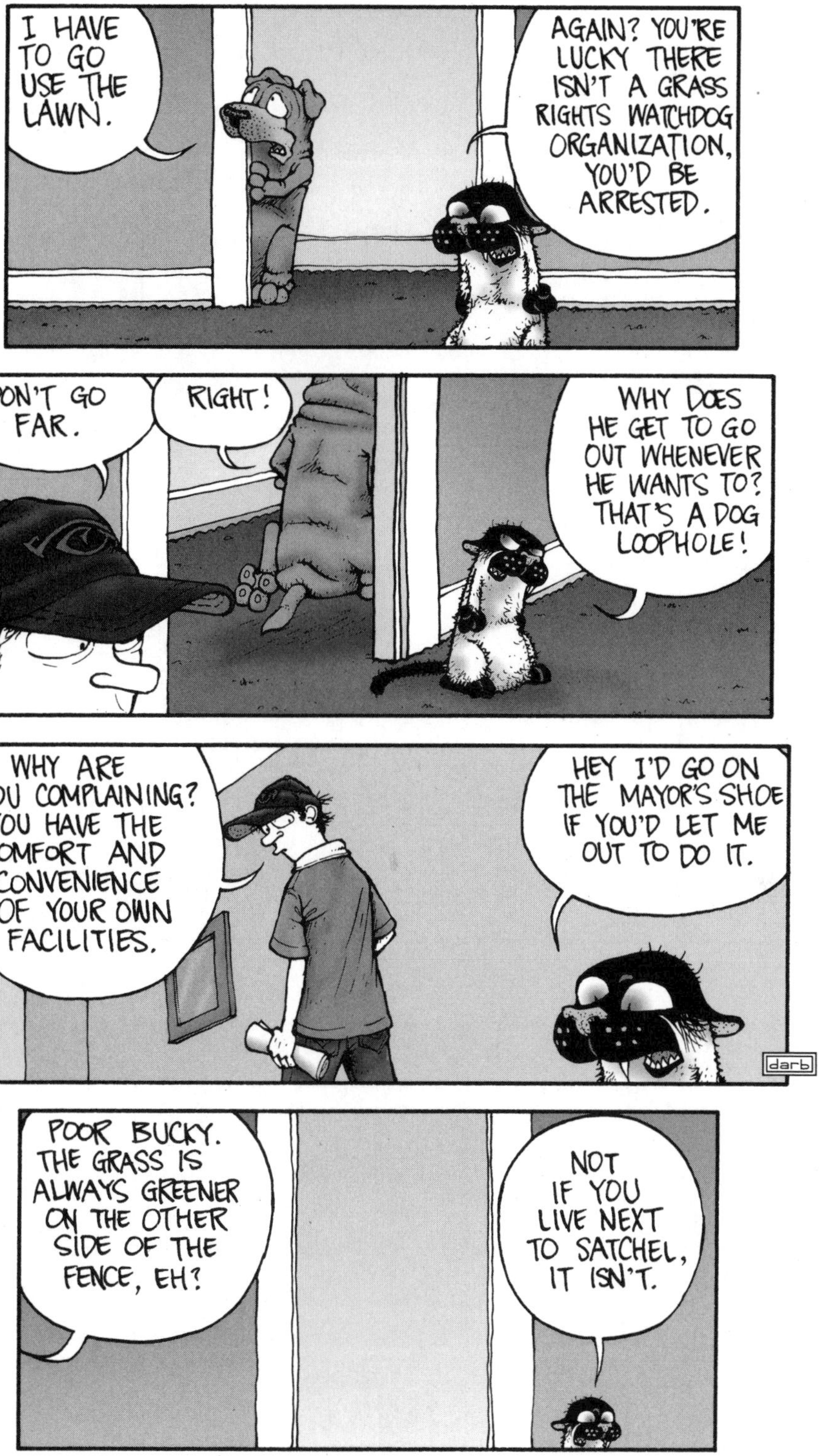
I HAVE TO GO USE THE LAWN.
AGAIN? YOU'RE LUCKY THERE ISN'T A GRASS RIGHTS WATCHDOG ORGANIZATION, YOU'D BE ARRESTED.
DON'T GO FAR.
RIGHT!
WHY DOES HE GET TO GO OUT WHENEVER HE WANTS TO? THAT'S A DOG LOOPHOLE!
WHY ARE YOU COMPLAINING? YOU HAVE THE COMFORT AND CONVENIENCE OF YOUR OWN FACILITIES.
HEY I'D GO ON THE MAYOR'S SHOE IF YOU'D LET ME OUT TO DO IT.
darb
POOR BUCKY. THE GRASS IS ALWAYS GREENER ON THE OTHER SIDE OF THE FENCE, EH?
NOT IF YOU LIVE NEXT TO SATCHEL, IT ISN'T.

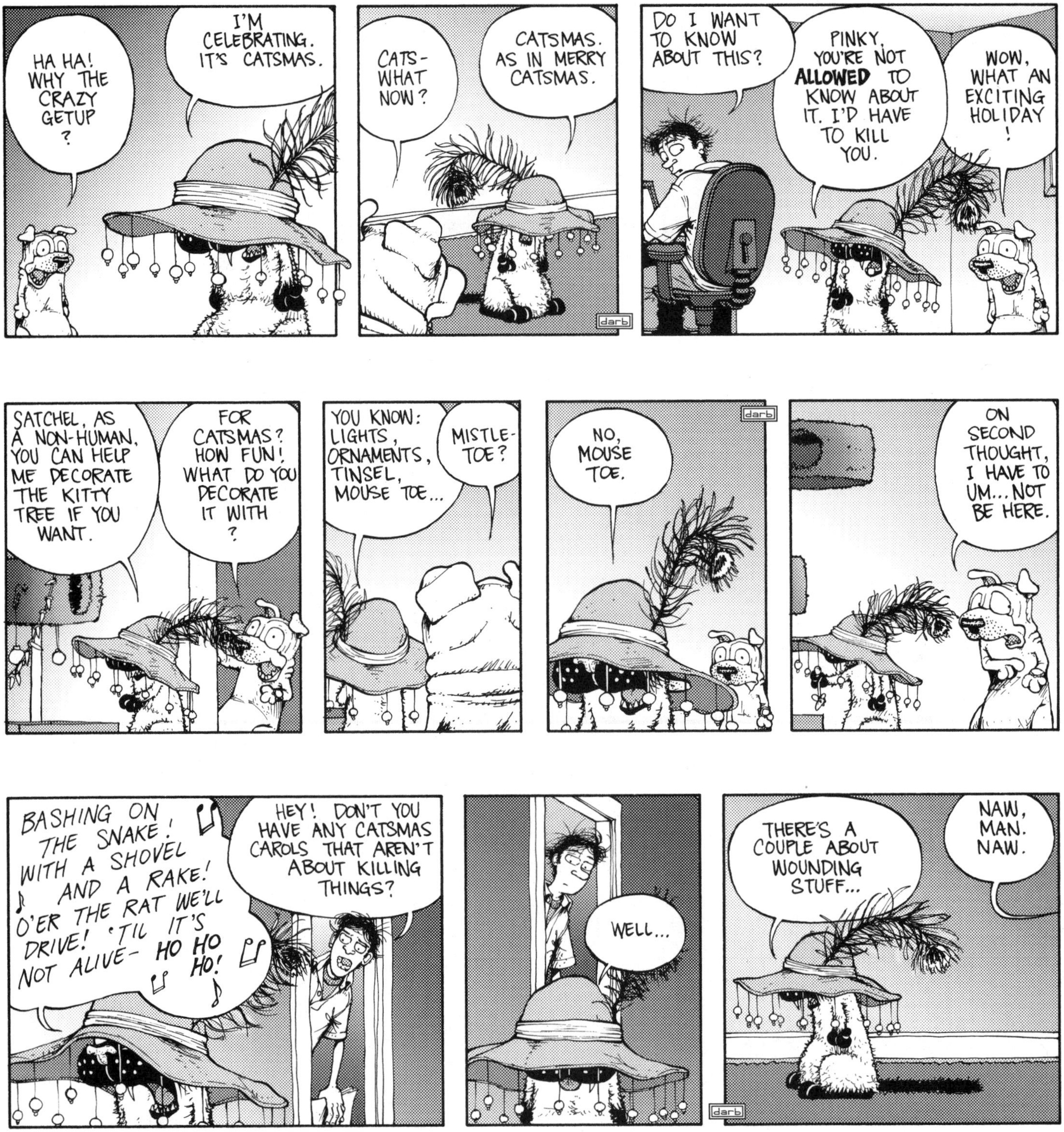
HA HA! WHY THE CRAZY GETUP ?
I'M CELEBRATING. IT'S CATSMAS.
CATS- WHAT NOW?
CATSMAS. AS IN MERRY CATSMAS.
darb
DO I WANT TO KNOW ABOUT THIS?
PINKY, YOU'RE NOT **ALLOWED** TO KNOW ABOUT IT. I'D HAVE TO KILL YOU.
WOW, WHAT AN EXCITING HOLIDAY !
SATCHEL, AS A NON-HUMAN, YOU CAN HELP ME DECORATE THE KITTY TREE IF YOU WANT.
FOR CATSMAS? HOW FUN! WHAT DO YOU DECORATE IT WITH ?
YOU KNOW: LIGHTS, ORNAMENTS, TINSEL, MOUSE TOE...
MISTLE- TOE?
darb
NO, MOUSE TOE.
ON SECOND THOUGHT, I HAVE TO UM... NOT BE HERE.
BASHING ON THE SNAKE! WITH A SHOVEL AND A RAKE! O'ER THE RAT WE'LL DRIVE! 'TIL IT'S NOT ALIVE- HO HO HO!
HEY! DON'T YOU HAVE ANY CATSMAS CAROLS THAT AREN'T ABOUT KILLING THINGS?
WELL...
darb
THERE'S A COUPLE ABOUT WOUNDING STUFF...
NAW, MAN. NAW.

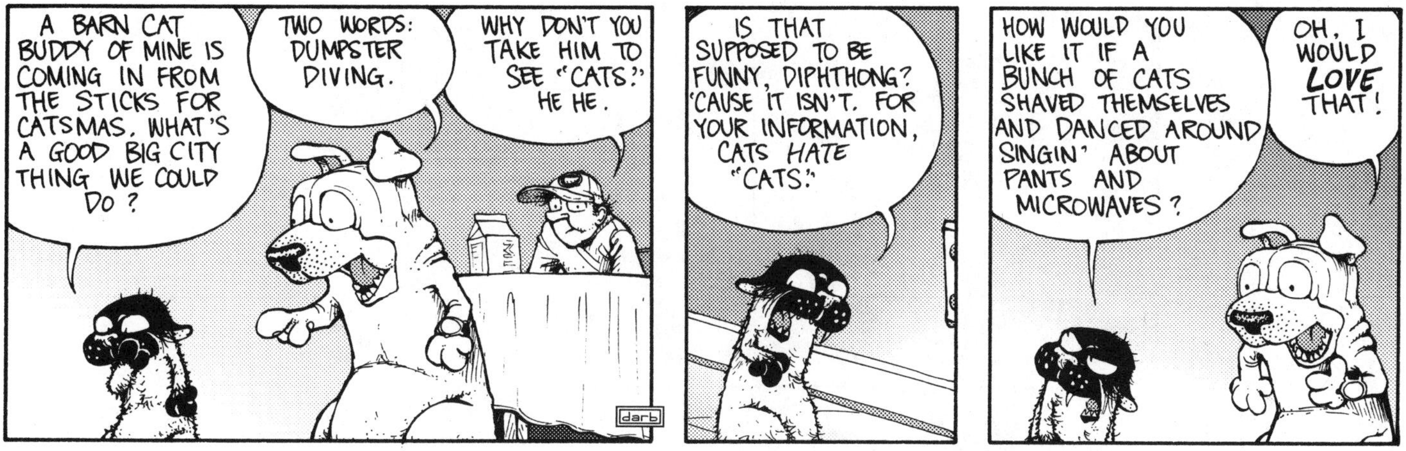
A BARN CAT BUDDY OF MINE IS COMING IN FROM THE STICKS FOR CATSMAS. WHAT'S A GOOD BIG CITY THING WE COULD DO?
TWO WORDS: DUMPSTER DIVING.
WHY DON'T YOU TAKE HIM TO SEE "CATS." HE HE.
darb
IS THAT SUPPOSED TO BE FUNNY, DIPHTHONG? 'CAUSE IT ISN'T. FOR YOUR INFORMATION, CATS *HATE* "CATS."
HOW WOULD YOU LIKE IT IF A BUNCH OF CATS SHAVED THEMSELVES AND DANCED AROUND SINGIN' ABOUT PANTS AND MICROWAVES?
OH, I WOULD ***LOVE*** THAT!

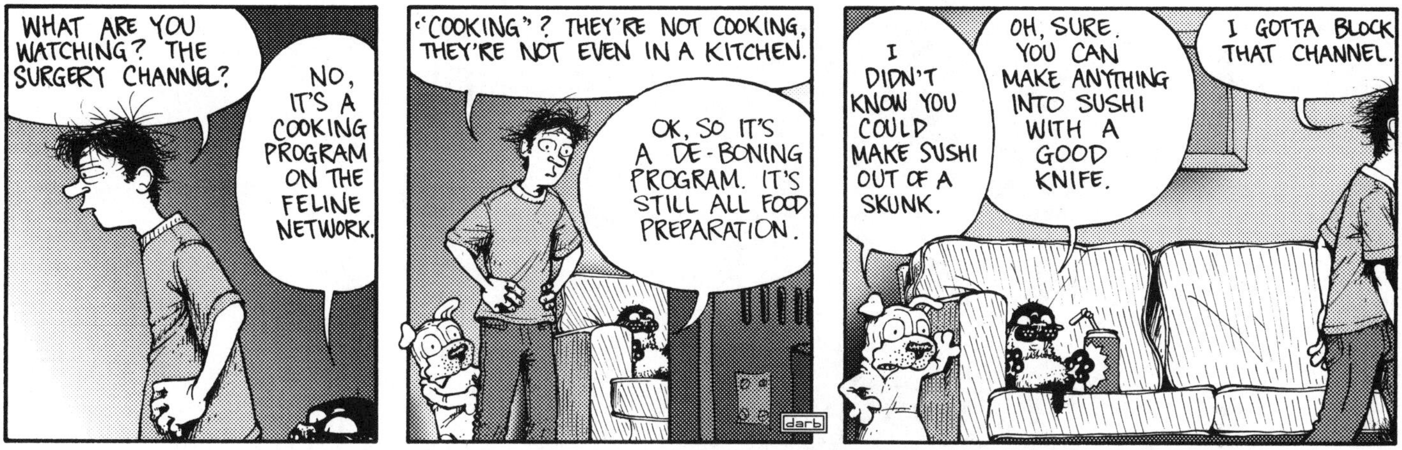
WHAT ARE YOU WATCHING? THE SURGERY CHANNEL?
NO, IT'S A COOKING PROGRAM ON THE FELINE NETWORK.
"COOKING"? THEY'RE NOT COOKING, THEY'RE NOT EVEN IN A KITCHEN.
OK, SO IT'S A DE-BONING PROGRAM. IT'S STILL ALL FOOD PREPARATION.
darb
I DIDN'T KNOW YOU COULD MAKE SUSHI OUT OF A SKUNK.
OH, SURE. YOU CAN MAKE ANYTHING INTO SUSHI WITH A GOOD KNIFE.
I GOTTA BLOCK THAT CHANNEL.

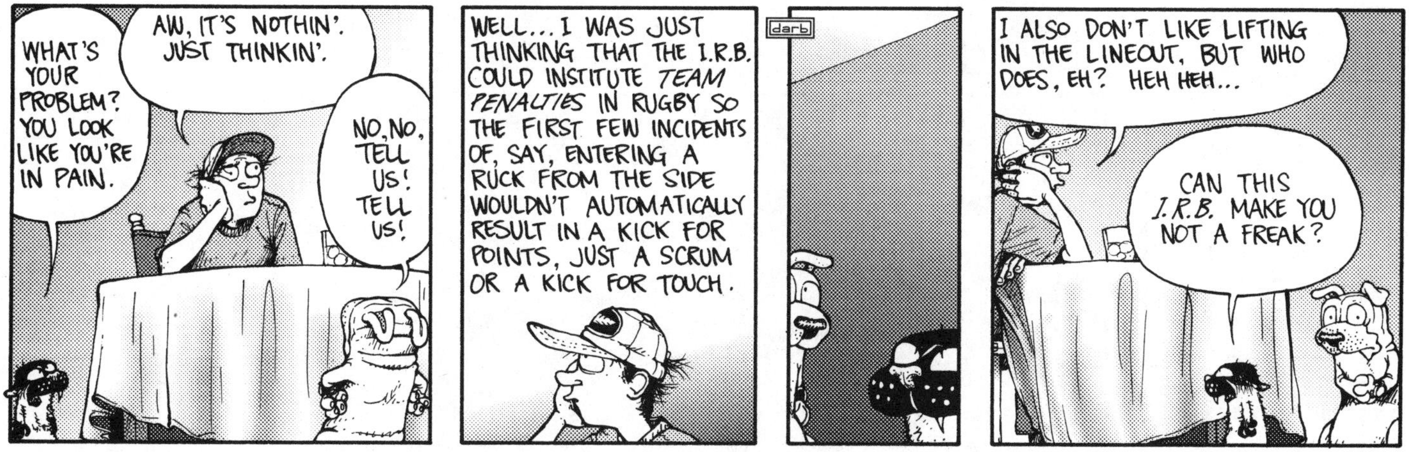
WHAT'S YOUR PROBLEM? YOU LOOK LIKE YOU'RE IN PAIN.
AW, IT'S NOTHIN'. JUST THINKIN'.
NO, NO, TELL US! TELL US!
WELL... I WAS JUST THINKING THAT THE I.R.B. COULD INSTITUTE *TEAM PENALTIES* IN RUGBY SO THE FIRST FEW INCIDENTS OF, SAY, ENTERING A RUCK FROM THE SIDE WOULDN'T AUTOMATICALLY RESULT IN A KICK FOR POINTS, JUST A SCRUM OR A KICK FOR TOUCH.
darb
I ALSO DON'T LIKE LIFTING IN THE LINEOUT, BUT WHO DOES, EH? HEH HEH...
CAN THIS *I.R.B.* MAKE YOU NOT A FREAK?

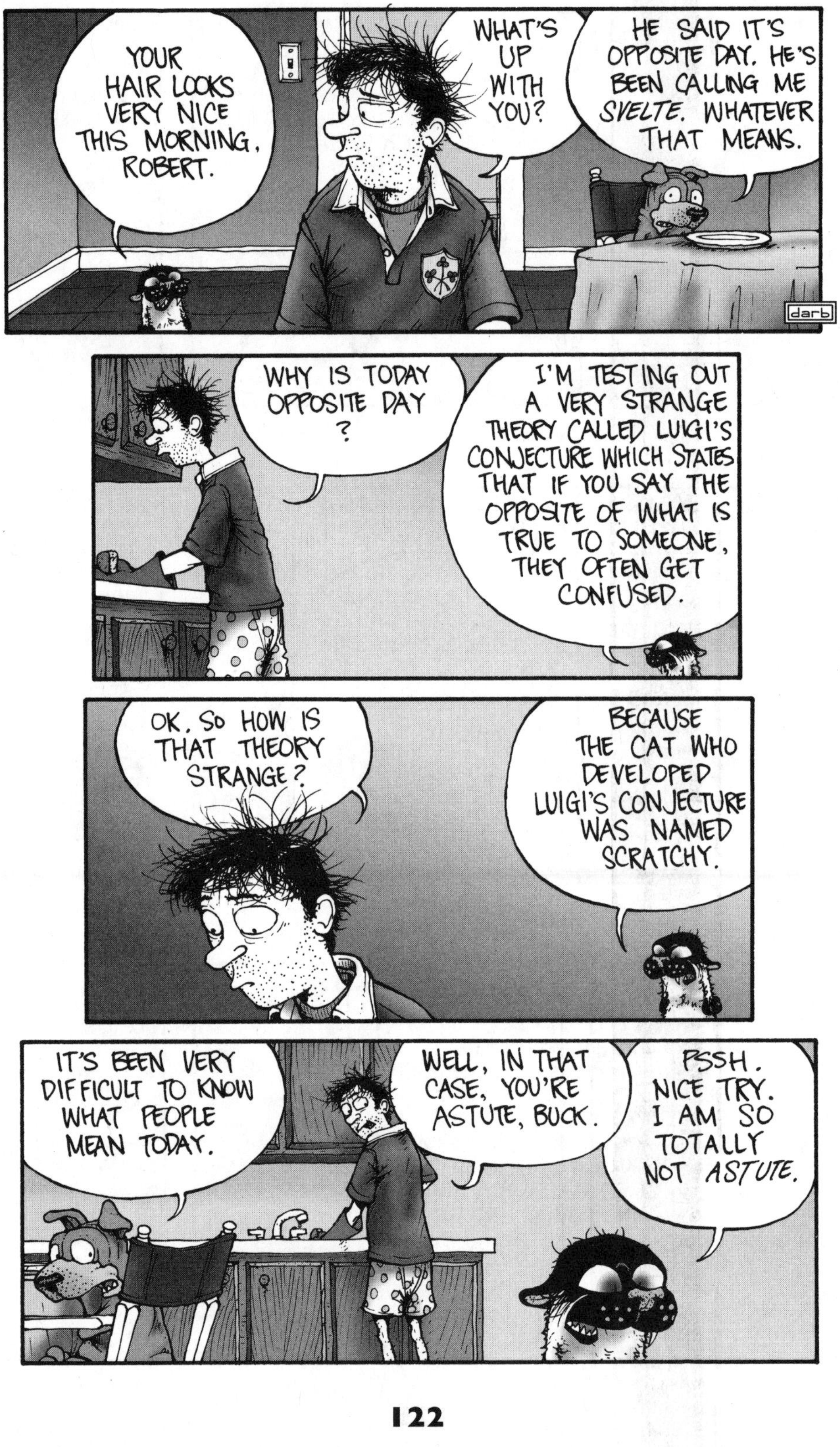
YOUR HAIR LOOKS VERY NICE THIS MORNING, ROBERT.
WHAT'S UP WITH YOU?
HE SAID IT'S OPPOSITE DAY. HE'S BEEN CALLING ME *SVELTE*. WHATEVER THAT MEANS.
darb
WHY IS TODAY OPPOSITE DAY ?
I'M TESTING OUT A VERY STRANGE THEORY CALLED LUIGI'S CONJECTURE WHICH STATES THAT IF YOU SAY THE OPPOSITE OF WHAT IS TRUE TO SOMEONE, THEY OFTEN GET CONFUSED.
OK, SO HOW IS THAT THEORY STRANGE?
BECAUSE THE CAT WHO DEVELOPED LUIGI'S CONJECTURE WAS NAMED SCRATCHY.
IT'S BEEN VERY DIFFICULT TO KNOW WHAT PEOPLE MEAN TODAY.
WELL, IN THAT CASE, YOU'RE ASTUTE, BUCK.
PSSH. NICE TRY. I AM SO TOTALLY NOT *ASTUTE*.

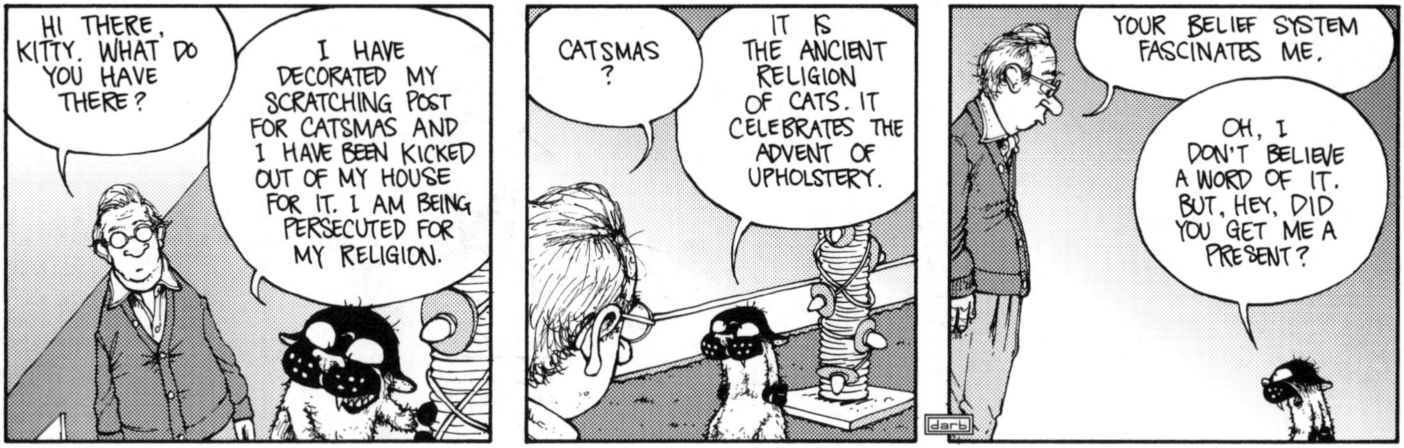
HI THERE, KITTY. WHAT DO YOU HAVE THERE?
I HAVE DECORATED MY SCRATCHING POST FOR CATSMAS AND I HAVE BEEN KICKED OUT OF MY HOUSE FOR IT. I AM BEING PERSECUTED FOR MY RELIGION.
CATSMAS?
IT IS THE ANCIENT RELIGION OF CATS. IT CELEBRATES THE ADVENT OF UPHOLSTERY.
YOUR BELIEF SYSTEM FASCINATES ME.
OH, I DON'T BELIEVE A WORD OF IT. BUT, HEY, DID YOU GET ME A PRESENT?
darb

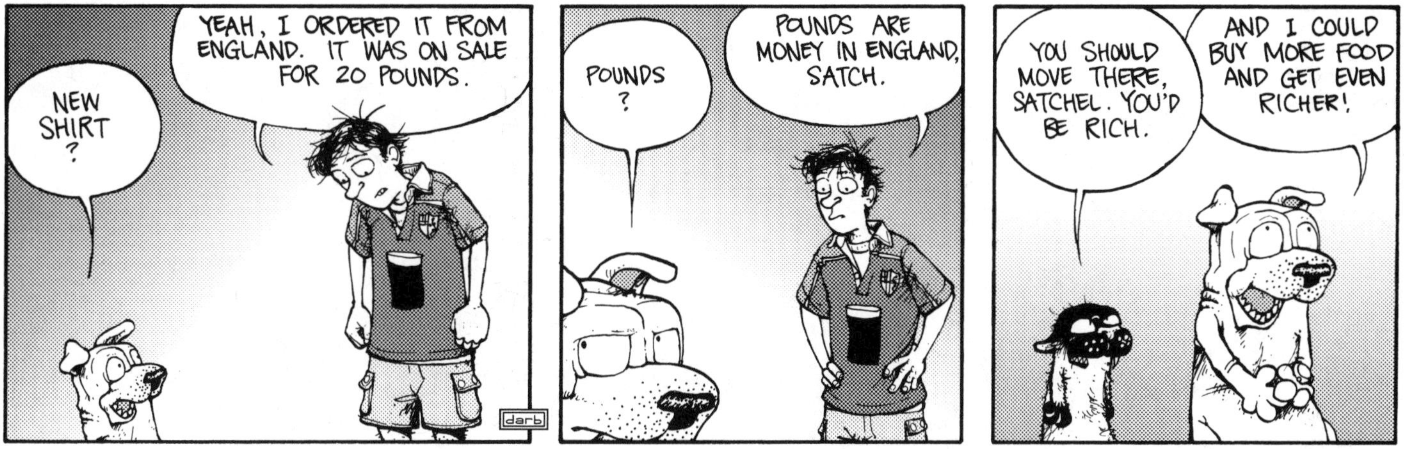
NEW SHIRT?
YEAH, I ORDERED IT FROM ENGLAND. IT WAS ON SALE FOR 20 POUNDS.
darb
POUNDS?
POUNDS ARE MONEY IN ENGLAND, SATCH.
YOU SHOULD MOVE THERE, SATCHEL. YOU'D BE RICH.
AND I COULD BUY MORE FOOD AND GET EVEN RICHER!

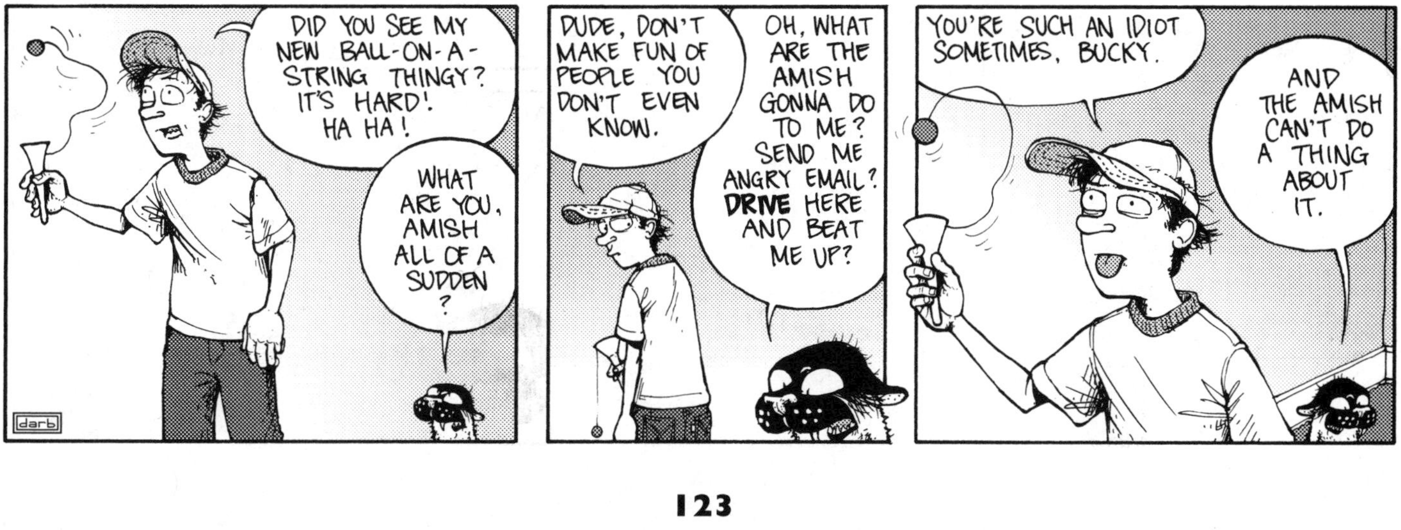
DID YOU SEE MY NEW BALL-ON-A-STRING THINGY? IT'S HARD! HA HA!
WHAT ARE YOU, AMISH ALL OF A SUDDEN?
darb
DUDE, DON'T MAKE FUN OF PEOPLE YOU DON'T EVEN KNOW.
OH, WHAT ARE THE AMISH GONNA DO TO ME? SEND ME ANGRY EMAIL? DRIVE HERE AND BEAT ME UP?
YOU'RE SUCH AN IDIOT SOMETIMES, BUCKY.
AND THE AMISH CAN'T DO A THING ABOUT IT.

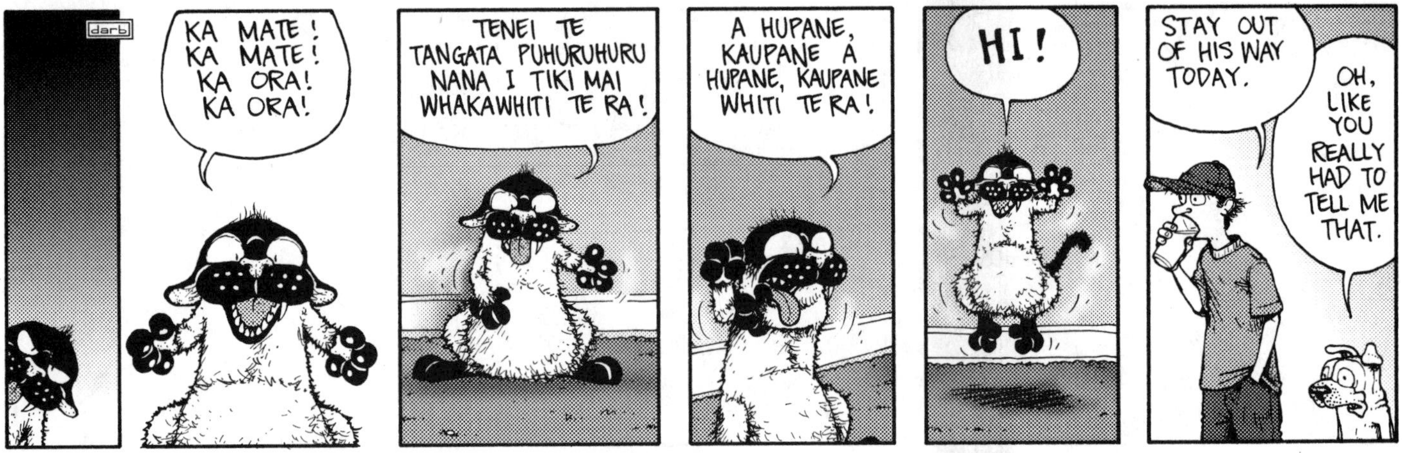
KA MATE! KA MATE! KA ORA! KA ORA!
TENEI TE TANGATA PUHURUHURU NANA I TIKI MAI WHAKAWHITI TE RA!
A HUPANE, KAUPANE A HUPANE, KAUPANE WHITI TE RA!
HI!
STAY OUT OF HIS WAY TODAY.
OH, LIKE YOU REALLY HAD TO TELL ME THAT.

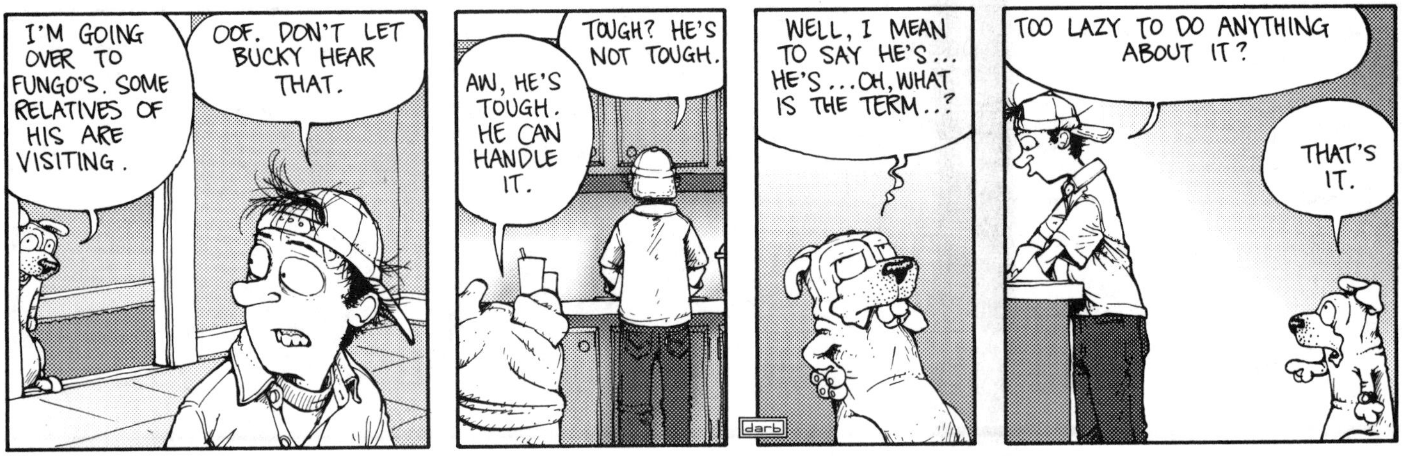
I'M GOING OVER TO FUNGO'S. SOME RELATIVES OF HIS ARE VISITING.
OOF. DON'T LET BUCKY HEAR THAT.
AW, HE'S TOUGH. HE CAN HANDLE IT.
TOUGH? HE'S NOT TOUGH.
WELL, I MEAN TO SAY HE'S... HE'S...OH, WHAT IS THE TERM..?
TOO LAZY TO DO ANYTHING ABOUT IT?
THAT'S IT.

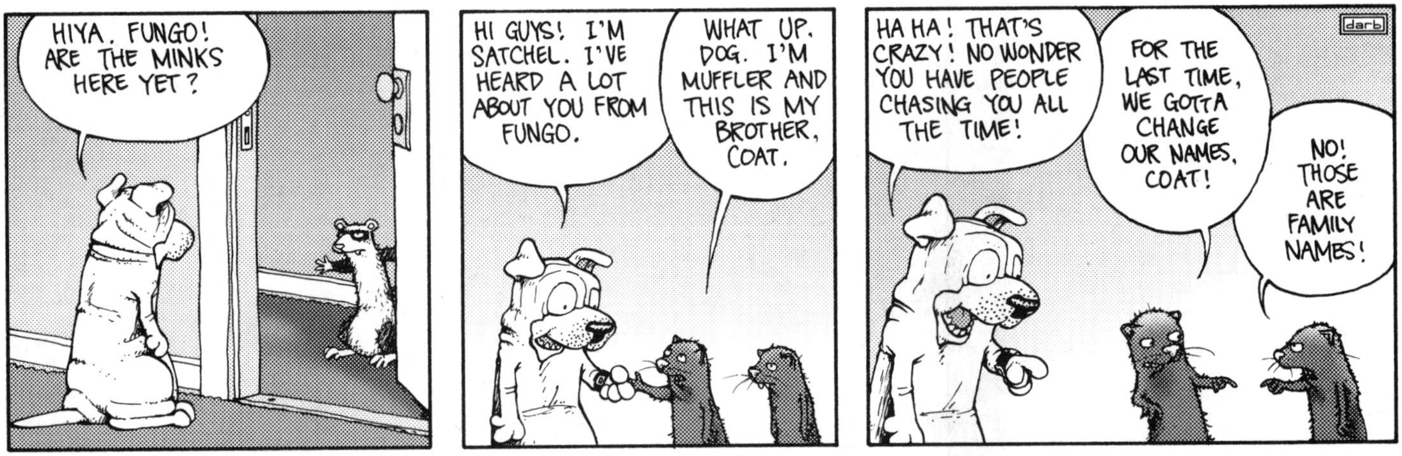
HIYA, FUNGO! ARE THE MINKS HERE YET?
HI GUYS! I'M SATCHEL. I'VE HEARD A LOT ABOUT YOU FROM FUNGO.
WHAT UP, DOG. I'M MUFFLER AND THIS IS MY BROTHER, COAT.
HA HA! THAT'S CRAZY! NO WONDER YOU HAVE PEOPLE CHASING YOU ALL THE TIME!
FOR THE LAST TIME, WE GOTTA CHANGE OUR NAMES, COAT!
NO! THOSE ARE FAMILY NAMES!

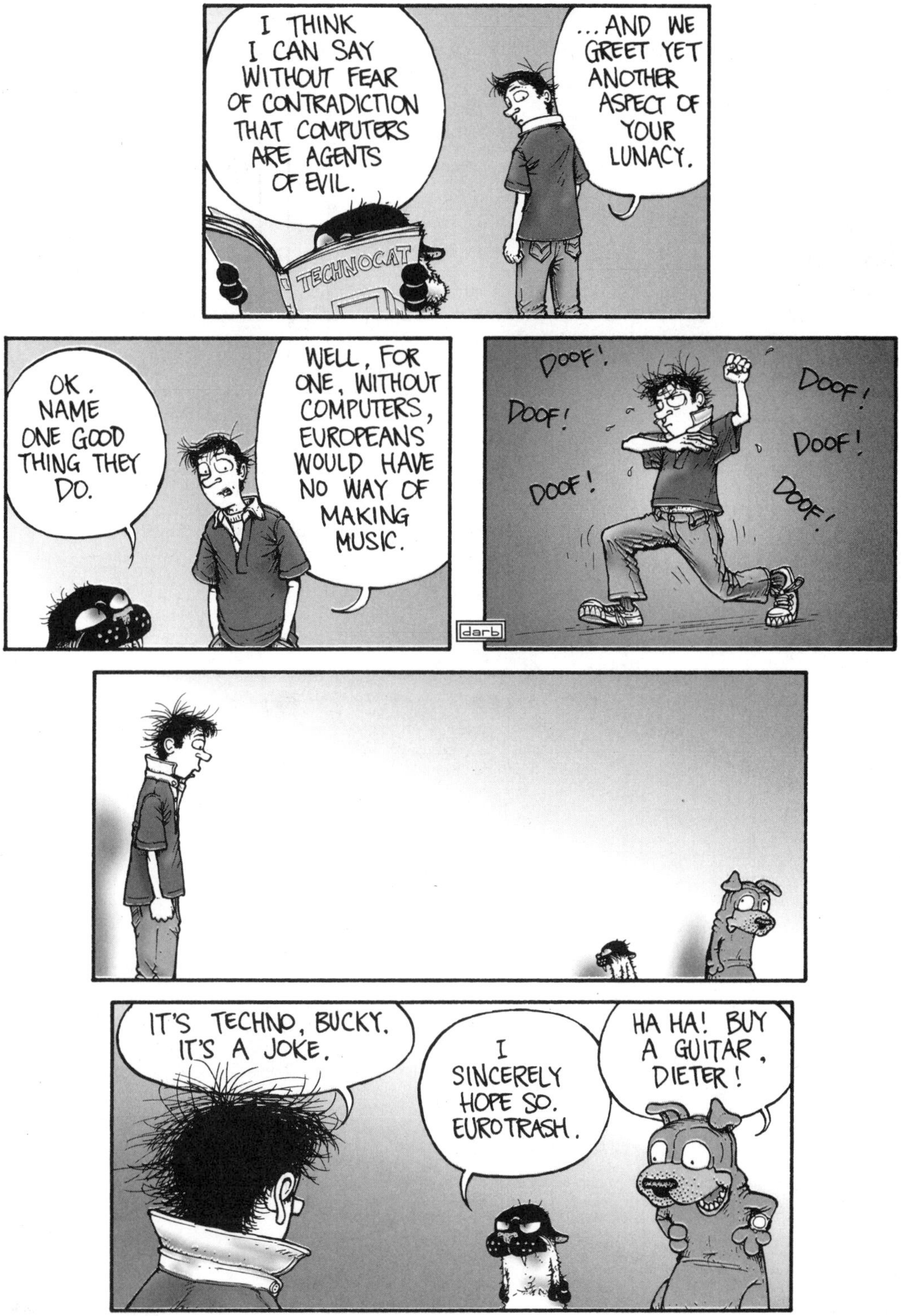
I THINK I CAN SAY WITHOUT FEAR OF CONTRADICTION THAT COMPUTERS ARE AGENTS OF EVIL.
...AND WE GREET YET ANOTHER ASPECT OF YOUR LUNACY.
TECHNOCAT
OK. NAME ONE GOOD THING THEY DO.
WELL, FOR ONE, WITHOUT COMPUTERS, EUROPEANS WOULD HAVE NO WAY OF MAKING MUSIC.
DOOF!
DOOF!
DOOF!
DOOF!
DOOF!
DOOF!
darb
IT'S TECHNO, BUCKY. IT'S A JOKE.
I SINCERELY HOPE SO. EUROTRASH.
HA HA! BUY A GUITAR, DIETER!

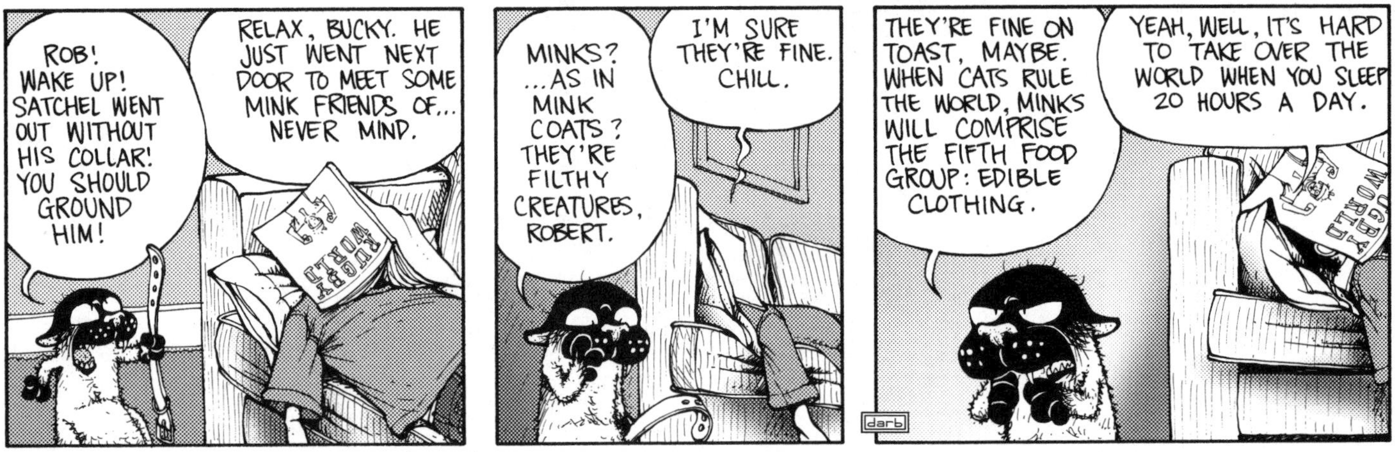
ROB! WAKE UP! SATCHEL WENT OUT WITHOUT HIS COLLAR! YOU SHOULD GROUND HIM!
RELAX, BUCKY. HE JUST WENT NEXT DOOR TO MEET SOME MINK FRIENDS OF... NEVER MIND.
RUGBY WORLD
MINKS? ...AS IN MINK COATS? THEY'RE FILTHY CREATURES, ROBERT.
I'M SURE THEY'RE FINE. CHILL.
THEY'RE FINE ON TOAST, MAYBE. WHEN CATS RULE THE WORLD, MINKS WILL COMPRISE THE FIFTH FOOD GROUP: EDIBLE CLOTHING.
YEAH, WELL, IT'S HARD TO TAKE OVER THE WORLD WHEN YOU SLEEP 20 HOURS A DAY.
darb

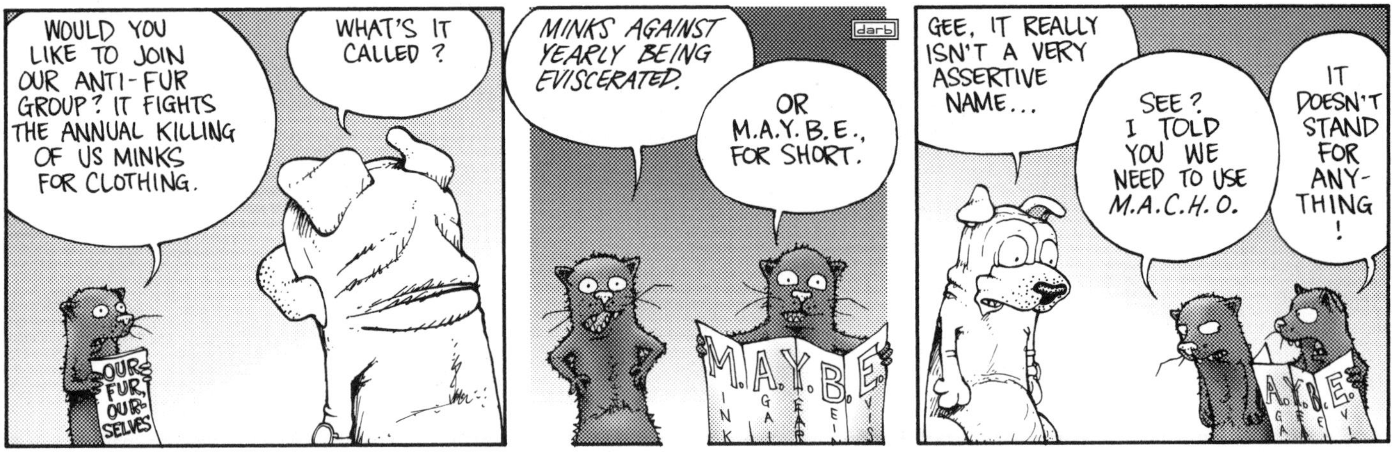
WOULD YOU LIKE TO JOIN OUR ANTI-FUR GROUP? IT FIGHTS THE ANNUAL KILLING OF US MINKS FOR CLOTHING.
OUR FUR, OUR-SELVES
WHAT'S IT CALLED?
MINKS AGAINST YEARLY BEING EVISCERATED.
OR M.A.Y.B.E., FOR SHORT.
M.A.Y.B.E.
darb
GEE, IT REALLY ISN'T A VERY ASSERTIVE NAME...
SEE? I TOLD YOU WE NEED TO USE M.A.C.H.O.
IT DOESN'T STAND FOR ANY-THING!

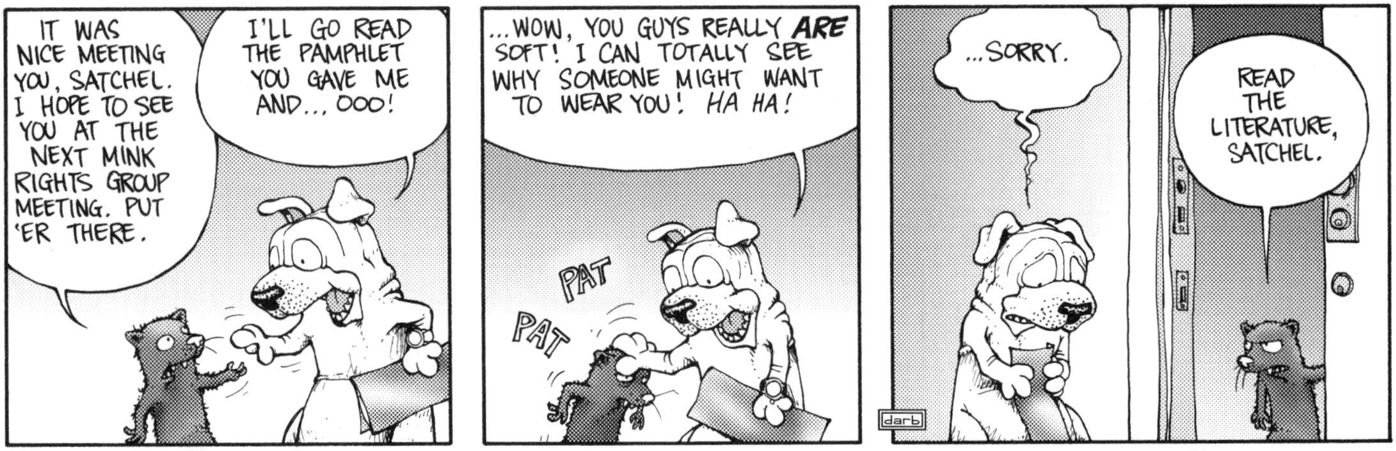
IT WAS NICE MEETING YOU, SATCHEL. I HOPE TO SEE YOU AT THE NEXT MINK RIGHTS GROUP MEETING. PUT 'ER THERE.
I'LL GO READ THE PAMPHLET YOU GAVE ME AND... OOO!
...WOW, YOU GUYS REALLY ARE SOFT! I CAN TOTALLY SEE WHY SOMEONE MIGHT WANT TO WEAR YOU! HA HA!
PAT
PAT
...SORRY.
READ THE LITERATURE, SATCHEL.
darb

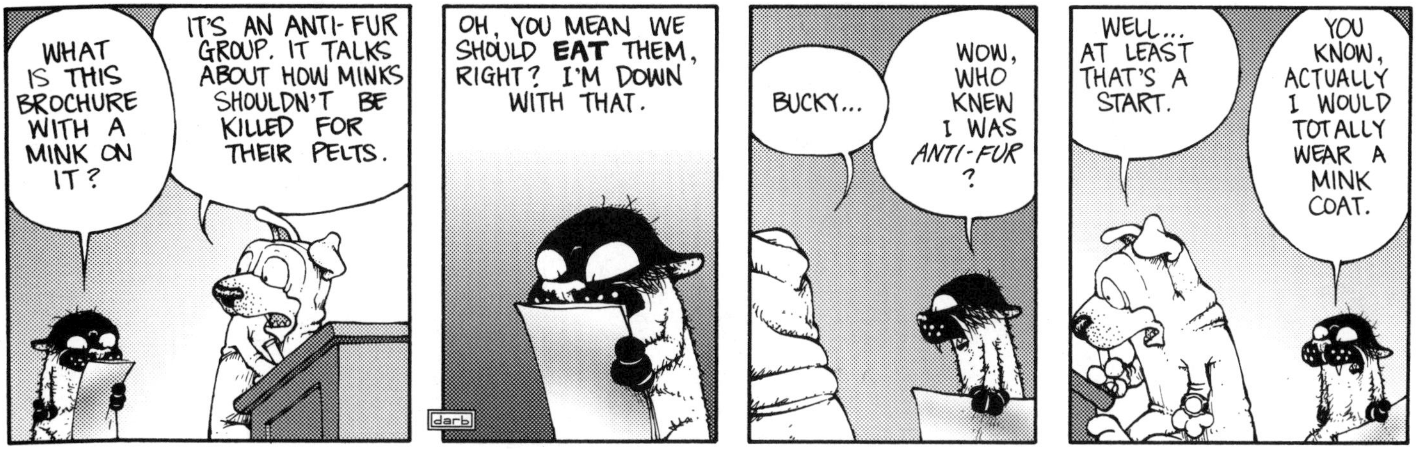
WHAT IS THIS BROCHURE WITH A MINK ON IT?
IT'S AN ANTI-FUR GROUP. IT TALKS ABOUT HOW MINKS SHOULDN'T BE KILLED FOR THEIR PELTS.
OH, YOU MEAN WE SHOULD EAT THEM, RIGHT? I'M DOWN WITH THAT.
BUCKY...
WOW, WHO KNEW I WAS ANTI-FUR?
WELL... AT LEAST THAT'S A START.
YOU KNOW, ACTUALLY I WOULD TOTALLY WEAR A MINK COAT.
darb

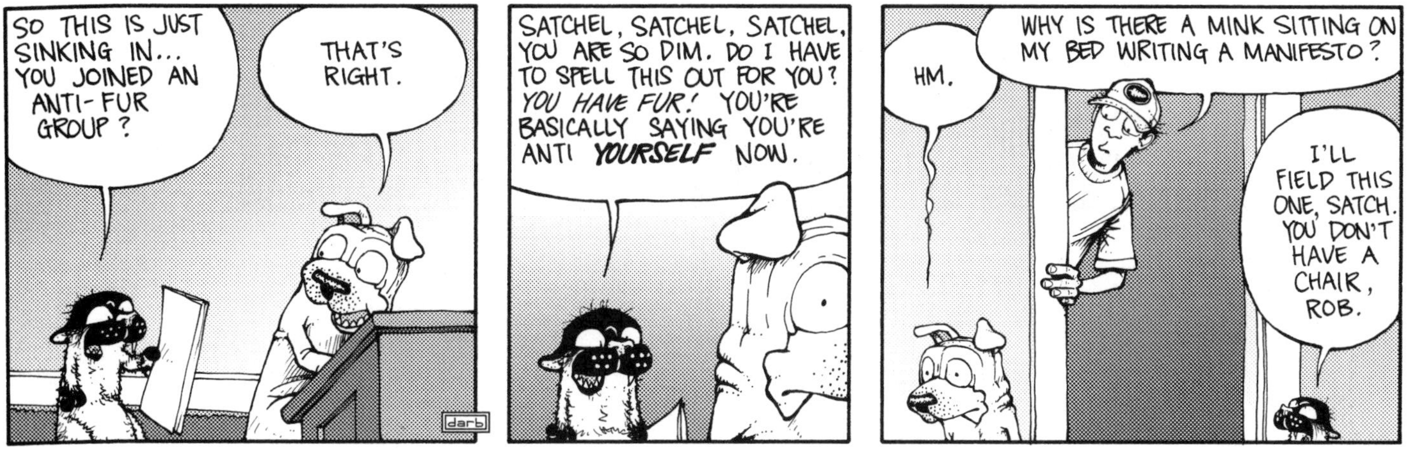
SO THIS IS JUST SINKING IN... YOU JOINED AN ANTI-FUR GROUP?
THAT'S RIGHT.
darb
SATCHEL, SATCHEL, SATCHEL, YOU ARE SO DIM. DO I HAVE TO SPELL THIS OUT FOR YOU? YOU HAVE FUR! YOU'RE BASICALLY SAYING YOU'RE ANTI YOURSELF NOW.
HM.
WHY IS THERE A MINK SITTING ON MY BED WRITING A MANIFESTO?
I'LL FIELD THIS ONE, SATCH. YOU DON'T HAVE A CHAIR, ROB.

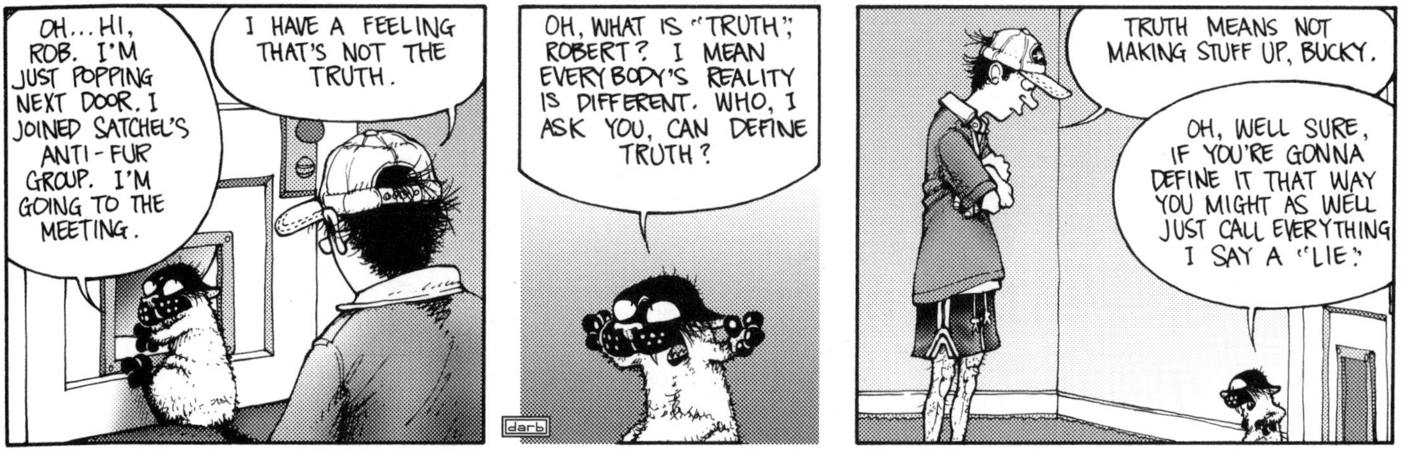
OH... HI, ROB. I'M JUST POPPING NEXT DOOR. I JOINED SATCHEL'S ANTI-FUR GROUP. I'M GOING TO THE MEETING.
I HAVE A FEELING THAT'S NOT THE TRUTH.
OH, WHAT IS "TRUTH," ROBERT? I MEAN EVERYBODY'S REALITY IS DIFFERENT. WHO, I ASK YOU, CAN DEFINE TRUTH?
darb
TRUTH MEANS NOT MAKING STUFF UP, BUCKY.
OH, WELL SURE, IF YOU'RE GONNA DEFINE IT THAT WAY YOU MIGHT AS WELL JUST CALL EVERYTHING I SAY A "LIE."

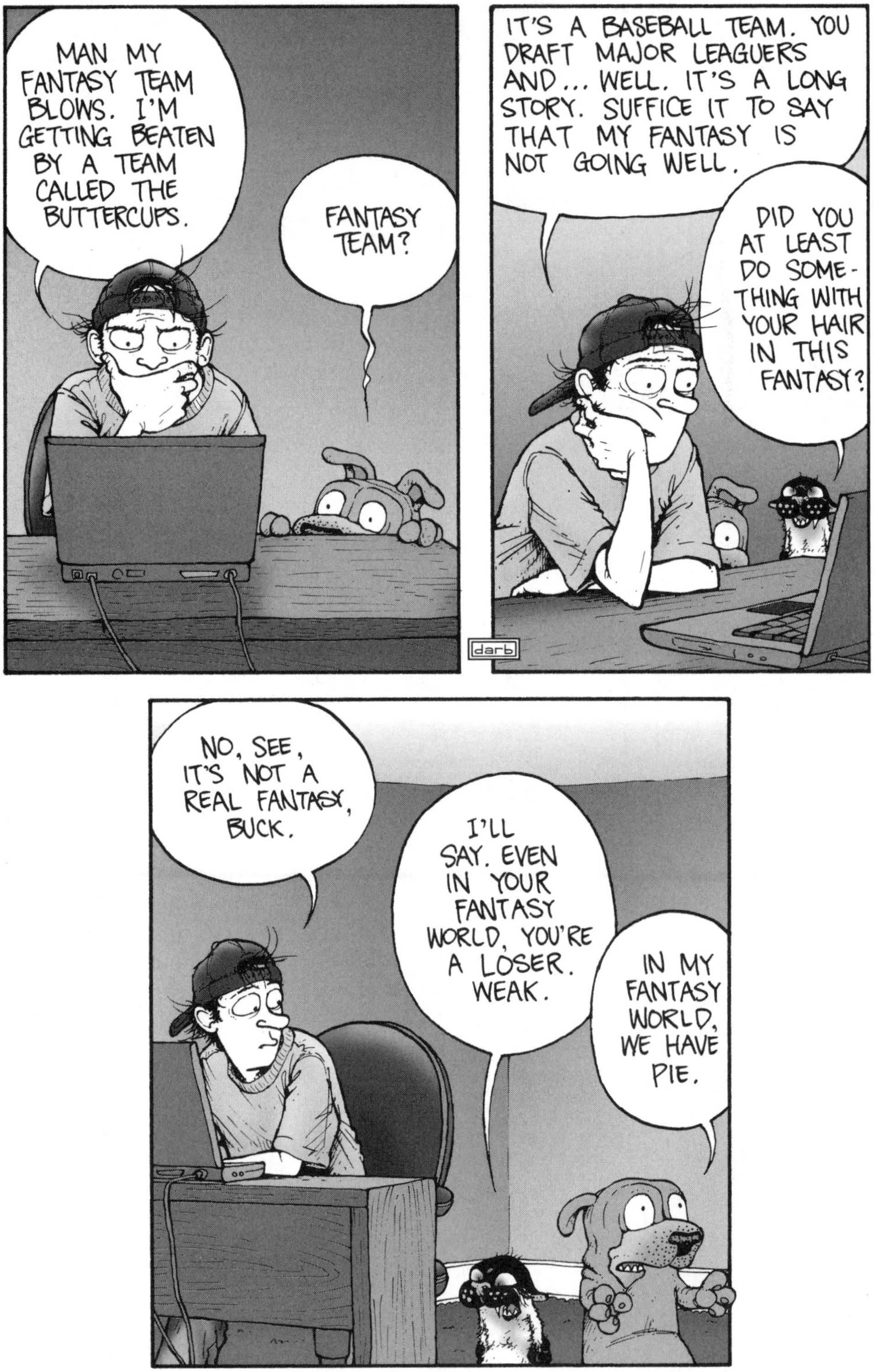
MAN MY FANTASY TEAM BLOWS. I'M GETTING BEATEN BY A TEAM CALLED THE BUTTERCUPS.
FANTASY TEAM?
IT'S A BASEBALL TEAM. YOU DRAFT MAJOR LEAGUERS AND... WELL. IT'S A LONG STORY. SUFFICE IT TO SAY THAT MY FANTASY IS NOT GOING WELL.
DID YOU AT LEAST DO SOME-THING WITH YOUR HAIR IN THIS FANTASY?
darb
NO, SEE, IT'S NOT A REAL FANTASY, BUCK.
I'LL SAY. EVEN IN YOUR FANTASY WORLD, YOU'RE A LOSER. WEAK.
IN MY FANTASY WORLD, WE HAVE PIE.